INDIGENOUS PEOPLES
AND ARCHAEOLOGY
IN LATIN AMERICA

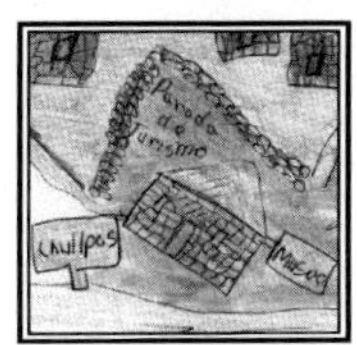

ARCHAEOLOGY AND INDIGENOUS PEOPLES SERIES

Sponsored by the World Archaeological Congress

Series Editorial Board:

Sonya Atalay, Indiana University, Bloomington
T. J. Ferguson, University of Arizona
Dorothy Lippert, Smithsonian Institution
Claire Smith, Flinders University
Joe Watkins, University of Oklahoma
H. Martin Wobst, University of Massachusetts, Amherst
Larry Zimmerman, Indiana University, Indianapolis

Books in this series:

Kennewick Man: Perspectives on the Ancient One, Heather Burke, Claire Smith, Dorothy Lippert, Joe Watkins, and Larry Zimmerman, editors

Indigenous Archaeologies: A Reader on Decolonization, Margaret M. Bruchac, Siobhan M. Hart, and H. Martin Wobst, editors

Being and Becoming Indigenous Archaeologists, George Nicholas, editor

Indigenous Peoples and Archaeology in Latin America, Cristóbal Gnecco and Patricia Ayala, editors

INDIGENOUS PEOPLES AND ARCHAEOLOGY IN LATIN AMERICA

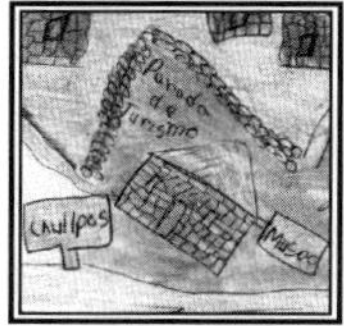

Editors

Cristóbal Gnecco

Patricia Ayala

Walnut Creek, California

LEFT COAST PRESS, INC.
1630 North Main Street, #400
Walnut Creek, CA 94596
http://www.LCoastPress.com

ISBN 978-1-61132-015-2 hardcover
ISBN 978-1-61132-017-6 electronic

Library of Congress Cataloging-in-Publication Data:

Indigenous peoples and archaeology in Latin America/Cristóbal Gnecco, Patricia
Ayala, editors.
     p. cm.
   Includes index.
   ISBN 978-1-61132-015-2 (hardcover : alk. paper)
1. Indians—Antiquities. 2. Indigenous peoples—Latin America—Antiquities.
3. Archaeology—Government policy—Latin America. 4. Cultural property—
Latin America. 5. Nationalism and collective memory—Latin America. 6. Latin
America—Antiquities. I. Gnecco, Cristóbal. II. Ayala Rocabado, Patricia.
   E65.I4757 2011
   980'.01—dc22

                         2011006966

Printed in the United States of America

♾™ The paper used in this publication meets the minimum requirements of
American National Standard for Information Sciences—Permanence of Paper
for Printed Library Materials, ANSI/NISO Z39.48–1992.

Contents

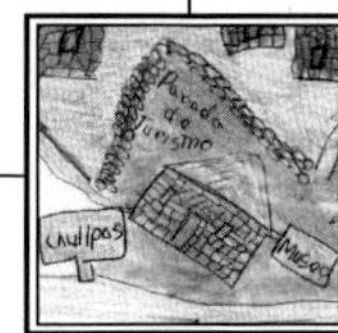

List of Illustrations

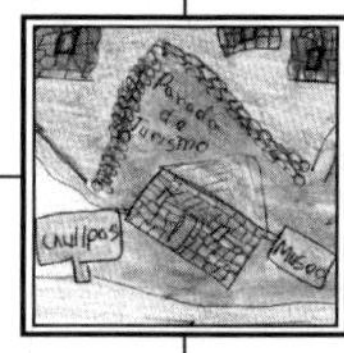

INTRODUCTION

WHAT IS TO BE DONE? ELEMENTS FOR A DISCUSSION

Cristóbal Gnecco and Patricia Ayala

The relation between archaeology and native communities is ambivalent: it either is problematic, more and more a battleground, or a place for intercultural encounters. While it did not exist before or it was directional, nowadays the global trend of indigenous empowerment has renewed history, has made it a tool of cultural meaning and political legitimacy, and has turned the relation with archaeology into a contested and polemical topic. The interest of indigenous peoples for archaeological matters, ignored (when not proscribed) until recently, has widened the conception of "heritage" to make it truly historical and to make it rest in different worldviews; now several conceptions confront themselves on the rhetorical battleground. The national one, to which many archaeologists subscribe, implies that the history of *others* is transformed into the history of *we all*; although it is only just one amidst many—and cannot be imposed over the others without symbolic violence or, as in the case of legal prescriptions, without tangible and direct violence—it still has the support of the institutional apparatus and the blindness of the state about an issue in which other actors are also interested. The state has confined heritage to legal frames and to a policelike functionality, producing a fetishism of objects and a worrisome saturation of museums and storerooms (exponentially increased in the last years due do CRM projects).[1] Yet, the state bypasses the consideration that the protection and valuation of heritage can involve the preoccupations, expectations, and dissents of local communities. This will not be achieved by building museums everywhere, as if their mere existence would guarantee the polysemization[2] of heritage. It will not be achieved, either, by getting local actors to participate in institutional spaces created to control the definition and management of heritage—that is how one of the main mechanisms of multiculturalism, participation without participation, is fulfilled. Although the meaning of museums as theaters for the *mise en scène* of the national past has expired, their insatiable reproduction says as much about their ignorance of contextual transformations than about their refusal to contemplate their distorted face in the mirror.

In Latin America the debate between indigenous peoples and archaeology is younger than elsewhere, but it has already reached comparable levels of intensity and visibility. Although it has resulted in several academic publications in the last years (e.g., Ayala 2008; Benavides 2005; Endere 2002; Gnecco 2006; Monné and Montenegro 2003; see several papers in *Chungará* 35 [2003] and *Textos Antropológicos* 15 [2004]), it was preceded by criticism of archaeology by native intellectuals (Mamani 1989; Rivera 1980). Several related events have also been organized: local and national meetings and forums (a meeting at Ollagüe, Chile; a forum in Río Cuarto, Argentina) and symposia at the 51st International Congress of Americanists in Santiago de Chile (2004) and at a WAC Inter-Congress in Catamarca, Argentina in 2006.

The purpose of this book is to show the variety of approaches to the topic in different Latin American countries. Unlike other similar works, this book shelters radical, antithetical and even improper postures from the standpoint of political correctness but that show, "realistically," the wide spectrum in which they are situated; such a "realism" is militant (in different positions and politics) and dodges a complacent and accommodated distance. The 19 papers and the declaration forming this volume come from various countries in the region (Mexico, Colombia, Ecuador, Peru, Bolivia, Chile, Argentina, and Brazil) and are structured around the relations between indigenes and archaeology in the frame of national histories and from the perspective of the emergence of the native interest for matters, things, and scenarios that they disdained before and that archaeologists considered exclusively their own, without questioning and challenge. The recent history of the region, which echoes global multicultural policies, shows that the archaeological establishment has been forced to relax the control it had over the production of historical meaning from objectified time; it has done this by establishing ethical standards and by responding to legal prescriptions and indigenous activism.

Some authors defend the institutional posture, preoccupied by the irruption of indigenous interests in archaeological matters; others believe that it is possible to establish scenarios in which the actors arriving at the production of archaeological discourses can live side by side without interfering; others think that the hour has come to plan strategies for participation and to build bridges of interdiscursive understanding. Taking the pulse of such diverse postures does not exhaust the dimensions of the matter; this cartographic (but not moral) exercise only strives to contribute to feeding its fires. This introduction, which shamelessly steals the title of a book by Lenin, has a simple structure, a board over which we display the arguments of the papers, perhaps just hints that others can follow or avoid. We will write about ruptures and discontinuities; about repatriation and fetishism; about representation. We will begin with a bit of context, making an outline—possibly vague and surely schematic—of the relations (or the lack of them) between archaeology and indigenous communities.

FROM MESTIZO TO MULTICULTURAL ARCHAEOLOGY

An observation of Pursewarden in *Clea* can serve as a starting point: "The Other does not exist; there only exists oneself facing, eternally, the problem of the discovery of the self!" (Durrell 1981:131). Endless self-contemplation is doomed to ignore different symbolic configurations. There lies part of the (non)relation between native peoples and the discipline: while the latter used things indigenous to build its history from a logocentric gaze (but ignored their local meanings), the former did not pay attention to what archaeology did because their preoccupations were elsewhere and because asymmetrical relations of power were at stake. If indigenous disinterest for things "archaeological" is not a starting point but a matter that cries to be interpreted, so the archaeological disdain for other histories merits analytical attention.

Since the struggles for independence started at the beginning of the nineteenth century, an objectified time (for museums, writings, and image reproduction) by national discourses helped to build mestizo communities (except in Argentina). Archaeology built a new temporality—that of a celebrated pre-European past casted on Western terms, by Western means, and to serve Western needs—to make denser the novelty of the recent nations. That temporality, typically modern and typically Latin American, quickly overpowered other coexisting temporalities: those of the natives, of the slaves, of the avowedly pure whites. It did away with the dark times of the conquest and colonization by uplifting a glorious indigenous past. Bourgeois modernity, that of the rising mestizos, condemned the centuries of European rule as brutal, barbaric, criminal, backward, and isolationist. The time span that stood between past indigenous societies and modernity was effaced. Extraordinary paradox: the period that made possible Westernized South American societies was stigmatized and banished while the Indians, despised and subjugated, were elevated in the past.

A past needed by the nation, stripped bare of European roots but full of European referent-making strategies (objectification, universality, progressive temporality), was provided by well-chosen pre-European things and by the romanticized societies that produced them, shown and vindicated as the (well-hidden) roots of the national tree. Yet, the appropriation of indigenous achievements by national storytellers, all members of elites that despised the Indians and considered themselves white, was a brutal paradox. José Carlos Mariátegui (1929) put it this way when writing about world revolutions:

> In Indo-America ... the Creole aristocracy and bourgeoisie do not feel solidarity with the people by the link of common history and culture. In Peru the aristocrats and the white bourgeois scorn the popular, the national.

The storehouse of time is full of surprises: the objectified time of despised individuals was used as the roots of the national tree, as the foundation of an imagined community that built and reinforced the articulation of populations with diverse origins, subduing their own temporalities. Latin American archaeologies, made by and for mestizos, were tools of glorification and densification of a national unity from which native societies were excluded. For Bolivian activist Carlos Mamani (1989:48), nationalisms "take possession of what is not theirs in order to lay the foundations of their 'nation' in a past which does not belong to them and whose legitimate descendants they continue to oppress." The nationalist appropriation of the pre-European archaeological heritage, severing the relation of continuity with contemporary indigenous peoples, implied that only the mestizos (the national community) were rightful heirs of the pre-Columbian splendor and stewards of its custody and promotion. Contemporary indigenes, unworthy and degraded inheritors of past greatness, were represented on the margin of history as condemned and distanced subjects, owners of an arrested, if not dead, temporality. Their presence in the national imagination was a marginal and museum-bound commentary to pre-European societies, a proof of their precarious (but not surprising) survival—the tenacity of the savages, anachronistic and arbitrary to the modern logic but necessary for its rationalization.

Archaeologists cannot elude their role in the construction of colonial discourses. Archaeology has helped anthropology to turn the social into text and culture at the expense of the politics and context that define it. In the process of studying (creating) cultures, archaeologists execute an extraordinary clinical operation: they isolate them from present times and relegate them to a remote past, only accessible with the tools of archaeology. Such a decontextualizing and aestheticizing process ignores the operation of the colonial machine and lends arguments to an order that it only fights, if that, in its more peripheral statements. Said (1996:44–45) put it more directly:

> There is no way I can perceive the world from within our culture (a culture, besides, with an exhaustive history of extermination and annexation behind) without perceiving, at the same time, the imperialist conflict. This

is a cultural fact of extraordinary importance, both political and interpretative, because it is the true horizon that defines us and, by extension, the condition of possibility of concepts such as "alterity" and "difference" which would be abstract and unfounded otherwise.

This situation apparently changed with the advent of the multicultural order three decades ago. Postnational (multicultural) archaeology opens its practice to the participation of local actors (in research, CRM, and decision making), it widens the spaces of circulation of its discourse (especially with the promotion of local museums, printed materials, and audiovisuals), and it includes other historical horizons in its interpretations; besides, it tolerates different symbolizations of the past, the way of representing them, and the widening of their scenic deployment. But all that much goodness is deceiving: mestizo archaeology has been refunctionalized to adequate itself to the demands of a context it has not contributed to transform but that calls for its accommodation. The tolerance of non-academic histories by multicultural archaeology is crossed by the demand for authenticity, producing canonical intransigence that establishes new limits to rhetoric legitimacy. The indigenes recognized, sanctified, and promoted by expert discourses must be as Western definitions want them to be. For multicultural archaeologists, the "permitted Indian" (*sensu* Hale 2004) is a bearer of an authentic and pure culture, a jealous guardian of nature and history. This demand for authenticity, always circumstantial and malleable, portrays local histories as a locus for the reactivation of a temporal sense that postmodernity pretends to annihilate. In a paradox that can only be postmodern, indigenous histories, previously arrogated and transformed by national history, are valued in their own terms as discourses of continuity and sacrality, alternative to the brutal dehistorization of the past. But when the indigenes adventure outside the new canon of multicultural representation (narrower and more watched over than the colonial and modern canons), their authenticity is questioned and their rights are limited.

ON RUPTURES AND CONTINUITIES: THE MORAL SCENARIO

Several papers in the book show how archaeology ruptured the continuity of indigenous histories and how they were transformed by the colonial apparatus.[3] Although some modern archaeologists attributed to contemporary indigenous peoples the character of heirs and continuators of the very cultural traditions they studied, they did not do so to make indigenes participate in their historical enquiry (as interlocutors or as empowered actors) or accompany their research, but to obtain interpretative hints, especially from myths. Alejandro

Haber warns that archaeological practice is based in the rupture of historical continuity and that the preterization of indigenes is one of its main tenets; this metaphysical exercise, by means of which archaeology builds its object (the indigenes as a part of the past), is the same by which it conceives itself as objective. Alexander Herrera, Federico Navarrete, Hugo Benavides, Fernando López, and Marcelo Fernández-Osco also refer to the tight relation between archaeological discourses and the construction of national histories. For Navarrete, for instance, the symbiosis between ruins, archaeologists, and the state in Mexico explains how the Creole national conscious was fed by pre-Hispanic culture material at the expense of indigenous historical continuity and their meaningful relation with archaeological remains. The paper written by one of us (CG) suggests that the rupture of historical continuity was a strategy that colonialism used to transform local histories and to impose a new sense of time (that is, an origin and a destiny); the role of the Catholic Church in this process seems to have been fundamental because it led to the devaluation and, eventually, to the proscription of the relation of the indigenes with their ancestors (turned Others by colonialism). This may explain why Latin American indigenous communities (at least those influenced by Catholicism) have a problematic relation (although the matter is changing) with what expert knowledge calls the archaeological record. Native peoples reproduced and many still reproduce the rupture with the pre-Columbian past and with the things that render it material; some of them refer to archaeological sites as "things of the Indians," as places occupied in remote times by different Others with whom they feel neither historical nor cultural ties. That is what the other of us (PA) argues for the case of the Atacameños in Chile regarding the social proscriptions of the "grandparents," entities of another time that local populations fear and that inhabit archaeological sites. A similar case is that of the *awilitus* in Peru, who, according to Herrera, are conceived of as dwellers of a past previous to humankind.

Multicultural rhetoric has changed this order of things: while the nation-state is happy to emphasize the ruptures in continuity, multiculturalism sides with continuities, something that is supposed to be reflected in legal bodies that recognize ethnic groups or communities if they prove their link with the pre-Hispanic past (as Luis Cornejo, María Luz Endere, Plácido Cali, and Pedro Funari describe for Chile, Argentina, and Brazil). But appearances are deceptive. Multicultural legal dispositions, apparently altruistic and repairing of the injustices committed by colonialism, are poisoned. While the law demands the demonstration of historical continuity, archaeologists claim that objectivity be established with their tools (another example of the articulation of the law and the expert). But the fact that native populations think that continuity does not need to be proved by experts (still users of epistemic violence) but only to side with identity and history indicates that something is wrong. Such a dysfunction (what some believe is not what the others think) is a multicultural characteristic that, we are told, ceases to be a problem when arbitrated by the state, the guarantor that the symphony of so many different musicians be more or less harmonic. "Historical continuity" (proved through "cultural affiliation") as a legal precept is a multicultural operation, an example of the limits that multiculturalism imposes and of the rights it reserves for itself: it permits the state and its experts to decide who is an inheritor of whom, what can be given, and what can be withheld. The opposition to the legitimacy of a continuity that is not established by means of scientific rhetoric demonstrates that this issue has become one of the most highly disputed grounds of the contemporary struggle for the control of historical narratives. The countries that have consecrated native rights over "archaeological materials" consider that cultural affiliation is a determinant element in the establishment of historical continuity. For many archaeologists, historical continuity is a disputable argument of the indigenous demand for the control of the vestiges and discourses about the past, a fact that has to be demonstrated by those who pretend to be heirs of the pre-Columbian past and especially by those who demand the ownership of the archaeological record. Luis Cornejo holds that it is academically impossible to establish an unequivocal link between most archaeological remains and specific contemporary indigenous cultures in Chile; he states that such a link could only be established on the base of demonstrable continuities in essential cultural aspects, such as ideology and social organization, as in the case of the Rapanui of Easter Island.

The matter of continuity or rupture does not end there. It has more nuances. Appealing to a mentality that dates back to colonial times but that was refined by nationalism, some processes of self-identification do not recognize links with the pre-Columbian past and do not want to assume a stigmatized Indian identity. Such is the case described by Alexander Herrera for Peru, where non-indigenous peasant authenticity gives way to histories that emphasize discontinuities between present people and past Indians, precisely when legal benefits demand continuities. A similar situation was observed by Denise Gomes in Parauá, Brazil; although the commoners did not show interest in archaeology when it stressed the very cultural continuities they reject, subsequent archaeological interpretations that referred to the lack of a direct historical continuity provided elements that were appropriated as a positive argument to reinforce a self-image of modern citizens that negates a connection to the indigenous past.

Repatriation: Between Fetishes and Meanings

Repatriation has been the legal (sometimes also ethical) battleground in which the struggle for power between native communities and archaeologists has taken place worldwide for the past two decades; it has also been the scenario to which the relations between the two have for the most part been confined. Native communities have turned political the search of historical meaning through the dispute for the biological and cultural remains of their ancestors with archaeologists and research institutions. The potential of this discourse in favor of indigenous struggles is unquestionable, as Juana Paillalef points out in her paper.

From a legal point of view, repatriation is just a matter of human remains and their associated objects (not just things but also places). Although it could well be the point of entrance to a larger issue—the challenge to the monopolistic control of historical narratives exercised by archaeology—it has rarely occurred so. Repatriation has raised things to a category different than that mobilized by archaeologists and museums, which are now centers of litigation and contestation.

Few cases of repatriation have occurred in Latin America, but they are enlightening. It is noteworthy that these cases are so few in spite of the strength, visibility, and legitimacy of indigenous movements. This may be due to the above-mentioned ruptures: many indigenous peoples are simply not interested in the very topics and objects cherished by archaeologists due to the imprint of colonial temporality. But the fact that repatriation is occurring indicates that such a position can be changed, as Endere, Cali, and Funari point out while discussing the return in Argentina of indigenous remains to their descendants. Although there are no laws or ethical guidelines on repatriation in Chile, some years ago the Atacameños reinterred pre-Columbian human remains, appealing to their beliefs about the "grandparents" and to protect them from tourists (Ayala 2008).

The struggle for the "material record" (especially for burials and their associated paraphernalia) can shift from a purely legal matter (although its origin is political) to other arenas, such as the creation and legitimacy of a wide political economy of historical narratives. The more publicized ethical principles (those of the Canadian Archaeological Association, World Archaeological Congress, and Australian Archaeological Association) state that this is only possible if native groups participate and control the production of archaeological narratives and if natives are trained to be archaeologists. Some indigenes share this belief (Watkins 2000). As Mamani (1989:58) noted:

> An Indian archaeology, under our control and systematized according to
> our concepts of time and space, could perhaps form part of our enterprise
> of winning back our own history ... Archaeology has been up until now

a means of domination and the colonial dispossession of our identity. If it were to be taken back by the Indians themselves it could provide us with new tools to understand our historical development, and so strengthen our present demands and our projects for the future.

But these statements, which seem to set a bridge and fill a void, leave intact the core of the problem: the archaeology that appears on them is the same that produced historical schizophrenia (the good Indian of the past and the bad Indian of the present). It is the same that objectified beings and lives. How can the discipline be invited to the party if it is wearing its same old clothes? The hour has arrived to think of alternatives. One alternative is intercultural: a renovated relationship between indigenes and archaeology can be the occasion to coproduce something new (this is the plain sense of dialectics) instead of reproducing what we already know. In such a coproduction, the discipline would have to think itself over and see how it can be transformed; to begin with, it should find out where in its metaphysical building the colonial phantom is hiding. For Haber, a critical archaeology without the consequent corrections in a decolonial practice is sterile; thus, one of the things we can do to expunge colonialism from the discipline is to expose its philosophical bases to other worldviews. The least we can expect from such an exposition (and from such an encounter) is the transformation of the discipline, a long stroll outside its well-guarded gates.

IN THE WORLD OF REPRESENTATIONS: ARCHAEOLOGY *OTHERWISE*

Representations create discourses and practices[4] whose characterization depends of frames of interpretation that transcend the limits of their own display and determine, to a great extent, the course of social life. Modern historical discourses are performative acts of colonialism. Mignolo (1995) argued that the analysis of representations as practices of colonialism should be centered on colonial semiosis. Analyses made from a distance and exteriority do not capture the wide range of semiotic interactions that take place in colonial situations and negate the self-representations of the Other:

> The concern with the representation of the colonized focuses on the discourse of the colonizer, and one forgets to ask how the colonized represent themselves, how they depict and conceive themselves, as well as how they speak for themselves without the need of self-appointed chroniclers, philosophers, missionaries, or men of letters to represent (depict as well as speak for) them. (Mignolo 1995:332)

This call for attention leads us to think (1) how the discipline arrogated the representation of the history of the Others, and (2) how the Others represent it for themselves. It leads us to think about the politics of representation. Although for archaeologists, paraphrasing Said (1996:50), it seems easier to talk about sherds than about politics, the appearance of indigenous peoples at their table force them to talk about politics, while still talking about sherds. Sherds become the entry point to politics.

The 1980s saw the consolidation of social movements that vindicated cultural differences, especially indigenous movements. The empowerment of alterity (dynamizing its fights against state integrationist politics and claiming the right to difference and autonomy) included the challenge to the narrative monopoly of storytellers, such as archaeologists, and to their role in cultural mediation: now the Others can represent themselves. This does not mean that indigenous historical self-representations necessarily resort to archaeology; they more frequently appeal to their own histories (which Western typologies call myths) or build official histories modeled in messianic heroes. But in the last two decades some indigenous communities have come to archaeology for political and cultural expression, accompanied by non-indigenous archaeologists (such as the case described by Luis Guillermo Vasco) or training their own people. Indigenous communities are interested in archaeology (as a producer of discourses about a given past) or, more often, in the "archaeological heritage" (as a repository of basic meanings for the social fabric), not because it is the only road to historical sense but because it can help them to read their purposes and expectations.

Until the beginning of political decolonization, especially in the last three decades, indigenous history had been written by outsiders. This phenomenon has not been entirely eradicated; as Wilhelm Londoño notes, in the archaeological museum of Antofagasta de la Sierra, in northeastern Argentina, a poster states, "If archaeologists recuperate lost memories, the people are their owners and custodians." Archaeologists the "retrievers" of lost memories? This is a curious arrogance: the memory they say to recuperate ends up being just an opaque exhibit of things. Archaeologists make a rare entity of memory, a thing (or something else of an elusive character, but turned into a thing) that can only be recovered by the magic stroke of disciplinary genius. But the orbit of representation has been widened and indigenous communities, freed of the rhetoric yoke of the expert impersonator, represent themselves. A privileged locus of such a representation is history, both as what it was and should not have been (colonialism) and as what it was, must have been, and can happen again (the possible worlds of utopian imagination). Historical self-representation has used archaeology as one road (another one) to revitalize temporal meanings.

The growing visibility of the *mise en scène* of indigenous archaeologies (made by, for, and from indigenous peoples) casts light on something that academic archaeology has ignored: the concrete character of the processes of historical production more than abstract preoccupations about the nature of history (*sensu* Trouillot 1995). For decades archaeologists carried out their work (writing history from things) without paying any attention to native communities. That disdain was based on two reasons: (1) the supposed absence of temporal continuity between contemporary indigenes and those of the past, and (2) the making of national histories by mestizos who, purposefully, excluded things indigenous from their accounts (other than some "things" left by pre-Columbian societies). However, in the last years many archaeologists and the institutions in which they operate (universities, museums) have transformed their attitude toward indigenous communities, noting—perhaps for the first time—that they exist in the same field of knowledge. But the issue is a more notorious preoccupation of archaeologists than of indigenes, and it is centered in the material heritage (objects again), not in the communities and their histories; it is, in sum, a disciplinary preoccupation.

The involvement of Latin American indigenous communities with archaeological matters is recent (their contestation is older); that is why few of their members have reflected on related issues or, at least, have written about them. Such a fact is evident in this book: only two indigenes have agreed to write their views. This does not mean that they are not interested in historical meanings attributed to "objects"; it means that their means of representation transit other roads.

Antiestablishment discourses formulated before the advent of multiculturalism, such as those by Rivera (1980) and Mamani (1989), were few but categorical: archaeology is a colonial tool. Like those authors, and from their own ethnic realities, Paillalef and Fernández-Osco in this volume criticize the discipline, especially for its reluctance to consider the interests of local communities: archaeology worked and works from monocultural but not relational bases; the interest of archaeologists prevails, subordinated to the institutional interests of research centers that do not reflect the pluridiverse character of knowledge.

There are other forms of relation besides the confrontation of essences (the science of archaeologists against indigenous sensibility, the rationalism of expert knowledge versus the irrationality of native thinking). The bridge of collaboration and, to a certain extent, of interdiscursive comprehension is not only stretched out over political terrain but even over the constitution of meaning. Even so, the possibility of a more horizontal relation between native communities and archaeologists is not always based upon the dissolution of the idea, shared by archaeologists and indigenes (although with different valuations), that on one side lays rationality and the discovery of truth and on the other sensibility and the transcendence of the sacred. The radicalization in essentialist trenches is not necessarily a threat; it may be necessary for a much-needed confrontation.

The frame of collaboration established in some countries revolves around agreement (joint revision of legislation and operative politics as much as control over research), participation (in research teams, CRM projects, and interinstitutional committees) and collaboration per se (in research, exhibits, and legal battles against commodification). Several papers in this book show how this participative/collaborative process is taking place, and how archaeology changes its practice and discourse. With differences corresponding to the academic and social contexts in which they unfold, such experiences tell about indigenous participation in research, about the need to carry out long-term investigations to comprehend local processes, and about dialogue and discussion. Interdiscursive proposals seek mutual benefits and respond to the diversity of interests at stake. Some papers are more optimistic than others. While Salazar is convinced that a productive collaboration can be achieved between transnational capitalism, archaeology, and native societies in joint ventures centered on heritage, Dante Angelo portrays collaboration as the cure for colonial guilt, as a concession to a political correctness that reproduces disciplinary autism. Angelo's arguments (overtly critical and soundly skeptical about roles, power, and positioning) may be unfair with some endeavors, but his refreshing extremism shows that the archaeological engagement with indigenous peoples is (sometimes) irresponsibly naive and built upon selective criteria of authenticity and purity, true multicultural brands. Take the case described by Francisco Gil; two Bolivian communities resignify their links with formerly proscribed ruins in order to gain the benefits of tourism. Those who hold that archaeological concessions to native communities demand their adherence to the prefabricated script of the authentic Indian scorn this kind of behavior, labeled as strategic opportunism. Other outcomes and expectations are ignored and castigated when the script is not strictly followed. Power relations are rarely at stake. Most archaeologists are content to offer cultural crumbs to the communities (a local museum, a video, a booklet) while preserving the control of key issues (research design, destination of finds, production and dissemination of narratives). Such is the case of some projects in San Pedro de Atacama, Chile, which promote a communitarian and participative archaeology yet do little more than reproduce old power relations: the natives still are excellent informants, diggers, or lab assistants but they do not participate in decision making about their past and its built materiality (Ayala 2008). Multicultural archaeology accommodates the new participative language, repeating non-reflexively practices inherited since the very beginning of the discipline, although nowadays using the tag of a non-exclusive archaeology (according to its particular conception of exclusivity), open to an indigenous participation without participation.

In some cases collaboration is more peripheral: it involves how one party can put to use the work of the other. The research of Flavia Prado Moi and Walter Fagundes Morales in the Paresi territory, Brazil, shows how much indigenous peoples can profit from archaeological findings. In such a relationship, the metaphysical building blocks and the ontological limits of the different histories involved are not confronted. What would happen if philosophical transformation were at the core of the encounter? What would occur if philosophical armors were left aside? The paper by Lesley Green, David Green, and Eduardo Neves is a reflection on the transformations that occurred to the archaeology they were practicing in an indigenous territory in Brazil; research questions, methodologies, and practices changed, along with their engagement with local needs and aspirations.

Collated words: collaboration, participation, disdain, contempt, isolation. They describe situations that have happened or are now happening between archaeologists and natives. None of them have comprehensive meaning if the context is ignored; none of them can faithfully describe interests, expectations, and fears if considered in utter isolation. Whatever relationship there is, it can never be fully understood and, thus, fully dissected for the good of everyone if considered outside the larger context where it occurs. In such a context, postnational states, postmodernism, and multiculturalism thrive alongside ethnic empowerment, the politicization of the cultural, and the culturization of the political. "Spectral reflections" of the postmodern condition shine in the paper by Hugo Benavides, who exposes a complex interplay that is not exhausted by victimization and stigmatization. In Ecuador, as elsewhere, different historical meanings and historical vehicles cannabalize, ignore, or selectively use each other. All possible scenarios cannot be foreseen (although they can be assessed while they occur), but they have in common the constitution of power in the very spaces where identities collide with the market.

Collaboration has become a scenario nowadays much discussed by archaeologists, who have different concerns and agendas—so many, indeed, that the meanings attributed to the term are multiple and emerge from the various ways in which archaeologists engage with local communities.[5] Yet neither this nor any other form of collaborative research has been regularly pursued in archaeology. For one thing, it demands concerted agendas (at least between scholars and local actors), something most archaeologists are unwilling to accept, accustomed as they are to a previously unchallenged monopoly. For another, it implies sharing control not just of things but of narratives. Collaborative approaches are no longer rare, but they are still a minority of academic pursuits.

A truly collaborative archaeology is a major challenge, one that will require archaeologists to relinquish control (both physical and rhetorical). But what is a *truly* collaborative archaeology? For most archaeologists "collaboration" is more a way of alleviating their guilt (and getting on with their work) than a way of embarking on the path of different practices. Native societies do not necessarily require non-native archaeologists to work with in historical matters, in which case "collaboration" is meaningless and may be just a disciplinary need (urged to go public). More often than not the collaboration that archaeologists have in mind is a way of mitigating the discipline's colonialism by passing along to the lay public what they have found, without giving up their privileges.

Coproductions of historical discourses can hardly be uprooted from contextual transformations. The openness of archaeology to indigenous interests is not a generous concession but a conscious role: the discipline can unfold its wings in the political struggle for cultural and territorial rights (aren't they the same, after all?). The meanings of archaeology in a wide project of decolonization show that this is not an academic issue (the legitimacy and potency of archaeology) as much as a political one (decolonizing history and society at large). Decolonization is not just another academic adventure, not a trivial matter, not a new trope added to the encounter of archaeologists with literature, not a programmatic statement. It is a contextual demand that some archaeologists accept while others ignore. The consequences of expanded, horizontal, and politicized relations between archaeology and indigenous peoples are not limited to the arena of representation; if their impact is not felt in all social spheres they will be useless, academic fireworks.

To talk about current indigenous peoples and archaeology in the same phrase is to chart a relationship that the disciplinary complicity with national colonialism (by commission, not by omission) made impossible until recently. Those archaeologists who engage native communities outside any modern pretension transform old directionalities, turn the gaze to an *inside* that recognizes the steps taken, imagine different forms of representation (not the vehicle as much as the content) and, above all, new relational forms, and expose the skin and the entrails to others. They want to escape the colonial hug and to adopt relational alternatives. Hugo Achúgar (1998:271–272) remembered an African proverb ("Until the lions have their own historians, hunting histories will keep glorifying the hunter") to talk about positionality, localization, and memory, "the centers of the political and intellectual debate," because they lead us to a discussion about power and about the power of representation: positionality because it is a matter of assuming positions beyond disciplinary limits; localization because logocentrism (exteriority, neutrality, and distance) is forced to see from the geopolitics of knowledge; and memory because

> we are in a new process of construction of the future national that, surely, could not have the characteristics of the 19th century project and which demands the revision of the past. It is also possible that we are in a new foundational moment but the "foundational effort" cannot be based, neither only nor fundamentally, in the power of the scholars. It cannot because that power, as much as the word of the scholar, is questioned. It cannot because nowadays the owners of memory are not the scholars anymore. It cannot, besides, because memory is not just one and the owners of words are many and diverse. It cannot because the owners of the nation are not—they should not be—the owners of the word. (Achúgar 1998:83)

The indigenous challenge to the disciplinary monopoly (both of narratives and things) strips bare what the discourse of archaeologists refuses to say: it measures their silence. The silence of archaeologists before the transformations of society (their evasive game with sherds) is not their disciplinary strength but their weakness. Shutting up eludes contextual pressures, hides the head in the sand. Neither indigenous challenge nor disciplinary impairment should lead to the sad show of an archaeology that does not represent (or that pretends not to represent), that moves to one side avoiding its responsibility, either as a cynic opportunism or as an autistic isolation. Spivak (2003) already said it: transparency is the outfit of the new colonizer. The opportunity is wide open—to represent and to relate otherwise. To find the indigenes is not to arrogate their representation, as archaeology did for so long, but to accompany it. This self-examination does not exhaust the matter, however. Instead of silence (not of scientific cleanliness this time but of multicultural cynicism), recolonizing because it assimilates and patronizes, archaeology can talk differently, just as indigenous peoples begin to talk from previously unused platforms of enunciation. Let's clean the house, then: neither intellectual charity nor abusive appropriation. Because Nicholas Thomas (1994:28) has already put it well we will not pretend to say it wrong:

> My aim, though, is not to "sympathize with" Aborigines, as though they should be grateful recipients of such intellectual charity; still less is it to attempt to rewrite colonialism from the other side, on their behalf, as it were; that has been done often enough. My departure point is not the "problems" or "experiences" of blacks, but the problematic ways in which contemporary white culture deals with Aboriginality.

The relations of archaeology with the outside world—that not-so-amorphous entity lying outside disciplinary borders—are not limited to indigenous peoples, neither are they the only actors interested in things archaeological. Although indigenous societies have organized visible, empowered, and successful social movements (the very reason why this book is dedicated to explore their relationships with the discipline), the reflections set forth here can be more valuable if understood in a wider frame: that of the relations between archaeology and non-academic, non-logocentric, non-capitalist historical and social projects.

A different archaeology emerges out of those diverse encounters. Archaeology *otherwise* reaches out for different relations, away from disciplinary locks and close to a transforming militancy. Such an archaeology is still marginal (as measured against institutional power) but it cannot be negated, in spite of the intolerance of those archaeologists who still believe in the goodness of modern knowledge, who circumvent the activism of an antisystemic militancy that searches for people instead of looking for research objects, who evade doing archaeology with the people instead of getting people to archaeology.[6] Archaeology *otherwise* (which seeks relations with other visions, other histories, other worlds) fights for the transformation of the discipline, gets involved with the people, and engages their struggles for a better world.

> *Curse: That this book remains closed to the apathetic greedy who do not read to verify their intuitions but their prejudices.*

NOTES

1. The problem of space is not the point, of course, but the lack of reflexivity around a senseless and purposeless accumulation. What is the meaning of accumulating more and more objects if not to please a fetishist vocation?
2. This is not a minor matter. Lewis Carroll in *Through the Looking Glass* wrote: "'When I use a word,' Humpty Dumpty said, in a rather scornful tone, 'it means just what I choose it to mean, neither more nor less.' 'The question is,' said Alice, 'whether you can make words mean so many different things.' 'The question is,' said Humpty Dumpty, 'which is to be master—that's all.' Alice was too much puzzled to say anything; so after a minute Humpty Dumpty began again. 'They've a temper, some of them—particularly verbs: they're the proudest—adjectives you can do anything with, but not verbs—however, I can manage the whole lot of them!'" (Carroll 2008:66).
3. For Frantz Fanon (2007:168) "colonialism is not happy with imposing its law to the present and the future of a dominated country. Neither is it happy with pressing the people in its nets, with emptying the colonized brains of all form and all content. By a sort of a perverse logic it turns to the past of the oppressed people to distort it, disfigure it, and annihilate it."
4. This separation is a concession to customary use to make sure that neither term is left out of the argument. Foucault (1972) showed that discourses *are* practices.

5. By "local" we mean non-academic—uninterested in the universal narratives cherished by scientific archaeology.
6. That is what ethnoarchaeology has been doing for decades: just widening the discipline's hermeneutic horizon. To do so, it instrumentally brings people to archaeology. Ethnoarchaeology strengthens logocentrism, avoids an intersubjective way, and subdues multiplicity, just producing inputs for expert knowledge.

REFERENCES

Achúgar, Hugo 1998 Leones, cazadores e historiadores. A propósito de las políticas de la memoria y del conocimiento. In *Teorías sin disciplina. Latinoamericanismo, poscolonialidad y globalización en debate*, edited by Santiago Castro and Eduardo Mendieta, pp. 271–285. Porrúa, Mexico.

Ayala, Patricia 2008 *Políticas del pasado: indígenas, arqueólogos y Estado en Atacama*. Ediciones IIAM, Santiago.

Benavides, Hugo 2005 Los ritos de la autenticidad: indígenas, pasado y el Estado ecuatoriano. *Arqueología Suramericana* 1(1):5–48.

Carroll, Lewis 2008 *Through the Looking Glass*. Forgotten Books, Charleston.

Durrell, Lawrence 1981 *Clea. El cuarteto de Alejandría*. Edhasa, Buenos Aires.

Endere, María Luz 2002 Management of Archaeological Sites and the Public in Argentina. Unpublished Ph.D. dissertation, Department of Archaeology, University of London, London.

Fanon, Frantz 2007 *Los condenados de la tierra*. Último Recurso, Rosario. First published 1961.

Foucault, Michel 1972 *The Archaeology of Knowledge and the Discourse on Language*. Pantheon, New York.

Gnecco, Cristóbal 2006 Ampliación del campo de batalla. *Trabajos Antropológicos* 15:183–195.

Hale, Charles 2004 Rethinking indigenous politics in the era of the indio permitido. *North American Congress on Latin America Report* 38(2):16–21.

Mamani, Carlos 1989 History and prehistory in Bolivia: What about the Indians? In *Conflict in the Archaeology of Living Traditions*, edited by Robert Layton, pp. 46–59. Unwin Hyman, London.

Mariátegui, José Carlos 1929 Punto de vista antiimperialista. Paper read at the Primera Conferencia Comunista Latinoamericana, Buenos Aires.

Mignolo, Walter 1995 *The Darker Side of the Renaissance: Literacy, Territoriality, and Colonization*. University of Michigan Press, Ann Arbor.

Monné, Merardo, and Mónica Montenegro 2003 He preguntado a los indios para conocer sus creencias acerca de las ruinas... *Pacarina* 3:235–239.

Rivera, Silvia 1980 La antropología y arqueología boliviana: límites y perspectivas. *América Indígena* 40(2):217–224.

Said, Edward 1996 Representar al colonizado. In *Cultura y Tercer Mundo*. Vol. 1, *Cambios en el saber académico*, edited by Beatriz González, pp. 23–59. Nueva Sociedad, Caracas.

Spivak, Gayatri 2003 ¿Puede hablar el subalterno? *Revista Colombiana de Antropología* 39:297–364.

Thomas, Nicholas 1994 *Colonialism's Culture*. Princeton University Press, Princeton.

Trouillot, Michel-Rolph 1995 *Silencing the Past: Power and the Production of History*. Beacon Press, Boston.

Watkins, Joe 2000 *Indigenous Archaeology: American Indian Values and Scientific Practice*. Altamira Press, Walnut Creek.

ENTRANCE (EXIT)

INDIGENOUS ARCHAEOLOGY AND PEASANT POWER

Alejandro F. Haber
Translated from the Spanish by Lilén Malugany

I am disturbed by the archaeologies that talk about power, as if power were there to be observed, measured, weighted, as if archaeology were not of this world, a world in which practices and discourses are about power but at the same time they are power. I am unsettled, in general, by naivety. I am sad with the peasants who, devoid of their power, convinced that they live at the mercy of the powerful, lose their lands, their rights, and their culture, and end up at the mercy of the powerful. I wonder what the practices and discourses of indigenous archaeology say about peasant power, as if I had not the answer prepared already. Only basing itself on geographical, cultural, and social distance between the situation of archaeological intellectual labor and the communities among which archaeology expands its strategy of observation of reality, can archaeology see itself as having only indirect and secondary social consequences.

The archaeology of northwest Argentina (I might write here the archaeology of Argentina, yet I would rather, vainly, arouse an image of prudence) had as its first task the naturalization of distance, in such a way that even more than distance it would be a break, and even more than nature, metaphysics. The first discussion about the archaeological objects found in Calchaquí was held by illustrious precursors like Inocencio Liberani, Florentino Ameghino, Samuel A. Lafone Quevedo, Juan Bautista Ambrosetti, Adán Quiroga, Julián Toscano, Eduardo Holmberg, and Francisco Pascasio Moreno, and it was centered on deciding if the drawings on the surface of the pottery, the bronze discs, and the rock engravings, all these remains of the indigenous civilizations of the area, were or were not forms of writing (Holmberg 1893; Lafone Quevedo 1890; Liberani and Hernández 1950 [1877]; Moreno 1890–1891; Quiroga 1893).

Instead of reducing the question of writing on artifacts to a purely academic discussion, it was, in fact, an attempt to cut out the academic domain itself. They discussed what was to be known of the history of the indigenous people and how. Thus, it was decided among these writers if there would be a Rosetta Stone that would allow them to read the texts with which they would write the indigenous history. At that time in the late nineteenth century, the indigenous people who lived in northwest Argentina, and who also worked for the above-mentioned pioneers of archaeology, hardly read the alphabet of the Spanish language and although they spoke at least Quechua (among other indigenous languages), they could neither read nor write it. The issue at hands was to delineate the indigenous history as an object of knowledge and the reading of hieroglyphs as method. Soon, given the evident difficulty of sustaining the writing hypothesis, some of these authors, most of them living in northwest Argentina, devoted themselves to the interpretation of the drawings not in terms of a codified system of notation and record but as meaningful expressions whose representations were, at least, conventional (Ambrosetti 1896, 1899; Lafone Quevedo 1902; Quiroga 1898).

The introduction of the folklore narrative of northwest Argentina gave these authors an interpretative framework for the archaeological objects, implying that although the indigenous people had lost their ability to make objects, at least they had not lost the meanings their ancestors had represented in them. The discussion about writing became a discussion about meaning and, in fact, about the position of the knowledgeable subject regarding meaning (Haber 1995). I will take three different cases to see in their differences the things they share: the understanding of the object given by the preunderstanding of the knowledgeable agent.

Adán Quiroga sustained that archaeological objects were meaningful and corresponded to the Calchaquíes, who inhabited northwest Argentina when the European invaders arrived and to whom they offered fierce resistance during 140 years (Quiroga 1893, 1899). Their descendants inhabited the area, although the history of dismemberment, defeat, and exploitations had reduced their warlike culture to folkloric contents. Nearly at the antipodes from Domingo Faustino Sarmiento's *Facundo*, Adán Quiroga even considered the indigenous as underaged at the moment he wrote his legal treatise on *Crime and Punishment* (Quiroga 1886). National historiography, Adán Quiroga said, should be centered on the Calchaquí epic, for the formation and education of the citizens.

Samuel Lafone Quevedo (1890, 1891), even more prolifically than Adán Quiroga, had been devoted to interpreting the ancient objects of northwest Argentina, which he attributed to an admired civilization. This civilization was not made up of warriors and heroes but clever handicraftsmen, wise people who knew myths and legends, intelligent farmers of the desert. The Calchaquí warriors destroyed this dragon-inspired (for the motif he interpreted as the depiction of a firedrake) civilization. He considered the Calchaquís more akin to the barbarian than to the civilized, and ancestral to the indigenous people who worked for him in his metal refinery at Pilciao. In this way, he reconciled his aesthetic and intellectual admiration for the objects with his class prejudices toward the indigenous peasantry of Andalgalá who he strove to introduce to the moral benefits of the industrial discipline.

Francisco Moreno (1890–1891) declared in the programmatic manifesto of the Museum of La Plata (which he had created) that whether the Calchaquí objects had some meaning or not was not relevant to science, since science should be devoted to describing, classifying, ordering, and exhibiting them to the citizens for their general knowledge of the Indians "who were extinguished from this soil." It is not surprising, then, that the favorable resolution to Francisco Moreno's position gave rise to the archaeological discipline (thus the formative character of this stage).

In the first discussion about the archaeological object, the observer's position was a fundamental element. It was not a discussion about the object but about the different visions of the relationship between archaeology as an enterprise oriented toward the discovery of truth and archaeology as an enterprise aimed at provoking consequences in society. Different visions of the relationship between archaeology both as knowledge and as social practice, to say it in our jargon, were then juggled out.

Adán Quiroga believed that present-day society should appropriate the indigenous culture and obtain from it its own character, history, and identity. Maybe he was a forerunner of indigenism in America, yet his work and his political career were truncated by his unexpected early death. Bartolomé Mitre, general of the war against the indigenous peoples of the Pampas and of the equally shameful war against Paraguay, as well as founder of the Argentinean national historiography (and intellectually and politically admired by Adán Quiroga), had criticized the poetic vehemence of Quiroga's style (Cáceres 1963), preferring the cold distance of one who describes the world as if he were out of it.

Samuel Lafone Quevedo, with whom Adán Quiroga talked at length when the old wise man visited the city of San Fernando del Valle from his refuge beyond the Ambato mountains, positioned himself as a capitalist entrepreneur in a peasant indigenous world and put the blame of his bankruptcy on the indigenous people's laziness and the shortage of promotion policies from the national government (Márquez 1959).

Lafone Quevedo was appointed in charge of the management of the Museum of La Plata when Joaquín V. González created the university, absorbing the former creation of Francisco Moreno and displacing him. Lafone Quevedo's long stay in La Plata was a retirement more than the coronation of his work, which remained in Pilciao (Haber and Delfino 1995–1996).

Francisco Moreno, in turn, related with the object according to the model he already knew: the natural sciences, as well as diplomacy, were the continuation of war by different means. The indigenous peoples, who were before objects of study (in those very same years and by the same people), were now objects of war. The dictum that "the best Indian was the dead Indian" is reaffirmed when the archaeological, as well as the dead, do not speak. His position, which archaeology inherited, is the position of one whom, methodically and patiently and on behalf of the whole nation, ascertains the death of the indigenous.

Perhaps what I have written so far is enough to show certain things about the distance in the demarcation of the object of archaeology regarding the archaeologist. The metaphysical break through which archaeology builds its object of knowledge (the indigenous as part of the past) is the same through which it is understood as objective (an intellectual, present, and white activity). Both objectivism and the object of archaeology are the result of the uncritical practice of an agent already and previously made of the measure of a society that understands itself as white and that knows itself through the scientific method. The search for knowledge does not only have social consequences but is itself a consequence of a hegemonic *doxa*.

Though my brief commentaries were reduced to the formative stage of Argentinean archaeology, I want to imply that, with other theories, other methods, other techniques, archaeology and the archaeological object seem to have kept the same form since then. Two recent passages would suffice to show the doxical and prescriptive character of the metaphysical rupture and the place of archaeology within it.

In the first place, the following: "Around 1600, when the Spanish colonial system is already established in northwest Argentina, after 10,000 years of independent development, the aboriginal world becomes extinct" (Hernández 2001:97); this was published only ten years ago in a text about the archaeology of the Quebrada de Humahuaca. It is quite difficult for me to comment on this passage, as I am afraid it would not be sufficiently underlined; I suggest, in turn, that we may think on the effect that the phrase, coming from the mouth of archaeology, might have on the indigenous communities of the area.

In the second place, the metaphysical break over which archaeology has built its object as well as its objectivism is, since 2003, consecrated in Act no. 25,743, the Act of Protection of Argentinean Archaeological Heritage. It is legislated there that "the movable and immovable things or vestiges of any kind that are on the surface, subsurface, or under jurisdictional waters that could give information about the sociocultural groups that inhabited the country from pre-Columbian times to more recent historical periods are considered to be archaeological patrimony," without giving a damn if any person or community could have any other interest, not necessarily the information, about the same objects in case they would form part of the same "sociocultural group." In the countries originated from colonial processes, the categories of race, ethnic group, gender, culture, and class are partially overlapped and are reproduced among themselves in such a way that the structures of domination remain naturalized and the privileges reproduced. It would be good if archaeology could undertake a criticism of its role in the formation and reproduction of the representations through which these categories are established and endure. Who are the "sociocultural groups" that the law euphemistically makes reference to? The break must be here in order to let the question be answered. The euphemism, the unsaid, speaks of the metaphysical character of the break.

The current context is one of expansion of the real estate market over community lands, whose uncertain possession is presented in the form of the commons or other figures of public dominion. Such a context is only possible once the indigenous communities have been declared to be dead and the peasants have been considered devoid of identity, classified as mestizos, as was customary in the old times of Spanish colonial racism, or as fake Indians (*indios truchos*), as the new Argentinean racism has hastened to designate, being their offspring separated from their traditional knowledge due to the secularizing and amalgamating effects of school.

No one can explain how the peasants managed to arrive at the place they now live. The archaeological and anthropological representation of peasantry at northeastern Argentina as devoid of traditional ties with the land is the offspring as well as the breeder of colonialism. It is not a matter of which side you choose to be: archaeology—i.e., the game of language through which the material marks of the traditional relationships of the indigenous peasantry with the land are turned into archaeological heritage and as a result, potential sources of information about anodyne "sociocultural" groups of the past—is already politically laden.

We are worried by the fact that the capitalist mining and agro-industrial expansion destroys the archaeological heritage that is defined by our particular and circumstantial academic practice, but we are not worried by, at least in the same way, the fact that these expansions are produced over the lands that are snatched from the indigenous peasant communities. We bear witness in silence, as they are doomed to proletarization in the same lands that were theirs not long ago or to migration to the poorest quarters of the cities to beg for the always-insufficient social aid.

If archaeology expects to develop itself as a practice for decolonization, it is necessary to decolonize it in the first place. This requires self-reflection before theory, before archaeology. That is to say, critical archaeology, if it has to decolonize itself, should be formulated into a deep cultural self-criticism; if not, it will be condemned to reproduce the same representations of the world that constitute us as social agents before archaeologists. Left unrevised, those representations blur the critical capacity of theory. And, only by correcting archaeology's practices in the sense of decolonization can the critical revision of the social consequences of our practices and our discourses be expected to be fertile.

There is no search for knowledge without social consequences; remaining stuck to this belief cannot be considered an academic luxury anymore, nor a political naivety. The theory of knowledge is, at the same time, the theory of society; knowledge is also social practice. Decolonizing archaeology is to deconstruct its object, and this is equal to a crisis of objectivism. Our relationship with reality must be rethought as a condition of a reconstruction of our relationship with knowledge; in this sense, it is fundamental to redirect knowledge within the current of life.

In the southern Andes, everything that exists is within the current of life. All beings are living beings, and they relate to each other as such. This includes the earth, the atmospheric phenomena, crops, animals, hills, water, the stars and the constellations, the living and the dead, the ancestors and the ancient beings. Knowing how to breed/nurture life is the same as knowing how to be bred/nurtured by life. To pass on the seed of life is every being's duty. In the southern Andes, the sense of knowledge is to know how to relate with other beings of the world that could be more powerful than oneself; thus, there is an indistinguishable relationship between knowledge and power. Interpreting its signs, influencing favorably in its action, reestablishing the "balance" in the relationships, knowing how to breed and knowing how to be bred summarizes the sense of knowledge of the Andean peasantry.

It is not about a type of knowledge that could be logically linked to other types of knowledge in order that it can eventually account for the world and in this way operate technically on it. The southern Andean peasant lives in a world whose center is the farm, a living world that germinates, grows up, blossoms, yields fruits, and dies to be born again. Those beings are carrying out conversations in the world and they are becoming in these conversations.

Archaeology, as all Western scientific disciplines, assumes a universal world that can be, well or badly, known, predicated, operated.

Knowledge is based on the technomethodological control of the world, of the object, and not in the conversation among beings. The object can be decomposed; its integrating parts, as well as its relationships with other objects, are relationships that can be enunciated according to the logics of non-contradiction, of the third excluded.

Seeing the panorama in this way, it seems that an insurmountable abyss is opened between those two approaches to the world. This is why I would rather not see the panorama in this way. I would rather think that it is possible to dispossess myself of the observer's arrogance and to return to the world of life. This does not mean to unlearn all the way; on the contrary, it entails settling down again after the oblivion of the earth.

A critical archaeology supposes the deconstruction of archaeology's basic assumption, the one that sets archaeology as the discourse that preterizes the indigenous, that is, imposes a unique mode and one verbal tense to predicate the indigenous. But if that assumption has been reproduced at the same time that archaeology has got its share of recognition in the academic distribution of reality, this is because the assumption is not merely academic but cultural. Therefore, the archaeology of archaeology is not without a cultural criticism.

It is not about entering into a dialogue between archaeologists and indigenous people. Or, rather, it is not as simple as that. It is about recognizing in our cultural constitution the negotiations, the Othering, the preterizations of the indigenous, of which archaeology is, on a large scale, nothing but a reproduction mechanism.

The words "peasant" and "indigenous" are not synonyms. In Argentina, at least, the category peasant has come to replace the category indigenous, to the same extent that the regulations of a colonial tax system have been replaced by regulations based on capitalist relationships. The expansion of the real estate market considers formerly marginal lands—those of the peasants—as an appealing commercial objective. A number of communities are repossessing their lands and self-recognizing their indigenous identity as a form of resistance to imminent or consummated dispossession.

The use I make of "peasant" and "indigenous" is a mark of the fleeting character of such categories nowadays. The language with which we describe the world is also the legacy of that colonial world we wish to abolish; its inadequacy is, for the moment, unavoidable. The gap between socioeconomic (peasantry) and cultural (indigenous) definitions is, in the end, another colonial mechanism that makes it possible to understand the people who breed the farm and the land where people are bred as two separate objects and to put them separately at the disposal of knowledge and the market. Yet, more important than achieving a correct and definite word to designate reality is to delineate the sense of practice and academic discourses in relation to their wanted effects in reality.

This text describes the contribution of archaeology to the conceptual detachment that, in the short or long run, justifies the conceptual dispossession of the traditional resources of indigenous communities and the violation of their rights. It aims at pointing out, at the same time, the road to return to the land and the potential contribution of archaeology to the peasants' processes of seizing the land through, for example, the consolidation of their traditional indigenous rights. What is reality? How do we know it? What is our place in it? How do we speak about it? Which effects do we expect in reality? Those questions are aspects of the same critical task. In the present tenses where there were only pasts, in subjunctive modes where there were only indicative modes, conjugated like the peasant prayer, archaeology has a different place in another reality.

But why do we have to tell what reality is? A poet's words are more pleasant than an archaeologist's—in this case Paco Urondo's words (1989) at the prison of Villa Devoto, April 1973, when he wrote: "At the other side of the iron bars lies reality; at this side of the iron bars also lies reality; the only unreal thing is the iron bar."

Note

A number of colleagues contributed with ideas, comments, or simply—though not less importantly—with their encouragement and affection, without them these words would have not been aligned in the text: Heather Burke, Pedro Funari, Rafael Gassón, Cristóbal Gnecco, Gary Jackson, Des Kahotea, Carlos López, Santiago Mora, Javier Nastri, Eduardo Neves, Emilio Piazzini, Marta Ruiz, Ernesto Salazar, Mario Sanoja, Nick Shepherd, Claire Smith, Iraida Vargas, César Velandia, Joe Watkins, Verónica Williams, Martin Wobst, and Andrés Zarankin. Lilén Malugany and Lee Steadman made a great effort to put this text into English language. None of them should be blamed for my excesses. My excesses are due to Silvina.

References

Ambrosetti, Juan Bautista 1896 El símbolo de la serpiente en la alfarería funeraria de la región calchaquí. *Boletín del Instituto Geográfico Argentino* 17:219–230.

———. 1899 *Notas de arqueología calchaquí; (1ª serie)*. Imprenta y litografía Buenos Aires, Buenos Aires.

Cáceres, Julián 1963 Palabras del Director del Instituto Nacional de Antropología. *Cuadernos del Instituto Nacional de Antropología* 4:11–15.

Haber, Alejandro F. 1995 Supuestos teórico-metodológicos de la etapa formativa de la arqueología de Catamarca (1875–1900). *Arqueología* 47:31–54.

Haber, Alejandro F., and Daniel D. Delfino 1995–1996 Samuel Lafone Quevedo and the construction of archaeology in Argentina. *Revista de História da Arte e Arqueologia* 2:31–43.

Hernández, María Isabel 2001 Formulación de hipótesis arqueológicas a partir de la evidencia rupestre: un caso de la quebrada de Humahuaca, Jujuy. In *Actas del XIII Congreso Nacional de Arqueología Argentina*, pp. 91–110. Universidad Nacional de Córdoba, Córdoba.

Holmberg, Eduardo 1893 Munaysapa. Lo que dice un fragmento de vaso calchaquí. *Revista del Jardín Zoológico de Buenos Aires* 1(4):102–115.

Lafone Quevedo, Samuel 1890 *Notas arqueológicas á propósito de un objeto de arte indígena*. Anales del Museo de La Plata, La Plata.

———. 1891 Las huacas de Chañar Yaco (Provincia de Catamarca). *Revista del Museo de La Plata* 2:353–360.

———. 1902 Las "manoplas" del culto de Viracocha. Estudio de arqueología calchaquina. In *Actes du XII Congrès International des Américanistes*, pp. 285–291. Paris.

Liberani, Inocencio, and Rafael Hernández 1950 [1877] *Excursión arqueológica en los valles de Santa María, Catamarca, 1877*. Universidad Nacional de Tucumán, San Miguel del Tucumán.

Márquez, Fernando 1959 Noticias antropológicas extraídas del "Diario íntimo" de D. Samuel A. Lafone Quevedo. *Runa* 9:19–30.

Moreno, Francisco Pascasio 1890–1891 *Exploración arqueológica de la Provincia de Catamarca. Primeros datos sobre su importancia y resultados*. Revista del Museo de La Plata 1, separata.

Quiroga, Adán 1886 *Delito y pena*. Talleres Gráficos, Tucumán.

———. 1893 *Calchaquí y la epopeya de las cumbres*. Revista del Museo de La Plata 5, separata.

———. 1898 El simbolismo de la cruz y el falo en Calchaquí. *Boletín del Instituto Geográfico Argentino* 19:305–343.

———. 1899 *Calchaquí*. Tucumán.

Urondo, Francisco 1989 *Poemas de batalla*. Planeta, Buenos Aires.

PART I

WHEN MATERIAL CULTURE MATTERS: THE STATE, INDIGENOUS PEOPLES, AND ARCHAEOLOGISTS

CHAPTER 1

RUINS AND THE STATE: ARCHAEOLOGY OF A MEXICAN SYMBIOSIS

Federico Navarrete

In 1978, an enormous monolith of the Aztec[1] goddess Coyolxauhqui was found in downtown Mexico City, a few yards from the main square. This accidental finding made it possible to determine, without a shadow of a doubt, the exact location of the old Templo Mayor—the main pyramid of the Aztec capital of Mexico, over whose ruins the modern Mexican capital was built. Given this extraordinary opportunity, Mexican president José López Portillo made the decision to acquire two blocks of buildings in the area by compulsory purchase and ordered their demolition, with the aim of excavating the old sacred site. That marked the birth of the Templo Mayor Archaeological Project, one of the greatest in Mexican history. A few years later, López Portillo himself defined his actions in a commemorative book:

> On that 28th of February, 1978, I felt power to its full extent: I could, at my own will, transform the reality that masked the fundamental roots of my Mexico, that lay at the very core of its history, mystical sphere, and of its still unresolved dialectic tragedy. This came as a fleeting opportunity to bring about its integration, at least symbolically. To open a square "akin" to the colonial square, the Zócalo of our independence, for all of

us Mexicans to understand that we come from the Omeyocan—Place of Duality—which we must accept so as to walk steadily through the paths of our destiny, recognizing our mixture as a condition and a force of our origin and our destination ... And I had the power to rescue the space and redeem our times ... Perhaps there would not be another chance. To discover, to bring to the light: to give new dimension to the central proportions of our origin. To open the space of our consciousness as an exceptional Nation. And I was able to do so, solely by saying, "Let us acquire the buildings. Let them be torn down. And let the Aztecs' Templo Mayor be unveiled to the day and the night." (López Portillo et al. 1981:25–27)

This act of authoritarianism for the service of archaeology, and the subsequent use of archaeology for the service of authoritarianism, illustrates, rather eloquently and spectacularly, the symbiosis that has existed throughout the twentieth century between Mexican archaeology and state power. Such symbiosis has entailed the almost exclusive institutionalization of Mexican archaeology into an agency of the Mexican federal government, the Instituto Nacional de Antropología e Historia (INAH) (National Anthropology and History Institute), which enjoys a legal and political monopoly on the exploration, preservation, and use of the country's archaeological remains. Given that the main duty of the INAH is managing and preserving such heritage, Mexican archaeologists have been forced to do salvage, reconstruction, and preservation activities, many times to the detriment of their research work. Moreover, state funding for archaeology has privileged the search and reconstruction of spectacular monuments, especially state architecture and artwork associated with pre-Hispanic elites, over problem-centered research and, in general, over a more holistic analysis of indigenous societies. In this paper I will endeavor to reconstruct the origin of this symbiosis between ruins, archaeologists, and the state in order to explain how it has managed to prevent other sectors in Mexican society, particularly indigenous groups, from having a meaningful relationship with the archaeological legacy of the pre-Hispanic past. To assess the importance of this monopoly, one must remember the fact that, beyond their marked regional, linguistic, religious, cultural, and political distinctions, almost all Mexicans deem pre-Hispanic ruins an essential symbol of their identity and roots. This is the result of the nationalistic vision of Mexican history, which I will call "monolithic," both because of its love of large stone monuments (which in Mexico we like to call monoliths) and because of an equally monolithic identification between the pre-Hispanic indigenous peoples and modern mestizo Mexicans, from which contemporary indigenous groups are paradoxically excluded (Navarrete 2004). This vision has undoubtedly reigned supreme in Mexico and has underpinned the laws regulating Mexican archaeological heritage, the institutions managing it, and archaeologists' practices and discourses.

THE EXPROPRIATION OF THE INDIGENOUS PAST

The oldest roots of the monolithic vision of Mexican history is found in the patriotism conceived by groups of Creoles, that is persons of Spanish descent born in the Americas, between the seventeenth and nineteenth centuries. In their quest to invent an identity of their own to distinguish themselves from the Spaniards and to lay the foundations of their nation, these groups glorified the Aztec empire destroyed by the conquistadors in the sixteenth century and turned it into the direct antecedent of the future independent Mexican state (Lafaye 1977).

In the eighteenth century, the discovery of two impressive Aztec sculptures under Mexico City buildings, the famous statue of the goddess Coatlicue and the equally celebrated "Aztec Calendar," created even further interest in the pre-Hispanic past and pride in its magnificence, providing a specific physical reference to the Creoles' ideological construction. Authors such as Antonio de León y Gama, Antonio Alzate, and Francisco Clavijero compare these monuments to those from classical times, creating a valuable analogy between pre-Hispanic indigenous cultures and the classic Mediterranean cultures, and between themselves, as explorers and heirs of that past, and European archaeologists and antiquarians. Contemporary indigenous peoples were excluded from that ideological construction. Clavijero proposed that the archaeological heritage be transferred to a museum, where it would foster Creole pride and study. However, when scholars found out that the indigenous people of the city had begun worshipping Coatlicue's image, they decided to bury it again. Bishop Benito Marín Moxo y Francoly explained this decision as follows:

> The indians, who look at all the monuments of the European arts with such stupid indifference, came to contemplate their famous statue with restless curiosity. At first, it was believed that they did not do so for a reason other than national love, present among savage peoples and civilized ones, and for the pleasure of contemplating one of the most remarkable pieces of work of their ancestors, appreciated even by well-read Spaniards. However, it was later suspected that their frequent visits had some secret religious reason. It became essential to forbid entrance altogether, but their fanatic enthusiasm and their incredible craftiness circumvented this restriction ... This fact, corroborated by persons of seriousness and learning ... forced us to take, as we have said, the decision to rebury the aforementioned statue. (cited by Matos 2005:11–12)

This episode marks the beginning of a clash between two different ways of relating to the archaeological heritage, a clash that still prevails: the indigenous religious cult is condemned from the intolerant perspective of learned Western thought, which defends the nationalistic admiration of a magnificent past, a form of "aura" that, as Walter Benjamin correctly states, is nothing more than a late transformation of religious worship, a "secularized ritual" (Benjamin 1973:26).

This project that sought to expropriate the social memory of indigenous groups in the name of science and nationalism is exactly like the one that has characterized modern Mexican archaeology and, in general, Latin American national archaeologies. David Brading (1980:39–40) has suggested that this expropriation, and the resulting reverence of the pre-Hispanic past from the Creole perspective, was possible thanks to the fact that Mexico, unlike Peru, lacked an indigenous movement seeking to revitalize that past, despite the religious interest in the figure of the goddess Coatlicue. Indigenous communities in central Mexico claimed that their origin lay in lands granted by the Spanish monarchy in the sixteenth century, in the establishment of their colonial towns, and in the election of their patron saint, but only referred vaguely to their pre-Hispanic past (López 2003). Maya groups to the south of the country repeatedly rebelled against colonial domination, but always in the name of the Catholic religion, without making any reference to their postcolonial past (Reifler-Bricker 1993).

During the nineteenth century it was not possible to perform many excavations given the political turmoil initiated by the lengthy war of independence and perpetuated by continuous civil wars and foreign invasions until 1867. However, the monolithic vision of Mexican history and the monopoly of Creole and mestizo elites upon it developed and consolidated. Nineteenth-century historians and archaeologists built a grand, unified narrative—akin to the nationalist histories being elaborated at that time in Europe—from known archaeological remains and written sources on pre-Hispanic history from the colonial period (Anderson 1983). This narrative posited the unity and continuity of all pre-Hispanic cultures known until then, from Teotihuacán and the Toltecs to the Mexico-Tenochtitlán Aztecs, and turned the pre-Hispanic period into the initial chapter of this national history. Just like the Creole patriotism of previous centuries, this narrative exalted the Aztecs as the culmination of the indigenous past (Pérez 2000). In the political context of the nineteenth century, this glorification laid the foundations of the country's territorial union and the centralization of political power in Mexico City.

Even though this historical elaboration was merely based on a few archaeological excavations, it proved to be deeply influential for the evolution of this discipline since the end of the nineteenth century, when excavations were resumed, for it defined two of its main features. Firstly, its dependency on historical sources produced at the start of the colonial period (sixteenth and seventeenth centuries), sources which, until today, have been fundamental for the identification, classification, and interpretation of archaeological cultures discovered in Mexico. Since then, one of the key debates in pre-Hispanic archaeology and history has been the identification of Toltec civilization, which according to the written sources was the epitome of indigenous civilization, with the archaeological remains of different cultures (López and López 1999). The second, equally defining, feature is archaeology's connection to the nationalistic discourse and its need to build a global, unified history of all pre-Hispanic indigenous cultures that is a referent of identity and a source of pride to the modern Mexican nation and its Creole and mestizo sectors.

Porfirio Díaz's administration, from 1876 to 1910, saw the birth of modern Mexican archaeology with Leopoldo Batres's excavations in Teotihuacán, near Mexico City. Díaz's regime also established the state monopoly on the administration of archaeological heritage and the control of archaeological exploration, although it also gave generous grants to foreign archaeologists, even allowing them to export their findings (Vázquez 2003:120–121).

There was also a sudden increase in the prestige and appeal of pre-Hispanic archaeological remains. Aztec, Maya, and Teotihuacán monuments and sculptures were displayed at art shows, international exhibitions, and museums as evidence of the existence of a Mexican "antiquity" that could be put on a level with classical times. That celebratory demonstration established Mexico's place in the "concert of civilized nations," on a par with European countries that, back then, strived to salvage and collect Egyptian, Greek, and Roman archaeological remains. This led to a complex dialectic between the claim of Mexico's exceptionality, proven by its singular pre-Hispanic heritage, and its cosmopolitism, proven by the capacity of its elites to construct a scientific discourse, true to Western cannons, about their own past (Tenorio-Trillo 1996:64–95). The dialectic relation between the object of study (the pre-Hispanic period, deemed extraordinary) and the subject studying it (the modern scientist aiming to be equal to archaeologists from the rest of the world) has been fundamental to the justification of the state monopoly on archaeological legacy.

THE CONSOLIDATION OF THE MONOLITH

During Díaz's prolonged administration and under the regimes risen from the Mexican Revolution since 1917, archaeology was linked to the ideology of *mestizaje* (racial mixing), which defined the racial and cultural identity of the nation. This ideology, defined by the state and its closest intellectual circles, proposed that the Mexican people were the product of a biological mixture of the indigenous and the Hispanic races, inheriting the best features of each one. The racial mix should cause the complete homogenization of the Mexican population and the disappearance of the racially distinct indigenous and European groups. However, the mestizo culture was always defined as purely Western, and it was stated that the mixture should lead to the elevation of the indigenous race to the superior level of the European (Knight 1990).

The ideology of *mestizaje* saw the indigenous past as glorious but extinct, overcome by the Spanish conquest of the Aztecs, which gave way to the birth of a new race, the mestizo race, and to the emergence of a new nation. Therefore, the indigenous past had been left behind and present indigenous groups were nothing more than its vestiges, degraded by centuries of Spanish colonization, who were incomparable to the splendor of their ancestors and should vanish as soon as possible in the melting pot of *mestizaje* (Navarrete 2004). For the mestizo, archaeological monuments were the evidence of the greatness of their forefathers, but they should belong to them (who were the only group qualified to study, rebuild, and appreciate them) and not to contemporary indigenous peoples, unworthy heirs of this magnificent legacy. The mestizo nationalism of the twentieth century was a direct descendant of the Creole patriotism of the eighteenth century.

After the Mexican Revolution, the ideology of *mestizaje* experienced a slight transformation, for it began to acknowledge the relative value of contemporary indigenous cultures, maybe as a reflection of the participation of indigenous and peasant groups in popular rebellions between 1910 and 1917. This acknowledgment, however, was limited, since the objective of homogenizing the nation culturally and racially through the integration (and extinction) of indigenous groups was not forgotten. The indigenous culture deemed valuable was a hand-picked, stereotyped version of the cultural and social realities of the Mexican indigenous peoples that privileged "handcrafts" and folklore. Manuel Gamio was one of the first to set forth this new vision, and also the first (and almost the only) Mexican archaeologist who sought to combine excavations with fieldwork among contemporary indigenous populations. His masterpiece *La población del Valle de Teotihuacán* (The population of the Teotihuacán Valley) encompassed archaeological, ethnological, ecological, and geographic studies in a superb description of the history and development of the region's dwellers from pre-Hispanic times until the present. At the same time, he established an educational project in the Teotihuacán Valley with a view to revitalizing the creative potential of indigenous populations, for he suggested that artistic talent was an essential feature of their identity. Nevertheless, Gamio's insistence on the relation between archaeological and ethnographic work came from a perspective that was alien to contemporary indigenous societies: the perspective of the scientist and the state agent. In Mexico, these roles are generally inseparable. Therefore, the indigenous people were presented as objects (the people of the past, the objects of study, and the people of the present, the objects of education), but never as subjects, a role that only corresponded to the mestizo scientist.

These ideas and this perspective were shared by several political and cultural actors of the time. Mexican muralists like Diego Rivera incorporated pre-Hispanic images and symbols into their spectacular visual discourses on Mexican identity, but always portrayed these images as past realities that should be a source of pride for the nation and integrated into modernity, as they were integrated into the entirely modern and cosmopolitan discourse of their murals (Rodríguez 2004). In cinema, Russian filmmaker Sergei Eisenstein and his Mexican imitators showed faces of contemporary indigenous people next to portraits of pre-Hispanic indigenous people to prove racial continuity. Still, in these depictions, the European or mestizo filmmaker was always the subject who compared and juxtaposed objects from the indigenous past and present without giving them a real voice or recognizing their specific agency.

In this way, the ideology of *mestizaje* and the monolithic conception of the national history coincided in defining the state and the intellectual groups associated with it as the sole legitimate agents for the use, management, and research of the archaeological legacy and in marginalized all indigenous groups from these activities. According to this idea, the pre-Hispanic past belongs, first of all, to Mexico as a nation, always represented by the state, and secondly to all mestizo Mexicans, but never to indigenous peoples as a particular group. This exclusive vision was also based on the idea of *patrimonialismo* of the Spanish monarchy, which held that all antiques in America were private property of the Crown and could only be given in concession to individuals. The independent Mexican state set itself up as the legitimate and indisputable heir of that monopoly (Vázquez 2003:95–145).

Around the middle of the nineteenth century, the monolithic vision was institutionalized and made into law by the revolutionary regime, which also institutionalized the bureaucratic apparatus of the single-party regime of the Partido Revolucionario Institucional (Institutional Revolutionary Party). The INAH was founded in 1939 and entrusted with archaeological excavations, safeguarding archaeological heritage, and conducting scientific and artistic research on the indigenous population of the country. Since its inception, the combination of research and heritage custody and management duties has inhibited the development of the former (Gándara 1992).

The Instituto Nacional Indigenista (National Indigenist Institute) was founded in 1948, with the responsibility of serving and studying existing indigenous societies. Since then, the Mexican state established an institutional division of labor: the INAH was charged with studying and celebrating dead indigenous peoples, a boundless source of nationalistic pride and identity, and the INI had to solve the "problem" of live indigenous peoples, using anthropology as the tool to integrate them fully into mestizo society, i.e., to achieve their disappearance as ethnically and culturally different groups (Navarrete 2004). It is significant that the INI's first director, Alfonso Caso, was one of the most remarkable Mexican archaeologists of the time, yet there was no organic link between his activities as a researcher of the pre-Hispanic past and his work as the administrator of the state policy on indigenous peoples.

In the historical and methodological arenas, the German anthropologist Paul Kirchhoff (1943) argued that archaeological and historical cultures in central and southern Mexico shared enough major cultural features to be considered part of the same cultural area, which he called Mesoamerica. His proposal has been immensely significant for the development of Mexican archaeology, since it made it possible to analyze the specifics of each archaeological culture and each site within a general framework of analysis that gave them meaning. In terms of space, it allowed for the definition of a vast cultural region with particular subregions. In terms of time, the concept of Mesoamerica has allowed for the use of historical sources of the early colonial period and contemporary ethnographic sources to interpret archaeological findings of times as remote as the Formative period (2000–200 BC). Even though these methodological procedures have been criticized (e.g., Kubler 1972), they have become common practice among archaeologists, historians, ethnologists, and art historians and have yielded valuable results. However, the generalized, noncritical adoption of this concept and the cultural history methodology associated with it has hindered the evolution of other theoretical and explanatory approaches and has turned archaeologists' interpretative work into a mere procedure: to place their findings in a predefined historical and cultural framework (Vázquez 2003:45–94). In my opinion, this is due to the fact that the concept of a Mesoamerican cultural area has been combined with the ideological vision of indigenous history, previously constituted by Mexican nationalism, and has therefore reinforced a monolithic vision of pre-Hispanic, colonial, and modern indigenous societies. An example of this combination is Guillermo Bonfil's book *México profundo* (1990), where he states that the true essence of the Mexican nationality is a "Mesoamerican civilization" that has remained essentially unchanged for three millennia and has been attacked and destroyed, but not transformed, by Spanish colonization and the policies of the Mexican state-nation. This has led to the emergence of a relation of symbolic identification between the archaeological remains of the former Mesoamerican states (from the La Venta Olmecs to the Mexico-Tenochtitlán Aztecs, Monte Albán Zapotecs, Teotihuacáns, and the Palenque and Chichén Itzá Maya) and the modern Mexican state. Along this line of argument, it is frequent for pre-Hispanic states to be seen as direct predecessors of the current Mexican state, be it with a negative connotation, as a source of its authoritarianism (Paz 1970), or a positive one, as a source of its undying identity (Florescano 1998). Archaeology has become an agent and a propagandist of state ideology and its monolithic vision of the national past. This has inhibited the appearance of more critical visions of pre-Hispanic societies. The monolithic vision has also entailed the virtual exclusion of societies from northern Mexico, which belong to the cultural area named Aridamerica, from the interest of Mexican archaeologists, even though the exploration of this region has grown over the last few years.

The monolithic vision of Mexican history reached its definite materialization in the building of the National Anthropology Museum (Museo Nacional de Antropología, or MNA) inaugurated in 1964, a monumental structure that set its essential features in stone. The museum established a direct link between the present glory of the Mexican state that built it and the past greatness of the pre-Hispanic states on display in its rooms, and it has become a privileged site for public ceremonies involving the President of the Republic and other officials. The museum established the Aztecs' supremacy in the nationalistic historical genealogy and made the room devoted to this culture and its emblematic monoliths (the "Piedra del Sol" [Aztec Calendar] and Coatlicue, finally rescued from indigenous idolatry to serve the lay religion of the Mexican state) the central and culminating piece of the museum exhibit. Moreover, it privileged the spectacular display and aesthetic admiration of the pieces over their cultural and historical explanation. Thus, it became a huge and magnificent collection of eye-catching pieces, fundamentally designed to strengthen the patriotic pride of its Mexican visitors and to present a linear and teleological vision of the nation's past. It is significant that the museum dedicated a second floor to "ethnographic" rooms that present ahistorical, folklorist visions of contemporary indigenous cultures. This space, much smaller than the massive archaeological section and separated from it, has become a marginalized sector of the institution, just as current indigenous groups are marginalized from society.

In this way in the second half of the twentieth century, legislation and institutional practices established and strengthened the state's monopoly over pre-Hispanic remains, which has palliated the devastating effects of plundering and the illegal trade of archaeological pieces but has also imposed a barrier on the participation of indigenous groups and other sectors of society in the management and research of these remains, making them the exclusive territory of official archaeologists. The "discovery" and reconstruction of numerous spectacular archaeological sites has proven to be highly lucrative to the Mexican state from an ideological point of view.

THE CRACKING OF THE MONOLITH

Over the last few decades, the monolithic vision of national history and the legal and institutional framework that consecrated the state monopoly on archaeological patrimony have experienced a profound transformation. This should come as no surprise, for both of them were historically and functionally linked to the consolidation of the postrevolutionary authoritarian state, which is why the recent political and social democratization has weakened them. Political centralism has lost strength, like the monolithic narrative of national history centered on the Aztecs and the supremacy of Mexico City as the historical, cultural, and political center of the country. In response, different regions and social groups have created particular historical discourses that entail a differentiated, plural relation with the indigenous past and the archaeological heritage. At the same time, the governments of states and municipalities have demanded greater participation in the management and use of that legacy.

The traditional definition of Mexican identity is no longer satisfactory for many sectors of society. Some groups attribute significance to their pre-Hispanic roots, conceived according to their particular religious beliefs and political ideologies, and increasingly use ruins for ceremonies and rituals that go beyond established institutional practices and are not always consistent with the canon of official history. Other groups recognize no links with that past, despite the state's attempts to convince them that their origin lies there. In general, the symbols of Mexican identity defined by the monolithic vision have become exotic and touristic commodities and are no longer culturally significant for many parts of Mexican society.

The institutions arisen from the postrevolutionary regime have had to make great efforts to adapt to this new reality. The INI has recently gone through a deep reform, for the encompassing concept of indigenism became obsolete in the face of the evolution of indigenous societies and their political movements that demand a new relationship with the state. The INAH has maintained its legal monopoly on the use of patrimony and has kept fostering spectacular archaeological projects, but has not been able to generate a new national historical discourse that could reach beyond the monolithic vision and integrate indigenous people and other sectors of society in a different way. Despite the adoption of policies that are more open to collaboration with civil society and indigenous and peasant communities, some researchers and authorities from the INAH have developed an attitude of rejection to the participation of other sectors in archaeological patrimony research and management, considering them "enemies" who threaten the duty of protection entrusted upon their institution. Therefore, in certain cases, the INAH's monopoly has been degraded to a form of *patrimonialismo* that makes its members treat national heritage as if it were their own. In this perverse logic, it is frequent for archaeologists to deny other scholars access to their field findings and to refrain from publishing the results of their work, so a great part of the excavations done in Mexico remain unknown to the scientific community and the general public (Vázquez 2003). Museum directors and people in charge of the INAH's vast collections arbitrarily restrict access to them or try to charge high fees for their reproduction, even if it is not-for-profit.

This attitude was manifest in a recent dispute over the destination of Papago human remains unearthed by a French archaeological expedition (authorized by the INAH, as all excavations done legally in national territory) in Quitobac and claimed by the Papago people who live in the state of Sonora, in northern Mexico. In the face of the repatriation demand made by the Papago, most probably inspired by similar demands by the "First Nations" of the United States and Canada over the last few years (Thomas 2000) and which were supported by a Mexican court, an archaeologist attached to the INAH responded:

> The authorization of the Archaeology Council suffices to do archaeological research in any part of the national territory; there is no need to consult with the descendants of native populations at all. Since we are all Mexican, there can be no talk of traditional territories. (quoted by Vázquez 2003:134)

This case is not unique. Archaeologists and museographers hired by the INAH have faced community demonstrations when trying to take away pre-Hispanic pieces considered by peasant and/or indigenous communities as part of their local patrimony. The best-known example is the transport of the monolith known as "Tlaloc," originally located in the town of Cuauhtinchan and currently on display in the National Anthropology Museum. One aspect worthy of consideration is that the changes in the dominion over the pieces also entail changes in their interpretation. Such is the case of the so-called "Señor de las Limas" (Lord of the Lemons), an Olmec sculpture (which archaeologists date to the first millennium BC) found in 1965 by members of the Las Limas community, who called it "Virgen de las Limas" (Virgin of the Lemons), since they considered it a miraculous image of the Virgin of Guadalupe. This sculpture was taken away from the community and now forms part of the collection of the Anthropology Museum at Jalapa, where it is displayed as an archaeological artifact, obliterating the religious value previously assigned to it by the population of Las Limas (Medina, n.d.).

Despite the fact that the law enshrines the state monopoly over archaeological heritage, it also allows for the organization and authorization of social groups as aids to its preservation. Therefore, ever since the 1970s, there has been an initiative to build community museums to house and exhibit some pieces in the towns where they were found. Self-regulated and focused on the interests and concerns of town dwellers, these museums are an example of cooperation between official agencies and the society for the management of this legacy (Morales 1994). However, these experiments have not spread to great institutions, where the idea of curatorships shared with indigenous people or of giving the people a voice of their own in the museographic discourse is not even considered.

Unfortunately, there is a lack of reflection, analysis, and proposals regarding the possibility of finding compromises between the demands of indigenous peoples and the practice of archaeology or archaeological heritage management. In such a scenario, it is not strange that response to conflict has been unsatisfactory, limited, or elusive (Medina, n.d.). There is also a lack of formal or official formulas of collaboration between archaeologists and indigenous communities in research and excavation projects, with a few exceptions involving Mixtecos in Oaxaca and Huicholes in Nayarit (Johannes Neurath, personal communication 2003).

In general, the issue of the relation between archaeology and indigenous societies is barely beginning to be addressed by a few researchers, and there are disagreements between them: some defend the INAH's traditional monopoly and deny the relevance of recognizing the rights of indigenous people over archaeological heritage, arguing that there is no proof of the existence of direct historical links between contemporary populations and the people who built the sites (Rodríguez 2005), while others suggest that, even though the state should maintain the essential right of property, it is necessary to propose specific collaboration programs tailored to the circumstances of indigenous societies (Medina, n.d.).

A profound reflection on the matter is therefore urgent, as well as a discussion of pragmatic, theoretical, and methodological aspects and a revision of specific cases. Based on that, it will be possible to define guidelines for involving communities in archaeological heritage research, management, and preservation in a respectful, informed, and responsible manner. It is important to mention, as do Medina (n.d.) and Rodríguez (2005) beyond their disagreements, that mimicking American solutions will not solve this problem, for the Mexican case is very different for historical and cultural reasons.

On the other hand, the scientific claim with which Mexican archaeology justifies its monopoly is very weak, given its scarce scientific output. Moreover, as has been argued by Cristóbal Gnecco (1999), and as has happened in Mexico since the eighteenth century, this type of claim in Latin America has only excluded *different* social groups from access to archaeological legacy and imposed the dominance of just one historical discourse, the official discourse, over local, subaltern, or ethnic histories.

In short, it is imperative to rethink the legal and institutional framework governing the use of Mexico's archaeological heritage to find one that is less exclusive and centralistic, more democratic and participatory, and less oriented toward economic and political profit. This redefinition must be done by the mestizo groups who consider themselves heirs of the pre-Hispanic peoples and by indigenous peoples, who have a different relationship with that past. This may be the only way to break with the monolithic vision of the Mexican past and with the dichotomy between dead and live indigenous people that has hurt the latter so much.

Note

1. Also referred to as *Mexica* in Spanish. The most common translation, *Aztec*, will be used for the purposes of this paper.

References

Anderson, Benedict 1983 *Imagined Communities: Reflections on the Origin and Spread of Nationalism*. Verso, London.

Benjamin, Walter 1973 La obra de arte en la época de su reproductibilidad técnica. In *Discursos interrumpidos I*, by Walter Benjamin, pp. 15–57. Madrid, Taurus.

Bonfil, Guillermo 1990 *México profundo. Una civilización negada*. Grijalbo/Conaculta, Mexico.

Brading, David 1980 *Los orígenes del nacionalismo mexicano*. Era, Mexico.

Florescano, Enrique 1998 *Etnia, Estados y nación. Ensayo sobre las identidades colectivas en México*. Aguilar, Mexico.

Gándara, Manuel 1992 *La arqueología oficial mexicana: causas y efectos*. INAH, Mexico.

Gnecco, Cristóbal 1999 *Multivocalidad histórica. Hacia una cartografía postcolonial de la arqueología*. Universidad de los Andes, Bogota.

Kirchhoff, Paul 1943 Mesoamérica: sus límites geográficos, composición étnica y caracteres culturales. *Acta Americana* 1:92–107.

Knight, Alan 1990 Racism, revolution and indigenismo: México, 1910–1940. In *The Idea of Race in Latin America*, edited by Richard Graham, pp. 71–113. University of Texas Press, Austin.

Kubler, George 1972 La evidencia intrínseca y la analogía etnológica en el estudio de las religiones mesoamericanas. In *Religión en Mesoamérica*, edited by Jaime Litvak and Noemí Castillo, pp. 1–24. Sociedad Mexicana de Antropología, Mexico.

Lafaye, Jacques 1977 *Quetzalcóatl y Guadalupe. La formación de la conciencia nacional en México*. Fondo de Cultura Económica, Mexico.

López, Alfredo, and Leonardo López 1999 *Mito y realidad de Zuyuá: serpiente emplumada y las transformaciones mesoamericanas del Clásico al Posclásico*. Fondo de Cultura Económica, Mexico.

López, Paula (editor) 2003 *Los títulos primordiales del centro de México*. Conaculta, Mexico.

López Portillo, José, Miguel León-Portilla, and Eduardo Matos 1981 *El Templo Mayor*. Bancomer, Mexico.

Matos, Eduardo 2005 *Estudios mexicas*. Vol. 1, bk. 4, *Obras maestras del Templo Mayor*. El Colegio Nacional, Mexico.

Medina, Isabel n.d. ¿Arqueología indigenista en México? Una discusión. Unpublished manuscript in possession of the author.

Morales, Teresa 1994 *Pasos para crear un museo comunitario*. Direccion General de Culturas Populares, Mexico.

Navarrete, Federico 2004 *Las relaciones interétnicas en México*. UNAM, Mexico.

Paz, Octavio 1970 *El laberinto de la soledad*. Fondo de Cultura Económica, Mexico. First published 1950.

Pérez, Adriana 2000 Arqueología y nacionalismo a la luz del discurso histórico mexicano: 1850–1910. Unpublished BA thesis, Department of History, Universidad Nacional Autónoma de México, Mexico.

Reifler-Bricker, Victoria 1993 *El Cristo indígena, el rey nativo*. Fondo de Cultura Económica, Mexico.

Rodríguez, Itzel 2004 *El pasado indígena en el nacionalismo revolucionario. El mural antiguo (1929) de Diego Rivera en el Palacio Nacional*. UNAM, Mexico.

Rodríguez, Daniela 2005 El derecho de las poblaciones indígenas sobre los monumentos arqueológicos: algunas consideraciones desde la arqueología. In *Los derechos de los pueblos indios y la cuestión agraria*, edited by Carlos Humberto Durand Alcántara, pp. 179–196. Porrúa, Mexico.

Tenorio-Trillo, Mauricio 1996 *Mexico at the World's Fairs: Crafting a Modern Nation*. University of California Press, Berkeley.

Thomas, David Hurst 2000 *Skull Wars: Kennewick Man, Archaeology, and the Battle for Native American Identity*. Basic Books, New York.

Vázquez, Luis 2003 *El leviatán arqueológico: antropología de una tradición científica en México*. CIESAS-Porrúa, Mexico.

CHAPTER 2

NATIVE HISTORIES AND ARCHAEOLOGISTS

Cristóbal Gnecco

The histories "imposed" by colonialism upon native societies were less imposed than woven into daily life. In that reticular weaving colonialism built its imperviousness: by creating more than destroying, by composing symbolic networks rather than just removing and replacing one with another, colonialism became hard to identify and confront. Outright domination and subjection can be confronted more thoroughly (though certainly not more easily) than cultural creations originating in semiotic encounters.

The conception of the past of the indigenous communities in Andean southwestern Colombia was shaped by the Spanish conquest, especially by the generalized ideological (and physical) violence exercised by the Catholic Church. We may never know how those communities conceived of their pasts before European colonization; yet, we know that Catholicism instituted a historical conception that condemned pre-conquest times with a moral evolutionism uttered from the project of civilization. The pejorative treatment of past inhabitants (not necessarily Others but also the communities' own ancestors; in other words, the ancestors turned Others) was and is extended wherever colonial domination occurred. Colonial domination destroyed local histories (and their associated paraphernalia, such as shrines and votive items) and their historians (by physical destruction or by rhetorical subservience) but it also created histories anew with new beginnings. Time and the inhabitants existing before such beginnings (cloaked in mystical terms and appearances) were condemned and loaded with negative meanings. Colonialism replaced native myths of origin with the genesis of civilization.

Several indigenous societies (especially those subjected to the domination of the Catholic Church) fear material referents linked to their

---

Portions of this chapter are excerpted from an article (coauthored with Carolina Hernández) originally published in *Current Anthropology* 49:439–467 (2008). © 2008 by the University of Chicago Press.

forebears, precisely what archaeologists call "archaeological materials," both biological and non-biological. That fear is translated into proscription, creating a curious scenario in which empowered native communities explicitly interested in historical matters disregard archaeological sites and materials.

Although the indigenous communities that were brought under the colonial yoke surely possessed theories of Otherness, maybe including dichotomous classifications of self and Other akin to those of the West—that is, the self as civilized, primordial, and exemplary and the Other as barbaric, referential, and negative—the way they perceived (and many still perceive) their own pasts as uncivilized and negligible was colonially produced. Yet such a conception is now being contested and subverted by native activism; what was previously feared and proscribed now assumes a positive valuation. I will discuss this process by showing how the Colombian Nasa are contesting and transforming colonial-national history through the resignification of what archaeology had turned into material referents (things archaeological, proscribed until recently), systems of representation (archaeology, especially its denial of local meanings), and colonial categories (histories that created new beginnings and condemned old practices).

THE NASA PEOPLE, THE JUAN TAMA *RESGUARDO*[1] AND THINGS ARCHAEOLOGICAL

Some 200,000 Nasa, whose relationship with the state (colonial and republican) has been marked by both capitulation and rebellion, live mostly in a region of the Andes of southwestern Colombia known as Tierradentro (see Figure 2.1 for the location of the places mentioned in the text). In 1994 an earthquake shook the heartland of their territory. Several communities were uprooted from their ancestral lands due to the destruction of agricultural fields and mounting geological risk. A relocation effort was then launched by the Colombian state with the aim of finding suitable lands (suitable in economic and cultural terms). After some initial hesitation and difficult negotiations with the state-run agency that directed the relocation, some 500 Nasa from Vitoncó (considered to be the heartland of Nasa territory) accepted resettlement in an area around Santa Leticia, a small frontier town between the provinces of Cauca and Huila that lies outside current Nasa territory. The community agreed to move after the *the' walas* (shamans) had given their approval. The new settlement was named after Juan Tama, an eighteenth-century Nasa leader and a fundamental referent in Nasa history.

Strengthening their sense of belonging (territorial and otherwise) and ethnic consciousness has become an urgent matter for the resettled Nasa.

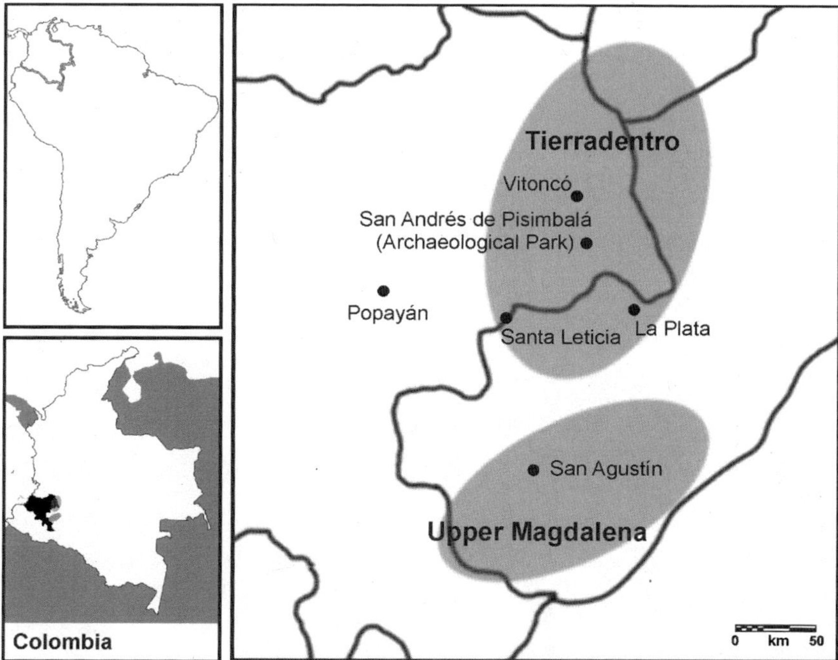

Figure 2.1 Map of southwestern Colombia showing locations mentioned in the text.

In these new settlements young generations face conflicting feelings about ethnicity, much more intensely than their parents faced a few decades ago when capitalism was encroaching upon their world and putting pressure on their ethnic identity. The ambivalence between being and not being Nasa can be dramatic. Overt conflict is more prevalent in the region around Santa Leticia than in the ancestral lands because the Juan Tama settlement is surrounded by mestizo peasants with different priorities and worldviews, rather than by other *resguardos*. In such a situation a sense of territorial belonging can make a difference, becoming one of the bases of cultural life. Gómez and Ruíz (1997) have shown that the territory is for the Nasa more than a spatial phenomena; it is a dynamic social process resulting from multiple interactions (economic, ecological, political, cognitive, and symbolic) and the main locus of social memory. The territory is lived history and history is territory played anew.

History is a model for the creation and revitalization of ethnic identity, which prominently includes the defense of territorial integrity. The relatively recent inception of an official native history[2] has been crucial in the revival of historical matters and the role accorded to it in the weaving of an empowered social fabric. Official native history and myths accord a central place to territory in Nasa life. The Nasa communities that were relocated after the 1994 earthquake have strategically displayed the relationship between history and territory in the process of giving meaning to a physical space that, at least in recent oral tradition, was not their own. Representations are recreated according to ancestral worldviews and are articulated and accommodated in order to provide a meaningful symbolic scheme to situational needs, such as territorial widening.

In 1995, a year after the Juan Tama settlement had been established, the community "confirmed" the mythical boundaries of the "new" zone. Although the area settled was devoid of indigenous peoples to the eyes of Westerners until a decade ago, there is a widespread belief that this *de facto* widening of pre-1994 Nasa *resguardos* is a redrawing of the preconquest limits of Nasa territory, which seem to have extended tens of kilometers eastward. The *the' walas*, elders, political officials (the governor and members of the *cabildo*, the corporate governing body), and some members of the community walked the territory, finding similarities with their heartland in Tierradentro and recognizing points of reference mentioned in myths, so deeply that they felt that they were not arriving in the Santa Leticia area but just returning. While performing this symbolic appropriation of the new *resguardo*, they came across La Candelaria, an archaeological site[3] with stone statues (located in a narrow valley in the upper reaches of the Aguacatal River, near Santa Leticia), up to then disregarded by Nasa history. The stone carvings from the site were given mythical meaning and the site itself was declared ancestral land. Angel María Yoinó, a *the' wala* of great esteem, claimed that the statues at La Candelaria

> take care of us and from now on we have to care for them, although we can't reach out or can't understand. If we the *the' walas* don't get together, we will never understand this way. We know that they loved and love us so we must do the same, to love and respect them. Stones have existed since the origin of the earth; they have been rearing us. We have been living for a long time and so we have to remember our forebears, but we forget and don't seem to remember them. But now that we have found them we must think with strength, walk with strength, and teach our grandkids. Only thus we will keep living.[4]

The stones are animated objects that evoke emotions and beings (the ancestors) that go beyond particular places and times, appealing to larger (and more permanent, although changing) structures of meaning; they are mythically recreated and displayed for the most part and link and supersede spatiotemporal contingencies, allowing "new" territories to be given meaning and to be appropriated by a sense of belonging. The symbolic meaning attributed to La Candelaria by the Nasa resettled around Santa Leticia has been important in this process for reflecting on temporality and cultural continuity. It has served as an anchor to people coming to a "new" territory that rapidly became their own because it is peopled by ancestors. History and territory recursively feed each other.

Until a few years ago, there were no records of Nasa relational meaning with the numerous archaeological remains that dot Tierradentro (mostly in San Andrés de Pisimbalá, where painted communal tombs and stone statues cluster).[5] Some three decades ago archaeologists Gerardo Reichel-Dolmatoff (1972:57) noted that "many archaeological sites in Páez [Nasa] territory are still greatly feared ... by the local Indians who attribute them to the ancient Pijao-jaguars." Reichel-Dolmatoff was noting what was to be widely known in multicultural times: many indigenous peoples disregard what expert knowledge calls the "archaeological record." In the case of the Nasa, this behavior may seem surprising given their strong involvement with the indigenous struggle, in which history is paramount, and given that the ancestors are central to their social life. Establishing historical continuity with imprints of the pre-Hispanic populations of the area would have fed territorial claims and cultural revival. But such continuity never developed. The reason is clearly not disinterest in historical matters: the indigenous movement considers the defense of native history one of its purposes (CRIC 1983:5), the Nasa think of themselves as heirs of the past peoples of the region (Rappaport 1990:18), and historical consciousness is one of the pillars on which Nasa worldview is built (Piñacué 1994:27–29).

A paradox is then at hand: the Nasa claim descent from the pre-Columbian inhabitants of Tierradentro, yet they made no effort to infuse the pre-Hispanic material culture found in their territory with local historical meaning, nor attempted to claim it back from state control,[6] as has happened worldwide in the last 30 years. Despite its large and politically active indigenous population, Colombia is still to see a strong confrontation of histories. Nothing comparable to the events prompted by NAGPRA in the USA or the consensual arrangements agreed upon by native peoples and the archaeological apparatus in Canada, Australia, and New Zealand has yet taken place in Colombia, where indigenous peoples' challenge to archaeology has been only marginal.

There can be several reasons for this apparent anomaly. The Nasa fear anything physically related to the dead (ancestors), so much that it is proscribed to be associated with or near their remains. One of the most dreadful diseases in Nasa medical systems is the *cacique* (chief) illness (Portela 2002:70). Whenever archaeological remains of any kind, especially burials,[7] appear (e.g., during the construction of houses, ditches, roads), the *the' walas* advise a change of location; if they happen to appear after construction, the *the' walas* perform the refreshment of the site and the cleansing of the people who have acquired *p'tanz* (dirt, in a very general sense).[8] The *cacique* disease stems from Nasa worldview, which posits the existence of three worlds, one of which is the underworld, where the ancestors, among other beings, have lived since they buried themselves to escape the Spanish invasion and domination.[9] The ancestors also live in a proscribed region of this world, the world of the Nasa; that region houses the untamed, the uncultivated, and the wild, but also the sacred. The forces dwelling in this region are spiritual, powerful, and feared. Both the underworld and the untamed region of this world are places where the Nasa can enter into contact with the order and forces of creation, a time before Catholicism (which for the Nasa is both an important cultural referent and, especially since the emergence of widespread political consciousness in the last three decades, the cause of cultural loss).

The power of the *caciques* over society could have elicited the fear manifest in the *cacique* illness. Yet the fact that the illness is related to the remains of the dead, with which the Nasa establish no positive links (as memory, guidance, or warmth), points to the operation of colonialism. Could it be the case that the active and meaningful relationship between indigenous peoples and some aspects of the contemporary materiality existing in their territories (archaeological remains) was severed at some point during colonial domination? The turning point in the European crusade against such a relationship was the *extirpación de idolatrías* (extirpation of idolatries), a task entrusted to the church, because the subsistence of native religious practices (and the corporate sense they conveyed) was a potential focus of resistance. The extirpation of idolatries created, above all, a widespread fear that was used by colonial authorities to break down the chains of symbolic meaning that may have existed between the natives and their material culture, including the things related to the ancestors. The fear of ancestors, a common feeling among indigenous populations in Colombia, resulted mostly from the preaching of Catholic missionaries. As Taussig (1987:373) has noted:

> The *infieles* or pagans of that other (preconquest, pre-European) time, have been enfolded and iconicized into the bowels of the Christian cosmos as Antichrist figures—so that they live on forever rustling the leaves of memory in the colonially constructed space of death.

Ramírez (1996:99) found the same attitude toward putative ancestors among indigenous communities of the eastern flanks of the Andes, where they are called *aukas* or *andaquíes*, and are considered savage Indians or cannibals, among a long list of pejorative terms. This image is built around the non-baptized, around those who confront domination, and has ancient, Judeo-Christian roots. *Auka, andaquí* or Pijao are not ethnic denominations but terms applied in different languages to the same phenomenon: the incarnation of behaviors repressed and punished in the self by the morality of civilization. For instance, *auka* is a Quechua word meaning "warrior, enemy, opponent, cruel, sadistic, bad, traitor, savage, rebellious, barbaric, mischievous, unworthy" (Torres 1982:39)—that is, a sum of the negative connotations attributed to the Other. The ancestors, therefore, are to be left alone, undisturbed, lest their evil powers awaken and threaten the fragile modernity of recently normalized subjects.

The *cacique* illness of the Nasa and its proscription of the physical proximity to the places of the dangerous and feared Other (the ancestors, but also the Pijaos, alien invaders) may be an instance of the colonial fear reaching beyond mere abstract symbolism to encompass physical referents. The fear of ancestors highlights a colonial wickedness: the invention of another Other within the Other, a sort of double alterity imposed by the construction of the civilized self. There is a *good Other*, leaning to colonial domination and to religious conversion; and there is a *bad Other*, rebellious and untamed, a permanent morality constantly reminding the perils of subversion. Ancestors occupy the ranks of the bad Other (that is, ancestors were turned Other). They belong to a time when alterity did not suffer colonial subjugation and therefore embody behaviors to be repressed in and by the good Other, on the verge of becoming part of the civilized self if just colonialism is capable of countering the courtship of the bad Other. The ancestors are among the non-baptized, the spirits, while the Nasa are baptized, that is, humans. Catholic influence on Nasa historical morality, which impinges upon the very classification of beings and non-beings, created two main eras: the time before Catholicism, dominated by spirits and danger, and the time of the civilized, converted self. The ancestors live in the former and were lumped, together with the Pijaos, as bad Others, so much so that they ended up being identified with each other and the terms used interchangeably.

A dangerous Other (embodied in the symbol of the jaguar, in the figure of the Pijaos, and in the ancestors) had to be kept at bay or tamed, whether it was outside or inside the social body. Western morality thus confronted the danger of the Other because it implied the dissolution of the bond that linked the self with the civilized order. The classification of bad and good Others had an instrumental end: severing the relationship of native societies with times before the advent of Christianity created a new beginning.

Colonial historical domination was not homogeneous among indigenous societies. For reasons that are case sensitive, some of them managed to escape the brutal transformation of their historical representations.[10] But even in cases in which colonialism condemned and proscribed pre-European times, feared ancestors can become positive forces once more. The Juan Tama Nasa mythical encompassing of La Candelaria may signal an ongoing change in the traditional relationship between native groups and archaeology in Colombia and elsewhere.

NATIVE HISTORIES: HISTORY IN THE MAKING

Colonialist archaeological discourse about native histories imposed the idea that indigenous peoples and cultures were part of the past. The basis of this discourse, upon which the exclusion and subordination of ethnic alterity was predicated to a large extent, was the idea that the subject matter of history is not the wishing future. Native resistance to this discourse faced a meaning-producing regime—national history—with local histories largely mobilized in the frame of ethnic struggles.

In the last two decades there has been a drift toward a restoration of the links with ancestral times turned material. In Colombia this still-developing process was started by the Guambianos, neighbors of the Nasa, who feared the Pishaus, the reputedly former inhabitants of their territory,[11] as much as the Nasa fear the Pijaos. The Pishaus were a colonial-produced incarnation of a feared alterity. Yet, the Guambianos have recently turned them into their own revered ancestors (Dagua et al. 1998). In this task they were accompanied by anthropologists and archaeologists. Material remains uncovered by a collaborative archaeological research were endowed with new meanings in the context of ethnic struggle for self-determination and cultural revival. The consideration of Pishaus as alien enemies was a colonial creation. For that reason, their recovery as ancestors is a political move of the greatest importance.

There is yet another interpretation of such an inversion: the bad Other is certainly feared, but also admired and made central to the symbolism of resistance (Taussig 1987). The bad Other embodies the powers to confront the colonial order. Otherness is potential resistance, something the state knew and knows well; it thus enlisted the Catholic Church to curtail deviations from the norm of civilization. The bad Other exemplifies everything feared and punished by the self, a moral void in which the good Other is always prone to fall. But the good Other, no matter how afraid, finds in the bad Other a model, a positive morality, an icon of struggle. The ancestors fooled the Spanish by burying themselves in the underworld, a sign not of cowardice but of ingenuity, and therefore avoided colonial subjugation. Burying in land or water (as Nasa myths tell about Juan Tama and other creation heroes), that is, patiently resting/escaping until the right time to return arrives, is a pan-Andean trademark of native messiahs, eagerly awaited in the symbolism of their societies. Thus, the negative categorization of the bad Other is, simultaneously, its sign of purity, the signature of the "true" native.

The indigenous organization has recently started to follow the trend set by the Guambianos, taking significant steps to signal the commitment with things archaeological previously proscribed and now part of a sacred landscape. The current events taking place in Juan Tama contribute to further and deepen this move. The Juan Tama community displays history in the making. Nasa history is cyclical, and one of its prominent features is times of renewal. It also is millenarist to a great extent, but not conceiving times of destruction and creation as much as occasions when the world and its order are fully reorganized; disasters may indeed occur, but they are propitious for the restoration of the correct order (Rappaport 1981). This idea seems to be widespread in Amerindian philosophy; the name it receives in the Andes is *pachakuti,*[12] a cyclical, cataclysmic destruction of the world followed by the return of the right order.

Millenarist movements of the eighteenth and nineteenth centuries in Tierradentro documented by Rappaport (1981), similar to others in the Andean realm, highlight the role of earthquakes in the reorganization of the world. The 1994 earthquake caused widespread destruction, but it also was a creative historical event: it has been thought of as a time of renewal and restoration, one capable of awakening history. This mythical renewal, moral in its postulation of the world *as it has to be,* sides with political struggle in forming a propitious time for the Nasa, a restoration of a lost order, a time in which historical meaning, through the symbolic appropriation of otherwise ignored and feared *things,* can be important. As Rappaport (1981:384) has noted, messianic thought is always present in Nasa culture, ready to become action when "available social conditions and cultural symbols coincide." In Juan Tama those social conditions exist, given the strong involvement of the people in political consciousness, bilingual education, historical revitalization, and promotion of communal practices. Archaeological things, such as those from La Candelaria, can be historical activators, anchors to memory and territory, meaning-creating beings. But, how is it that archaeology, a Western discipline, relates to peoples who challenge Western principles, striving to build their vital projects away from the lure of development and the market?

ARCHAEOLOGY AND INDIGENOUS PEOPLES

Western master narratives had at their core a historical operation: the birth of savages into civilization. In Latin America, archaeology participated by launching a "fair war" against indigenous history in the name of Aristotelian reason. Indigenes entered civilization held by the hand of a history told by others. But they entered it *not being.* The entrance requisite was their negation. The ontology of indigenes in the discourse of archaeologists is a long negative: they are not, they don't dwell within that discourse. Indigenous peoples, however, did not recognize themselves in a history that was crafted with the *things* their "ancestors" left.[13] The temporality crafted by archaeology was not an epistemic exteriority, nor a triumphant hegemony. It was not an exteriority because it was created within the expected epistemic limits of Western subjects: nothing of what it said was alien to Hegelian history. It may have surely been exterior to ethnic Others, but such a temporality was not created for them. Yet, precisely here lie its limits. As a hegemony-creating discourse, archaeological temporality was a failure: the consensus it created was feeble, partial, top-down, and only imposed with a high dose of violence (in museums, school curricula, mnemonic celebrations).

Archaeology became the notary public of the passing of pre-European "civilized" societies; it legitimized the disappearance of the Indians (something of the past), it paved the road to national ideologies.[14] The discipline buried the Indians and, when needed, exposed selected indigenous *things*, already its own. Yet, indigenous peoples want archaeology. But the plural is too general, too oblivious of particular sensitivities, too sententious, too academic. I can sense that what indigenous peoples and archaeologists think, feel, and want of their mutual concurrence to the archaeological realm is quite different. For archaeologists it is clear: the indigenous acceptance of an open and democratic archaeology is their best hope for the future of the discipline. Public archaeologists are delighted to share their knowledge with the lay masses—this time dressed with ethnic garments. Their illustrated move pleases them deeply, for they disguise their unwavering commitment to Western cosmology as altruism and multicultural correction.

The positioning of indigenous peoples before archaeology is not that consensual. Some value archaeological processes and results if they are part of their agendas, considering that material objects and features turned archaeological by academic or community-appropriated discourses can serve to strengthen historical reflection, central in social mobilization and life. Others confront archaeology altogether and reject any possible transaction with it. A perusal of the geographical distribution of these two antithetical positions will show that the former is mostly exercised by native groups in industrialized democracies, while the latter characterizes most indigenous peoples in what used to be called the Third World. Such a distribution is not odd; it closely responds to the differential effectiveness of multicultural policies and to how successful they have been in building strong hegemonies—accomplished more completely in those countries where nationalism was more aggressive and triumphant.

Those groups accepting archaeology and making it their own want it as another recourse to enliven the past—a cherished support of social life. Sometimes they even want it to fight *other* histories (national, that is) in their own terrain, with their own discursive objects. What they do is truly archaeology (a disciplined gaze into time turned material), but this time controlled and designed to serve native needs and expectations.[15] Although indigenous peoples had never lived in the archaeological house, multicultural (public) archaeology invites them to come over: it even offers them a new room, graciously labeled "indigenous archaeology." (The same happened with feminism: it aimed to change society and life, destroying their androcentric axes, but ended up living in the same old house, yet in a different wing, where males cannot hear its noise.) This is a classic multicultural scene. A "reformed" establishment is happy to concede to former marginal actors what it cherishes the most: epistemic disciplinary coherence. Its gains are numerous: it keeps practicing archaeology as it has been known (it changes nothing of its metaphysical fabric), it does it in public (generously), it feels more democratic (by *sharing*), it gets closer to what it used to call *the savage*, appeasing his/her desires and convincing itself that disciplinary nearness translates into spatial, temporal, and cultural coalescence.

Those who confront archaeology and want to know nothing about it raise their voice from a discursive emergence, from a distance, even from an assumed exteriority. They expose and challenge what the West has done and drag its institutions into the fight, including academia. Confrontation of the West is not new—it is centuries old—but it has gained more coherence and strength since the 1950s, starting with the anticolonial wars in Africa. It has increased its pace and intensity on the multicultural stage, where actors with opposed agendas concur. One of the actors concurring to the historical scene reconfigured by multicultural policies—of which repatriation is one of the most prominent—is archaeology. By its mere concurrence, it pretends to forget that other social disciplines reacted to anticolonial contestations some 40 years ago while it ignored contextual agitations by burying itself in its lab, its trench, its sherds. But it now notices, in panic, that something is happening, that some social movements challenge its work, unveil its dark face. Archaeologists then sink in utter silence—and keep on doing what they have always done, protected by a solid and conservative *esprit de corps* nurtured by esoteric meetings and publications—or talk the multicultural language. They talk about dialogue and participation. They talk an empty language, full of nothing. Such is their political correction, their shameless cynicism. Should archaeologists be surprised that their work is now contested, many times from an aggressive radicalism that they see as unjustified violence against their hygienic operation? They ask, with a grimace, "Why are the natives so angry if we did nothing to them, if we just limited our work to recount past deeds from material remains?" The naive good intentions of illustrated archaeologists, convinced that their sharing of archaeological secrets is the ultimate concession democracy can dispense, bounces back against a solid wall of rejection at the grassroots level.

In the interstices of the friction resulting from those two postures, there is yet another approach to the matter, very different than multicultural archaeology. While the latter deals publicly with disciplinary problems (most of them removed from social needs), the former devotes its efforts to recover the relationship between academia and society from a common agenda of problems to be resolved, the least pressing of which is not colonial domination. It is not a different disciplinary practice, perhaps complementary of traditional ways of doing; it seeks to build new relations, which can only be found outside disciplinary gates. In such a new political economy of truth there is power and subjects; there is a new house being built: modest, perhaps, but content to receive those who think that academic privileges ought to be questioned, those who side with social projects stressing solidarity and good living.

I am not quite sure what Juan Tama people think about archaeology, a discipline they know little about, other than that it ranks high in Western historical esteem. They are concurring to what some would call the "archaeological scene," not really interested in archaeology, perhaps not even interested in things archaeological. They know they have inhabited the south of what is now called Colombia since times immemorial. There they have been, lived, are being. Their collective memories dwell there, their roots, their projections into the future. When the 1994 earthquake forced them to leave their homes and settle near Santa Leticia, they knew they were not going away but returning to an origin. They left the heartland of the *cacique* Juan Tama, only to return. They left Vitoncó to return to Santa Leticia, further south, where the *the' walas* said they could keep weaving their lives according to ancestral roots. When they arrived in (returned to) Santa Leticia, they felt that ancestral collective memories were there, that they have always been there, waiting. They felt Juan Tama was there, caring for their lives. When their return to the territory had been anchored by Juan Tama, by the ancestors (some living in the archaeological things of La Candelaria), they understood that the territory returned with them; then their lives kept on making, weaving, celebrating.

Notes

1. *Resguardo* is equivalent to the English term "reservation," although it has precise connotations, both in colonial and republican terms; that is why I use the Spanish word instead of its English equivalent.

2. Such a history has created a sense of community that goes beyond the borders of particular *resguardos* by stressing the importance of grand individuals, political heroes who fought for the Nasa. Those leaders left memorable struggles to be remembered as models for political action; they also left, knowingly or not, a morality mobilized in contemporary ethnic agendas.

3. La Candelaria was "found" by German-born French archaeologist Henri Lehmann in 1943. Lehmann moved three statues from the site to Popayán, the provincial capital town, where they are still housed. Descriptions of the statues from La Candelaria can be found in Lehmann (1944) and Sotomayor and Uribe (1987:225–233).

4. This quotation has been excerpted from a 2003 video.

5. For an archaeological summary of Tierradentro, see Chaves and Puerta (1986).

6. Tierradentro is one of three archaeological parks that exist in Colombia, and it is managed by the Colombian Institute of Anthropology and History, a state-run agency. It was declared a World Heritage Site by UNESCO in 1995.

7. Known as *tumbas de pijaos* (Pijao burials). According to numerous reports, the Nasa and the Pijaos appear to have been allies against the Spaniards at the onset of the European conquest (Sevilla and Piñacué 2006). Yet, for the Nasa and other communities the Pijaos became feared enemies; it seems likely that the Spaniards enlisted the Nasa in their war against the Pijaos by manipulating old and new alliances (Bolaños 1994). The Nasa internalized their former allies as enemies, a move that went on to become fully metaphysical.

8. A Nasa linguist defined *p'tanz* as "a negative cosmic force" (Gómez and Ruíz 1997:133), thrust upon people who violate cultural proscriptions. It also implies a threat to the environment, the community, and the individual.

9. Although in some stories so-called "Pijaos" take the place of the ancestors and bury themselves to escape baptism, they are generally considered to be alien invaders, not the original inhabitants.

10. The native groups of the Sierra Nevada de Santa Marta on the Caribbean coast (Reichel-Dolmatoff 1985) and the Uwa from the Eastern Cordillera (Falchetti 2003; Osborn 1995), both in Colombia, constantly recreate the meaning of archaeological remains. The ancients are revered in agricultural terraces, mythological dwellings (such as pyramid-like hills), and large rocks (thought to be petrified mythical characters). Not coincidentally, both areas were relatively spared from church domination.

11. Considering the Pishaus as ancestors was not widespread. Some Guambianos thought the Pishaus were Kallimachik—ancient Nasa (see Vasco, this volume) with whom they fought, especially for territory, until relatively recent times. In either case the meaning given to the word is that of an enemy, a feared Other.

12. *Pachakuti* is a complex Aymara word: "*Pacha* could be interpreted as the energetic confluence of space and time, and therefore the radiation of life. *Kuti* could be interpreted as a violent turnaround, a 'revolution' in Western terms" (Mignolo 2005:165).

13. In another utter paradox, those ancestors were not theirs anymore once they became the odd forbears of national society (*our* Indians).

14. This also was the role played by museums. As Stavenhagen (2002:28) pointed out, "soon Latin American countries become modern and Indians would be only relics of a picturesque past (indeed, magnificent museums—such as the one in Mexico city— were built to pay homage to the great dead civilizations of the past and to symbolize the strong roots of the contemporary mestizo nation)."

15. I purposefully omitted stating that indigenous archaeology is performed by indigenous peoples because that is not always the case. Many instances are known, especially in

North America, of indigenous organizations hiring non-native archaeologists to perform an archaeology that can safely be labeled indigenous.

REFERENCES

Bolaños, Álvaro Felix 1994 *Barbarie y canibalismo en la retórica colonial. Los indios pijaos de fray Pedro Simón.* CEREC, Bogotá.

Chaves, Álvaro, and Mauricio Puerta 1986 *Monumentos arqueológicos de Tierradentro.* Banco Popular, Bogotá.

CRIC (Consejo Regional Indígena del Cauca) 1983 *Cómo nos organizamos.* CRIC, Popayán.

Dagua, Avelino, Misael Aranda, and Luis Guillermo Vasco 1998 *Guambianos. Hijos del aroiris y del agua.* CEREC, Bogotá.

Falchetti, Ana María 2003 *La búsqueda del equilibrio. Los uwa y la defensa de su territorio sagrado en tiempos coloniales.* Academia Colombiana de Historia, Bogotá.

Gómez, Herinaldy, and Carlos Ariel Ruíz 1997 *Los paeces. Gente territorio.* FUNCOP-Universidad del Cauca, Popayán.

Lehmann, Henri 1944 Arqueología de moscopán. *Revista del Instituto Etnológico* 1:657–677.

Mignolo, Walter 2005 *The Idea of Latin America.* Blackwell, Oxford.

Osborn, Ann 1995 *Las cuatro estaciones. Mitología y estructura social entre los u'wa.* Banco de la República, Bogotá.

Piñacué, Jesús Enrique 1994 Cosmovisión de la sociedad páez. In *Paeces por paeces*, edited by Carlos Osorio, pp. 27–32. Banco de la República, Bogotá.

Portela, Hugo 2002 *Cultura de la salud paéz: un saber que perdura, para perdurar.* Universidad del Cauca, Popayán.

Ramírez, María Clemencia 1996 *Frontera fluida entre andes, piedemonte y selva: el caso del valle de Sibundoy, siglos XVI–XVIII.* Instituto Colombiano de Cultura Hispánica, Bogotá.

Rappaport, Joanne 1981 Mesianismo y las transformaciones de símbolos mesiánicos en Tierradentro. *Revista Colombiana de Antropología* 23:365–413.

———. 1990 *The Politics of Memory: Native Historical Interpretation in the Colombian Andes.* Cambridge University Press, Cambridge.

Reichel-Dolmatoff, Gerardo 1972 The feline motif in prehistoric San Agustín sculpture. In *The Cult of the Feline*, edited by Elizabeth Benson, pp. 51–68. Dumbarton Oaks, Washington, DC.

———. 1985 *Los kogi. Una tribu de la Sierra Nevada de Santa Marta.* Procultura, Bogotá.

Sevilla, Elías, and Juan Carlos Piñacué 2006 Los nasa de Tierradentro y las huellas arqueológicas, primera aproximación. Paper presented at the IV Congreso de Arqueología en Colombia, Pereira, Colombia.

Sotomayor, María Lucía, and María Victoria Uribe 1987 *Estatuaria del Macizo Colombiano.* Instituto Colombiano de Antropología, Bogotá.

Stavenhagen, Rodolfo 2002 Indigenous peoples and the state in Latin America: An ongoing debate. In *Multiculturalism in Latin America: Indigenous Rights, Diversity and Democracy*, edited by Rachel Sieder, pp. 24–44. Palgrave Macmillan, New York.

Taussig, Michael 1987 *Shamanism, Colonialism and the Wild Man.* University of Chicago Press, Chicago.

Torres, Glauco 1982 *Diccionario kichua-castellano.* Casa de la Cultura Ecuatoriana, Cuenca.

CHAPTER 3

INDIGENOUS ARCHAEOLOGY ... IN PERU?

Alexander Herrera

INTRODUCTION

Does indigenous archaeology exist in Peru? An affirmative answer may seem obvious when considering a country whose indigenous people make up 30% of the population.[1] Many rural *campesinos* (farmers) maintain deeply embedded customs and traditions, and the majority are organized in communities with collective territories and rights formally recognized by the state. Additionally, they usually live close to some of the thousands of monumental archaeological sites that exist in Peru. And yet, even though the identity of traditional Peruvian *campesinos* is deeply rooted in the Andean past, it would be incorrect to speak of an indigenous archaeology in Peru, because their collective participation in the construction of historical discourse has been marginal, and as contradictory and complex as their relationship with the notion of indigeneity. From a legal standpoint at least, there are surprisingly few indigenous people in Peru, despite a strong tradition of indigenism in state policy. They are either understood as members of farming communities (*comunidades campesinas*) or, in Amazonia, of native communities (*comunidades nativas*). The term "indigenous people" (*pueblo indígena*) stems from the international jurisdiction that has evolved from the International Labour Organization's Convention No. 169. Therefore, contradictions between national and international law regarding the relative status of class and the indigenous identities of Peruvian citizens are rife, especially since Convention 169 was approved by Congress.[2] Additionally, Andean *campesinos* have a long tradition of shifting between multiple identities depending on the contexts of interaction (see below).

It may seem ironic that today's denial of indigenous identity in Peru is a result of indigenous reaffirmation policies, of state indigenism. At the start of the past century, in 1904, Manuel González Prada (1956:59) affirmed in *Nuestros Indios* that "the Indian question is more than pedagogical, it is economic, it is social." Paredes (2001) has interpreted González Prada's stance on identity in the materialist sense that "one is Indian in as much as one is poor and exploited, but if the Indian possess money he whitens; and vice versa, a poor white man turns Indian, turns *cholo*." Three decades later, José Carlos Mariátegui (1937) narrowed the focus on "the Indian issue," finding the fundamental root of the problem in the inequalities in land ownership. The protracted proindigenous battle in the name of the "forgotten mass" of the Republic fought by the Peruvian Left during the twentieth century, climaxed, in a sense, in the sweeping agrarian reform imposed by the de facto government of General Juan Velasco Alvarado in 1969.

The transformation of "Indians" into "citizens" in national discourse and legal settings alike effectively traded indigenous identities against land rights, giving rise to the modern *campesino* farmer, at least in theory. The Revolutionary Government of the Armed Forces tried to eliminate from above the root contradictions inherent in the idea of the Indian as a "problem" through a sudden and aggressive use of supreme decrees. Key among these contradictions was the contrast between a widely extolled indigenous past, the history of the "race" of "first Peruvians" who "conquered ... land, plant, and beast" and forged the "civilizations" that led to the Inca empire (Florián 1961), and the replication, since the colonial period, of conditions for the systematic and institutionalized exploitation of the indigenous population.

Partly as a result of the above, many *campesino* farmers today view the ethic rhetoric that focuses around that which is considered indigenous, upheld by visitors and foreign organizations alike, as a catalyst for a degrading racism that inspires a profound rejection in a complex management of multiple identities that are both opposing and complementary (de la Cadena 2000). In order to distance themselves from a long history of institutionalized discrimination, millions of Quechua and Aymara speakers in Peru have adopted a primary peasant-class identity. In other words, they consider themselves as members of a rural proletariat and thus rarely make use of their political capabilities in terms of ethnicity or indigenism. A recent exception, notable for its rising prominence over the last two decades, is the National Confederation for Communities Affected by Mining (CONACAMI), the only member of the Andean Coordination of Indigenous Organizations (CAOI) that makes no reference to indigeneity in its name. Shunning the discourse of indigeneity does not imply that local, rural identities are weak, however, or that indigenous cosmogonies and notions of self are not significantly manifest in the daily lives of *campesinos* in Peru.

Through mundane tasks many *campesinos* maintain a close, complex, and significant relationship with places and objects from the past—hat Peruvian archaeologists call "archaeological heritage"—but these places and objects form part of experienced landscapes, sets of meaningful relationships that are not mediated by the concept of heritage. Lakes, ridges, or ancient *waka* (sacred places) are often places of popular worship, both in the countryside as in the city, and there are thousands of archaeological sites at which soothsaying, curses, and offerings are regularly made; archaeological objects are also nearly always present on the desks of traditional *curanderos* (healers) (e.g., Camino 1992). Past inhabitants, variously referred to as *awilitu, awki, machukuna,* or *gentiles* (Gose 1994; Harris 1982), are frequently admired as erectors of the great *wanka* (standing stones), builders of terraces, canals, and imposing *marka* (villages) and *pukara* (fortresses) embedded on the summits of mountains and ridges. In the Ancash highlands of north-central Peru, sites and objects from the precolonial past are generally treated with respect, partly because the *awilitu* are understood as the protectors of *chakra* (fields) and flocks. But ancient sites are also avoided and tombs particularly feared, as they are associated with deadly diseases including syphilis and *wari* sickness (Walter 2006).

Dialogue between the scientific establishment and the *campesino* heirs of the indigenous past has been remarkably asymmetric and of little transcendence for the development of Peruvian archaeology. Archaeologists have tended to enrich their works with local knowledge, reciprocating with the offer of work, the delivery of technical reports, and the dissemination of their knowledge about the past. However, they have tended to be inspired by an educational drive toward those who they deem do not know their past in an adequate manner; thus they aim to "educate" following the colonialist belief that the only valid discourse on the past is that which is produced by archaeology.

It is rare to find joint and sustained initiatives between peasants and archaeologists that eschew a long tradition of endocolonialist paternalism and seek intercultural horizontal dialogues. Identification of archaeologists as *pishtaku* (also *ñakaj* in Quechua and *kharisiri* in Aymara), a demon that lives by stealing the essence of others (Herrera and Lane 2006; Lane and Herrera 2005), reflects the depth of the social gap that separates the discourse of professional archaeologists from indigenous lifeways and identity. The existence of this unfortunate perception also reveals the scarcity of the diffusion of archaeological knowledge among the closest descendents of the precolonial indigenous population, which is preoccupying when taking into account the social emphasis found in nationalist archaeological discourse and in Latin American social archaeology in particular.

In this chapter, I consider the practices of both archaeologists and *campesinos* with regard to archaeological sites and objects, focusing on points of agreement and disagreement that outline the breach between the heirs of the indigenous past and those who seek to study it, and the social contexts in which it is replicated. In order to follow the rise and development of this social gap, it is necessary to look back at the colonial beginnings of archaeological practices in Peru and the mining of monuments for material wealth. In order to understand how an emerging national archaeology, often framed as indigenous, became an accomplice (or mastermind) of an ethnophagic state indigenism (Bretón 2001:114–117), it also becomes necessary to review the history of the Indian figure's instrumentalization throughout the twentieth century. As a point of contrast, I touch upon a select group of *campesino* practices regarding both archaeological sites and remains. I focus on the activities that take advantage of both the spaces and objects related to the past that help establish indigenous identities through a discrete own-discourse, which is rarely expressed in interethnic discourse. To finalize, I discuss possible ways of building intercultural bridges on the base of established ritual practices at archaeological sites.

Peruvian Archaeology and the State

The history of Peruvian archaeology may quickly be summarized as a history of material and intellectual pillage, which mirrors the country's colonized position as an exporter of raw materials for foreign consumption. In this section, the development of Peruvian archaeology is situated in the complex relationship between the state, the material remains, and the peoples of the past and their current heirs, and reviewed by addressing the global, nationalist, and colonialist social contexts for its reproduction (Trigger 1996). There is doubt that nationalist archaeology is predominant, but this tradition coexists with global archaeology and endocolonialism. One may find aspects of the colonial tradition in the sacking and trafficking of cultural assets, the pacts between urban elite collectors and rural clients, and the foregrounding of the cultivated (artistic or scientific) that eschews local and regional aspirations and identities.

The objective of this section is to highlight critical elements in the history of Peruvian archaeology that may help sharpen focus on the current crisis of sense that afflicts national archaeology. In Peru, this crisis is directly related to the eclipse of centrality in the indigenous and "Andean" in the national discourse (Burga 2001) and, arguably, to the shallow penetration of the multiculturalist project attempted in the first decade of the twenty-first century. Despite the trajectory of the Peruvian archaeological academy and theoretical efforts to socialize Andean archaeology (Aguirre 2005; González Carré and del Águila 2005; Lumbreras 1974; Tantaleán 2004), Peruvian archaeology's discourse has tended to feed state-promoted projects and expositions on "the Indians of the past." The predisposition to reproduce nationalist discourses that emphasize economic difference and hierarchy, while eschewing cultural and ethnic difference, as well as historical trajectories and continuities, mirrors the denial of the existence of significant indigenous "others" in Peruvian politics.[3] The weakening power and credibility of state institutions brought about by neoliberal structural reforms during the 1990s has laid bare an archaeology unwilling to (or incapable of) loosening its historical bonds to reformulate critical postures in social science. The current crisis manifests itself in diminished theoretical debates in comparison to the forums open to cultural historicism and the alliance of archaeology to emergent parochialisms. The latter, tied to regionalist political projects, are at risk of reproducing, on a minor scale, paths of exclusion similar to those trodden on a national level throughout the twentieth century.

COLONIALIST ARCHAEOLOGY

Since the wars of the conquest and throughout the colonial era, the dominant perception of objects and sites from the past in the Andes revolved around the notion of treasure (Rostworowski 2002), denying any value or authenticity beyond material wealth. European domination was of course based on the ideology of racial and cultural inferiority of the American natives, which meant that there was simply no need, nor desire, to exalt the indigenous past (cf. Trigger 1996). The quest for the gold and silver that Cieza de León (1962) mentions as "buried in the sepulchers of kings and chieftains" gave rise to a centuries-long frenzy of sacking and pillaging (Zevallos 1994). Initially, during the late sixteenth and throughout the seventeenth centuries, the main limitation to this activity was the availability of a workforce (Rostworowski 2002:1141).

The Spanish Crown sought to control this situation early on, in part to ensure the taxes known as Quintos del Rey or Royal Fifth, which were levied on mineral products and constituted the main source of income from the American colonies well into the late eighteenth century. The entrepreneurs of colonial looting organized their activities in a way similar to mining, establishing mandatory shifts of *mita* (tributary) work to ransack pyramids and cemeteries, especially on the northern coast (Zevallos 1994; cf. Rostworowski 2002). The usual administrative procedure was simple: (1) filing a statement of intent to dig a particular site at the Reales Cajas (revenue office); (2) registration of the claim; (3) issuance of a license to dig; (4) naming of a *veedor* (inspector) to supervise extraction; and (5) transfer to the Reales Cajas of all silver and gold obtained for smelting, marking, and payment of dues to the royal treasury (Zevallos 1994:10, author's translation).

Initially, the church doubted the legality of this type of treasure hunt. In 1551 the Council of Lima ordered, under threat of excommunication, that the tombs and places of rest of the pagan natives were not to be dismantled (Zevallos 1994:11). The order had little effect over the long term, however, and the church eventually decided that since the sites were not sacred to the Christian faith, they could be dug if there were no apparent heirs to the treasures and under the provision that the bones of the deceased were to be rearranged as they were found originally (Zevallos 1994:11).[4]

Countless contracts were drawn up to pillage *huacas* (*waka* pyramids) with participation of both Creoles and mestizos, as well as native indigenous leaders (see below). Clerics and friars also took an active role in the above-mentioned looting, including the enlightened bishop Baltasar Martínez de Compañón (1978 [1735–1797]), whose interest in recording objects and contexts goes hand in hand with the famous illustrated manuscript and study collection sent to Madrid shortly after 1788 (Alcina 1995). His activities, however, mark a turning point in the colonial history of archaeological practice in Peru that foreshadows the rise of the evidential value of the materiality of the past (cf. Wylie 2005).

The legal framework for the extraction and taxation of metals did not impinge upon non-metallic artifacts and materials of the past, leading to the early establishment of a market for "antiquities." By 1820, when General José de San Martín disembarked in Pisco, one of the Republican expeditionaries, an Englishman by the name of James Paroissen, noted in his diary on September 24, "A man here gets his livelihood by selling the ornaments, etc., he obtains from those sepulchers, but unfortunately he was not then in Chincha" (Zevallos 1994:14).

One of the most challenging and under-studied aspects of the history of colonial looting is the direct and active role played by native leaders in the search for treasure. In 1569, the principal chieftain of the Chimo valley (Trujillo), Pedro Oxcahuamán, was granted permission to seek treasure, while in 1593 "a company made solely of noble and tributary Indians came together to excavate (sic) certain *huacas* near Mansiche (today Trujillo)" (Zevallos 1994:12). In 1634 after traveling to Spain, the chieftain of Luriguanca, Felipe Guacrapaucar, obtained a Real Cédula that included express authorization to hunt for treasures in the Jauja region (Espinoza 1981). By 1773, Francisco Solano Chayhuac Casamusa sought, and was granted, the viceroy's permission to charge for treasure hunting in Chan Chan.

The examples outlined above, as well as many others in Zevallo's (1994) landmark book, make it difficult to sustain the idea that indigenous looting was a direct response to urgent economic necessity. Throughout his historical review of cases, Zevallos (1994) expressed dismay at the innumerable instances of "Indians" practicing "sacrilegious" looting in ancestral places. In contrast, Rostworowski's (2002) study raises the issues of fear and need as conditions affecting an ideological transformation whereby certain *huacas* were seen to have lost power after being vanquished; they had become *atisca* (Rostworowski 2002:1140–1144). It thus seems as if the spatial and temporal distribution of indigenous looting may allow tracking the pace and rhythm of the destructuration of indigenous society, especially vis-à-vis the successive campaigns to "extirpate" idolatry. The persecution of indigenous practices related to ancestor veneration attacked a pivotal set of integrative practices that articulated collective memory, and it seems plausible to hypothesize that some indigenous leaders may have destroyed the material remains of their own past in an effort to escape a crushing social categorization; it was not only a viable economic activity, but also showed an active denial of the pagan past.

Collecting and looting are old,[5] widely spread, and interdependent practices that reduce the value of the past to the aesthetic or commercial value of selected pieces, and constitute the most salient continuation of the colonial tradition in Peru. A modern variant, which cloaks and justifies collecting on the basis of its evidential value, is the commissioning of looting for "cultural" or "educational" ends. Most widely spread is the looting of archaeological pieces as homework for the "study" of objects in school classes, usually history. The establishment of municipal museums through sponsored looting, as exemplified by the regional wave of ransacking unleashed by an elected mayor of the province of Asunción (Ancash) in the 1990s, is but an extreme variant. The pieces that today make up a significant regional collection (Minelli and Wegner 2001) were acquired with public funds and include items disdained by foreign collectors, who usually paid more. Such collecting may thus be understood as a strategy to resignify and deindigenize the past through the process of musealization.

Finally, present-day *huaqueros* (looters) are usually *campesino* farmers aiming to supplement their incomes by selling metal and pottery pieces to established collectors or providing the textile scraps used in handicraft manufacture (pendants, jewel boxes, and dolls) for the tourist trade. This activity, denounced as early as 1772 by Antonio Ulloa in *Noticias americanas*, has deep roots in history, as we have seen. Presently, it includes ritual codes of excavation and an established oral tradition enshrined in popular culture. The *marinera norteña* "El Huaquero" by composer Miguel Paz provides an example that is popular among foreign and Peruvian archaeologists:

> *Yo soy el huaquero viejo*
> *Que vengo de sacar huacos (bis)*
> *De la huaca más arriba, hay,*
> *de la huaca más abajo (bis).*
> *Huaquero, huaquero,*
> *Huaquero vamos a huaquear. (bis)*
> *Cova cova cova al amanecer,*
> *Cova cova cova al anochecer. (bis)*

NATIONALIST ARCHAEOLOGY

The main shared objective of national archaeologies worldwide is that of promoting patriotism and cementing national unity through the glorification of a supposedly common past (Trigger 1996:618–620; cf. Anderson 1991). The history of archaeology in Peru during the republican period provides a clear example of how the appropriation of the past is coupled to the changing fortunes of the state.

The publication of *Antigüedades peruanas* by Mariano Eduardo de Rivero in 1827, six years after independence, marks the rise in criollo and mestizo preoccupation with archaeological objects as alternative sources for studying the past (Coloma 1994). "The [colonial] historians of Peru do not convey anything positive about the governments, laws, uses, and customs prior to the establishment of Manco Capac's empire" (de Rivero 1994:8, author's translation). The perceived importance of knowing about this past was, and partly still is, rooted in culturalist genealogical thinking, wherein the Republic merely restored the sovereignty established by the "ancient Peruvians" of old (Herrera 2011).

With the surge of independentist discourse, the colonial double symbol of king and queen came to be replaced by the symbolic relationship between the (female) allegory of the nation and Inca Manco Capac (Quijada 1994). This prominent role in the construction of national identity afforded to ancient civilizations in general and to the Incas in particular began to wane toward the mid-nineteenth century, however. The War of the Pacific (1879–1884) finally ended this first, preprofessional phase of Peruvian nationalist archaeology.

The importance of the indigenous past as a source of national inspiration saw a strong resurgence in the aftermath of Peru's military defeat, a process of national reinvention that helped shape the beginnings professional archaeology in Peru. For the first time the national discourse about the past found its way onto the materiality of postage stamps, which have since and ever increasingly been used as vehicles for state propaganda, as they have across Latin America (Child 2005). Postage stamps are an integral part of the state's public façade at a national and international level, and they spread and reproduce the dominant self-conceptions of the time.

The first direct allusion to the past on Peruvian stamps was in a series of figurative postage stamps issued in the context of the Aristocratic Republic, the suite of oligarchic governments that oversaw the reestablishment of the institutions broken by the war. They represent "national personalities" (1896–1900) and "celebrated men" (1909) and include a stereotypical Inca, probably intended to represent Manco Cápac (Figure 3.1a). The face values assigned to the series printed from 1896–1900 and again in 1919 follow a chronological order. The stamp with the anonymous Inca has the lowest value, followed by Christopher Columbus, Francisco Pizarro, and figures from the wars of Independence and the Pacific (Figure 3.1b). Allusions to the precolonial past disappear from philatelic discourse until 1931,[6] when Manco Cápac appears in the series entitled "Natural Riches of Peru" with the series's lowest value (1 centavo). The inversion that occurred in the series issued between 1934 and 1935 is striking; the highest values were now reserved for allegories of the "Coronation [sic] of Huascar" (50 centavos) and "The Inca" (1 sol), a change that reflects the deep impact of Augusto Bernardino Leguía's indigenist policies in the self-conception of the Peruvian state.[7]

Figure 3.1   First direct reference to the precolonial past in the Peruvian stamps that circulated between 1896 and 1900. A stereotyped Inca appears on the less valuable stamps (1 and 2 centavos) (Figure 3.1a), Francisco Pizarro on those of 4, 5, 10, and 20 centavos (Figure 3.1b), and president La Mar on those of 50 centavos, 1 sol, and 2 soles.

The figure of Leguía, four times president of Peru (1908–1912, 1919–1924, 1924–1929, and 1929–1930), is key to understanding the development of later paternalist attitudes toward Peru's indigenous population. The 1919–1920 constitution established the protection of the "indigenous race" through the vindication of indigenous communities' collective property. The writings and thinking of José Carlos Mariátegui, Hildebrando Castro, and archaeologist Julio César Tello, widely regarded as the founding father of Peruvian archaeology, greatly influenced *leguiista* politics.

The intellectual development of the link between the indigenous past and the ethnographic present marks the beginning of the indigenist phase of professional archaeology in Peru. This second phase began in the second decade of the twentieth century with the work of Tello[8] (1880–1947), who "represents the nationalism of an archaeology committed to the present" (Morales 1993:19). From highland farmer origins, Tello was sent to attend secondary school in Lima and passed from medical school at San Marcos University—under the tutelage of Ricardo Palma, then director of the National Library—to the study of anthropology at Harvard University (Astuhuamán and Daggett 2005). A substantial part of his archaeological career coincided with his office as congressman from Huarochirí (1917–1929) during the Leguía government. From this position he garnered the necessary support for the foundation of the Museo de Arqueología Peruana, which was inaugurated in 1924 and is today known as the National Museum Anthropology, Archaeology, and History of Peru, where his remains lie buried.

In his work Tello contrasted an autochthonous vision of the origin of Andean civilization, in accord with the indigenist ideas of the time, to the diffusionist thesis of the "civilizing wave" of Mesoamerican origin, suggested by Humboldt and propagated by Max Uhle (1959:14–15 passim; see Kaulicke 1998) since the beginnings of the twentieth century. Uhle (1959) founded Andean archaeology's chronological edifice based on rigorous fieldwork and a theoretical predisposition toward diffusionism as an explanatory framework for Andean cultural developments. Tello's explorations (e.g., 1923, 1929), in turn, show a distinct sensibility toward local conditions and cultural traditions. He sought evidence for continuities in cultural trajectories and frontiers and focused on traditional and historical routes of transit, seeking to arrange archaeological remains, oral histories, folklore, and ethnohistorical sources into a single model of indigenous American cultural development.

The beginning of the third and current phase in the development of Peruvian nationalist archaeology is marked by the adoption of Marxist theory and political anti-imperialism, a position propounded since the 1960s by Emilo Choy, Rosa Fung, and Luis Guillermo Lumbreras, among many others. This "progressive" or "left" archaeology, thought of as an emancipating archaeology (Lumbreras 1974), was brought under the service of the state during the military government of General Velasco, who appropriated it in order to reformulate the official state discourse on the past.

In spite of the twists and turns of Peruvian politics, the influential offices and political positions successively occupied by Lumbreras and collaborators of the INDEA (Instituto Andino de Estudios Arqueológicos) over the last four decades have allowed the consolidation of a standard nationalist archaeological discourse in the political arena, scant methodological and theoretical innovation notwithstanding (Aguirre 2005; Tantaleán 2004).

Global Archaeology

Global archaeology has been largely associated with a small number of states that exact a powerful political, economical, and cultural influence in extensive areas of the world, while incorporating the propagation of the dominion of one country over another through the biased manipulation of the weight that discourses on the past innately carry; it was defined by Trigger (1996:623) in the image of that archaeology practiced by Soviet and North American archaeologists in their respective "areas of influence" during the Cold War. As such, global archaeology includes investigative questions driven by hegemonic academic centers, distance between local and foreign investigators, exacerbated by publication in foreign languages (usually English), as well as a lack of interest in local discourses and problems (Politis 2003). As is the case in most of Latin America, the imperialistic European trends of the past have given way to North American–style globalism that has had, and continues to have, a strong impact on Peru.

A known example in Peru is the Virú Valley Project (Willey 1953) led by Gordon Randolph Willey, globally considered the first regional archaeological study based on modern systematic survey (Billman 1999:1). This project pioneered the use of a Peruvian coastal valley as a laboratory to address questions derived from Julian H. Steward's (1955) theory of multilineal evolution using military technology (aerial photography and Willys Jeeps), Steward being one of Willey's collaborators at the American Bureau of Ethnology at the time. This investigation marked the consolidation of the first stage of global archaeological research in Peru, whose origins arguably lie in the work of George Ephraim Squier (1821–1888), State Department commissioner to Peru between 1862 and 1865, who complemented his diplomatic and commercial work with annotated visits to archaeological sites (Squier 1878). This first phase may be said to have continued until 1985, when a series of changes in legislation normalized the archaeological profession, forcing a transition that has yet to be concluded but that has already changed the practices of foreign archaeologists working in Peru.

The attempt to extend the state's control over archaeological practice marks the beginning of the current phase in imperialist archaeology in Peru. The first Rules and Regulations for Explorations and Archaeological Excavations, approved during the first months of the first government of Alan García Pérez (R.S. 559-85Ed) compels locals and foreigners to enroll themselves in an archaeological roster. The revised 2000 edition (R.S. 004-2000Ed) strengthens state control by establishing a norm whereby foreign projects must include a Peruvian codirector or academic subdirector, forcing linkages between investigators and national and foreign institutions. Unforeseen consequences include the eased emigration of Peruvian archaeologists and the emergence of a market for stooge coinvestigators, largely driven by foreign scholars trapped in a web of bureaucracy. The rulebook's chief weakness, however, is its blind spot toward the relationship between archaeologists and local populations, to courtesy at an interpersonal level, and to institutional interaction with local authorities and communities, as it implies a tacit negation of claims to the existence of preferential rights over heritage other than those of the state.

ARCHAEOLOGISTS, *AWILITUS*, AND *CAMPESINOS*

Many traditional practices at archaeological sites and with archaeological remains embody a vision of the past that is radically different from anthropological discourse in that it separates the indigenous element from the concept of the autochthonous as a strategy to overcome racism (de la Cadena 2000:6–7). In a way similar to the "unethnic ethnohistory" discussed by Frank Salomon (2002) for Huarochiri, the *campesino* discourse on the precolonial past in the Ancash highlands of Peru seeks to exorcize the indigenous elements from that past. In practice however, both sites and objects exert a considerable symbolic pressure that is directly linked to the figure of the *awilitus*. I will here address three aspects of traditional practices that are closely related to archaeology: the role of the ancestors, the rites performed at archaeological sites, and the habitual use of archaeological sites and objects.

The term *awilitu* is commonly used across the north-central highlands to refer to the inhabitants of a past before the present humanity whose graves, houses, canals, fields, and corrals are found dotted in local territories. It encapsulates an ambiguous and complex filial relationship that identifies ego as a direct descendant of a people that no longer exist and characterizes this relationship as one based on affection. This contrasts with the equally wide perception of the *awilitus* as primitive and savage pagans whose remains are a source of multiple diseases (Walter 2006). Archaeological sites and remains, and human bones in particular, are among the most highly charged and dangerous symbolic elements of local realities (Salomon 2002:478).

Archaeological sites that are home to the *awilitus* are places in which excavations are dangerous because of *antimoniu* or *amaa haaka*, a "foul air" that may emanate from tombs (Herrera and Lane 2006:163). The *awilitus'* outrage at an unsanctioned excavation may be considered a direct cause of illness or death (Walter 2006:184). Therefore, most archaeologists, both local and foreign, tend to sponsor and partake in ritual *pagu* offerings (Figure 3.2). The chief difference in the linkages established with the people of the past by archaeologists and *campesinos*, however, is that for the archaeologist the subjects of study are dead, whereas for the *campesino* certain remains may embody forces that act upon their everyday life spaces.

Ritual offerings sponsored by archaeologists have become a habitual sign of symbolic deference toward the past across much of Peru and

Figure 3.2 The archaeologist Wilber Rodrigo reads coca leaves and distributes *kintu* to colleagues and local collaborators as a part of an offering ritual or *pagu* previous to the start of research activities at the Yangón archaeological site (San Nicolás district, C. F. Fitzcarrald Province). The Cuzqueñan style of the ritual contrasts with the local custom of using rubbing for ritual cleansing, *pagu*, and protection against the *awilitus*.

the Andes. In *pagu* offerings the anthropological training of foreign archaeologists, the regional cultures of Peruvian coinvestigators, and local tradition and oral history often come together in efforts that seek to harmonize investigative practice in the local context. Fragments of prayers taken from ethnohistorical sources may be included, Cuzco (or Aymara)-style rituals performed, with modern esoteric elements commingling different practices, traditions, and languages. Neither is it uncommon to see surprise on the faces of the local people witnessing the activities of the *ingenierus* (engineers, a term often used to refer to archaeologists and other urban fieldworkers, such as geologists, biologists or surveyors, who come in cars, deploy equipment, and leave). It could be argued that archaeologists practice *pagu* offerings to foretell the trajectory of their investigations, much in the same way that the *campesinos* seek to foretell aspects related to their labor cycles. The *pagu* made by archaeologists, however, differ greatly from local practice, and their potential importance as spaces for intercultural and horizontal dialogue (Herrera and Lane 2006) has yet to transform archaeological fieldwork strategy and practices.

The meaning of sites and archaeological objects for rural highland farmers in Peru tends to fit an animist, relational vision of the surroundings as a landscape that is alive and lived in (Allen 2002; Bolin 1998). *Apu* tutelary mountains are a critical referent of collective Andean identities and, as such, they are present on the Peruvian coat of arms that dressed one of the nation's early flags (Figure 3.3). Mountains, like lakes and certain outcrops of rock, are considered entities that deserve to be treated with respect, which includes "feeding" them offerings. Offering rituals and divinatory practices at archaeological sites are quite common

Figure 3.3 Peruvian flag of General San Martín, October 21, 1820. The rising sun at the center of the red and white fields probably referred to the Inka past and to the mountains, following an Andean style.

(Figures 3.4 and 3.5), but their visibility is low. Rituals tend to be discrete and strictly private, undertaken at night at specific times in the lunar cycle by small groups of people. Angry, hungry mountains may open up and devour engineers, lawyers, trucks, and even helicopters to the sound of church bells or a traditional music band (*banda*).[9]

At a local and domestic scale, the propitiatory role attributed to tombs and ancient sculptures may be exemplified by traditional practices that might be banned under current heritage legislation. The construction of corrals next to or around ancient tombs in the Cordillera Negra region is one such example, even though the spatial association of tombs and corrals in this region dates back to the precolonial era. Their recurrent pairing is probably linked to the availability of pastures and may materialize some of the manifold linkages between flocks, corrals, grazing areas, and mortuary communities (Herrera and Lane 2006:Fig. 3). Driven by climate change and population pressure, the higher reaches of the Cordillera Negra are again being resettled, and corrals built by the tombs, invariably looted and destroyed "so the *awilitus* may help watch the flocks."[10]

A final example of the meanings given to archaeological objects by indigenous farmers is the use of a sculpture, the stone representation of a warrior in typical Ajia/Huaraz regional style (Schaedel 1952), to mate

Figure 3.4 Geoglyphs sketched on the ground near the Llamatsipunta archaeological site in the upper Cordillera Negra (Pamparomás district, Nepeña Province), probably as a part of a ritual of divination.

Figure 3.5 Material remains of a small *pagu* or *pagapo* performed at the Pukayaku archaeological site in central Conchucos (Ancash region); they include a little stone house and a vessel fragment.

cattle (Figure 3.6). The owner of the corral indicated that cows tied to it during the mating season were more fertile, leading others in the region to seek it regularly. The fact that the sculpture has been moved, probably from a tomb and possibly by the family of the present custodian, suggests that the essential qualities attributed to ancient places, buildings, and objects are still mobile.

In summary, the role of the ancestors in highland Peru may be broadly understood as tightly linked to the fertility that they may bring or impede. The offering rituals carried out at archaeological sites by indigenous farmers and archaeologists vary widely. The relationship of *campesino* farmers with archaeological objects and sites tends to be expressed in a subtle discourse about the past that is articulated out of view of outsiders through autochthonous worldviews and practice. The rituals performed at archaeological sites, however improvised, offer rare and important opportunities for engaging in horizontal intercultural

Figure 3.6 Anthropomorphic sculpture in the local Aija style (AD 400–800?) placed in a yard used as a corral. It is said that the sculpture increases the fertility of cattle tied to it during mating.

dialogue on site, not in an administrative office or a church in town; a dialogue that begins by taking the legitimate self-definitions of *campesinos* seriously.

FINAL REMARKS

Even though there is no indigenous archaeology in Peru, significant practices exist that testify to the tightly knit relationship between people of the present and places and objects from the past. Indigenous identities are rarely deployed and articulated explicitly in political initiatives due to the profound stigmatization of the indigenous in Peruvian society. Traditional practices, however, articulate substantive cultural differences that uphold strong local identities. Faced with the task of building a nation, Peruvian archaeology has tended to background identity and difference in the present, actively feeding the official history of a unified mestizo nation instead. This strong integrationist stance is at odds with the multiculturalism set in motion in the first decade of the twenty-first century. The chasm between the heirs of the indigenous past and those who study it is related to a mutual inability to understand the goals and objectives of the histories that each group upholds and constructs and deepened by weak understandings of the power relations that frame discourses about the past.

The remains of the past are key referents of *campesinos*' inhabited and lived-in landscape. Their presence provides one of the pillars that sustain the judicial legitimacy of *comunidades campesinas* (Salomon 2002:477), although "possession since time immemorial," a key requisite for official farming community recognition, may also be demonstrated by recourse to colonial heritage. The existence of non-indigenous *campesino* authenticity in the context of modernity, however, leads to oral and written histories that emphasize the discontinuities between the people (Christian and civilized) of the present and the Indians (pagan and savage) of the past, precisely where the law demands continuity. These deindigenized "indigenous" histories will necessarily differ from the culture-historical reconstructions of archaeologists.

The presence of an archaeologist in the field is commonly seen as a passing intrusion, often made dangerous by the process of excavation in the places where the *awilitus* inhabit. Since the removal of archaeological objects to museums in the capital is also frowned upon, it should not come as a surprise that *campesinos* tend to distrust archaeologists. The archaeological process, however, contrasts favorably with the more radical transformations of the landscape driven by mining firms, the use of mountain tops for electricity and telecommunications pylons, and the symbolic appropriation of places by sectors of the Catholic Church that continue to Christianize the landscape through the erection of crosses and the conducting of services on archaeological sites (Figure 3.7). In the best-case scenario, archaeologists seek to "educate" on their own terms, based on the premise that archaeology produces the only valid discourse about the past.

The educational quest of Peruvian archaeology will probably continue to have little impact as long as it remains imbued by indigenist paternalism. However, municipalities, schools, and other local authorities have increasingly begun to sponsor exhibits, museums, and even archaeological research projects. This tendency may continue, offering an important leeway for the development of archaeology in Peru during the remainder of the twenty-first century. Yet it is possible, and worthy of further investigation, that the displacement of objects and remains from the past to the controlled environments of museums may also continue to substantiate identities that have been exorcized of the indigenous element.

Figure 3.7   Rustic cross erected at the summit of an archaeological site to accompany open-air masses. The renovation of containment walls is directly linked to this practice, common in the Conchucos region (Asunción Province).

NOTES

1. According to linguistic data and census projections compiled for UNICEF's Sociolinguistic Atlas of Indigenous Peoples in Latin America (Sichra 2009) there were 8,466,229 indigenous people in Peru in 2010. The two strongest language groups are Quechua and Aymara with 434,372 and 3,262,137 speakers recorded in the 1993 census, respectively (Sichra 2009).
2. Supreme resolution RS 26253 was ratified by Congress on February 2, 1994.
3. The bloody repression of indigenous protests in Bagua on June 5, 2009, after the writing of this paper, has helped catapult an indigenous leader to presidential candidacy, but it seems too early to presage a reversal of the overall trend.
4. Zevallos (1994:11) suspected that this arrangement was linked to the participation in treasure hunts of several clerics and friars from Trujillo, but the matter appears not to have been investigated further.
5. Zevallos (1994:13) documented the existence of collections of archaeological objects among urban upper classes as early as the 1540s.
6. The high cost associated with the only stamp that recalled the colonial past in the series from 1917–1918, an allegory of the "Funerals of Atahualpa" (1 sol), is imperative as it alludes to the Inca's death as historically important.
7. The first series of postage stamps to depict archaeological motifs—a Paracas winged being (10 centavos), a Moche combat scene (15 centavos), and a stylized Inca keru (50 centavos)—dates from October 1932.
8. The most recent and complete biography of Tello was written by Astuhuamán and Daggett (2005).
9. This tale was picked up in 1999 from a peasant informer working for the Pierina Archaeological Project (Proyecto Arqueológico Pierina). The gold mining

operations in this zone processed entire mountains using the "heap" or "dump" technique.

10. T. Florentino, Comunidad Campesina José Carlos Mariátegui de Chorrillos, personal communication, August 2001.

REFERENCES

Aguirre, Manuel 2005 *La arqueología social en el Perú*. BAR International Series S1396, Oxford.

Alcina, José 1995 *Arqueólogos o anticuarios. Historia antigua de la arqueología en la América española*. Ediciones del Serbal, Madrid.

Allen, Catherine 2002 *The Hold Life Has: Coca and Cultural Identity in an Andean Community*. Smithsonian Institution Press, Washington, DC.

Astuhuamán, César, and Richard Daggett 2005 Julio C. Tello: una aproximación a su biografía. In *Paracas*, by Julio César Tello, vol. 1, pp. 3–14. UNMSM-Institute of Andean Research, Lima.

Billman, Brian 1999 Settlement pattern research in the Americas: Past, present and future. In *Settlement Pattern Studies in the Americas: Fifty Years since Virú*, edited by Brian Billman and Gary Feinman, pp. 1–5. Smithsonian Institution Press, Washington, DC.

Bolin, Inge 1998 *Rituals of Respect: The Secret of Survival in the High Peruvian Andes*. University of Texas Press, Austin.

Bretón, Víctor 2001 Capital social, etnicidad y desarrollo: algunas consideraciones críticas desde los Andes ecuatorianos. *Boletín de Antropología Americana* 37:111–117.

Burga, Manuel 2001 Lo andino hoy en el Peru. *¿Qué Hacer?* 128, Jan–Feb 2001, http://w3.desco.org.pe/publicaciones/QH/QH/qh128in.htm.

Camino, Lupe 1992 *Cerros, plantas y lagunas poderosas: la medicina al Norte del Perú*. CIPCA, Piura.

Child, Jack 2005 The politics and semiotics of the smallest icons of popular culture: Latin American postage stamps. *Latin American Research Review* 40(1):108–137.

Cieza de León, Pedro de 1962 *La crónica del Perú*. Espasa-Calpe, Madrid.

Coloma, César 1994 *Los inicios de la arqueología en el Perú o "Antiguedades peruanas" de Mariano Eduardo de Rivero*. Instituto Latinoamericano de Cultura y Desarrollo, Lima.

de la Cadena, Marisol 2000 *Indigenous Mestizos: The Politics of Race and Culture in Cusco, Perú, 1919–1991*. Duke University Press, Durham.

de Rivero, Mariano 1994 Antigüedades peruanas. In *Los inicios de la arqueología en el Perú o "Antigüedades peruanas" de Mariano Eduardo de Rivero*, by César Coloma, pp. 28–34. Instituto Latinoamericano de Cultura y Desarrollo, Lima. First published in 1841.

Espinoza, Waldemar 1981 *La destrucción del imperio de los Incas*. Amaru, Lima.

Florián, Mario 1961 *Los primeros peruanos*. Ministerio de Educación Pública, Lima.

González Carré, Enrique, and Carlos del Águila (editors) 2005 *Arqueología y sociedad*. IEP-INC-INDEA, Lima.

González Prada, Manuel 1956 Nuestros Indios. In *Manuel González Prada. Ensayos escogidos*, edited by Augusto Salazar. Scorza, Lima. First published 1904.

Gose, Peter 1994 *Deathly Waters and Hungry Mountains: Agrarian Ritual and Class Formation in an Andean Town*. University of Toronto Press, Toronto.

Harris, Olivia 1982 The dead and the devils among the Bolivian laymi. In *Death and the Regeneration of Life*, edited by Maurice Bloch and Jonathan Parry, pp. 45–73. Cambridge University Press, Cambridge.

Herrera, Alexander 2011 Heritage tourism, poverty and identity in Peru. In *The Ethics of Heritage Tourism, Archaeology and Identity in Latin America*, edited by Margarita Díaz-Andreu and César Villalobos, pp. 161–185. Oxbow Books, Oxford.

Herrera, Alexander, and Kevin Lane 2006 ¿Que hacen aquí esos pishtaku? Sueños, ofrendas y la construcción del pasado. *Antípoda* 1(2):157–177.

Kaulicke, Peter (editor) 1998 *Max Uhle y el antiguo Perú*. PUCP, Lima.

Lane, Kevin, and Alexander Herrera 2005 Archaeology, landscapes and dreams: Science, sacred offerings, and the practice of archaeology. *Archaeological Review from Cambridge* 19:111–129.

Lumbreras, Luis Guillermo 1974 *La arqueología como ciencia social*. Casa de las Américas, La Habana.

Mariátegui, José Carlos 1937 *Siete ensayos de interpretación de la realidad peruana*. Casa de las Américas, La Habana.

Martínez de Compañón, Baltasar Jaime 1978 [1735–1797] *La obra del obispo Martínez de Compañón sobre Trujillo en del Perú en el siglo XVIII*. Centro Iberoamericano de Cooperación, Madrid.

Minelli, Laura, and Steven Wegner (editors) 2001 *El museo de Chacas*. Editrice Compositori, Bolonia.

Morales, Daniel 1993 *Historia arqueológica del Perú (del Paleolítico al Imperio Inca)*. Milla Batres, Lima.

Paredes, Martín 2001 Asedios al indigenismo. *¿Qué hacer?* 128, Jan–Feb 2001, http://w3.desco.org.pe/publicaciones/QH/QH/qh128in.htm.

Politis, Gustavo 2003 The theoretical landscape and the methodological development of archaeology in Latin America. *Latin American Antiquity* 14:115–142.

Quijada, Mónica 1994 De la colonia a la república: inclusión, exclusión y memoria histórica en el Perú. *Histórica* 18(2):365–382.

Rostworowski, María 2002 Los infinitos tesoros del antiguo Perú. In *Sobre el Perú. Homenaje a José de la Puente Candamo*, edited by Margarita Guerra, Oswaldo Holguín, and César Gutiérrez, pp. 1141–1150. PUCP, Madrid.

Salomon, Frank 2002 Unethnic ethnohistory: On Peruvian peasant historiography and ideas of autochtony. *Ethnohistory* 49(3):475–506.

Schaedel, Richard 1952 An Analysis of Central Andean Stone Sculpture. Unpublished Ph.D. dissertation, Department of Anthropology, Yale University, New Haven.

Sichra, Inge (editor) 2009 *Atlas sociolingüístico de pueblos indígenas en América Latina*. UNICEF-AECID-FUNPROEIB Andes, Cochabamba.

Squier, George Ephraim 1878 *Peru: Incidents of Travel and Exploration in the Land of the Incas*. Macmillan, London.

Steward, Julian 1955 *Theory of Culture Change: The Methodology of Multilinear Evolution*. University of Illinois Press, Urbana.

Tantaleán, Henry 2004 La arqueología social peruana: mito o realidad. *Cota Zero* 19:90–100.

Tello, Julio César 1923 Wira Cocha. *Revista Inca* 1:93–320.

———. 1929 *Antiguo Perú: primera época*. Segundo Congreso Sudamericano de Turismo, Lima.

Trigger, Bruce 1996 Alternative archaeologies: Nationalist, colonialist, imperialist. In *Contemporary Archaeology in Theory: A Reader*, edited by Robert Preucel and Ian Hodder, pp. 615–631. Blackwell, Oxford.

Uhle, Max 1959 *Wesen und ordnung der altperuanischen kulturen*. Colloquium Verlag, Berlín. First published 1917.

Walter, Doris 2006 Los sitios arqueológicos en el imaginario de los campesinos de la Cordillera Blanca (Sierra de Ancash). In *La complejidad social en la sierra de Ancash*, edited by Alexander Herrera, Carolina Orsini, and Kevin Lane, pp. 177–190. Comune di Milano, Milán.

Willey, Gordon 1953 *Prehistoric Settlement Patterns in the Virú Valley, Perú*. Smithsonian Institution Press, Washington, DC.

Zevallos, Jorge 1994 *Huacas y huaqueros en Trujillo durante el Virreinato (1535–1835)*. Instituto Nacional de Cultura, Trujillo.

CHAPTER 4

TURNING TABLES IN SEARCH OF DIALOGUE: THE MAKING OF INDISCRETE SPACES IN LATIN AMERICAN CONTEXTS

Dante Angelo

This chapter is part of a bigger project in which I intend to touch upon the political aspects implicit in the archaeological practice and that, inherently, form part of the definition of the discipline and its members. The aforementioned project responds to the need to deal with these and other aspects and introduce them actively into the academic debate. Here, I am interested in emphasizing the experiences through which the relationships between archaeology, politics, and society become evident and in which the debate and decisions over the past is also claimed by other stakeholders. It is important, I argue, to trace the conceptual and practical frameworks (as well as their implications), power relations, and the social and economic connotations in which these relations take place, especially regarding the discourses of cultural plurality in nationalists and postnationalists contexts.

Archaeology is not exempt of such debates, directly or indirectly, since the past remains as a key element in the construction of identities and ethnicities in the present, as many authors have accurately shown (Trigger 1984, 1989; see also Díaz-Andreu 1999; Díaz-Andreu and Champion 1996). The convulsive social landscape, now experiencing deep and increasing changes fostered by global economics, has resulted in the acknowledgment of the "multicultural" more as a constitutive requirement of globalization than as a response to this process (Hale 2002; Žižek 1998); it has also led to a reemergence of identity projects (Jones 1997; Olsen 2001) permeating the practice and theoretical view of anthropology and archaeology (Appadurai 1996; Gupta and Ferguson 1997).

A democracy with neoliberal tinges has torn to pieces much of the direction of social critique, such as Marxism (Oyuela-Caycedo et al. 1997), on its return to those countries that were previously racked by dictatorships, as is the case of Bolivia, Argentina, and others in Latin America. An evaluation of this and other "trends of critique" is necessary, therefore, in the light of a critical position on the practice of archaeology. This, certainly, has a strong impact on the practice of the discipline that, in many cases, was forced to rethink its conceptual frameworks as well as the practice itself from a position that was subject to challenges, multiple interpretations, and different needs from the past. It is precisely these challenges that promote and open these "indiscrete spaces," turning tables and forcing us to consider a necessary repositioning as academics and individuals who work within different social contexts.

As Gnecco (2005:184) asserts, one of the most important aspects in the process of consolidation of the authority of science (assumed by archaeology) was the "delimitation of the site of enunciation, the space where the historical discourse was and still is legitimated" within the academy. This space of enunciation, worthy to keep in mind, is consolidated by academic events, like the one at which this paper was originally presented, and others to which I will make reference further ahead, where specific agendas are established. Usually in these scenarios, it is hoped that these agendas be dealt with according to a particular rhetoric—the academic—therefore defining the mechanisms of participations and, consequently, those of exclusion as well.

This is something that, for most of us, is crudely taken for granted. However, it is more and more evident that the diverse circumstances in which concepts like "heritage," "identity," "culture," and others, have overran the limits of what is conceived of as strictly academic, are now appropriated and rearticulated in different kinds of discourses held by a myriad of social actors. These discourses respond to political and ideological claims (be these vindicative, millenarist, exclusionist, and others), articulating themselves around old contingencies and promoting new ones.

Contrary to other studies, then, my work is not based in an analysis of a single, specific, case study. Instead of presenting a case that, from its dissection and objectification, is transformed in a case study, my work attempts to focus on the very fact that brought us to congregate in spaces of debate to discuss these themes. What is more, I argue that is important to conduct a reflexive analysis of the process in which we, whether we want it or not, are immersed. It is from this analysis of some of the reactions and attitudes that began to take shape in the academic world, following the formation of specific contexts, that I understand this emergent process as a process of emergency, a cry that calls us to assume new positions at the dialogue table.

Part 1

The current Latin American and global context of the last decades has been shaken by the arise of social movements and their subsequent acknowledgment within the public sphere in terms of the "multicultural" (Hale 2002). The emergence of critical trends within anthropological and archaeological thinking has brought their role as scientific disciplines within society into question. Thus, the preoccupation to challenge exclusionist discourses of fascist and neocolonialist nature (Arnold 1996; Díaz-Andreu 1999; Politis 1995) had a strong effect on the analysis of the relation between archaeology and nationalistic discourses (Díaz-Andreu and Champion 1996; Gnecco 1999, 2005; Jones 1997; Mamani 1996; Trigger 1984, 1989). The nation-states, a project to which archaeology had widely contributed (Jones 1997; Trigger 1984, 1989), besides being spaces in crisis (Bhabha 1990; Gupta and Ferguson 1997), became a fashionable theme of archaeological inquiry.

Nowadays, it is not news to find extremely sharp and mordacious critiques targeted against nationalism—as well as other similar specific topics (Michael Shanks, Bjornar Olsen, and Chris Witmore, personal communication 2003)—contesting exclusion and homogenization in order to attain the label of "critic." Nation-states, with their invented traditions (Hobsbawm and Ranger 1983) and their imagined communities (Anderson 1991), are now the object of a harsh, although not so effective, critique (Fernández 2003; Paz 2004; Zaburlín 2005). The result, nonetheless, is scarcely gratifying, especially when the critique to the positivist foundations of modernity of the nation-states does not offer an alternative to confront the results promoted by the burgeoning process of "balkanization" of some of these, or to confront the charge of neoliberal economic powers of transnational capital (Angelo in preparation; Kojan and Angelo 2005).

It is also impossible, within this very frame, to attempt to provide alternative answers along with these criticisms to nationalism. A case in point to clarify this claim, in my opinion, is the incapacity of archaeologists (and other social scientists) to deal critically with some of the hottest issues in Bolivian politics, such as the emergence of regionalist autonomist projects. These projects, echoing the critiques against the oppressive characteristics held by nation-states and their dominant discourses, have begun to forge separatist discourses with even more exclusionist and neo-fascist overtones (Antelo 2004; cf. *Tinkazos* no. 16, a journal edited by the Program of Strategic Research of Bolivia [PIEB], La Paz). In the face of this and other new social challenges, many of us (archaeologists and anthropologists) have decided to turn a blind eye and deaf ears, discretely, avoiding becoming part of this volatile and highly dynamic context that is being engendered in the social and politic realms in present-day Bolivia.

Related to the questioning of the asphyxiating nature of colonialist representations and the homogenizing structures of the nation-states, new interventions and representations, this time coming from indigenous groups and others—identified as these minorities historically displaced and subordinated—made their presence felt in the debate. These new actors and their claims for vindicative rights regarding the use (and abuse) of the past by science and anthropology were brought into the academic forums. This is the case of the work of Vincent Deloria (*Custer Died for Your Sins*, 1969) and others (see also Echo-Hawk 1997; Langsford 1983; Mamani 1996; Watkins 2002; Zimmerman 1989), making evident the need to consider critically the contributions of archaeology to a wider social context (Layton 1989; see Gnecco 1999, 2005; Politis 2001 for Latin American examples).

However, this seems to be a phenomenon that does not end there. Facing an apparently increasing process of homogenization, promoted by the advances of global capitalism, other different processes of empowerment and new (re)configurations in the social and cultural geography can be seen (auspiced, generally, under the problematic label of multiculturalism). The dynamics of the transnational movements and the emergence of diasporic or revivalist communities have turned categories such as "identity" or "local" into elusive ones, forcing archaeologists, and social scientists in general, to adopt a more informed perspective. As Hodder (2003:72) asserts:

> The increased concern with alternative perspectives, multivocality and identity issues in archaeology is linked to globalism, post-industrial societies, the information age and so on. Writers such as Castells (1996) have looked at broad globalizing trends in economic systems, and Arjun Appadurai (1996), working from an anthropological perspective, has discussed the cultural components of this process, describing a new fluidity whereby the emphasis is on transnationalism and diaspora.

It is from these intricate relationships between archaeology and society that definitions like cultural heritage, local communities, and others, have now attained considerable currency, being explicitly included as central themes within the agenda of academic and public debates (Shanks 2004; Ucko 1987). Nonetheless, even when there is an extensive literary production concerning these issues, impulsing a more reflexive and responsible practice of the discipline (see Hamilakis 2003; Meskell 1998), these issues have been largely absent—or have received scant attention—in the debate in countries like Bolivia, and others, where the heralds of multiculturalism and pluralism were already saluted and celebrated. Thus, despite the fact that these issues have been looming over (and kept at bay from) the academic and political domains for more than two decades, they are recently being incorporated into Latin American spaces of debate (Ayala 2005; Ayala et al. 2003; Gnecco 1999, 2005; Politis 2003).

Part 2

The influence of global factors affecting diverse local communities has resulted in its very reconfiguration, promoting at its turn identity claims related to their past and culture. As some authors argue, these claims have moved from aspects that have to do with *social politics* (class and social equality) toward those related more to *cultural politics* (identity politics and politics of recognition) (Fraser 1997). Identity politics—as is assertedly pointed out by Comaroff (1996)—are situated as part of complex interweaving and power equations, expressed in material, symbolic, and political terms. In some of the interpellating discourses, then, "ethnic identity must call on some shared sensibility, some latent cultural essence; a primordial infrastructure, as it were, from which appropriate signs, symbols, and sentiments may be extracted when necessary" (Comaroff 1996:165). In that sense, the past (and the archaeological discourse), no doubt, acquires a remarkable importance, becoming a field of strategic struggle (Preucel and Hodder 1996a:604). Four vignettes will help me to illustrate my analysis.

Vignette 1

"I have a question about how to make a difference" said a post by one of the participants of the World Archaeological Congress (WAC) electronic mailing list. This person's preoccupation had to do with the construction of the new airport in Quito, Ecuador, which was "beginning to take shape over hundreds of tombs, structures and villages. It is being plowed under, the whole lost civilization," and the lamenting of the potential loss of data that "would be worthy of any museum." The message also added:

> How can we protest the government and stop the construction? Also, TLC or The Free Trade talks are going on right now and we, as Americans, have been warned to stay low profile. So, did you know about this happening? Do people care? Because the Ecuadorian government does not? What is there to do? (G. H., quoted by A. P., March 20, 2006, WAC LISTSERV)

Different answers and comments followed the question. Some made evident the tense relationships between national and foreign archaeologists, the former being uncomfortable with the interference of the latter in "national affairs"; others stressed issues related to the source—whether private, international, or national—of funding for the project so as to determine who could be charged as guilty. Still, others emphasized the state, conditions, and limitations of the archaeological research, and even the need for a new airport. Thus, as one poster stated:

> I take offence at [his] communiqué disparaging the Ecuadorian government and archaeologists and the fact that it's being spread around all over the world. The new airport has been in the planning stages for the past 8 years or so. Quito's soon to be old airport is very dangerous due to its envelopment by the city [with] many accidents and deaths there in recent years. The National Institute of Cultural Patrimony conducted Phase 1, 2, and 3 studies and mitigation at the new airport site a couple of years ago now. (T. B., March 22, 2006, WAC LISTSERV)

Another poster would respond:

> With respect, I have to suggest that your response on this matter highlights a structural problem that characterizes the cultural heritage programs of many Latin American countries. While the laws trumpet the sanctity of the nation's cultural patrimony, it is left to the chronically under funded cultural ministries to protect and manage it. The construction and economic development agencies of government are assigned no responsibility whatever. (T. K., March 23, 2006, WAC LISTSERV)

In a matter of days the flow of e-mails escalated, heating up the debate and exposing serious tensions within the country's politics and the interweaving of global capitals and local interests found in contradiction between international standards and national legislation proceedings regarding cultural heritage. And, while some would remark that the archaeological finds at the site "[only] consist of utilitarian ceramics, of rustic manufacture, which are found on the surface (no more that one meter deep), and are fairly common in the area of Quito" (A.O., March 29, 2006), and that no architectural structures, neither houses nor ceremonial centers, were found—clearly privileging a monumentalist notion of valuable heritage—others would cry out, denouncing

> I was turned down permission by INPC to make some corrections [of mistakes made in phase 1], at that point INPC *officers told me that, Ecuador was a sovereign country with their own laws and that they will not allow anyone who claims to be enforcing World Bank Standards* … I am concerned since I do not know what will happen with the tombs? Are there physical anthropologists involved? What are the analyses Quiport [the project's name] will perform on those burials and to what extent the analysis will go? (P. L., March 28, 2006, my italics, WAC LISTSERV)

In my opinion, what this exchange of thoughts clearly evidences is that we, as archaeologists, are situated in different intersecting planes (political, economical, academic, national sovereignty, and so forth), where some of them demand from us immediate, protagonic, and well-informed action. However naive the initial question may sound, it exposes different concerns, which are differently echoed by different responses; on the one hand, the worries about the lost of irretrievable data reflects the high value that is still invested upon the archaeological object. On the other hand, the denouncement of inescapable responsibilities in which archaeology is globally involved would also come forward:

> Please, have a look on the news about thousands of indigenous peoples demonstrating against TLC in Ecuador, and then think about the government position regarding indigenous peoples and their heritage and future. Then also think about the warning you've received as Americans: "stay low profile." What are the roles of American archaeologists? To stay low profile and let your American government do whatever they want? Ecuadorians are struggling against what they see as an injustice. They do not stay low profile. (A. H., March 22, 2006, WAC LISTSERV)

It seems to be the case that the practice in the discipline remains immersed in tension. Seemingly, it is still hard to overcome the image of the discipline as concerned only with objectivity, the empirical data, and an agenda that privileges the academic, leaving politics aside (Latour 1993, 1999; Shanks 2004). This also reflects the different positions and the intricate networks in which we are trapped, where our work is instrumental for other stakeholders. In any case, we are tied to responsibilities we cannot deny and we need to make ourselves accountable in front of possible interpellations.

Vignette 2

To this scenario we must add the fact that many of the new emergences in the public space (and that now irrupt into the academic debate) pose a threat to our ethos as community, promoting deep anxieties that begin to reveal some of our deepest preconceptions and biases toward the Other(s) that emerge(s) to interpellate us. Thus, for instance, I was stunned by the degree of disillusion and disappointment of several of my colleagues about the relation between archaeologists and indigenous communities (especially the role of the latter in this relationship), a hot and recurrent topic in the academic sphere nowadays. In many cases, this disillusion has to do with a rather pragmatic and cynic perception (and prescription) of these relations and in other cases—perhaps the majority—with the romanticization of "the indigenous."

In the first case, some researchers seem to see the members of local communities as passive receivers of the knowledge of the past and think that—despite their rights over territories and material culture, sometimes sanctioned by state's legislation—they should have no opinion in the decisions about how research about the past must be done (Mamani 1996). Almost a 100% of archaeological investigations in countries like Bolivia, for instance, are conducted in rural areas or lands that belong to indigenous communities recently recognized by the state (Albó 2002). In many cases, the relationship is absent, aside from the bureaucratic paperwork, and the only thing that matters is to keep "good PR" with these communities, while making sure that they are kept at bay and do not interfere with research (e.g., Stanish and Kusimba 1996).

In the second case, local communities are framed within romantic and nostalgic conceptions of the Other. The "indigenous" or the "*originario*" (Spanish word commonly used to denote "aboriginal"), which are generally the terms used to make reference to members of these communities, is perceived as possessing an atavistic link with the past. Related to this conceptualization there are other concepts such as "purity" and "originality" for which, necessarily, this Other has to be good and docile, as in the myth of the "noble savage." Thus, when these local communities fall from these preconceptions and stereotypical images that prevail in most of us (thanks to anthropological views that privilege conceptions such as possession of communal lands, peasant economy, and some particular atavistic belief/relationship with ancestors, etc.), they are seen as "culturally contaminated by economic interests," which results in their becoming "greedy," "corrupt," and other much less kind epithets—as commented in conferences halls, corridor chitchat, and informal meetings among scholars. Nostalgically, then, the "noble savage" is announced as dead. Of course, all these comments are carefully cleansed and removed from any academic or technical monograph or report.

This, necessarily, derives from the imposition of negative connotations that point to the compartmentalization and seclusion of these communities and their members within primordialist categories (Benhabib 2006; Said 1989; Van Buren 1996). These categorizations are usually based on essentialist conceptions of "culture" subject to scrutiny, whose characteristics are generally presented within synchronic models of sociocultural analysis (e.g., Bastien 1978; Isbell 1977; Murra 1975). These analyses, nonetheless, are challenged by the very members of the represented societies in the practice due to, among other reasons, the rapid pace of globalization and the diverse historical and social changes taking place within it (Appadurai 1996; Paine 2000; Starn 1991, 1994). Commonly, this results in a nostalgic disappointment in the ideal of the "indigenous" for some archaeologists.

Vignette 3

On the other side of the discussion, reacting to these challenges to the nature of history and the irruption of new political actors, the response has been (a forced) openness and inclusion. This is the case (and the reason) for many of the conferences and meetings recently held, such as the "Encuentro de reflexión sobre patrimonio cultural, comunidades indígenas y arqueología" (Cultural heritage, indigenous communities and archaeology: A reflexive encounter) in Ollagüe (Chile, at the end of 2002) and, more explicitly, the 51st International Congress of Americanists (ICA) in Santiago (Chile, July 2003) and the "Reunión de Río Cuarto" (Río Cuarto meeting), Río Cuarto (Argentina, May 2005) (Ayala 2005; Ayala et al. 2003; see also *Arqueología Suramericana* 1:287–293). In other cases, the questionings had a more disruptive character, fueling internal tensions in the discipline—see, for instance, Politis (2001) about the case of the mummies of Llullaillaco in Salta, Argentina. Since then, scholarly practice is trying to open spaces to include these new voices in the archaeological discourse so they can take part in the interpretation and use of the past (Hodder 1999, 2003). Nonetheless, this openness risks being no more than a strategic move, a gambit, in the articulation of a new hegemonic discourse that only seeks to include these voices while reaffirming its authority.

As Hodder points out, this liberal trend that now attempts to portray itself as self-critical "continues a colonial impulse. It tries to engage the subaltern in a Western discourse that is not only elitist but also difficult, specialized and abstract" (2003:24). Despite the fact that some authors have manifested their worries (and some their pleasure) about the new role that local communities are beginning to assume regarding the control and management of archaeological resources (Monné and Montenegro 2003), it is still hard to delineate the frame within which these relationships take place. Apparently for many of us, accepting that these communities become the *owners* of *our objects* of study is no more than a formality with which to comply. Undoubtedly, the relations between local communities and archaeological projects are determined by unequal power relations, which are usually defined by the authority, cultural capital, and academic credentials of the researchers (Bourdieu 1984; Bourdieu 1991). It is worth mentioning some of the assumptions usually held aprioristically by some researchers: (1) local communities, in spite of their intrinsic relation with the past, are dispossessed of the knowledge to approach it; and (2) therefore "they can benefit"—from a very positivistic view—from knowledge that academia can provide regarding ("their") history.

In other cases, the economic advantage held by these projects, especially when they are backed by international agencies and/or foreign universities, clearly set unequal relationships between the projects and the economically depressed communities, affecting the balance in the decision making regarding the objectives and agenda of research (however, see Pyburn 2002:121). Sometimes, these projects are economically endowed to afford local museums, which can or cannot have clear policies about tourist impact on the sites and where results are presented as contributions of science to these local communities (Bauer and Stanish 2001; Muñoz 2002; Nielsen et al. 2003; Stanish and Kusimba 1996). This is mainly because one of the aspects in which archaeological investigation has gained relevance is related to the increasingly oversaturated tourist market (Lima 2003; Nielsen et al. 2003).

The results can be significant in terms of providing economic alternatives to these communities so they can insert themselves (successfully or not) in tourism circuits (Nielsen et al. 2003). Additionally, besides opening a path to insertion into the tourist economy for local communities, archaeological investigations have also become instrumental for political discourses related to territory and identity claims (Capriles 2003; Hodder 1999; Lima 2003). Nonetheless, a majority of these projects scarcely consider the repercussions that these types of actions can have. Neither the political consequences of the forms of representation nor the processes of bracketing off these communities are considered critically. Generally, these communities are encouraged (if not forced), for the sake of tourism, to represent primordialist images of themselves, as the following paragraph shows:

> In December the community celebrates the Khapac Raymi[1] festival in the archaeological [s]ite [of Inkallajta]. While in previous years it was a rather popular party, with electronic music and all, since 2002 *they [the people of the community] have recovered [in the festival] their own customs as well as their autochthonous musical instruments emphasizing these rituals and offerings to Pachamama, despite the influences of a protestant church that has a strong presence in the region.* (Muñoz 2002:16, my italics)

In front of this statement it may be useful to ask whether a possible decision to turn their backs on these cultural practices would define the people of this particular community as less authentic and, therefore, not fit to possess this heritage.[2] I must acknowledge that, in many cases, this essentialist representation (or self-representation) acquires certain strategic characteristics that are played by these communities, either as a group or individually (Spivak 1988; cf. Benhabib 2006).

The problem I see, in any case, is that this type of (self)representation is becoming more and more the only possibility rather than an option among many others to choose from. This, evidently, has to do with the demand and consumption of this kind of cultural product (Shanks 2004; Shanks and McGuire 1996), whose success or failure depends on the credibility of these new inventions of the "authentic and natural" where local and global unite in complicity (Castañeda 1996; also Angelo, in preparation). Critical approaches that could count with the participation of fellow archaeologists about these economic strategies—which ultimately promote the insertion of these communities in global economy in unequal conditions—are scarce. Therefore, power relations defined in this type of relationship between the local and its counterparts are unbalanced, resulting in the infliction of a subtle but effectively symbolic and neocolonialist violence (Bourdieu 1991).

Vignette 4

Recently, *Chungará* has dedicated a complete issue (vol. 35, no. 2) to presenting the results of academic projects that initiated debate around cultural heritage and the relationship between members of indigenous and academic communities.[3] These experiences of collaboration are still incipient to providing accurate evaluations; nonetheless, the framing, the representations, and conceptualizations of the relations between what is defined as "the indigenous" and "the academic" scarcely receive critical consideration in the whole publication. Thus, the imbalance generated by this kind of conceptualization of the power relations, stereotypically dualistic and conservative, is barely called into question, which risks the possibility of reinforcing existing power structures through the consolidation of a system of knowledge about the past (that of archaeological science) that, in this case, becomes fortified as dominant at the expense of the subjection and passivity of its alleged interlocutors (Gnecco 1999; Preucel and Hodder 1996a).

The critique to postmodernist's pretensions of hyperreflexivity provided by Crapanzano (1991) is worth considering. This author argues that postmodernism, with its critical baggage toward metanarratives and the positions of authority held by rationalist epistemology and its economic and political power networks, has promoted a discourse that describes for us (i.e., analyzes critically) the intricate relations of power but, at the same time, prescribe us (i.e., constrains us) to a fixed way of approaching reality. According to Crapanzano, it is possible to assume a position regarding this prescription but, as long as this is confused with description, is not possible to reject it completely, which defines a confrontation, or rather an "[incorporation] into a totalizing hermeneutic—a sort of epistemological antinomianism—which rejects totalization, questions the authority of any hermeneutic, and refuses any transcendental position" (Crapanzano 1991:435). This, certainly, provokes a type of closure to the debate that does not allow the effective articulation of discourses nor the challenging of dominant structures, since it does not acknowledge the subversive potential of the different individual positionings (Wylie 2003) and, according to Crapanzano, promotes this critical stand as a sort of fundamentalism.

Crapanzano's work alerts us to an argument that could become problematic and susceptible of being easily co-opted by liberal discourse, if we are going to understand this space of critique as framed solely within a cultural critique that only blends positivistic postures as necessary—that is, demagogically celebratory of a discoursive diversity (Hale 2002; Žižek 1998:176). In this sense, it is important not to cordon off or contain these claims, such as the vindicative claims of indigenous groups regarding their past, by defining them as fundamentalist expressions (leading to their disqualification), especially if these claims phrase their critique in postmodern jargon[4] or, even worst yet, to include them demagogically as samples of recent academic openness to local claims (e.g., Ayala 2005; Ayala et al. 2003).

Undoubtedly, Crapanzano is informed about this possibility when he warns us against the insistent discourse of equality and reflexivity promoted by postmodernism or, better said, by multiculturalist neoliberalism, about which Butler et al. (2003), Hale (2002), and Žižek (1998), among others, talk to us. For this author, the notion of egalitarian dialogue, or the so-called "dialogical space," has been overestimated, where, apparently,

> [interlocutors] pretend that they are equals and have equal rights in the exchange. *This dialogical egalitarianism may in fact be purely ideological, a mystification of "real" differences in power, and these real differences may—certainly do—affect the plays of power that occur within egalitarian-framed dialogue.* (Crapanzano 1991:436, my italics)

The result of this idealization, he goes on to say, is that it produces a "double indexing that occurs within any exchange: an intra- and extra-dialogical indexing of the participants, for example, *as equal within the dialogue but as unequal outside the dialogue*, in real life, as we say" (1991:436, my italics). In other words, these differences and power relations that two or more parties get into, in any exchange, are concealed by the idealized pretension (the pretense) in which this kind of dialogue is conceived or represented.

This is the problem that I see in many of the collaborative projects presented in Ayala et al. (2003), which, through a change in the academic attitude toward local notions regarding cultural heritage, pretend to show an opening in the spaces of debate, to be occupied by those groups historically disenfranchised. Whereas it is evident that one of the objectives of the reflexive trend inside the discipline was to promote the inclusion of "local voices," opening up multiple interpretations and uses of the past (Hodder 1999, 2003), it is necessary to differentiate between dialogue and ventriloquism (Castañeda 1996). The latter implies the legitimation of the dominant discourse through the incorporation of subaltern voices, subsuming their potential critique to subvert and challenge hegemonic views, resulting in what Spivak refers to as the impossibility of the subaltern to speak (Spivak 1988; cf. Hodder 2003).

Part 3

Certainly, in the last decade we have witnessed a change in the attitude concerning the position academia and especially disciplines like anthropology and archaeology have taken in relation to this new social context in which they are situated. Nevertheless, it is necessary to maintain a suspect attitude and constant scrutiny. Apparently, in many of the new dialogue situations that are being promoted, it is assumed that much change is not necessary and that business can be carried on as usual, but only to assist (paternalistically?) these communities. As Hodder sarcastically, but rightly, puts it, "Dialogue and collaboration and multivocality on their own are not enough. Many discussions of dialogue assume that we just [need to] add a bit of collaboration and stir" (Hodder 2003:2).

Yet, there is a strong reticence to accept that the battlefield, as Gnecco (2005) argues, is widening. For some, it seems, these kind of interpellations are still uncomfortable, producing indiscrete spaces and disturbing our usual *habitus*. In this sense, the response so far has been generally to make special room, opening spaces to debate (dialogue) these issues. The results of this response have included the organization of the "Foro de Pueblos Originarios de Río Cuarto" (Forum of the Originary Peoples of Río Cuarto, which resulted in the Declaración de Río Cuarto 2004) or the session in which this work was initially presented.

Thus, for instance, the following happened during a recent academic event in Tilcara where some voices that questioned archaeologists and their interpretations emerged.[5] In some cases, the critique was directed, generically, to the colonialist nature of archaeology; in others, the archaeological interpretations and epistemological foundations were questioned (one of the speakers, for instance, assumed a rather romantic, messianic, and totalizing view of the Inkas and the Tawantinsuyu, now very common in discourses that seek to promote a pan-Andean identity). Amidst a hot peak in the discussion created by this indiscreet participant, and addressing the interrupting voice, one of the archaeologists in the conference room respectfully said, "Sorry for interrupting.

This certainly is an interesting and much-needed discussion, but, back to where we were," and then, turning around and addressing the colleague who was dissertating, asked, "what is the chronological framework for the region?" (Tilcara, 2005).

The organizers of the event were compelled "to open" a space of debate at the end of the presentations so this inescapable issue could be discussed but, at the same time, unwittingly perhaps, the very debate was removed from the context in which the presentation and discussion of academic works was being contested.

Thus, this "interesting issue" was treated at the end of the event, after several dozens of academic lectures, in front of a tired audience of archae-ologists and the public. Rhetorical participations followed, deriving from a dialogue that was closer to those of multiculturalist type auspiced commonly by international agencies like the World Bank (Hale 2002). By that time, the dissident "non-academic" voices had been attenuated, becoming less confrontative; many of them valued and thanked the fact that "they were being allowed to participate in the event," receiving a general ovation from the academic audience (see also Ayala et al. 2003 for a similar situation). From my perspective, the inclusion of other voices can result, in cases like this, in a cacophony where everybody can speak without prejudice since differences are already neutralized.

It is necessary, I contend, to accept the enlargement of the spaces of discussion that, from challenges and interpellations like those described above, could allow us to sustain a more committed and active dialogue, keeping a critical eye open for possible compartmentalization of the debate. To restrict the discussion of these and other issues that could emerge in which other stakeholders' interests are involved, would be to promote a normative and disciplinary process, that is, bracketing them off within a shell. Reactionary positions would clearly applaud these (unwitting?) actions by which science, once again, is put in charge of establishing the limits and conditions that entitles its authority. Our actions are always political, so there should be an explicit participation toward the decolonizing of our discipline.

Conclusions

It is from the works of Nancy Fraser and Seyla Benhabib that I reflect on the limitations as well as the scope of recent attempts at the inclusion of alternative perspectives and their debate in academic realms. Benhabib (2006), following Nancy Fraser (1997) and Marion Young (2000), argues for the search for a universalist deliberative democracy that could emerge from the recognition of public expressions of cultural identities in civic spaces (Benhabib 2006:50). In order to do this, she contends, it is also necessary to consider the faculty of the(se) peoples to elaborate their own narratives and cultural resignifications—positioning them within interlocutive networks from which that very subjectivity can be also be called to question—so that their cultural legacies are in constant transformation and the production, reproduction, as well as the reappropriation of these legacies, therefore, escapes totalization (Benhabib 2006:144).

Gnecco (2005:187–188) argues that, in certain way, "historic subordination has displaced the place of enunciation of the past" through local narratives that began to acquire acceptance within new normative legislations, both nationally and internationally. Even though I concur with this observation, I also share Gnecco's own skepticism expressed in another publication (Gnecco 1999); I fear that this acceptance is but another strategy of assimilation through which difference and conflict are neutralized and demobilized. For Benhabib (2006:44), "According to the interactive universalism, I can learn who the other(s) is(are) only through their narratives of self-identification and I can be conscious of this otherness, and these aspects of their identity that present them as others in front of me, only through their own accounts." It would be necessary, then, to be more careful and to pay closer attention to these narratives to grasp the subjectivities that they represent.

However, in many cases, conditions of equality in the production and valorization of these narratives are quickly assumed, which, as we have seen, is largely critiqued and debated by authors like Crapanzano (1991; see also Preucel and Hodder 1996b:667–677 passim). On the other hand, it is helpful to remember that the number of local communities and stakeholders (among which archaeologists and other professionals can be found) in front of whom we are accountable is large and varied (Hodder 2003:25). A close evaluation of these aspects, carried out in a very explicit way, would be necessary in order to promote a dialogue in which the needs and priorities can be verbally uttered and dealt with. Evidently, this is not an easy task and, again, considerations about whom and what should be given priority in this dialogue makes it a strategic field of negotiation.

In that sense, I see two inherent problems that we need to deal with before these public expressions of identity could achieve these public and civic spaces having enough power to contest domination. These are, first, the pretensions of equality and the representations we sometimes keep in mind at the beginning of any dialogue for which we will probably need

> to understand these group identities in a much more dynamic way, keeping in mind that, in reflecting about identity politics and politics of difference, we need to concentrate less in what the group *is* by paying more attention to what their political leaders *demand* from the public sphere. (Benhabib 2006:47, italics in the original)

Second, it is also important to remember that, despite the fact that liberal democracy now heralds equal opportunities and equal access to resources among the individuals of any given society through their juridical system, this "equality" depends on the resources that individuals will possess and be able to mobilize to justify their choices and decisions (Hall and Held 1990).

In previous paragraphs I mentioned the nostalgic character that leads many archaeologists to see, disappointedly, how different local communities are abandoning their cultural practices that before tied them to the past, or how they became "non-authentic," losing their "purity and innocence." This nostalgic view, according to Rosaldo (2000), is a key element and plays a fundamental role in the acritical repetition of synchronic sociocultural analysis that reifies the orientalist image of the Other (Said 1989), neglecting the historical processes of cultural and economic interaction. Thus, regardless the extensive debate about the archaeological role related to collaborative works with local communities, it seems that, in many cases, the production and consolidation of cultural essentialisms is still one of the aspects that archaeology is able to promote and reify, dangerously. I would argue that it is extremely risky to follow this path, for it only reinforces seclusion and museifies the Other. Therefore, this should be avoided if we pretend to make a real contribution to the acknowledgment of diversity, and if we attempt to make this relevant in terms of promoting real spaces of encounter.

NOTES

I want to thank to Vero Seldes and Clarita Rivolta for inviting me to participate in their session "Nuevos desafios en arqueología: los espacios de interacción con la comunidad" (New challenges in archaeology: Interacting with communities), held in Salta as part of the 8th National Congress of Argentinean Anthropology in September of 2006. This session provided the space where these ideas were initially exposed. Alejandro Haber read previous versions of this paper, providing his critical insight. As several other times before, the discussion of this and other themes has benefited from conversations with Angela Macías, José Capriles, Ewa Domanska, and Alfredo Gonzáles-Ruibal, who also provided me with their time and patience to read early drafts of this paper and offered insightful comments. I have tried to incorporate their suggestions the best I could; needless to say, the paper's shortcomings are my own.

1. The Khapac Raymi festival became popular in the last decades as one of the commemorative celebrations of the indigenous identity that takes place in the archaeological site of Inkallajta. Similar versions of this festival include Inti Raymi, popularized since the 1940s in Cuzco, Peru, as is mentioned by Marisol de la Cadena (2000), or the celebrations of the Andean New Year, held in Tiwanaku and other parts of Bolivia and, recently, Ecuador, Argentina, and other countries.

2. A similar case is shown in the work of Rivolta (2004), in which she discusses the cultural practices recently (re)introduced to the Quebrada de Humahuaca and the celebration of the Andean New Year in the region, and its variations throughout the last years.

3. This issue of *Chungará* presents the insertion of this thematic in Chilean, and—to certain extent—Latin American academic spaces (Ayala et al. 2003); the volume incorporates experiences both inside and outside the Chilean borders (Fernández 2003; Lima 2003; Nielsen et al. 2003).

4. Many recent claims for the restitution of human remains made in recent years in Latin America (Politis 2001) have been commonly dismissed by conservative factions of academia under the presumed vinculation of these claims with postmodern thinking. Thus, for example, some of the arguments of this conservative trend hold that "these claims are part of a *gringo* fashion," clearly trying to allude to the nationalities of some of the representatives of the postmodern perspective; others would assert that "this is not a real problem in Latin America where [local and indigenous] communities not only see this as part of archaeological work but also participate, very enthusiastically, as assistants in scientific excavations" (comment made by conference participant, Stanford University, 2002).

5. While I was conducting my Ph.D. research in the Quebrada of Humahuaca, Argentina, I attended the workshop "Procesos sociales prehispánicos en los Andes Meridionales," held in Tilcara in August of 2005. The brief ethnographic references included in this part of the text come from the notes I had taken there; of course, the interpretation of the events may or may not be shared by other participants.

REFERENCES

Albó, Xavier 2002 *Pueblos indios en la política plural*. CIPCA, La Paz.

Anderson, Benedict 1991 *Imagined Communities: Reflections on the Origin and Spread of Nationalism*. Verso, London. First published 1983.

Angelo, Dante 2005 La arqueología boliviana: reflexiones sobre la disciplina a inicios del siglo XXI. *Arqueología Suramericana* 1(2):185–211.

Antelo, Sergio 2004 *Los cruceños y su derecho de libre determinación*. Levi Libros, Santa Cruz.

Appadurai, Arjun 1996 *Modernity at Large: Cultural Dimensions of Globalization*. University of Minnesota Press, Minneapolis.

Arnold, Bettina 1996 Nazi archaeology. In *Contemporary Theory in Archaeology*, edited by Robert Preucel and Ian Hodder, pp. 549–569. Blackwell, London.

Ayala, Patricia 2005 Pueblos originarios y arqueología: discursos en torno al patrimonio arqueológico en San Pedro de Atacama (Segunda Región, Chile). *Textos Antropológicos* 15(2–3):249–262.

Ayala, Patricia, Sergio Avendaño, Mónica Bahamondes, Ulises Cárdenas, and Álvaro Romero 2003 Comentarios y discusiones en el encuentro "Reflexión sobre patrimonio cultural, comunidades indígenas y arqueología." *Chungará* 35(2):379–409.

Bastien, Joseph 1978 *Mountain of the Condor: Metaphor and Ritual in an Andean Ayllu*. West Publishing, Saint Paul.

Bauer, Brian, and Charles Stanish 2001 *Ritual and Pilgrimage in the Ancient Andes: The Islands of the Sun and the Moon*. University of Texas Press, Austin.

Benhabib, Seyla 2006 *Las reivindicaciones de la cultura. Igualdad y diversidad en la era global*. Katz, Buenos Aires.

Bhabha, Homi 1990 Introduction: Narrating the nation. In *Nation and Narration*, edited by Homi Bhabha, pp. 1–9, Routledge and Keegan Paul, London.

Bourdieu, Pierre 1984 *Distinction. A Social Critique of the Judgment of Taste.* Harvard University Press, Cambridge.

———. 1991 *Language and Symbolic Power.* Harvard University Press, Cambridge.

Butler, Judith, Ernesto Laclau, and Slavok Žižek (editors) 2003 *Contingencia, hegemonía, universalidad. Diálogos contemporáneos en la izquierda.* Fondo de Cultura Económica, Mexico.

Capriles, José 2003 Arqueología e identidad étnica. Articulando el pasado con el presente. Reflexiones en torno a la violencia. Paper presented at the 15th Reunión Anual de Etnología, Museo de Etnografía y Folklore, La Paz.

Castañeda, Quetzil 1996 *In the Museum of Maya Culture: Touring Chichén Itzá.* University of Minnesota Press, Minneapolis.

Comaroff, John 1996 Ethnicity, nationalism, and the politics of difference in an age of revolution. In *The Politics of Difference: Ethnic Premises in a World of Power,* edited by Edwin Wilmsen and Patrick McAllister, pp. 162–183. University of Chicago Press, Chicago.

Crapanzano, Vincent 1991 The postmodern crisis: Discourse, parody, memory. *Cultural Anthropology* 6(4):431–446.

de la Cadena, Marisol 2000 *Indigenous Mestizos: The Politics of Race and Culture in Cuzco, Peru, 1919–1991.* Duke University Press, Durham.

Deloria, Vincent 1969 *Custer Died for Your Sins.* MacMillan, New York.

Díaz-Andreu, Margarita 1999 Nacionalismo y arqueología: del Viejo al Nuevo Mundo. *Revista do Museu de Arqueologia e Etnologia* 3:161–180.

Díaz-Andreu, Margarita, and Timothy Champion (editors) 1996 *Nationalism and Archaeology in Europe.* UCL Press, London.

Echo-Hawk, Roger 1997 Forging a new ancient history for Native America. In *Native Americans and Archaeologists,* edited by Nina Swidler, Kurt Dongoske, Roger Anyon, and Alan Downer, pp. 88–102. AltaMira Press, Walnut Creek.

Fernández, Soledad 2003 Comunidades locales y la enseñanza de la arqueología: una experiencia en Bolivia. *Chungará* 35(2):355–359.

Fraser, Nancy 1997 *Justice Interruptus: Critical Reflections on the Postcolonial Condition.* Routledge, London.

Gnecco, Cristóbal 1999 Archaeology and historical multivocality: A reflection from the Colombian multicultural context. In *Archaeology in Latin America,* edited by Gustavo Politis and Benjamin Alberti, pp. 258–270. Routledge, London.

———. 2004 La indigenización de las arqueologías nacionales. In *Teoría arqueológica en América del Sur,* edited by Gustavo Politis and Roberto Peretti, pp. 119–128. INCUAPA, Olavarría.

———. 2005 Ampliación del campo de batalla. *Textos Antropológicos* 15(2):183–195.

Gupta, Akhil, and James Ferguson (editors) 1997 *Culture, Power and Place: Explorations in Critical Anthropology.* Duke University Press, Durham.

Hale, Charles 2002 Does multiculturalism menace? Governance, cultural rights and the politics of identity in Guatemala. *Journal of Latin American Studies* 34:485–524.

Hall, Stuart, and David Held 1990 Citizens and citizenship. In *New Times: The Changing Face of Politics in the 1990s,* edited by Stuart Hall and Martin Jacques, pp. 173–188. Lawrence and Wishart, London.

Hamilakis, Yannis 2003 Iraq, stewardship and "the record": An ethical crisis for archaeology. *Public Archaeology* 3:104–111.

Hobsbawm, Erick, and Terence Ranger 1983 *The Invention of Tradition.* Cambridge University Press, Cambridge.

Hodder, Ian 1999 *The Archaeological Process: An Introduction.* Blackwell, Oxford.

———. 2001 *Archaeological Theory Today.* Polity Press, Cambridge.

———. 2003 *Archaeology Beyond Dialogue.* University of Utah Press, Salt Lake City.

Isbell, Billie Jean 1977 *To Defend Ourselves. Ecology and Ritual in an Andean Village.* University of Texas Press, Austin.

Jones, Sian 1997 *The Archaeology of Ethnicity*. Routledge, London.

Kojan, David, and Dante Angelo 2005 Dominant narratives, social violence and the practice of Bolivian archaeology. *Journal of Social Archaeology* 5(3):383–408.

Langsford, Rosa 1983 Our heritage—your playground. *Australian Archaeology* 16:1–6.

Latour, Bruno 1993 *We Have Never Been Modern*. Stanford University Press, Stanford.

———. 1999 *Pandora's Hope*. Harvard University Press, Harvard.

Layton, Robert (editor) 1989 *Who Needs the Past? Indigenous Values and Archaeology*. Unwin Hyman, London.

Lima, Pilar 2003 Participación comunitaria, desarrollo sostenible y arqueología: el caso de Quila Quila (Chuquisaca, Bolivia). *Chungará* 35(2):361–367.

Mamani, Carlos 1996 History and prehistory in Bolivia: What about the Indians? In *Contemporary Archaeology in Theory*, edited by Robert Preucel and Ian Hodder, pp. 632–645. Blackwell, Oxford.

Meskell, Lynn (editor) 1998 *Archaeology under Fire: Nationalism, Politics and Heritage in the Eastern Mediterranean and Middle East*. Routledge, London.

Monné, Merardo, and Mónica Montenegro 2003 He preguntado a los indios para saber sus creencias. *Pacarina* 3:237–240.

Muñoz, María 2002 *Arqueología, desarrollo e identidad*. Fundación del Banco Central de Bolivia, La Paz.

Murra, John 1975 *Formaciones económicas y políticas del mundo andino*. Instituto de Estudios Peruanos, Lima.

Nielsen, Axel, Justino Calcina, and Bernardino Quispe 2003 Arqueología, turismo y comunidades originarias: una experiencia en Nor Lípez. *Chungará* 35(2):369–377.

Olsen, Bjornar 2001 The end of history? Archaeology and the politics of identity in a globalized world. In *Destruction and Conservation of Cultural Property*, edited by Robert Layton, Peter Stone, and Julian Thomas, pp. 42–54. Routledge, London.

Oyuela-Caycedo, Augusto, Armando Anaya, Carlos Elera, and Lidio Valdez 1997 Social archaeology in Latin America? Comments to T. C. Patterson. *Latin American Antiquity* 62(2):365–374.

Paine, Robert 2000 Aboriginality, authenticity and the settler world. In *Signifying Identities: Anthropological Perspectives on Boundaries and Contested Values*, edited by Anthony Cohen, pp. 77–116. Routledge, London.

Paz, José Luis 2004 Arqueología y nacionalismo. Paper presented at the 69th Annual Meeting of the Society for American Archaeology, Montreal.

Politis, Gustavo 1995 The socio-politics of the development of archaeology in Hispanic South America. In *Theory in Archaeology: A World Perspective*, edited by Peter Ucko, pp. 197–228. Routledge, London.

———. 2001 On archaeological praxis, gender bias and indigenous peoples in South America. *Journal of Social Archaeology* 1(1):90–107.

———. 2003 The theoretical landscape and the methodological development of archaeology in Latin America. *American Antiquity* 68(2):245–272.

Preucel, Robert, and Ian Hodder 1996a Constructing identities. In *Contemporary Archaeology in Theory*, edited by Robert Preucel and Ian Hodder, pp. 601–614. Blackwell, Oxford.

———. 1996b Theoretical archaeological discourse. In *Contemporary Archaeology in Theory*, edited by Robert Preucel and Ian Hodder, pp. 667–678. Blackwell, Oxford.

Pyburn, Anne 2002 Altered state: Archaeology under siege in academe. In *Teaching Archaeology in the Twenty-First Century*, edited by Susan Bender and George Smith, pp. 121–124. Society for American Archaeology, Washington, DC.

Rivolta, Clara 2004 La celebración del Inti Raymi en la quebrada de Humahuaca: prácticas ancestrales y tradiciones recientes. Paper presented at the 3rd Congreso Argentino y Latino Americano de Antropología Rural, Tilcara.

Rosaldo, Renato 2000 *Cultura y verdad. La reconstrucción del análisis social*. Abya Yala, Quito. First published 1989.

Said, Edward 1978 *Orientalism*. Routledge and Kegan Paul, London.

————. 1989 Representing the colonized. *Critical Inquiry* 15:205–225.

Shanks, Michael 2004 Archaeology/politics. In *The Blackwell Companion to Archaeology*, edited by John Bintliff, pp. 490–508. Blackwell, Oxford.

Shanks, Michael, and Ian Hodder 1995 Processual, postprocessual and interpretive archaeologies. In *Interpreting Archaeology: Finding Meaning in the Past*, edited by Ian Hodder, Michael Shanks, Alexandra Alexandri, Victor Buchli, Joe Carman, Jonathan Last, and Gavin Lucas, pp. 3–29. Routledge, London.

Shanks, Michael, and Randall McGuire 1996 The craft of archaeology. *American Antiquity* 61(1):75–88.

Spivak, Gayatri 1988 Can the subaltern speak? In *Marxist Interpretations of Literature and Culture: Limits, Frontiers, Boundaries*, edited by Lawrence Grossberg and Cary Nelson, pp. 271–313. University of Illinois, Urbana.

Stanish, Charles, and Chapurukha Kusimba 1996 Archaeological research and community participation. *SAA Bulletin* 14(3):20–21.

Starn, Orin 1991 Missing the revolution: Anthropologists and the war in Peru. *Cultural Anthropology* 6(1):63–91.

————. 1994 Rethinking the politics of anthropology: The case of the Andes. *Current Anthropology* 35(1):13–38.

Trigger, Bruce 1984 Alternative archaeologies: Nationalist, colonialist, imperialist. *Man* 19(3):355–370.

————. 1989 *A History of Archaeological Thought*. Cambridge University Press, Cambridge.

Ucko, Peter 1987 *Academic Freedom and Apartheid: The Story of the World Archaeological Congress*. Duckworth, London.

Van Buren, Mary 1996 Rethinking the vertical archipelago: Ethnicity, exchange, and history in the south central Andes. *American Anthropologist* 98(2):338–351.

Watkins, Joe 2002 Marginal native, marginal archaeologist: Ethnic disparity in American archaeology. *SAA Archaeological Record* 2(4):36–37.

Wylie, Alison 2003 Why standpoint matters. In *Science and Other Cultures: Issues in Philosophies of Science and Technology*, edited by Robert Figueroa and Sandra Harding, pp. 26–48. Routledge, London.

Young, Marion 2000 *Inclusion and Democracy*. Oxford University Press, Oxford.

Zaburlín, María 2005 El proceso de activación patrimonial del Pucará de Tilcara. Unpublished Master's thesis, Universidad Internacional de Andalucía, La Rábida.

Zimmerman, Larry 1989 Made radical by my own: An archaeologist learns to accept reburial. In *Conflict in the Archaeology of Living Traditions*, edited by Robert Layton, pp. 60–67. Unwin Hyman, London.

Žižek, Slavok 1998 Multiculturalismo, o la lógica del capitalismo multinacional. In *Estudios culturales. Reflexiones sobre el multiculturalismo*, pp. 137–188. Paidós, Buenos Aires.

CHAPTER 5

THE INDIGENOUS OTHER IN ATACAMEÑO ARCHAEOLOGY

Patricia Ayala
Translated from the Spanish by Fernanda Kalazich R.

INTRODUCTION

From the 1990s and onward, the Chilean state has found itself in a process of reconfiguration, since the old discourse of national identity oriented toward the control and suppression of cultural differences has been left behind, moving to a multicultural and pluralist discourse that not only promotes diversity but also constructs it. This is a new ideological, legal, and institutional scenario in which the relationship between the state and indigenous peoples has changed from policies of denial, integration, and assimilation—which characterized the Chilean state from its birth in the nineteenth century until the 1990s—to policies of recognition and promotion of ethnic diversity with the promulgation of the Indigenous Law in 1993. From a position of power different from that of the previous period, indigenous groups emerged as new social actors, making visible and claiming a series of demands and struggles of signification and power around their cultural rights and the existing resources in their territory. For this matter, there are now new actors interested in archaeological remains and discourses about the past that vindicate their rights and claims for respect for their cultural meanings and visions of the past, and also their participation in the control and production of the meaning of archaeological heritage.

The understanding of this process in which we as archaeologists are involved requires an introspective and retrospective approach of the discipline and the social context in which we operate. In this sense, it is necessary to think about the role we play in the process of ethnicity, analyze the construction of the indigenous Other in archaeology and the type of relationships established, together with the critical approach to the interpretations and the images of the past we create. The problems between archaeologists and indigenous peoples in the past years require a reflection upon the historical, political, and epistemological development of our discipline, taking clear stances on how we want to relate with originary peoples and what kind of archaeology we want to practice.

Only in the past years have these issues have been dealt with in Chilean archaeological debate, and works referring to the anthropological problem of how and why archaeological heritage and discourses from the past gain relevance in the process of ethnic emergence are scarce. Likewise, and besides some descriptive approaches, the relationships established between the actors in this process have not been considered as a way to deal with the aformentioned problem. For this reason, in recent years I have carried out anthropological research in the Atacameño region of northern Chile oriented to the understanding of how and why archaeological heritage and the discourses of the past are part of the current movements of ethnic vindication at the same time that these elements contribute to shape and gives sense to these movements. Complementarily, I studied the way in which ethnic concerns about heritage have had an effect on conflicts and readjustments in the relationships between indigenous peoples, archaeologists, and the state in circumstances in which the latter has had a decisive participation in the definition and control of archaeological heritage. This chapter is an extract of that research and is centered specifically on the modalities of interaction between Atacameños and archaeologists.

Transiting between Archaeological and Anthropological Practice

The first time I was faced with the issue of the relationship between archaeologists and indigenous communities was in 1998 when excavating the Aldea de Talikuna archaeological site in Caspana, Chile, with an archaeological team led by Leonor Adán and Mauricio Uribe. On this occasion, a young Atacameño leader approached and inquired about what we were doing and if we had a permit to work there. It was a tense moment in which Leonor talked to him and we continued our work without difficulties. The questions posed by the ethnic leader attracted my attention since the people of Caspana were informed about our work through conversations with the leaders, outreach talks at the school, and colloquial conversations with people from the locality. Back in Caspana, we gave an account of what had happened to Julian Colamar, an adult leader with whom we maintained a close relationship from the beginning of our archaeological research in Caspana in 1995. His answer was that young leaders were very distrustful. After this episode, and until the end of the project, we did not experience any more similar situations; nevertheless, we were aware that there were delicate issues for the Atacameño community of Caspana, such as working in the cemetery of the *abuelos* (ancestors). For that reason, we only carried out an architectural study and analyzed the collections obtained in previous excavations. This work allowed me to get to know Julian Colamar's perception of the excavation of cemeteries and archaeological work through different conversations at his home or around Caspana. His beliefs on the *abuelos*, entities that inhabit archaeological sites, were similar to those expressed by Maria Paniri, shepherdess of Turi, whom I met in 1992 at the archaeological excavations led by Victoria Castro, Carlos Aldunate, and Luis Cornejo at the Pukara of Turi. Afterwards I continued to visit Maria and her family, although it was in one of the field campaigns led by Francisco Gallardo and Carol Sinclaire in the Salado River area that I learned about the *mal de chullpa* (illness given by the ancestors). For Maria, the allergy that covered my body on that occasion was due to the *mal de chullpa,* since the *abuelos* had cast an evil eye because I did not make an offering before beginning the excavations at the archaeological sites. Despite going to a medical center and taking medicine for two weeks, the allergy persisted. Maria performed a traditional procedure, and two days after the cleansing and the corresponding offering my allergy was gone.

In the following years I was part of different research projects in the Atacameño region together with the aforementioned professionals and others led by Barbara Cases and Carolina Agüero, parallel to which the first apprehensions on behalf of ethnic leaders about the archaeological discipline began, and also the first measures from the archaeologists. Nevertheless it was only in 2001 that I began to deal with this issue concretely through a project carried out with Ulises Cárdenas and Sergio Avendaño, oriented toward the connection of archaeological work with indigenous communities through three lines of action: the creation of museum spaces, workshops about cultural heritage, and the organization of a meeting entitled "Encuentro de reflexión sobre patrimonio cultural, comunidades indígenas y arqueología" (Encounter of reflection on cultural heritage, indigenous communities, and archaeology), which took place in Ollagüe that same year. In that meeting it became clearer than ever that the situation experienced in Caspana years before was not an isolated case, since different Atacameño leaders made strong critiques of archaeology, although there were some that demanded joint work (Ayala et al. 2003). Some years ago, when I made the decision to pursue a Master's degree, my interest in understanding this topic led me to choose the specialization of social anthropology as a way to study it from an academic perspective. A year after beginning this graduate program,

I organized the symposium "Originary peoples and archaeology" at the 51st International Congress of Americanists and began to work as coordinator of the Andean School outreach program at the Instituto de Investigaciones Arqueológicas y Museo of San Pedro de Atacama (IIAM), later taking the position of Coordinator of Relationships with the Atacameño Community at this institution until 2006.

ARCHAEOLOGY AND ORIGINARY POPULATIONS IN AMERICA

The context of discussion in which this study is framed has been dealt with from different perspectives, such as the construction of ethnic identities in the past and its effects and political uses in the present (Trigger 1984), the interpretation of this context as a power dispute around legitimate knowledge (Gnecco 1999, 2006), and its analysis from the process of social appropriation of heritage (Endere 2002). Other authors have shown how archaeological discourse has constructed an image of indigenous peoples and how it is associated with the social context of the author (Preucel and Hodder 1996; Trigger 1980, 1984). Other works stress the kind of relations established with originary peoples (Bray 2001; Ferguson 1996; Trigger 1980; Zimmerman 1989a, 1989b), these being the most related to the subjects dealt with in this chapter.

According to Trigger (1980), the beginnings of North American archaeology came with a stereotyped image of the Indians, since this discipline was highly influenced by the stereotypes that characterized them as members of static societies without progress in a primitive state of development and as reminiscences from the past. This perception was associated with a relative absence of relations between archaeologists and indigenous peoples. The manifestation of this prejudice would be reflected in an archaeological discourse that denies the notion of cultural change among the natives.

The interest of processual archaeology in ethnoarchaeology did not provide the necessary bases for the improvement of relationships between indigenous peoples and archaeologists, since this approach led to an instrumental relationship in which the native data was used to confirm the archaeologists' hypotheses and the natives were seen as objects of study (Trigger 1980). To this critique, Endere (2002) adds the definition of archaeological site as material culture unrelated to present-day societies and the ignorance with respect to the social meanings that contemporary indigenous peoples confer to the remains of the past. The universal objectives of this archaeological approach denied the possibility of studying the development of indigenous peoples as an end by itself, which affected the native vision about the archaeologists' disinterest in the problems of their society. Processual archaeology gave no importance to indigenous perspectives on cemetery excavations and archaeological constructions of the past; besides, New Archaeology coincided with an increase in indigenous demands for the control of archaeological remains (Ferguson 1996), which were boosted from the 1970s and onwards with the emergence of indigenous movements in the United States and Canada that led to ethnic vindications that questioned archaeological practice. In both countries, this process was echoed in the creation of ethical and legal dispositions.

In Latin America, legislations on the subject are practically inexistent, although some ethical norms that regulate the relations between indigenous communities, archaeological heritage, and archaeologists have been established (Gnecco 2006). In countries like Peru, archaeology has not been contested by indigenous populations, in contrast to the situation of Ecuador (Benavides 2004). In countries such as Colombia, although ethnic policies are inexistent, some indigenous groups have demanded the return of the material culture of their ancestors (Gnecco 2006) similar to the situation taking place in Argentina, where certain ethnic groups have claimed the repatriation and reburial of archaeological bodies, together with the administration of pre-Hispanic sites to insert them in tourism circuits (Endere 2002). In Bolivia, indigenous intellectuals have criticized archaeology since it has been used to legitimize colonial practices and nationalism (Mamani 1989). Also, Tiwanaku settlers confronted governmental employees and archaeologists for the administration of the archaeological site of the same name and their opposition to the international loan of archaeological pieces.

The context of ethnic mobilizations together with the impact of Marxism, feminism, and other alternative streams in archaeology echoed in the discussions at the end of the 1970s (Hodder 1994), when approaches different to that of positivism emphasized the role of social actors in the past and of the archaeologist in the present, together with stating the subjectivity of the reconstructed pasts, and raised the debate on the construction of the Other in archaeology and the importance of the past in the construction of current identities. These tendencies, known as postprocessual archaeology, abandon metanarratives and increase the acceptance of a diversity of perspectives in the interpretation of the archaeological record, advocating for a process of continual reinterpretation of the past. They also generated a major reflection on the role of the archaeologist in her/his social context and criticized the supposed neutrality of archaeology, in the understanding that the archaeologist has her/his own sociohistorical context and ideology that influence the interpretations made (Hodder 1994; Leone et al. 1987). They sustain that archaeology has been manipulated politically throughout its history, since it has been oriented and even controlled by different states, social movements, and religious tendencies and its discourses used in favor or against racial, ethnic, and social inequality, as well as in the justification or critique of colonization processes, together with its role in nationalist and indigenist discourses of different countries, and in the establishment and defense of rights over certain territories (Benavides 2004; Trigger 1980, 1984).

The configuration of a political and disciplinary context more favorable to the recognition of the demands and rights of originary peoples generated a redefinition of the relationships between the actors involved. In the last years, this issue has been analyzed from different perspectives; the relations of negotiation and collaboration between indigenous peoples and archaeologists has also been treated (Bray 2001;Gnecco 1999). In the case of the United States and Canada, indigenous claims for repatriation and/or reburial of archaeological remains led to the promulgation of a federal law in the former country and the creation of ethical principles and recommendations in the latter. Forums and discussions have taken place between archaeologists and indigenous peoples at an international, national, and regional level; in some countries, standards or protocols of behavior have been established.

RELATIONS BETWEEN ARCHAEOLOGISTS AND ATACAMEÑOS

The problem of this research, of how and why archaeological heritage gains relevance in the process of ethnic emergence, was approached from the Atacameños, since their leaders had made a series of demands to the state and the archaeologists regarding property, control, and economical use of this heritage. Likewise, in recent years the Atacameños have criticized archaeology, a discipline that has been practiced in the area from the end of the nineteenth century and of which Gustavo Le Paige, who lived and carried out archaeological research in the area between 1954 and 1979, is one of its most distinguished figures. In this section I analyze and discuss six categories of relations between archaeologists and indigenous peoples, which I identified and characterized from written information and ethnography. By dealing with human relations, these characterizations have different nuances and their limits are superposed in some cases. Furthermore, this is not about a historical process in which relations change in a unidirectional manner, but mostly about a complex system of relations that can occur synchronically or diachronically in time and that can be practiced by the same or different actors at any one time.

First Category: Denial

The Other is acknowledged but remains unrecognized, her/his existence not admitted. This form of interaction implies a distance between the actors, the inexistence of relations and/or the exclusion of the Other in practices referring to archaeological remains. We can observe this kind of relation when (1) the Other is denied as social subject; (2) the Other is not considered someone to establish a relationship with; (3) the archaeologist does not recognize the cultural meanings, values, and interests of the Other associated with archaeological remains; and (4) the Other is not considered as a subject with the right to know and express opinions regarding the practices related to archaeological remains.

This kind of relationship can be identified at least from 1950s. The critique of the Atacameños referring to Le Paige's archaeological work is mainly associated with the excavation of hundreds of burials, a fact that, seen in the context of local practices and discourses from that time, went against their values and beliefs (Figure 5.1). The Atacameños refer to archaeological sites as places of the *abuelos*, the *gentiles*—spaces and things that must be respected and feared in which the "land or the *abuelos* can catch you" and get you sick, for which reasons they should not be disturbed nor visited, nor objects taken from them.

Le Paige was aware of these local beliefs; however, his scientific interest for Atacameño prehistory led him to deny the practices and discourses of the indigenous population, together with the cultural meanings that archaeological remains portrayed for them. His attitude was not only

Figure 5.1 Collection of skulls recovered by Le Paige in the 1960s and 1970s (IIAM Archive).

coherent with the political context as well as with the development of archaeology in those years, but also with his practice as a priest: he must have considered it important to eradicate these "pagan beliefs" in a crusade of his own, similar to the "extirpation of idolatries."

Taking into account the power of Le Paige as a scientific-religious authority in a social and political context that did not favor indigenous peoples, it was difficult for Atacameños to express their disagreement on the excavation of the archaeological burials: "With Father Le Paige many people drifted apart from the church when he started to work the archaeological part because well, the father did not hide much what he had; he had a lot of skulls" (Atacameño 2, interview, 2003).[1] For people to stop attending mass, the discontent of the local population must have been strong, since it not only meant an act of disapproval toward Le Paige's archaeological work but also their estrangement from his religion. Discrepancies surrounding archaeological practices also rose in the private realm in the families where children who accompanied Le Paige to archaeological sites were reproached, a context in which these fears were not expressed to Le Paige.

After the death of Le Paige in 1980, the excavation of pre-Hispanic cemeteries continued in the oasis of San Pedro de Atacama, although on a smaller scale that in previous years and with methodologies and research problems belonging to professional archaeology. In this way, the values and beliefs of the Atacameños continued to be denied and in those years they did not manifest publicly their disagreement with archaeology. The archaeologists also continued the exhibition of human bodies in museums or, in the words of the Atacameños, "exhibiting the *abuelos*" without considering their cultural meaning for the local population.

The categories, interests, and scientific values of archaeologists were imposed over those of the Atacameños, generating a hegemonic discourse of the past from which the past of the Other was constructed. Archaeology has tried to write the history of these peoples, disdaining the ways in which these same peoples perceive and construct their own history (Gnecco 2006:185). The problem lies not only in the denial of other perceptions of the past, but also in the reproduction of the stereotype of indigenous peoples as members of societies without history. Some professionals have even stated that "without archaeologists Atacameños would not have history." Oral histories that define archaeological sites as places of the *abuelos*, of the *gentiles*, are not validated as another form of historical production, nor are the interpretations that indigenous peoples can make of the archaeological record, since only one knowledge that can confer meaning to the objects is recognized, that of the archaeologist.

Once the Indigenous Law was promulgated in 1993, the Atacameños made public demands on archaeology. It was not about small talk in corridors anymore in which archaeologists were criticized; after this law went into effect the discussion was about ethnic demands presented at meetings (i.e., the First National Atacameño Congress in 1998) and in documents (Documents of the Commission of Historical Truth and New Deal, 2003). Also, for four consecutive years, every October 12th the Atacameños lit candles in front of the museum in San Pedro de Atacama, considering that this institution keeps "their ancestors." Leaders of the indigenous group Zhali Lickan Ckappur of Calama once took over the museum, in circumstances that the professionals of this institution do not acknowledge: "It was not a proper takeover." According to the archaeologists, these events were treated with indifference because "we were very distanced, we had devoted ourselves to the scientific academic work" (Archaeologist 7, interview, 2004). This distancing of relations or their nonexistence evidences a denial of the Other as a subject of interaction, the denial of their right to have an opinion about archaeological practice, and a lack of acknowledgment of the value of such opinion, since despite the existing demands and critiques to the discipline, the archaeologists have ignored them and self-marginalized from the process.

In 2000, on the eve of October 12th, there was an attempt to burn down the Museum of San Pedro de Atacama. Until now the authorship of this attempt has not been legally determined, although there are interpretations of the incident. For the archaeologists from the museum this was a manifestation of the Atacameño community, "the climax of the rupture between the institution, academia, and the indigenous community" (Archaeologist 7, interview, 2004). The situation was not handled as an institutional problem associated with the relations established with the community, but as a danger for the museum and the archaeologists. Some Atacameños publicly condemned this attack; for them it was unforgivable since their ancestors and heritage could have burnt down.

This modality of interaction is also associated with the fact that archaeology has been practiced without communicating the objectives of the investigations to the Atacameños, despite the fact that research takes place in the territories they inhabit. This evidences a denial of the spaces of the Other since, in the words of an ethnic leader, "archaeologists come here without saying anything to anyone, as if this was their backyard," and, even though archaeological work requires a significant amount of labor, without letting local inhabitants take part in the activities.

Finally, I have to mention an aspect that has been treated by other colleagues but remains to be studied in more depth in the Atacameño case, that is, the critique related to the imposition of a linear time on the construction of the indigenous past. According to Fabian (1983), scientific discourses express knowledge in terms of temporal categorizations; in this way, the object of study is constructed as distant and objective (pre-Hispanic societies, societies from the past, natives from the past) whose way of life is seen in terms of primitive/savage. However, for indigenous populations the past is not behind us. It is not something that stopped being or something static; the past is dynamic. The past is perceived as circular: it is not necessary to rescue the past because it is present all around (Gnecco 1999; Mamani 1989; Zimmerman 1989a). In the Atacameño case, this perception is associated with the belief that the ancestors are in the surrounding hills and archaeological sites. The past is in front of our eyes and not behind in a distant and far space; the *abuelos* are from "other times" and "cohabit" with the Atacameños in the present.

Second Category: Acknowledgment

This category refers to the establishment of interactions between actors who create this relationship and mutually recognize each other through time, sharing social spaces and generating reciprocal knowledge. This form of interaction implies different degrees of relations with and knowledge about the Other: closeness, participation, involvement, trust, and credibility. According to the degree of interaction, this kind of relation allows a minor or major level of recognition of cultural meanings, values, and interests of the Other. This category is observed when (1) relations are established and the Other is known independent of archaeological practice; (2) the Other is known within a framework of archaeological research that integrates ethnography as one of the aims of the study; and (3) interaction takes place in formal spaces of archaeological outreach such as talks, workshops, and courses and in activities oriented toward the establishment of such relations.

As a priest and communal leader, Le Paige established relations of acknowledgment and proximity with the Atacameño population as he participated, shared, and got involved in communal activities, even promoting some of them. Despite the existing disagreements with his archaeological work, people did not take away their support from welfare activities. The way in which Le Paige related with the community created favorable and positive opinions about him, always mediated by his role as the priest of the village. This led to the creation of close and trustful relations, friendship, partnership, and affection, which allow us to understand how elder Atacameños participate in the ceremonies for Le Paige's anniversaries of birth or death and get emotional when remembering him and speaking of his social and priestly work.

In the 1980s outreach activities developed for the local community on behalf of the professionals of the Museum of San Pedro de Atacama generated a relation of closeness between archaeologists and Atacameños: "Look, I think it was a pretty relationship; at least I had a good experience, but that was me. This was around 1982" (Atacameño 2, interview, 2003). An important aspect of this relationship is that the participation of some Atacameños in archaeological duties generated a major defense and positive perception of the work carried out by archaeologists.

This kind of interaction is also related to an archaeology practiced together with ethnography (formal and informal), since the relation with indigenous peoples generates knowledge of their cultural meanings, values, and interests. This is associated with the ethnographical time of sharing and knowing as well as with the investigation of anthropological problems, such as the use of space, beliefs about the dead, and oral histories of the Inca occupation, among others (Aldunate et al. 2003). In this way, it is recognized that indigenous knowledge is as valid as scientific knowledge and so is its historical production. This kind of relation has antecedents previous to 1990 in Toconce, where indigenous perceptions about archaeological practice were considered at the moment of choosing the issues and methodologies of study.

This process of mutual knowledge has led the archaeologists to make themselves known as researchers, presenting the aims of their studies to the community and delivering their results. These situations have occurred in archaeological projects carried out in Ayquina-Turi, Caspana and, recently, San Pedro de Atacama.

Third Category: Collaboration

Through the development of archaeology in Atacama, it is also possible to establish collaborative relations between archaeologists and indigenous peoples. This form of interaction is relevant for the Atacameños and the archaeologists through the contribution of knowledge or practices, aiming for a more reciprocal and balanced relation from both parties. It is associated with the recognition and assessment that the contribution of the Other can be beneficial for the achievement of a determined project or aim.

This type of relationship can also be traced back to the time of Le Paige, who worked on numerous occasions with the Atacameños in projects of social relevance; although unrelated to archaeological practice, they evidenced other ways of interaction with indigenous peoples. The relations established with his Atacameño assistants could also fall within this category, though it is different from the relations established later, when archaeologists contributed to the Other from their own practices and knowledge. In the case of Le Paige, several Atacameños collaborated as informants and field assistants in his work. Without any doubt this situation was embedded in asymmetrical power relations, since Le Paige was invested with a double authority: religious and scientific.

This form of interaction is also identified in the 1980s, when professionals from the museum developed outreach activities and the local population began participating in archaeological practice (as guides at archaeological sites). This event had an influence in the formation of the "Committee for the Defense of Atacameño Heritage" which, together with professionals of the museum, would later negotiate the repatriation of the Larache gold artifacts from Santiago to the museum in San Pedro de Atacama. The constitution of this committee is evidence that back in those years there already existed a heritage consciousness among the inhabitants of San Pedro de Atacama from which they stated that "everything here belongs to us; it is the legacy of our ancestors and should therefore stay in our land" (*El Mercurio de Calama*, May 30, 1991).

It is also important to mention the recognition of Atacameño identity by the Chilean state. In the first political struggles to gain legitimacy from the state at the beginning of the 1990s, Atacameños went to the Museum of San Pedro de Atacama looking for antecedents as originary people. Together with archaeologists they gathered information that could guarantee their chronological depth. They eventually traveled to Santiago to process their recognition.

In more recent years one of the most valuable fields of collaboration between archaeologists and indigenous people has been the institutional formalization of a program of heritage training called the "Andean School" and of professional consultation within the fields of research and museology, as required for the management and valorization of archaeological sites, the insertion into the tourism market, and the creation of exhibition rooms or community museums in Atacameño communities. The Museum of San Pedro de Atacama has responded to several demands made by ethnic leaders, especially regarding access to information and knowledge generated by archaeology. One of the petitions lately formulated by the Atacameños deals with consultation in the evaluation of environmental impact studies, a conflictive issue that produces problems between archaeologists and indigenous people. The researchers that work in the area, by petition of members of the Atacameño communities, have collaborated in the formulation of territorial demands; in such case the valorization of archaeology as a useful tool for this purpose is evident. The use of archaeological data in the constitution of Atacameño indigenous communities is also recurrent.

Fourth Category: Visibilization

With the emergence of indigenous subjects in Chile in the 1990s, the relations between the state and originary populations were redefined, passing from policies of denial, integration, and assimilation to one of recognition and promotion of ethnic identities. Indigenous peoples were recognized and visibilized by the state, constituting another social actor interested in archaeological heritage. Within a framework of multicultural and pluralist policies, the Atacameños count with legal support (the Indigenous Law) and a favorable political and social context for the vindication of their rights and ethnic demands. As a result of this shift in established relations with indigenous peoples, the Other cannot be denied without consequences. Within the framework of this "new deal," Atacameños make claims related to their cultural meanings, physical and intellectual property rights over archaeological heritage, opposition to the excavation of cemeteries and to the exhibition of human remains in museums, management of archaeological sites, access to the information generated by archaeology, participation in archaeological work, the need to obtain communal permits in order to excavate, and the administration of the Museum of San Pedro de Atacama.

One of the aspects most discussed by archaeologists is that the demands presented by the Atacameños are related to a discourse of cultural continuity and the chronological depth of their people. Despite the fact that archaeologists have spread the idea of Atacameño identity and continuity in journals, exhibitions, books, and tourism leaflets (i.e., Le Paige 1958; Llagostera 2004; Núñez 1991), this continuity has been questioned from the point of view of its scientific validity. The legitimacy of this argument constitutes a contested subject in this struggle for the signification and control of the past and the archaeological record, ignoring that historical continuity is not a "fact" but a cultural and political statement constantly signified by the indigenous subject (Gnecco 2006). In order to rebate this Atacameño demand, archaeologists have recurred to what Zimmerman (1989b) calls "lineage arguments," that is, the necessity of a genetic demonstration of the links between pre-Hispanic and contemporary populations, giving preference to legal arguments when demanding repatriation of archaeological collections because museums are considered as guardians of national heritage.

The conflicts arisen have been influential: although the excavation of cemeteries has been halted, the stereotype of the archaeologist as a tomb looter still remains from the times of Le Paige and the scientific expeditions to the Loa River. The Atacameños continue to use this argument as a battle cry toward the discipline. Despite their apprehensions regarding the exhibition of human bodies in the museum, which exist from the times of Le Paige, it was only made public after the 1990s (Figure 5.2). A few years ago a group of ethnic leaders demanded the removal of human remains from the permanent exhibit of the Museum of San Pedro de Atacama, which initially resulted in the replacement of one of the bodies

Figure 5.2 Exhibition of human remains at the Museum of San Pedro de Atacama in the 1960s and 1970s (IIAM Archive).

with a replica. As I was writing this paper, the Museum of San Pedro de Atacama made public its decision to remove human remains from the permanent exhibition (Declaración Pública IIAM, September 4, 2006).

Some of these demands have been labeled by some archaeologists as "purely political," thus denying the cultural meanings that the Atacameños confer to the dead and the burials and failing to recognize that these demands, in the context of ethnicity in which they have been manifested, are cultural, political, and identity related. Besides, these disputes expose the problem of the ownership of archaeological heritage: Who is the legitimate owner? Who should manage it, the state or indigenous peoples? In the case of Chile, legal property is in hands of the state (Law 17.288) and symbolic property is in hands of indigenous communities through the management of archaeological sites and collections. For more than five years, now Atacameños have managed archaeological sites under the legal figure of *commodatum* or concession, which is interpreted by them as a recognition of indigenous property. For some of the ethnic leaders, archaeological ruins have a territorial valorization in their vindications since they are "hectares of their community"; every activity done in these places must be decided upon by the members, some of whom see archaeological work as a usurpation of their land. While archaeologists defend the state property of archaeological sites and are apprehensive regarding their protection and the potential of their object of study, indigenous peoples vindicate the property of the land, and the goods and benefits they can get from its management for tourism. The dichotomy of legal property/symbolic property has not been free of conflict.

In the context of indigenous visibilization, the problems between archaeologists and Atacameños have been radicalized. Ethnic leaders deny archaeologists by rejecting the possibility of relating to them, working jointly with them, or validating the contribution that archaeology can make to this process, replicating the form of interaction that led them to question archaeologists and the Chilean state. Such a denial by archaeologists and Atacameños has produced conflicts based on essentialist stands, prejudices, and disqualifications. Some Atacameños say that archaeologists "cheat" on the community; that they are "looters with a degree"; that they take "usufruct" "get rich" and "make profit" with the Atacameño's culture; that they are not concerned with the needs of the people; that they "appropriate," "sell" and "steal" their heritage; that they "make promises but don't keep them"; that they "take advantage of them"; that they are "usurpers" and "predators" of their "culture"; that they "do what they want to at the sites"; that they "don't respect us"; that they are people that Atacameños "don't trust" and, in the case of Le Paige, that they "fear." Some archaeologists believe that the Atacameños are "only interested in the money" they get from the sites; that "they have the peso sign in their eyes"; that they are "fundamentalists" and "sell their heritage"; that they "don't have a discourse"; that they only seek "political benefit"; that they have to "get a grip"; that they are "resentful and suspicious about archaeologists"; that they "hate us and see us as oppressors." Indigenous communities are branded as fundamentalists and as working against scientific knowledge, and archaeologists are characterized as enemies of indigenous interests in a context in which both actors defend their own interests and values. The radicalization of these stances means that as the validity of archaeological discourse is vindicated, indigenous peoples stop accepting archaeological production as equally meaningful (Gnecco 2006).

Fifth Category: Dialogue and Negotiation

The partial and/or momentary truce in the conflicts and radical positions between archaeologists and indigenous peoples has generated a favorable atmosphere for the redefinition of their relations. For this reason, spaces of dialogue (meetings, "dialogue tables," congresses, symposiums) oriented toward the construction of a relation based on mutual valorization and legitimization of ethnic and archaeological discourses have been created, as also of negotiation of the indigenous cultural meanings, valorizations, and interests associated with archaeological heritage. This has been evident in the organization of meetings in Cupo, Lasana,

Caspana, and Ollagüe by Atacameños as well as by archaeologists in which both actors have stated their critiques and concerns or, in some cases, have presented projects for managing sites. This has opened the dialogue between archaeologists and Atacameños, which, although not free of tensions, has eventually been instrumentalized by archaeologists.

From 2001 onwards, the Museum of San Pedro de Atacama has organized "dialogue tables," political moments of encounter and discussion with Atacameño representatives. Some participants in the first of such tables found it somehow "cathartic," with moments of tension between archaeologists and Atacameños. At the second table, according to some ethnic leaders, a new museum project was announced without much dialogue; for the archaeologists it was an opportunity to communicate about the activities they were carrying out. In 2005 the third table took place with the aim of acknowledging the perceptions, interests, and sensibilities of the local population, due to the discussion of an institutional policy regarding relations with the community.

Repercussions of this process of dialogue and negotiation become evident in the selection of research problems and archaeological methodologies, as well as in the implementation of outreach programs and participation of the local community in research projects. Currently there are no excavations in the cemeteries of the oasis and the projects that have found burials have communicated about them to the local community in order to make joint decisions. The insertion of archaeological sites in the tourism market has led to joint work between archaeologists and indigenous peoples, since some communities are more open to archaeology because they believe the finding of sites can give them the chance to access the economic benefits of tourism.

Sixth Category: Delegation and Mediation

The ethnic appraisal of the past has stirred a new modality of interaction between archaeologists and indigenous peoples. It is a relationship in which a third party is in charge of linking a museum or a team of archaeologists and their research project with the Atacameños, mediating between the interests of archaeology and those of indigenous communities. To this position, which was created in 2004 at the Museum of San Pedro de Atacama, falls the formulation and execution of outreach programs, the organization of dialogue tables with the Atacameños, and the reception of petitions for professional consultancies or the participation in activities prepared by the local community or related organizations. Until now the work developed through a mediator has been welcomed by indigenous communities and associated organizations, since they have a specific person to whom they can make demands and petitions. However, an important issue brought about with this modality is that it is a way of establishing a link with the Other from the outside, since the direct relation is delegated to a facilitator or mediator. In this sense, the political and strategic character of this modality, which was created as a response to the conflicts between archaeologists and members of the Atacameño community of San Pedro de Atacama, must not be overlooked.

BACK TO ARCHAEOLOGY

The results of this case study evidence a larger diversity in the modalities of interaction between archaeologists and indigenous peoples in Atacama with respect to the cases reported in the literature in other American counties, in which the relations described are of conflict and, in the last years, of negotiation and collaboration. Although the relations of denial are not characterized as such in the context of discussion presented, it is possible to identify them from the descriptions of the absence of relations between archaeologists and indigenous people, of distance and conflict between these actors, of the lack of awareness of archaeologists about the ties between indigenous communities and archaeological sites, together with the failure to recognize ethnic beliefs about the dead. This type of interaction has been present in the development of archaeology in the Americas since its birth, whereas the relations of dialogue and mediation are particular to vindication contexts in general. A specificity of the Atacameño case is the relation of mutual acknowledgment; denial and collaboration have antecedents here previous to the 1990s and can be traced back at least to the 1950s. Also, it is in the process of Atacameño appraisal that the modalities of interaction between archaeologists and indigenous peoples diversify, since besides the aforementioned modes, the relations of negotiation, visibilization, and mediation are constructed.

The history of relations between archaeologists and indigenous peoples in Atacama is characterized as dynamic and ever changing, since in a single period different forms of interaction can be activated, which can be synchronic or diachronic. These modalities of relationships are developed in a distinctive way through time, that is, in some moments more than in others, just as they activate differentially in a single actor. For example, it is possible to observe that an archaeologist relates in different ways and changes his or her stances regarding the Other through time. Actually, from relations of denial some actors move on to relations of acknowledgment, collaboration, and negotiation or vice versa, since this depends of the interests of the parties at a single time. On occasions, archaeologists whose stance has been that of acknowledgment and joint work with indigenous communities can later deny or disregard their interests if it serves their research purposes. So, instead of being able to label archaeologists in only one category of interaction, it is necessary to consider that these relations coexist in a single period or actor. Likewise, it is evident that the process is not unidirectional; relations do not necessarily change from denial to acknowledgment, collaboration, or dialogue. This is a process made of a complex system of relations of which the directions and turns are uncertain and hard to predict.

Relations of denial are directly associated with the conflicts between archaeologists and Atacameños and have been activated in different political contexts since the birth of archaeology. Failing to recognize indigenous peoples, not establishing relations with them, not acknowledging their cultural meanings, values, and interests associated with archaeological practice, and denying their right to know and have an opinion about the discipline have been characteristic of how archaeology relates to the Other. This kind of relation reflects the colonial origins of our discipline and evidences the asymmetries of power between archaeologists and indigenous peoples more than other modalities. It is precisely the historical denial by archaeologists that has led the Atacameños to question our work in the framework of the new multicultural policies of the Chilean state. Nevertheless, it cannot be assured that this modality of interaction will cease to exist in the present; the most likely scenario is that, with the redefinition of relations between the state and indigenous peoples and its subsequent recognition and political visibilization, the Other will not be denied without consequences for archaeology.

Ceasing to reproduce relations of denial requires the establishment and reinforcement of other kinds of relations with indigenous populations in which the need to acknowledge, visibilize, dialogue, negotiate, collaborate, and mediate would allow the consolidation of more constructive relations. One path in this direction may be to promote ethnographic work in archaeological research projects, since they would generate mutual knowledge and help to establish relations of trust between archaeologists and indigenous peoples. Ethnography integrated into archaeological practice, more than studying the Other to understand the archaeological record, works *with* the Other, tackling questions such as, how do indigenous communities relate to their past and to archaeological remains? How is the past constructed and what resources do they use for it? What are the categories of time and space? What are the cultural meanings regarding death and the dead? This is, trying to cross to the other side of the mirror. Likewise, a study of this kind will recover information on the image that indigenous peoples have about archaeology, for example, what ideas or "myths" circulate about our profession. This will allow us to know and evaluate what aspects of our work affect, worry, or generate the interest of indigenous communities and consider these aspects at the moment of research (Ayala 2008). Through this method, archaeology is provided with an anthropological value, a link that has been left aside by some of us. By providing anthropological characteristics to Atacameño archaeology, theoretical and methodological changes could be generated, since we would be relating to indigenous populations in a different manner and the past would be approached from a different perspective.

The above is related also to what in the last years has been labeled "public archaeology," a construction of knowledge that considers the interests, values, and benefits of the local community and of the archaeologists. Research projects are carried out simultaneously with socialization and outreach of the information generated, although not in a unidirectional manner in which the "experts" teach the Others their own history but by mutual feedback in which archaeologists communicate their construction of the past and native communities communicate their own. Outreach programs and heritage education are spaces that increase an active participation of both parties. Public archaeology implies the generation and maintenance of discussion throughout the discipline on contingent problems about their work, such as the uses of the past, the construction of identities, the production of and demand for essentialisms and exoticism in the market, heritage policies, conservation, protection and management of heritage, and ethics in the discipline.

This way of approaching archaeology requires a constant monitoring of the kind of relations established with the indigenous Other. Despite the diversification of interaction modalities developed within the framework of multicultural policies, in some cases the same relations of power continue to be reproduced within archaeology. This does not ignore the advances made by the relations of visibilization, collaboration, dialogue negotiation, and mediation, but questions us about the kind of participation, the interests involved in them, and how this affects archaeological practice. Although it is true that these relations have included the Atacameños in archaeological works, they are also used to neutralize ethnic conflicts and demands. Archaeological discourses on community participation are mechanisms of control more than changes in disciplinary practice: with certain rearrangements, the same kind of archaeology continues to be reproduced. The openness to dialogue or integration of indigenous peoples is made via "let's do it to avoid trouble" more than by a real motivation of working jointly or seeking horizontal dialogues with the Atacameños. In most research projects, the Atacameños continue to play the same role they played in the times of Le Paige, that is, as field assistants or informants. Research processes that fully integrate indigenous peoples are still lacking. The meetings and dialogue tables in which these issues are dealt with are approached from archaeology, and the power to make decisions is still in the hands of archaeologists. Thus, it is necessary to question the kind of dialogue and negotiation we are creating. Openness to dialogue turns into a "go and listen" for the Atacameños, without generating a proper dialogue or seeing their opinions reflected in decisions regarding archaeological projects and institutions. The archaeologists that value communal voices in the execution of their studies still constitute a minority. We have to ask ourselves whether archaeology has really opened itself to the Other and his or her cultural meanings. In the current context of the political visibilization of indigenous peoples, old archaeological practices related to the denial of the Other are reproduced along with others that promote an arguable level of participation, disciplinary disclosure, and dialogue between the actors involved.

The transit I made between archaeological and anthropological practice not only makes me believe strongly in the need for a complementary work between these disciplines, but also to think that the problems between indigenous peoples and archaeologists can take different directions if we take the chance to know each other. Who is the indigenous Other for the archaeologists? Who are we for them? What do Atacameños think, disapprove of, or like about our work? What are we archaeologists looking for in our investigations about the past and why are we interested in these issues? These are some of the questions that arise by knowing each other.

This is only possible if the Atacameños are willing to establish relations of acknowledgment, dialogue, negotiation, collaboration, and mediation. Since these modalities of interaction have been in operation, there have also been cases in which ethnic leaders reproduce relations of denial. Evidently some Atacameños repeat the same mode of interaction that motivated their critiques to archaeology and reject the possibility of relating to archaeologists, working jointly, or validating the contribution that these professionals can make to the process. So, it is important to communicate to indigenous peoples the changes produced in the history of the discipline in order to end stereotypes of archaeologists as "tomb looters" or as "exploiters of Atacameño culture," besides recognizing the changes in archaeology and its internal diversity.

Personally I believe that in order to generate substantial changes in our discipline it is necessary to work jointly with indigenous peoples, pointing toward a more horizontal dialogue and opening up other possibilities and ways of practicing archaeology. In this sense, it is important to consider the experiences developed in the last years in countries such as Australia, United States, Colombia, Argentina, and Brazil that evidence the possibilities and potential of a participative archaeology that integrates indigenous communities in research process, from the outline and definition of the problem to the interpretation of the data. In general terms, this way of practicing and conceiving of archaeology has been labeled in different contexts as "ethnocritical archaeology," "community archaeology," or "participatory archaeology," making central the work with indigenous communities. The challenge is to adapt these practices to the case of Atacama and construct an appropriate line of action supported by these approaches and also contributing to them. Besides, it is necessary to learn from local experiences that come close to this line of research through ethnoarchaeology and social archaeology.

NOTE

1. By request of most people interviewed, names remain concealed.

REFERENCES

Aldunate, Carlos, Victoria Castro, and Varinia Varela 2003 Oralidad y arqueología: una línea de trabajo en las tierras altas de la región de Antofagasta. *Chungará* 35(2):305–314.

Ayala, Patricia 2008 *Políticas del pasado: indígenas, arqueólogos y Estado en Atacama.* Línea Editoral IIAM, San Pedro de Atacama.

Ayala, Patricia, Sergio Avendaño, and Ulises Cárdenas 2003 Vinculaciones entre una arqueología social y la comunidad indígena de Ollagüe, II Región. *Chungará* 35(2):275–285.

Benavides, Hugo 2004 Los ritos de la autenticidad: indígenas, pasado y el Estado ecuatoriano. *Arqueología Suramericana* 1(1):5–48.

Bray, Tamara 2001 American archaeologists and native Americans: A relationship under construction. In *The Future of the Past: Archaeologists, Native Americans, and Repatriation*, edited by Tamara Bray, pp. 1–8. Garland, New York.

Endere, María Luz 2002 Management of Archaeological Sites and the Public in Argentina. Unpublished Ph.D. dissertation, Institute of Archaeology, University of London, London.

Fabian, Johannes 1983 *Time and the Other: How Anthropology Makes Its Object.* Columbia University Press, New York.

Ferguson, T. J. 1996 Native Americans and the practice of archaeology. *Annual Review of Anthropology* 25:63–79.

Gnecco, Cristóbal 1999 Archaeology and historical multivocality: A reflection from the Colombian multicultural context. In *Archaeology in Latin America*, edited by Gustavo Politis and Benjamin Alberti, pp. 258–270. Routledge, London.

———. 2006 Ampliación del campo de batalla. *Textos Antropológicos* 15:183–195.

Hodder, Ian 1994 *Interpretación en arqueología: corrientes actuales.* Crítica, Barcelona.

Le Paige, Gustavo 1958 Antiguas culturas atacameñas en la Cordillera Chilena. *Anales de la Universidad Católica de Valparaíso* 4–5:15–143.

Leone, Mark, Parker Potter Jr., and Paul Shackel 1987 Toward a critical archeology. *Current Anthropology* 28(1):283–302.

Llagostera, Agustín 2004 *Museo Arqueológico de San Pedro de Atacama: compromiso con el pasado, presente y futuro de una etnia.* Universidad Católica del Norte, Antofagasta.

Mamani, Carlos 1989 History and prehistory in Bolivia: What about the Indians? In *Conflict in the Archaeology of Living Traditions*, edited by Robert Layton, pp. 46–59. Unwin Hyman, London.

Núñez, Lautaro 1991 *Cultura y conflicto en los oasis de San Pedro de Atacama*. Editorial Universitaria, Santiago.

Preucel, Robert, and Ian Hodder 1996 Constructing identities. In *Contemporary Archaeology in Theory*, edited by Robert Pruecel and Ian Hodder, pp. 599–614. Blackwell, Oxford.

Trigger, Bruce 1980 Archaeology and the image of the American Indian. *American Antiquity* 45(4):662–676.

———. 1984 Alternative archaeologies: Nationalist, colonialist, imperialist. *Man* 19(3):355–370.

Zimmerman, Larry 1989a Human bones as symbols of power: Aboriginal American belief systems toward bones and "grave-robbing" archaeologists. In *Conflict in the Archaeology of Living Traditions*, edited by Robert Layton, pp. 211–216. Routledge, London.

———. 1989b Made radical by my own: An archaeologist learns to accept reburial. In *Conflict in the Archaeology of Living Traditions*, edited by Robert Layton, pp. 60–67. Routledge, London.

CHAPTER 6

BUILDING DIALOGUES ACROSS CONTRADICTING INTERESTS IN NORTHERN CHILE: AN EXPERIENCE AND SOME PRELIMINARY THOUGHTS

Diego Salazar

INTRODUCTION

In Latin America, particularly in Chile, indigenous communities, archaeology, and private companies have confronted each other regarding the control and management of critical resources such as land, water, or archaeological heritage. In northern Chile these conflicts have been especially visible and complex between indigenous communities and private companies due to the economical importance of the copper deposits in the desert, the lack of water resources in these arid territories, the vulnerability of the communities, and the legislations that have favored the interests of the investors to the detriment of indigenous groups.

One would expect to find a different relationship between archaeologists and indigenous communities, since anthropology during the last decades has aligned itself with minorities and the defense of their rights and interests. Nevertheless, other researchers have already seen that, at least in Chile, this is not the case (Ayala 2003; Ayala et al. 2003; Westfall 1998). Although there are some exceptions (see Ayala 2008), scientific research has been traditionally considered as the only aim of our discipline. The legitimacy of the scientific discourse has justified archaeological control both over cultural heritage and the "real past." Indigenous groups have at best participated as sources of information (as in ethnoarchaeological research) or have been simply absent from our investigations, while archaeological sites are still, by definition, property of the Chilean state and can be excavated only by professional archaeologists, with previous authorization from the National Monuments Council.

There were virtually no concrete experiences of relations between private companies and archaeologists before the 1990s; on the contrary, it is known that some mining companies have been important agents in the destruction and deterioration of archaeological heritage in northern Chile and elsewhere.

Considering this background, why should we consider the possibility of building dialogues between indigenous communities, private companies, and archaeology? Is there any way to deal with such contradictory interests? During these last years, transformations in the sociocultural environment in which these conflicts of interest are negotiated have created some modifications in the power balance and, as a consequence, we have witnessed certain changes in the practices of each of these actors that allow me to think that building dialogues is indeed possible. It is unclear what will happen at an institutional level, but the recent transformations in Chilean archaeology are noteworthy, some of which question traditional disciplinary scopes and limits. It is a difficult time for archaeology: a scientific community that has been reluctant to give up the privileges of academic legitimacy and the institutional system is now under threat. But rather than simply adapt to current social transformations, what is really needed for archaeology is a redefinition of our discipline from values, principles, and purposes different to the ones that gave its meaning during the nineteenth century. I offer some reflections on this regard as a result of my work in the contemporary social context of the discipline in northern Chile. Since 1999, I have had the opportunity to coordinate a project whose central challenge has been to construct a dialogue and a lasting relationship among the Atacameño indigenous community of Conchi Viejo, a private mining company (SCM El Abra), and archaeology (Salazar 2005).

MINING, COMMUNITIES, AND ARCHAEOLOGY IN THE DREAM OF MODERNITY

Conflicts between archaeologists, indigenous communities, and mining companies are not exclusive to northern Chile; rather, they occur throughout the world. Thus it is necessary to understand them in the wider sociocultural context of Western modernity. In capitalism, large-scale mining is an enormous source of wealth for private investors as well as for the state, generating working places and implementing important transformations in urban areas in terms of infrastructure, works, and higher levels of capital circulation. These consequences are considered beneficial when we observe them from a materialist point of view that considers economic development and technological advance as necessary goals in order to reach wellbeing. This way of thinking is proper to European modernity and has expanded throughout the world through the intellectual, political, and economic elites that have tended to universalize it. Because of this, it is not strange that in northern Chile an important number of citizens continue to value positively the contribution of large-scale copper mining (it is the "salary of the country," they say).

This logic and this economic model have been an incentive to the development of the mining industry in many other parts of the world. Because of geological circumstances, the principal industrial-scale mining operations tend to be located in "marginal" territories, far off from the principal urban centers. This is an important factor in understanding the support of national states for colonization projects of mining industries in these territories. This situation has experienced a notable growth in the last decades due to soaring international prices of many metals, stimulating a productive "boom" without precedent in the principal mining countries of the world (Ballard and Banks 2003), including northern Chile. This productive increase generated wealth and economical prosperity, but also produced conflictive consequences, among which stand out what Ballard and Banks (2003) call "resource wars" between mining companies and indigenous communities. In many cases the "marginal" territories where the great mining projects are being developed have been inhabited by indigenous communities for centuries. Such is the case in the Atacama Desert in northern Chile. Contamination and the dispute for territories and, above all, for water are the axes of conflict until the present day.

The conflict between archaeologists and indigenous communities has also increased during the last 10 years as a result of the growing dispute over the control of heritage resources and, to a lesser extent, the legitimate discourses about the past of indigenous communities (Ayala 2008). This conflict shares many characteristics with the one existing between indigenous communities and mining companies. As a consequence, it is not strange that indigenous communities have denounced an equally colonialist and discriminatory attitude from both companies and archaeologists (Ayala 2008).[1] The aftermath of colonial discrimination has differed, but the principles that legitimate it and the worldview that gives sense to it are similar in both cases. After all, scientific thinking (as a privileged way of representation) and capitalism (as a fundamental economical system of the new bourgeois order) were a simultaneous result of a new rationality and a new cosmology consolidated with the European Enlightenment.[2]

It seems unavoidable to propose a redefinition of our discipline if we are to promote a dialogue with indigenous communities. Current conditions are more favorable for reaching this goal: since the end of the twentieth century, the crisis of modern rationality allowed the development of a deeper "critical self-conscience," as well as new values that are not totally coherent with the traditional conception of archaeology. This change has also affected the great mining companies because they have seen themselves increasingly questioned by public opinion. Even when the negative impact that this industry generates has increased as a consequence of the "mining boom," social questioning is due, above all, to the contemporary crisis of modern values (which articulate the neoliberal economy) and to the increasing valuation of minorities, the environment, and local heritage within the national society. During the last years new legislations have appeared; they try to balance economic development with preservation of the environment, protection of the archaeological heritage, and the maintenance, reproduction, and sustainable development of indigenous communities. We are, then, in a more favorable situation for negotiation, at least on paper.

The "Postmodern Condition" and the New Scenarios for Archaeology

Since the 1990s, external situations have forced archaeology to consider the social background in which it develops and, even more, to relate with new actors such as indigenous communities and private companies (Merriman 2002). These changes are part of social and cultural phenomena entailed to the "postmodern condition" of the contemporary postindustrial society that has gained strength in Chile since the recovery of democracy. One of the most evident and better-studied consequences of the crisis of the modern project is related to the increasing importance of social minorities. The claims of indigenous minorities have found echo and support in the society at large, in which an increasing number of people identify with their cause (Benavides 2005). In this context new legislation has been enacted, favoring to some extent the demands of indigenous groups. Such is the case of the Chilean Indigenous Act of 1993, which has allowed significant amount of "ethnogenesis" in indigenous and rural communities, improving their capabilities for dialogue and negotiation. This fact has had important consequences for archaeology: empowered indigenous communities have begun to claim their rights over heritage, questioning the traditional behavior of archaeologists and the legitimacy of their activity and of discourses about the past (Mamani 1989). It has also had consequences in the economic model: private companies have been forced to develop new values and concepts such as "social responsibility," "citizen participation" or "community relationships" that have promoted a greater relationship with indigenous communities.

Environmental issues have also marked the crisis of modernity. In 1994 Chile issued the Environmental Act, aiming to regulate and moderate the environmental impact of all investment projects; it has meant an important change in the relationship between private companies and archaeology because archaeological remains are now considered as an environmental component to be protected. Damage has to be mitigated and compensated by the investors when it cannot be avoided. This act marked the beginning of contract archaeology in Chile.

The contemporary social background in Chile, mainly after the recovery of democracy in 1990, is altering the traditional way of doing archaeology in the country. Maybe, without noticing it, the discipline has gained more consciousness of its social responsibility, setting the foundation for a less hierarchical relationship with indigenous communities and private companies. Nevertheless, the discipline has not generated a systematic reflection about its praxis in order to achieve a critical and conscious adaptation to the new sociocultural environment.

El Abra Archaeological Project

The localities of San José del Abra and Conchi Viejo, where our project has been developed, are located in the Calama Commune, El Loa Province, II Region of Antofagasta, at the extreme north of Chile (Figure 6.1). Since the eighteenth century, a multiethnic community of miners and shepherds was formed here and became the source of the current Atacameño indigenous community of Conchi Viejo (Melero and Salazar 2003; Salazar et al. 2004). Early in the twentieth century, most members of the community emigrated to Calama, Chuquicamata, or other cities, while the territories of Conchi and El Abra became property of the Chilean Exploration Company. After the nationalization of copper in 1971, these territories were given to the newly created state's mining company, Codelco. As has occurred in many other historical situations, indigenous communities saw themselves legally displaced from their traditional territory; new owners acquired, legally, the exploitation rights of those territories without knowing or recognizing the existence of indigenous communities. In 1996, after an international bid, SCM El Abra started operating at El Abra and Conchi, with the aim of producing cathodes of fine copper for the international market.

More than 250 archaeological sites are currently known to exist in the lands of SCM El Abra. The colonial indigenous community of Conchi Viejo was limited to an island surrounded by territories belonging to the company. The town church (Figure 6.2) and some places in the surrounding area were designated archaeological sites in 1995, and protected according to the standards of the Environmental Law. Although

Figure 6.1   Map of the II Region in northern Chile showing San José del Abra, Conchi Viejo, and other locations mentioned in the text.

Figure 6.2   General view of the current village of Conchi Viejo with the church in the middle distance. The facilities of SCM El Abra can be seen in the background.

today the town of Conchi Viejo is inhabited permanently by only two people, it constitutes the social and symbolic center of the indigenous community settled mostly at Calama, some 80 km away. The members of the community come to Conchi Viejo for the celebration of certain religious ceremonies and feasts and in order to visit their dead, buried in the cemetery of the local church. After the Indigenous Act was passed, the members of the community living in Calama reorganized themselves in order to defend the community's interests and their traditional spaces from the productive activities of SCM El Abra and were legally recognized by the Chilean state in 1994, obtaining rights over a small territory surrounding the town (as already stated, an island within the mine's property). The community feels linked, historically and culturally, to the past of these localities and considers that archaeological and historical sites of the area are part of their identity (and, as a consequence, are their own), even though they are not aware of the majority of existing sites.

In spite of this complex political context, the community and the mining company agreed to cooperate. On the other hand, the company holds a good relationship with the National Monuments Council (the public organism in charge of watching over Chilean cultural heritage). A fluid relationship also exists between the community and the archaeologists. Although it has not been free of conflicts and tense negotiations, the history of the relationships between the actors involved in this project makes it feasible to build more permanent dialogues.

From the point of view of archaeology, this has been made possible through a CRM (cultural resource management) project aiming to do scientific research and to contribute to the community's social and identity process. The main components of the project are (1) scientific research; (2) a management plan of archaeological and historical sites, demanded by the Environmental Act; and (3) education and diffusion. Scientific research is an important part of the project since we are working with an indigenous community that knows little about their past, given that oral memory becomes diffuse as we go back in time beyond the nineteenth century. Research has been supported by the mining company according to the usual standards of traditional archaeological and ethnohistorical investigations. The results have been shared with the community, thus contributing to the ongoing process of the recuperation of its tradition. This has been done through the publication of a book and several articles, guided visits to the archaeological sites, talks and conferences both in El Abra and Calama, and a video about the community's past. This video was requested by the community, and we worked together on the script in order to decide what to show and how to present the data.

Thus, the project has found some points of agreement between the different actors through a management program of the archaeological heritage that exceeds the limits imposed by current legislation. The project searches for common ground between the interests of the mining company, the National Monuments Council, and Conchi's indigenous community. Furthermore, we have tried to identify the interests and needs of these actors and articulate the project in such a way that its results are able to satisfy them, at least to some extent.

From Theory to Practice: Facing Challenges and Difficulties

Although the project has achieved some of its goals, difficulties and contradictions have emerged during the process. In this section, I will point out some of these difficulties in order to evaluate the possibility of building dialogues between communities, companies, and archaeology. I will emphasize two topics, leaving aside the problems related to CRM (Cáceres 1999; Criado 1996, forthcoming).

The first topic I will discuss refers to the internal division of the indigenous community and how it has affected our work. This is an important topic to deal with, especially considering that throughout these pages I have spoken about the indigenous community of Conchi as a homogeneous and undifferentiated totality. As other archaeologists who work with indigenous communities have recognized (Green et al., this volume; Moser et al. 2002), communities usually are internally fragmented, generating a dilemma for the archaeologist who wants to carry out a project together with them: which "factions" must we work with? To which internal projects shall we commit? The articulation with neoliberalism in urban centers and the systematic contact that many Andean communities maintain with modernity have been a hard test for the persistence of traditional institutions, which are losing importance before the individualism of the market economy and the development of new economic networks not founded on social bonds.

In our case, fragmentation is perhaps best seen in the community of Conchi in the distance between urban and rural members of the community.[3] Although both groups were listed in the 1994 constitution of the community, during many years the families living in the Loa River valley complained that private and public funds received by the community rarely brought effective benefits to them (Villaseca 2000). The impasse led the inhabitants of the Loa River valley to look for legal recognition as an independent indigenous community. The Chilean state gave a partial recognition to the community of Taira, which nowadays channels private and public funds independently and negotiates directly with mining companies. After the breakup, the authorities of Conchi Viejo requested us not to mention or include images of the people from Taira in the video or any publications.

The neighboring communities of Chiu-Chiu and Lasana supported the "independentist" project of Taira, generating a new breakup in their relations with Conchi. This fact also has affected our project because in the past some Chiu-Chiu members have worked on our field team, but since 2004 the authorities of Conchi asked us to suspend these relationships and exclude people from Chiu-Chiu from working on archaeological sites linked historically to Conchi.

The cause of the dispute between Conchi and Taira is access to the economic resources and financial benefits granted by the state and the mining companies. Similar disputes, for the same causes, can be seen in other Atacameño communities in the Loa River drainage and in the San Pedro de Atacama area. These internal conflicts are the outcome of the traditional policy of "divide in order to govern" that the mining companies and the state have implemented in their negotiations with the Atacameños (Barros 2004).

Nevertheless, collaboration with mining companies and the state has also brought about a reorganization of the communities, now striving to recover their identity and fight for their rights (Rivera 2006). Yet, direct benefits of development projects implemented by local leaders does not always reach all community members; thus, internal disputes and distrust are generated.

Another confrontation occurs between authorities of the community and the only two inhabitants of the colonial town. The latter have expressed their criticism and discontent with respect to SCM El Abra's policy, not only because the support they receive is insufficient but also because its security staff does not allow them to access some of their traditional herding sites because they are now the mining company's "private property." Yet, the indigenous authorities have not brought up this problem to the company; in fact, their public discourse is usually favorable toward the mining company. How can these facts be interpreted? The inhabitants of the town blame indigenous authorities of negligence and unwillingness and, as did Taira before, consider that the authorities support only those projects beneficial to them. The authorities argue that they seek to avoid the confrontational-style characteristics of other Atacameño communities or organizations and highlight that they have other ways of achieving their objectives. Some authorities point out that their style is typical of the Andean social relationships—pacific negotiations and search for mutual benefits—that would have characterized Tawantinsuyu (the Inca empire). It is odd, though, that this style has been used with the mining companies but not with other communities or with Conchi's rural groups. What leads Conchi's directive to look for stable relationships with companies that compete for critical resources but to confront and divide regional communities? This is an important fact because the positive relationship with the company explains, in part, the success of our project. Why hasn't Conchi demanded the Chilean state legalize their rights over the territories disputed with the mining companies, a promised made by the Indigenous Act (Barros 2004)? Why have the indigenous communities defined the immediate improvement of their material life conditions as the principal horizon of negotiation even over territorial and patrimonial claims? More than an Andean political model, it seems to me we face here the principles of modern rationality expressed in the indigenous leaders' discourse. This suggests that the dialogue between communities and companies is possible only when the same language and rationality is used and when critical resources are not at stake. But, would it be possible to build a new language for building dialogues in a context characterized by the overcoming of modern rationality? I will return to this point in the conclusions.

The second and last aspect that I would like to comment on, and that has also been recognized by other archaeologists working with indigenous communities in northern Chile, is an integration of two different visions about the past: one emanating from scientific research and the other coming from oral memory and mythology (Aldunate et al. 2003; Castro and Varela 2000). Although it has not been possible to recognize myths in the urban community of Conchi, oral memory is quite strong and is based on local tradition, and in some cases on old documents. This oral memory is meaningful for the community as a source of tradition and identity. In some aspects, oral memory has proved contradictory between the different families that make up the community, because it offers different versions of the same facts. It may also be contradictory with respect to the archaeological and historical data we have recovered from the field and from archives. We are far away from having solved this problem in a satisfactory way. We have tried to conciliate different discourses, but it has not always been possible.[4] It is a delicate situation because archaeological knowledge is a system of interpretations with varying degrees of epistemological validity, frequently dynamic as new data appear or when new articulations of data are made possible by new concepts or theoretical models. So it is unclear if and how to promote scientific interpretations over local memory as a source of legitimacy for our discourses on the community's past. My opinion is that we must promote critical thinking in local communities by understanding the fundamental differences between archaeological discourse and oral memory.

This last topic is even more relevant in the case of myths, whose differences with archaeological discourse seem to be even more evident. In this context I agree with Gnecco (1999) and other authors when they suggest that they are incommensurable discourses because of different truth criteria and goals. Nevertheless, the certainty of archaeological interpretations of the past is often greater than that of myths. Yet, myths were not meant to preserve the memory of empirical events but rather to organize and transmit a cosmology, a cultural interpretation of history and of the world. While myth contributes a deep philosophy of cosmos and history, useful for understanding our own position in the world, archaeological reconstructions give us a relatively certain picture of concrete historical events without existential interpretations that may be personally meaningful. Myth is a metaphorical and symbolic knowledge of history. Literally interpreted it is generally false, but contributes answers that archaeology will never be able to propose about our position in the cosmos and the meaning of our lives. Today many communities face discredit of their mythic knowledge as they become more acquainted with scientific discoveries about the past and present. This is indeed a great threat to their identity and to their social links. As archaeologists we cannot accept the historical validity of mythical interpretations[5] but, at the same time, we must also contribute to the preservation of that traditional knowledge. This will not be achieved by stating that both these discourses are valid according to their own standards of truth, but by showing the real worth and importance of mythic discourse in a domain where scientific interpretations lack authority.

CONCLUSIONS

Can we advance toward the construction of dialogues between indigenous communities, archaeology, and private companies? In spite of difficulties, our project in El Abra has been auspicious; it gives an account of a non-frequent experience in northern Chile that has been able to consolidate a relationship of cooperation and dialogue for more than seven years between the academic field, an indigenous community, and a mining company. Even though scientific research is not at home in CRM projects in Chile (Cáceres and Westfall 2004), we have been able to develop a research strategy based on academic criteria that has already produced more than 20 publications and presentations in national and international congresses. Two Master's theses, one honor's thesis in social anthropology and two in archaeology, and four professional practices in archaeology have been carried out. In Conchi Viejo we socialized our knowledge about the past of Conchi and El Abra to contribute to the reconstruction of their identity. This has been valued by community members on different occasions. We have also spoken to the workers and executives of the mining company of the importance and value of the community. Our project has done scientific research and social archaeology within the frame of environmental impact studies. I thus conclude that dialogue is possible between archaeology, communities, and private companies. Certainly we have not changed the balance of power, which still benefits mainly the mining company, but at least we have been able to find some strategies within the system that have managed to satisfy some of the expectations and demands both of the indigenous and the archaeological community. In fact, this project has been recognized as exemplary by members of both.

Is it possible to replicate this experience in other places in northern Chile or Latin America? In order to answer this question, I first identify the main factors that explain our preliminary achievements. One is related to the fact that the indigenous community of Conchi is mainly based in Calama, that is, it is not fighting with the company for critical resources such as water or territory. A "resource war" (*sensu* Ballard and Banks 2003) has not yet occurred between the community and the mining company, nor between the community and the archaeologists, because the community values the contribution of archaeologists and historians in the reconstruction of their past. We have been supported by high executives of the company, who have shown sincere commitment and interest in the archaeological heritage. The authorities of the community privilege negotiations over confrontations for gaining long-term support from the company. These structural conditions have been key for the continuity and feasibility of the project; thus, any replication of this experience should rest on similar conditions.

It is also important to account for two additional factors: in the first place, the continuity of the project and the collaboration among different parties around the cultural heritage of Conchi and El Abra have been possible by the conscious search for mutual benefits. This is equivalent to say that the structure of our project has been articulated around the principles and language of a neoliberal economy in which the mining company has adopted the privileged position, while we have searched in the gaps of the system for spaces in which to develop a project that is more related to our own conception of archaeology and cultural heritage management (the latter is the second factor I will mention below). In the neoliberal logic we have found bridges to negotiate the conflicts arising between the mining company, the communities, and archaeology. Whether we like the model or not, the implicated parties share aspects of the neoliberal rationality by being immersed in a dominant and coherent system.

We archaeologists work within a dominant social and economic rationale, but can take advantage of structural possibilities for developing spaces of collaboration and participation; those spaces are not part of the traditional expression of this rationale in Chile, nor of the dominant archaeological praxis. This is the second factor I would like to mention before analyzing the possibility of replicating this experience in other contexts. It has been our conception of archaeology that has made us look for a new praxis within the dominant system. Thus, in order to replicate this experience or to promote the social contribution of our discipline, a different notion of archaeology is needed, one that goes beyond traditional disciplinary limits. This option is clear to many archaeologists in Latin America and elsewhere, mainly because the crisis of modernity has led them to question the traditional (modern) model of doing archaeology.

What is, then, an alternative to modern archaeology? One possibility is to get lost in the emptiness of the nonsense or in extreme postmodern relativism. Although postmodernity comes out of the crisis of modernity, it is not a real alternative. Postmodern solutions by Anglo-Saxon archaeologists (Hodder 1999; Merriman 2002; Thomas 2004; Tilley 1989) adequately reflect the current context but are not coherent alternatives to overcome key problems inherited from modernity. Archaeology cannot be unaware of the contemporary social context, so certain adjustments are necessary in order to assure disciplinary survival. The extraordinary importance of archaeology as a "technoscience" is a reflection of its successful adaptation to the social and legal scenarios characteristic of the crisis of modernity, normally called postmodernity. But applied knowledge is not enough. As part of the social sciences, archaeology has a responsibility toward society; today it must include showing alternatives to a system in crisis.

How can archaeology accomplish this role within the social sciences? Which one is, after all, the true "archaeology of the future" (Criado 1996)? If pure research characterized modern archaeology, we should reformulate the discipline to integrate—in its disciplinary definition and in the institutions that articulate it—the diffusion of results and heritage education; by doing so we can achieve a greater democratization and socialization of specialized knowledge. This is what has been called "heritage management," an interesting alternative for contemporary archaeology (Criado 1996, forthcoming). Such an approach gives value to heritage. Scientific research, conservation, protection, diffusion of results, heritage education, and even CRM are ways to reach this fundamental objective, relevant and necessary as research itself. So archaeology (academic or by contract) has as its purpose the generation of valid knowledge that must be diffused inside the local communities through different mechanisms in order for it to play a role inside their contemporary realities. The consequence of this point of view is obvious in respect to the archaeology of the future: the social dimension of the discipline must be a fundamental axis of its existence.

This approach was already present in Latin American social archaeology and also has been defended by representatives of the Anglo-Saxon postprocessual archaeologies. Nevertheless, the former was a modern political project that did not give the foundations for a true alternative to the crisis of modernity. Actually it was unable to consider the "otherness" of indigenous worldviews in its own right, subsumed under the homogenization of class and an economy determined by its material expression. Postprocessual archaeologies have tended to fall into relativism and hyperfragmentation, neither being an alternative to the modern crisis, but rather their expression. So the point I want to make is that social responsibility is not enough in itself for the archaeology of the future. We must also reflect on the kind of knowledge we generate and the effects this may have in local communities.

When the World Archaeological Congress was born, many archaeologists felt that at last archaeology was assuming its social role by expressing its public condemnation of racism. Twenty years later, and still with some discrepancies and reservations, such a position is still an integral part of WAC's principles. Although I value the increasing participation of archaeologists, I notice that we are contributing to the political debate as citizens, not as producers of knowledge about the past. So this cannot be considered a social effect of archaeology.

More than getting archaeology to achieve multivocality as an aim in itself, as most postprocessualist and postcolonial archaeologists seem to propose, the social responsibility of the discipline must be directed toward the production of valid knowledge about the past. Although archaeological knowledge has limits and is dynamic, it cannot be diluted in extreme relativism; empirical data restrict interpretation and allow claims with a greater or lesser degree of coherence and legitimacy. I am aware that this argument reproduces the modern canon, at least by rescuing the validity of scientific knowledge and its emancipating potential. But the crisis of modernity does not lie so much in the role of knowledge, nor in the existence of metanarratives or hegemonic discourses. The crisis is more a consequence of the universalization of a materialistic conception of reality and of an excessive emphasis on rationality and individualism (De Castro 2005). Thus, it is not contradictory to look for an alternative in modernity itself, lest we include those aspects directly responsible for the crisis. That is, precisely, my criticism to Latin American social archaeology: it preserved fundamental elements of modern cosmology, assuming that economic and social transformation would solve the problems of our civilization without considering the necessary changes in our materialistic worldview.

Giving voice to and empowering the oppressed and forgotten are not the final solutions to the conflicts and cannot be the ultimate disciplinary goal. Access to power and self-determination may be more transcendental because they refer to the meaning of life and wellbeing for communities; yet, they are not aims by themselves. The increasing integration of indigenous societies in extant power structures has meant that the leaders have been absorbed by state bureaucracy or have left their communities, searching for the support of the private sector (Barros 2004). Empowerment has not always been the solution to indigenous problems; it has also produced new conflicts within the communities. What does our system have to offer once power positions have been conquered by indigenous societies? Are elites really capable of conceiving definitive solutions to the problems generated by modern rationality? Isn't the crisis also expressed, and in occasions almost as violently, inside these same social segments, with all their economic and political power?

The most important social transformation to be made is changing our thinking, and social sciences have a role to play in this regard. Archaeology can contribute to this debate if the theoretical schemes from which we observe and interpret the past escape the prison of modern reality. Only then will we be able to glimpse a different past that, eventually, gives us some clues about the future that we must build. This is the final ingredient required for the "archaeology of the future." This implies, at least, two things. First is the need to recover the holistic dimension of knowledge about the past. The final aim of archaeological research should contribute to the global understanding of human beings. The hyperspecialized knowledge characteristic of contemporary science would not be justified socially unless it points, explicitly, toward the construction of holistic interpretations of global processes. Second, if the interpretative horizon of archaeology must be holistic, we might have to look for uniform concepts within the social sciences rather than reproduce the eclectic and endless diversity of approaches about the past that presently characterize us. This proposal may not be really democratic (Thomas 2004), because it establishes anew dominant paradigms and hegemonic axes in the production of scientific discourse, just as the modern project did. But this time conceptual schemes should not be articulated with the principles of modern rationality; they must be built upon non-Western worldviews. It is in this context that I think traditional indigenous knowledge and mythology can and must play a role in understanding the past: not by providing historical facts but by providing non-Western worldviews from which to understand and reconstruct past behaviors and social change. The process of researching and understanding these worldviews must be made together with community members. Not so much for them to recover traditional ways of life, but to have a standpoint from which to think critically about their current social processes and to make informed decisions regarding the future of their communities.

The reconstruction of historical development from the point of view of the "evolution" of conscience or rationality (De Castro 2005; for an archaeological reflection of this perspective, see Criado 2001, forthcoming and Hernando 2002) seems to me a good alternative for a really postmodern archaeology that assumes a social role in order to contribute to the construction of a future for our society. It is based on a coherent integration of content from different scientific disciplines that allow it not only to understand the "otherness" of indigenous worldviews, but also to contribute with a solid diagnosis of the actual state of Western society. Thus it has the potential to integrate worldviews and historical development into a holistic, explicative frame of human behavior. This is, of course, a pending task for all of us.

NOTES

I would like to express my gratitude to my colleagues Patricia Ayala and Cristóbal Gnecco for inviting me to participate in this publication and for their important comments on a previous version of this work. I would also like to thank the numerous colleagues, students, and friends who have participated in different stages of our work for their exemplary support, commitment, and enthusiasm, especially Hernán Salinas. I thank Andrés Troncoso, who commented on previous versions of this chapter and helped me to clarify the conclusions. I thank the authorities of Conchi, in particular President Manuel Ávila Galleguillos, for accepting us and the SCM El Abra Company for their support and commitment. Above all I would like to thank Leandro Aymani for his friendship and teachings.

1. See also Layton (1989) for other similar cases worldwide.
2. For a deeper analysis of the archaeology-modernity relationship see Gnecco (2008), Patterson (1999), Thomas (2004), and Trigger (1980).
3. At the beginning of the twentieth century, most members of Conchi migrated to Calama or Chuquicamata. Yet, some families went back to their original territories in the Tarapacá region, losing links with Conchi. Others chose to settle at the Loa River, where they maintained a rural lifestyle with traditional economic activities, such as herding (Villaseca 2000).
4. The recovery of the oral memory of the oldest members of the community and the presence of some of them at the archaeological sites studied by us have been enormous contributions to the knowledge we have generated about the most recent past of the localities and the history of the community of Conchi.
5. If we accept that each discourse has its own truth criteria and, thus, is valid by itself, we embrace extreme postmodern relativism. If so, it would be necessary to accept that the Hispanic conquest of America was completely justified because, under European truth and rationality, American natives benefited for having been rescued from darkness, ignorance, and immorality or that the dramatic "colonization" of the Bolivian high plateau was also legitimate by the modern accounts espoused by political, economic, and military nineteenth-century Bolivian elites (Barros 2004). I can infinitely extend the list of examples, from the Jewish Holocaust to current conflicts between native communities and mining companies for water in the desert.

REFERENCES

Aldunate, Carlos, Victoria Castro, and Varinia Varela 2003 Oralidad y arqueología: una línea de trabajo en las tierras altas de la región de Antofagasta. *Chungará* 35(2):305–314.

Ayala, Patricia 2003 Arqueología y sociedad: el caso de las comunidades indígenas en Chile. *Werken* 4:59–73.

———. 2005 La voz indígena en las investigaciones arqueológicas. Paper presented at the Primer Taller de Teoría Arqueológica en Chile, Santiago.

———. 2008 *Políticas del pasado: indígenas, arqueólogos y Estado en Atacama*. Ediciones IIAM, Santiago.

Ayala, Patricia, Sergio Avendaño, and Ulises Cárdenas 2003 Vinculaciones entre una arqueología social y la comunidad indígena de Ollagüe, II Región. *Chungará* 35(2):275–285.

Ballard, Chris, and Glenn Banks 2003 Resource wars: The anthropology of mining. *Annual Review of Anthropology* 32:287–313.

Barros, Alonso 2004 Crónica de una etnia anunciada: nuevas perspectivas de investigación a 10 años de vigencia de la Ley Indígena en San Pedro de Atacama. *Estudios Atacameños* 27:139–168.

Benavides, Hugo 2005 Los ritos de la autenticidad: indígenas, pasado y el Estado ecuatoriano. *Arqueología Suramericana* 1(1):5–48.

Cáceres, Iván 1999 Arqueología y Sistema de Evaluación de Impacto Ambiental. *Boletín de la Sociedad Chilena de Arqueología* 28:47–54.

Cáceres, Iván, and Catherine Westfall 2004 Trampas y amarras: ¿es posible hacer arqueología en el Sistema de Evaluación de Impacto Ambiental? *Chungará* 36, suppl.:483–488.

Castro, Victoria, and Varinia Varela 2000 Los caminos del "reinka" en la región del Loa Superior: de la etnografía a la arqueología. *Actas del XIV Congreso Nacional de Arqueología Chilena* 1:815–840. Copiapó.

Criado, Felipe 1996 El futuro de la arqueología, ¿la arqueología del futuro? *Trabajos de Prehistoria* 53(1):15–35.

———. 2001 Walking about Levi-Strauss. Contributions to an archaeology of thought. In *Philosophy and Archaeological Practice*, edited by Cornelius Holtorf and Hakan Karlsson, pp. 277–284. Bricoleur Press, Gotemburg.

———. Forthcoming *Arqueológicas. La razón perdida*. Bellaterra Ediciones, Barcelona.

De Castro, Luis Osvaldo. 2005 *El ocaso del titán. Las tres travesías del cambio*. Aguilar, Santiago.

Gnecco, Cristóbal 1999 Archaeology and historical multivocality: A reflection from the Colombian multicultural context. In *Archaeology in Latin America*, edited by Gustavo Politis and Benjamin Alberti, pp. 258–270. Routledge, London.

———. 2008 Manifiesto moralista por una arqueología reaccionaria. In *Sed non satiata II*, edited by Félix Acuto and Andrés Zarankin, pp. 93–102. Encuentro/Universidad de los Andes/Universidad Nacional de Catamarca/Universidad Federal de Minas Gerais, Córdoba.

Hernando, Almudena 2002 *Arqueología de la identidad*. Akal, Madrid.

Hodder, Ian 1999 *The Archaeological Process: An Introduction*. Blackwell, Oxford.

Layton, Robert (editor) 1989 *Who Needs the Past? Indigenous Values and Archaeology*. Unwin Hyman, London.

Mamani, Carlos 1989 History and prehistory in Bolivia: What about the Indians? In *Conflict in the Archaeology of Living Traditions*, edited by Robert Layton, pp. 46–59. Routledge, London.

Melero, Diego, and Diego Salazar 2003 Historia colonial de Conchi Viejo y San José del Abra y su relación con la minería en Atacama (II Región, norte de Chile). *Revista Chilena de Historia Indígena* 7:55–86.

Merriman, Nick 2002 Archaeology, heritage and interpretation. In *Archaeology: The Widening Debate*, edited by Barry Cunliffe, Wendy Davies, and Colin Renfrew, pp. 541–566. Oxford University Press, Oxford.

Moser, Stephanie, Darren Glazier, James Phillips, Lamya Nasser, Mohammed Saleh, Rascha Nasr, Susan Richardson, Andrew Conner, and Michael Seymour 2002 Transforming archaeology through practice: Strategies for collaborative archaeology and the Community Archaeology Project at Quseir, Egypt. *World Archaeology* 34(2):220–248.

Patterson, Thomas 1999 The political economy of archaeology in the United States. *Annual Review of Anthropology* 28:155–174.

Rivera, Francisco 2006 Entorno neoliberal y la alteridad étnica antiflexibilizante de los atacameños contemporáneos. *Revista Chilena de Antropología* 18:59–89.

Salazar, Diego 2005 Investigación, rescate y puesta en valor del patrimonio arqueológico en El Abra. In *Primer Seminario Minería y Monumentos Nacionales. Patrimonio Arqueológico, Paleontológico e Histórico*, edited by Gastón Fernández and Paola González, pp. 105–118. Ediarte, Santiago.

Salazar, Diego, Diego Melero, and Carolina Jiménez 2004 Los últimos 200 años en Conchi Viejo y San José del Abra (II Región): reflexiones sobre arqueología histórica y etnografía. In *Actas del XVI Congreso Nacional de Arqueología Chilena*, pp. 227–238. Concepción.

Thomas, Julian 2004 *Archaeology and Modernity*. Routledge, London.

Tilley, Christopher 1989 Archaeology as theatre. *Antiquity* 63:275–280.

Trigger, Bruce 1980 Archaeology and the image of the American Indian. *American Antiquity* 45:662–676.

Villaseca, Mauricio 2000 Dos historias, un paisaje: transformación y persistencia en el Alto Loa. Honor's thesis, Department of Anthropology, Universidad de Chile, Santiago.

Westfall, Catherine 1998 ¿Sólo indio muerto es indio bueno?: arqueólogos, pehuenches y Ralco. *Boletín de la Sociedad Chilena de Arqueología* 26:35.

CHAPTER 7

REFLECTIONS ON CHILEAN LEGISLATION AND THE INDIGENOUS ARCHAEOLOGICAL HERITAGE: AN ARCHAEOLOGIST'S VIEWPOINT

Luis E. Cornejo

To advance the discussion of cultural heritage, different perspectives are needed to help shed light on the political, social, academic, and ideological aspects in play, in addition to the more obvious, strictly legal ones. The viewpoint I present herein is founded upon Chile's cultural heritage laws, but is not that of a jurist. It can best be appreciated as one that takes into account the complexity of the problem; it is the perspective of an archaeologist attempting to approach current legislation from a critical standpoint with reference to both anthropological and archaeological elements. Hopefully, the paragraphs below will contribute to deepening the discussion of the uniqueness of our archaeological heritage, while recognizing it as part of a greater whole: Chile's cultural heritage (Aguilera 1998; Aldunate 1998). Specifically, my analysis will focus on discussing the implications of the notion of indigenous archaeological heritage, which has recently emerged as a strong component of the ethnic demands of Chile's different indigenous communities. This issue was only partially addressed in the Indigenous Law enacted in 1994. Indeed, as I will show below, the policy implications of various articles of this law have raised expectations and engendered disputes that were not foreseen when the bill was drafted. Above all, however, the discussion should not be based on a specific archaeological heritage, as any consideration of the archaeological heritage of Chile's native communities should seek only to enhance and enrich the criteria already established for the entire range of the country's archaeological heritage.

The legal framework governing the protection, promotion, and management of Chile's archaeological heritage includes a broad range of legal provisions found in the constitution, current legislation, and international conventions. Notable among these are the Ley de Monumentos Nacionales

(Law of National Monuments 17.288) and the Ley Indígena (Indigenous Law 19.253), and their respective regulatory systems.

THE LAW OF NATIONAL MONUMENTS

The most important law for Chile's archaeological heritage is the Law of National Monuments (LMN), a legal text dedicated to the protection, promotion, and management of Chile's cultural heritage (Law 17.288). The law was first enacted in 1970 and the regulations pertaining to archaeology were added in 1990 (Ministry of Education Decree 484/90, Regulations on Law 17.288 on Archaeological, Anthropological, and Paleontological Excavation and Prospecting).

The LMN establishes the framework for ownership of archaeological heritage by defining in its Article 21 that "by the sole operation of the law, anthropological-archaeological places, ruins, sites, and pieces existing on the surface and underground within the national territory are considered state-owned Archaeological Monuments." This definition delimits the discussion of ownership by making the state the sole owner of Chile's archaeological heritage, declaring that heritage a national monument, whether it is discovered or not and regardless of the nature of the place or ownership of the location where such heritage is found within the country's borders (Art. 1 and 21). What I find especially interesting here is the wording of the first article of the LMN, which states that "national monuments include all ... burial sites, cemeteries, and other remains of aboriginal peoples," regardless of whether these have already received official recognition. Such a broad definition has been accused more than once of violating private property rights enshrined in the constitution, because it ignores ownership of land containing archaeological heritage sites, establishing an ownership scheme similar to that in the mining sector, where land ownership is separate from ownership of the natural resources found therein.

The LMN sets out detailed provisions for the protection, promotion, and management of the archaeological heritage as national monuments and concentrates in a state institution—the Council of National Monuments—all decisions related to this heritage. Such decision-making power includes the authority to "regulate access to National Monuments" and "grant permits and authorizations for historical, archaeological, anthropological, and paleontological excavations anywhere within the national territory" (Art. 6).

Just as the LMN affirms that the state is the owner of all archaeological heritage, so too it establishes the state as the sole entity responsible for the protection of all archaeological heritage recovered from archaeological sites. The Council of National Monuments has the authority to determine which institutions may act as repositories of such objects. These institutions, mostly museums, must ensure that the heritage is conserved and exhibited and guarantee access to researchers interested in studying it (Regulations Art. 21). Under this framework the Council of National Monuments is responsible for museums and other institutions that have charge of archaeological collections (Art. 37).

The Environmental Framework Law of Chile (Law 19.300) considers archaeological heritage as an element that must be protected when projects are proposed that could have environmental impact. All new projects are subject to approval under the Environmental Impact Assessment System, and the assessment process may result in measures being established to prevent impacts on archaeological heritage and, where impacts have already resulted, to mitigate them and compensate for the harm they have caused.

The body of law referred to above makes the Chilean state the sole owner of archaeological heritage found in national territory, defining this heritage as a national monument under the direct control of the state. The legislation lays out specific procedures for regulating access to sites containing national heritage elements and the activities that may be carried out on national monument sites, prioritizing scientific investigation in the use of such sites.

INDIGENOUS LAW

Law 19.253, enacted in 1993, established legal norms for the protection, promotion, and development of Chile's indigenous peoples and brought into being the Corporación Nacional de Desarrollo Indígena (National Indigenous Development Corporation, CONADI), an institution "responsible for promoting policies to foster the comprehensive development of the social and cultural identity of Chile's indigenous peoples" (CONADI 2006). Among the law's provisions are three articles that make reference to archaeological heritage. These articles stipulate that the recognition, respect for, and protection of Chile's indigenous cultures require the protection of the indigenous archaeological, cultural, and historical heritage (Art. 28, Clause f). Article 29 establishes that, in order to protect the historical heritage of Chile's indigenous cultures, a report must be submitted to CONADI prior to any change in possession of the indigenous archaeological heritage (Clause a), its removal from the country (Clause b), or the excavation of historical indigenous cemeteries for scientific purposes (Clause c). The last of these provisions also affirms that any such scientific studies must have the approval of the indigenous community involved and be conducted in accordance with the provisions of the Law of National Monuments and its regulations (Law 17.288).

Before directly addressing the issue of archaeological heritage, there is one concept running through the entire law that must be analyzed: that of indigenous cultures. The legislation addresses this concept via three main criteria for classification as an indigenous culture: descendance from a pre-Columbian group, preservation of unique ethnic and cultural expressions, and attachment to the land (Art. 1). This analytical definition is complemented by a list of seven legally recognized indigenous groups in Chile (Art. 1), namely the Mapuche, Aymara, Rapanui, Atacameña, Quechua, Colla, Kaweshkar, and Yamana. Today, another group is seeking official recognition as an indigenous group, claiming to be descendant from the Diaguitas.

The legal definition of what constitutes an indigenous group assumes the independent and exclusive development of an ethnic identity. In other words, the Mapuche identity is separate from the Atacameña identity. This definition has meant that to enjoy the benefits granted under the Indigenous Law, a group must be an ethnic group with a well-known historical or prehistoric point of reference. This is how the Colla ethnic group was established. The Collas are an indigenous people that migrated from the eastern side of the Andes to the highlands around Copiapó in the late nineteenth century and had to construct their cultural practices (such as belief systems and dances) by recurring to a blend of cultural elements from other ethnicities. In the process of obtaining official recognition as an indigenous people, the inhabitants of the semi-arid northern valleys of Chile have chosen the name Diaguitas, about whom there is a tradition of historical and archaeological studies. However, this appellation derives from an error in interpretation on the part of early researchers (in the early twentieth century) and is not the name of the ethnic group that inhabited that territory before the European arrival; we do not know the name of that group.

As well as being exclusive, however, the definition of indigenous cultures is also inclusive, as it envelops the diversity within each culture, whether Mapuche or Atacameño. Since the law was enacted, each community and individual has had to define its membership in a particular ethnic group, which has been a somewhat problematic issue. For example, before the enactment of the law, the indigenous inhabitants of the Salado River (Upper Loa River) basin saw themselves as distinct from the populations inhabiting the Salar de Atacama oasis; today, however, they are both considered part of the Atacameño ethnic group defined for these territories.

This is one phenomenon in the ongoing process of building identity, a process that is traversed by situational factors, especially political and social ones (Jones 1997; Martínez 1998), not the least of which was the enactment of the Indigenous Law. Thus, the ethnic fusion and fission that we have witnessed and will doubtlessly continue to see in the future as a result of the Indigenous Law, are part of the long history of ethnic identity building in the indigenous world. This process is more flexible and dynamic than nation building in the Western world, which is a function of geopolitical regimes whose central mechanisms have been the definition of borders.

Defining Indigenous Cultural Heritage

With the concept of indigenous cultures established, I will now address aspects of this notion that are related to indigenous archaeological heritage. One of the implications of recognizing, respecting, and protecting indigenous cultures, as provided for in Article 28, Clause f of the Indigenous Law, is the protection of "indigenous archaeological heritage." This term establishes a foundation for the notion (e.g., Olivera et al. 1998) that indigenous communities have a kind of property right over the archaeological remains that make up their cultural legacy. This interpretation, and the demands that have arisen from it, makes it necessary to debate the scope of the concept of indigenous archaeological heritage from an archaeological perspective. Such a discussion is necessary in light of the increasingly common disputes between archaeologists and indigenous communities, as well as in anticipation of the actions of Chilean political and legislative authorities, whose counterparts abroad have demonstrated their view that archaeological heritage is a less valuable commodity than the land, the core issue in indigenous claims. The following discussion seeks to offer a possible pathway toward fulfilling legitimate indigenous aspirations to own the archaeological heritage left by native ancestors, while addressing the difficulties of this road from an archaeological perspective.

Following the same legal rationale used to identify and delimit different indigenous cultures, we should think in terms of a generic indigenous archaeological heritage, but one that is specific to each of Chile's recognized indigenous cultures. This reasoning coincides with the general view that each indigenous group that inhabits and inhabited Chilean territory has its own cultural, linguistic, and social differences. Present-day archaeological science defines archaeological heritage as the material evidence representative of a particular form of life or human activity. This definition is a departure from the old view, which focused on prehistory, especially with the development of areas of study such as historical archaeology, industrial archaeology, and forensic archaeology.

It is not easy to draw the line between archaeological and historical heritage, whether indigenous or not, especially where written history has not been forthcoming in providing information about certain events or human groups. Such written records tend to ignore not only indigenous groups and their most recent history, but also the disenfranchised social classes and inhabitants of remote territories; they have also attempted to hide certain events, especially systematic human rights violations. In all of these cases, and most obviously in the case of prehistoric societies, material remains are an important part of our heritage because they are special and even unique expressions of the cultural legacy of these people and evidence of those events. Having made this clarification, I now wish to offer a way of defining the archaeological heritage of Chile's different indigenous cultures. First of all, it seems correct to define it as the collection of material evidence left by the ancestors of today's indigenous peoples; however, this simple approach is complicated by the not so simple task of determining who the ancestors of each indigenous culture are. For historical times, the problem is less complex; documents and memory can prove the descent of today's indigenous people through material cultural heritage, even back to early colonial times. Analysis becomes more complicated when we go further back than the historical record. The profound changes prompted by the European arrival and, in some parts of the country, the population movements resulting from the previous Inka reign make it difficult to trace a clear historical and cultural line between the present and the past. As we go further back in history, other sociopolitical occurrences make the process even more conjectural.

As we go back in time the cultural linkages become more difficult to prove. The emergence of sedentarism and agricultural economies in most of Chile marked a strong cultural shift that in many cases broke permanently with a past dominated by a hunter-gatherer lifestyle. In most cases there is insufficient evidence to categorically determine whether such changes resulted from the incorporation of new populations or from the development of new ways of life within the same cultural groups. The long history of hunter-gatherers, which goes back some 14,000 years, offers an infinite variety of historical and cultural combinations, making it virtually impossible to follow the trail of today's indigenous cultures into this remote past.

It is academically impossible to draw an indisputable line between most archaeological remains and a specific contemporary indigenous culture. Such a line would have to be based on demonstrated continuities in key cultural aspects like ideology or social organization and rule out those that are more strictly environmental, such as subsistence. This is really only possible where a specific set of remains has been left by later populations in places where the same indigenous culture has been present for a long time. By way of examples, we can point to the evident connection between the San Pedro archaeological culture and the present-day Atacameños or that between the people that archaeologists call El Vergel and the present-day Mapuche. In both cases—the first from the Atacama Desert and the second from Chile's temperate southern rainforests—contextual evidence of archaeological cultures, early Spanish chronicles, and continuous occupation up to the present-day offer strong linkages between archaeological and present-day cultures. Special mention must be made here of Easter Island, where there is no doubt about the direct relationship between the archaeological heritage found on the island and today's Rapanui indigenous group.

Identifying which elements of the archaeological heritage constitute the cultural legacy of a given indigenous culture will require much more archaeological and anthropological investigation aimed at answering this specific question. This task will not be lacking in challenges, both scientific and political. Given its basic uncertainty principle, modern science is only rarely able to offer unquestionable affirmations of the kind expected by many of the stakeholders in this debate (such as jurists and indigenous peoples). Furthermore, the use of certain techniques that have proven highly useful for discussing legacies—particularly mitochondrial DNA or general bioanthropological studies—have negative political and ideological implications for many indigenous peoples, making their use unlikely in the near future.

This problematic situation makes it likely that, from an academic perspective (in other words, based on the results of scientific investigation in archaeology and anthropology) it will be possible to legally ascribe only a portion of Chile's archaeological heritage to a specific indigenous culture. Of course, there will be some exceptions, such as the Rapanui or, conversely, the so-called Colla, to whom it will likely be impossible to attribute any archaeological remains found in the territory that they inhabit.

The last point that must be addressed here is the compatibility of the above interpretation of what constitutes indigenous archaeological heritage and the Law of National Monuments, which contradict each other in one key aspect. The LMN defines as state property all archaeological remains, including those that could be defined as "aboriginal remains," which is not in line with the wishes of the heirs of the particular archaeological heritage that can be assigned to a given indigenous culture. Although it is more a political than a legal issue, in principle this question calls for a legal analysis. Indeed, such disputes could be resolved by adjusting the LMN to specify that some kinds of archaeological heritage in Chile are not state property per se but in certain circumstances could belong to a recognized indigenous culture. Such declarations should be made on a case-by-case basis with regard to specific indigenous cultures and be scientifically accredited, where at all possible.

The LMN also offers a way of guaranteeing the preservation of that heritage, which is one of its main objectives, by applying the same legal logic that is used for historical monuments. Title III of the LMN refers to "state-, municipal-, or privately-owned places, ruins, constructions, and objects" that should be considered monuments, affirming that regardless of whether or not the property belongs to the state, it should remain under state control through the Council of National Monuments. This emphasizes that regardless of who owns a monument, the state is called upon to protect its heritage and as a result to put in place measures to do so. To a certain degree this idea already exists in the Indigenous Law, which indicates (Art. 29, Clause c) that scientific excavations of historic indigenous cemeteries, as well as being governed by the provisions of the Indigenous Law, should follow the procedure established in the LMN.

AN ARCHAEOLOGICAL PERSPECTIVE (OR, THE ARCHAEOLOGIST'S PERSPECTIVE)

This discussion is of interest to archaeologists from all angles, especially as one of the most interesting anthropological issues today is redefining the identity of human groups. But I will limit myself here to a couple of key elements related to archaeological investigation and the discussion and interpretation of Chile's indigenous archaeological heritage. Before addressing these topics, it is worth pointing out that many years ago archaeology in Chile and in many other parts of the world left behind the colonial legacy of "original sin" that had stained anthropology as a whole. Today archaeology—and anthropology too, I understand—is better defined as mestizo practices, rooted in our Latin American socie-ties' more than 500 years of mestizo culture and carried out by and large by individuals who in one way or another, to a greater or lesser degree, are heirs of the pre-Columbian cultural tradition. This has mostly been the product of systematic archaeological studies conducted in public uni-versities since the mid-1970s, which ushered in a more democratic and professional approach to the scientific study of the past.

From the standpoint of archaeological scientific investigation it should be noted that, in principle, it is irrelevant whether the ownership of archaeological evidence rests with the state or a given Chilean com-munity. The real concern of archaeologists is ensuring that this heritage is well protected and accessible to foster the advance of our knowledge of human history as a whole. This is the main objective of this science and in my opinion can be achieved using the interpretation I have sug-gested. However, this also means that archaeological practice must adapt to and recognize the legitimate cultural rights and views of the com-munities who are the inheritors of a given heritage; indeed, a number of my colleagues have advanced in this issue already.[1] Obviously this will involve taking a stand on a couple of sensitive issues: the unwillingness of some indigenous groups to facilitate archaeological interventions at archaeological sites, especially cemeteries and ritual sites, and the exhibition in museums or publication of objects considered sacred by indigenous groups, especially human remains. In general, these issues should be resolved through negotiations between the communities involved and the archaeologists themselves, who can emphasize the scientific value of the knowledge generated by archaeological studies and its dissemination, as well as its value for the communities themselves. But the issue of exhibiting human remains speaks to more widely held beliefs: respect for the dignity of humans, whether modern or ancient, known or unknown, is never compatible with the exhibition of their remains. When addressing the thorny issue of the archaeological heritage of indigenous cultures, it is necessary to consider the place of the different types of knowledge available: oral tradition, historical studies, and archaeological investigations. The overlay of two or more of these kinds of knowledge can produce disconnectedness due to the nature of their respective records and the interpretations on which they are based. Often they have different historical depths or may focus on different cultural aspects. A good example of this is the historical imagery of the territory of south-central Chile, where the highly unified cultural viewpoint presented by the early Spanish chroniclers contrasts with the culturally diverse perspective that emerges from analyses of the archaeological record.

It is important to consider the present state of the knowledge we are going to use, basing this on the principles of scientific investigation. Building knowledge in archaeology does not simply involve accumulating information; rather, it is a constant process of redefinition in which some affirmations are given more weight and explored in more detail, while others are considered somewhat and still others ruled out altogether. In effect, the constructs of science never are more than hypotheses eternally open to discussion; there are no absolute formulas.

In brief, the criteria for defining the archaeological heritage of a particular indigenous culture should come from the bodies of evidence most relevant to the historical moment to which that heritage belongs. Taking into account the most recent findings of archaeological investigation and the opinions of experts in each cultural context should allow us to arrive at these criteria.

Final Thoughts

The preceding discussion has sought to outline some of the problems I see as an archaeologist when I examine the legal definition of the archaeological heritage of Chile's indigenous cultures. Rather than be politically correct, I have sought to be faithful to my ideas, which do not claim to represent the opinion of archaeologists or any other group of people, but have developed to a large extent through the debates and ideas in current circulation in Chile's archaeological community.

NOTES

I wish to thank archaeologists Carlos Aldunate, Lorena Sanhueza, and Héctor Vera for their comments on this manuscript, and the editors of this volume for their comments and for inviting me to contribute to this work.

1. Such as Victoria Castro and Carlos Aldunate in the Upper Loa, Mauricio Uribe in the Aymara region, and Leonor Adan in the Mapuche area.

REFERENCES

Aguilera, Nelson 1998 Patrimonio cultural indígena de Chile: aproximaciones iniciales desde el Estado. In *Patrimonio arqueológico indígena en Chile. Reflexiones y propuestas de gestión*, edited by Ximena Navarro, pp. 47–59. Universidad de La Frontera, Temuco.

Aldunate, Carlos 1998 Patrimonio cultural indígena. In *Patrimonio arqueológico indígena en Chile. Reflexiones y propuestas de gestión*, edited by Ximena Navarro, pp. 17–19. Universidad de La Frontera, Temuco.

CONADI (Corporación Nacional de Desarrollo Indígena) 2006 *Nuestra misión*, http://www.conadi.cl/mision.html, accessed January 2006.

Jones, Sian 1997 *The Archaeology of Ethnicity: Constructing Identities in the Past and Present*. Routledge, London.

Martínez, José Luis 1998 *Pueblos de Chañar y el Algarrobo. Los atacamas en el siglo XVII*. Centro Barros Arana, Santiago.

Olivera, Ana María, Claudio Colivoro, and Manuel Muñoz 1998 Alcances al anteproyecto sobre monumentos nacionales: elementos para una discusión. In *Patrimonio arqueológico indígena en Chile. Reflexiones y propuestas de gestión*, edited by Ximena Navarro, pp. 87–91. Universidad de La Frontera, Temuco.

CHAPTER 8

ARCHAEOLOGY AND INDIGENOUS COMMUNITIES: A COMPARATIVE STUDY OF ARGENTINEAN AND BRAZILIAN LEGISLATION

María Luz Endere, Plácido Cali, and Pedro Paulo A. Funari

INTRODUCTION

During the second half of the nineteenth century, Argentina was thought of as a nation composed of European immigrants. Existing indigenous descendants in the territory were considered as part of a wild race, condemned to disappear. In fact, the cultural homogeneity model adopted by the ruling elite denied the existence of any ethnic difference that could endanger national consolidation (Slavsky 1992). Pre-Hispanic material culture, however, was not outside the national political project. In 1913, Law 9080 was passed creating the basis for a legal system of heritage protection founded in the state ownership of ruins and archaeological sites of scientific value. The creation of the great national museums and the development of scientific positivism (Podgorny 2000; Politis 1995) made archaeological heritage an intellectual property owned exclusively by academic institutions, thus depriving indigenous descendants of all access to their ancestors' cultural heritage.

In the 1930s, pre-Hispanic archaeological heritage and archaeological and ethnographic collections lost importance in the construction of a national history oriented toward the reinforcement of Hispanic tradition and national heroes. At that time, the legal status of indigenous descendants changed from being regarded as enemies and icons of an inferior race (e.g., Zeballos 1986 [1878]), to having no rights, and finally to being members of the nation, without any ethnic consideration. However, from the social perspective, the stigma of being indigenous descendants was made evident by the color of their skin and the language itself. The derogative term "black heads," usually used to refer to working men, made apparent indigenous ancestry the cause of degradation.

In the second half of the twentieth century, the legal status of indigenous people was improved by the ratification (Law 14.932/59) of the ILO Convention 107 concerning the Protection and Integration of Indigenous and Other Tribal and Semi-Tribal Populations in Independent Countries and the creation of a government agency to deal with indigenous matters in 1961, as well as the first indigenous census in 1966. This shift in the official policy and the general atmosphere of social turmoil encouraged the appearance of indigenous movements between 1970 and 1975 (Serbín 1981), which were abruptly interrupted by the coup d'état in 1976. With the return of democracy in 1983, a change was perceived, defined in the official ideology tending to emphasize Argentina's character as a "multicultural nation" and confirmed by Law 23.302 on indigenous communities in 1985 and the constitutional reform in 1994.

In Brazil, indigenous people have represented national ancestry since independence in 1822, when the European monarchy who settled there began to idealize them. This view evolved for many decades until the advent of so-called *"indianismo"* at the end of the empire in 1889. With the proclamation of the republic and the change of authority from the court of the empire in Rio de Janeiro to the new elites from São Paolo, indigenous people began to represent the secular backwardness of the country. For many decades, the indigenous presence was put aside. With the redemocratization that followed the dictatorship of the Estado Novo (1937–1945), it was possible to propose an indigenous acceptance together with the foundation of the Brazil Anthropology Association (ABA) and the action in defense of preconquest archaeological remains headed by the humanist Paulo Duarte, who was in contact with the French Rivet e Emperaire (Funari 1994, 2002). In this context, the archaeological heritage protection law was passed in 1961, which is still into force. During the military dictatorship (1964–1985), indigenous people were again left out of the official issues, although indigenous rights remained present among the aims of the ABA, as well as the social movements and those in defense of human rights, such as the church in indigenous territory. With the restoration of civil government, indigenous rights were again in the political agenda through public discussions and the limiting of their territory. However significant the indigenous presence in the country was—a third of the population has Amerindians ancestors—it has not always received due attention or recognition.

As part of a common process in almost all of South America, the return of democracy in the 1980s and 1990s came with important constitutional amendments and legal changes on issues that had been postponed for years, as in the case of indigenous people's rights (see Barié 2003). The significance of this impact on the constitution and its derived legislation in Argentina and Brazil are a valuable indicator of the way that official policies have changed in each country in the last decades. This research seeks to discuss indigenous participation in relation to cultural heritage in Argentina and Brazil from an analysis of the legislation in each country and how this engagement is reflected in ethnic standards and archaeological practice.

The Case of Argentina

Constitutional Regulations

In 1994, the amendment of the national constitution (NC) included valuable regulations in relation to heritage preservation and the recognition of indigenous communities' rights, although some of them still require a national law to be operative.

Cultural heritage is explicitly considered in Article 41, which establishes that "the authorities will provide for the preservation of natural and cultural heritage," specifying that "the state has the duty to develop policies for the management and protection of this heritage in coordination with the provinces." On the other hand, it allows exerting protection when collective rights are at risk, among which the preservation of cultural heritage would be included. It is worth noticing that this action can be exerted by the ombudsman, or the associations whose objective is protecting these rights (Art. 43).

In Article 75, Clause 17, the national constitution recognizes the "ethnic and cultural preexistence of Argentinean indigenous communities," ensuring—together with the provinces—"respect for their identity and the right to participate in the management of their natural resources and other matters of their interest." This paragraph has been interpreted as giving indigenous communities the right to participate in the management of the cultural heritage of their ancestors (Endere 2000:56). Likewise, in Clause 19, fourth paragraph, the Congress has the authority to "state laws that protect identity and cultural diversity." Moreover, constitutional hierarchy is given to many international treaties, such as the International Agreement of Economic, Social, and Cultural Rights (Art. 75, Clause 22, second paragraph). To conclude, the national constitution, though not expressly stated, has a number of rules that would enable the recognition of the rights of the indigenous community in relation to their cultural heritage.

Indigenous Legislation

Law 23.302/85 on "indigenous policy and support to indigenous communities" introduced a substantial change in the subject prior to the constitutional reform. It recognized the legal status of indigenous communities[1] and declared "of national interest the attention and support to indigenous people and indigenous communities in the country, and their defense and development for their total engagement in the socioeconomic and cultural process of the nation, respecting their own values and customs" (Art. 1). This regulation also created the National Institute of Indigenous Affairs (INAI) as a decentralized entity whose aim is the enforcement of the law; it must hold a Record of Indigenous Communities to whom legal status is granted to act as such and it must also elaborate plans of allocation and exploitation of the lands, as well as educational and health programs. Indigenous communities participate in the implementation of these policies through representatives in a consulting Coordination Counsel (Decree 155/89 Art. 7i and Art. 10) (see Carrasco 2000).

It is also worth mentioning that Law 23.592, passed in 1988, prohibits any kind of discrimination based on ethnic or racial criteria. In 1992, Argentina ratified the ILO Convention 169 concerning "Indigenous and Tribal Peoples in Independent Countries" through Law 24.071. Nevertheless, it was not enforced until 2000, when Argentina finally deposited the instrument of ratification with the ILO. This convention not only coincides with the criteria of self-recognition or ethnic self-recognition of Law 23.302 as a basis for the definition of indigenous people, but it also states that "governments shall consult the peoples concerned, whenever consideration is being given to legislative or administrative measures that may affect them directly" and shall also "establish means by which these peoples can freely participate at all levels of decision making in elective institutions and administrative and other bodies responsible for policies and programs which concern them" (Article 6, Clauses a and b) (Hualpa 2003).

As it can be seen, there is a significant recognition of the indigenous communities' rights in the national constitution as well as in some key laws in Argentina. However, those rights are not always observed in the derived legislation and, least of all, in practice. In fact, those rights have not been considered in the law concerning archaeological heritage protection, which still recognizes the exclusive validity of scientific value and expert opinion when defining needs and modes of protection.

Indigenous Claims and Legal Recognition

The process of legal recognition of indigenous communities in Argentina initiated with the return of democracy changed considerably the perspectives of the indigenous claims on human remains held in museum collections.

The paradigmatic case in Argentina is the La Plata Museum, part of La Plata National University, which possesses a collection of indigenous Tehuelche and Araucano skeletons and skulls from the Pampa and Patagonia regions, who perished or were taken prisoner during the conquest of their territories in the late nineteenth century. These skeletons—especially the remains of historically well-known chiefs, such as Callfulcurà, Inakayal, Mariano Rosas, Manuel Guerra, Gherenal, Indio Brujo, and Chipitruz—have been claimed not only by different indigenous groups, but also by descendants since the 1970s. The University of La Plata has always rejected these claims, alleging that the remains were part of the state public domain. In other cases, the rejection was due to the impossibility of legally proving kinship (Podgorny and Miotti 1994; Podgorny and Politis 1992).

The fact that the collections of human remains were part of the national heritage made it necessary to pass a law of repatriation that would release them from the public domain in order to allow a legal restitution. In 1991, the first law of repatriation was passed (Law 23.940/91), which prescribed the restitution of the Tehuelche Chief Inakayal to its homeland in Tecka, Chubut Province, where he was buried in a mausoleum in 1994 after being accorded military honors and indigenous rituals. A new restitution was carried out in 2000 by Law 25.276, which prescribed the devolution of the remains of the Ranquel chief Mariano Rosas to his community in Leubucó, La Pampa Province. This restitution was carried out in June 2001 during an official ceremony called "historical reparation to the Ranquel community," in which numerous indigenous leaders and national and provincial politicians participated (Endere 2002).

Finally, Law 25.517/01 attempted to generate a substantial change in the subject when it established that the museums must make indigenous human remains available to "indigenous people or communities that claim them" (Art. 1). In this way, it claims that "to carry out any scientific project whose objective is concerned with indigenous communities, including their historical and cultural heritage, the express consent of the interested community will be necessary" (Art. 3). In 2010 the national government stated that the Instituto Nacional de Asuntos Indígenas (INAI) was the authority in charge of putting into practice Law 25.517. The INAI has the faculty of doing all the necessary actions in order to carry out the restitution of human remains, as well as providing opinion about scientific projects concerning indigenous communities, being able to coordinate actions with the Instituto Nacional de Antropología y Pensamiento Latinoamericano (INAPL) (Decree 701).

Legislation on Archaeological Heritage Protection

Facing a situation that seemed to encourage the recognition of the indigenous communities' rights in relation to its cultural heritage, the new Law 25.743 on archaeological heritage protection in Argentina passed in 2003 is surprising. This law, which amended the legendary Law 9080, regulates the preservation and protection of archaeological heritage and its scientific and archaeological use as part of the cultural heritage of the nation. It determines the responsibility of both state and provinces, and it establishes that the national enforcing authority is the Instituto Nacional de Antropología y Pensamiento Latinoamericano, (INAPL) creating, at the same time, the National Register of Archaeological Sites, Collections, and Objects. However, the new law completely ignores indigenous communities' rights and it does not make any differentiation among archaeological sites located on the lands of indigenous communities and ones located on private lands.

The contradictions between this law and the repatriation Law 25.517 show, once again, that the changes in the legislation and heritage management produced in the last years have not been part of an integral policy concerning cultural heritage: they came about in response to the effort made by an institution or to the particular project of some legislator, thus having limited effects in practice.

Standards in Professional Ethics

The possibility of organizing a professional association of archaeologists bearing registration control has been widely discussed in Argentina, although the results have not been encouraging. There is an unavoidable legal obstacle: an association should be created in each province and if professionals work in more than one province, which is very common among archaeologists, they would have to enroll in each of them simultaneously.[2] Hence, in 1999 it was decided to create a voluntarily integrated civil association called AAPRA (Association of Argentinean Professional Archaeologists). After many efforts, a few principles of professional ethics could finally be adopted in 2009.

Real Participation of Indigenous Communities

Respect for traditional beliefs in relation to archaeological sites and the fear of removing the human remains of their ancestors have been considered for years the product of people's ignorance and a hurdle to scientific investigation. However, there have been examples of researchers who have been sensitive to the demands of the local people and allowed the realization of rituals.

There are not many examples in Argentina of joint works with indigenous communities concerning investigation and preservation of archaeological sites. Nevertheless, it is worth mentioning the case of the Province of Neuquén, which has been a pioneer in this type of participation through the creation of site museums under the communities' custody (e.g., Añelo Site Museum in the Mapuche community Painemil [Biset 1989]) or communal museums (Communal Museum of the Cuenca del Curi Leuvú [Cúneo 2004:86]). Another significant fact was the decision adopted by the Administration of National Parks to give back to the Mapuche community Ñorquinco the custody of a sacred site in Lanín National Park (Neuquén), due to a joint agreement in 2000. The devolution of an area within the park—where there is a *rehue* (monument with ritual value) and a cave with rock paintings—was agreed upon, and a committee was formed to discuss a site management plan (Molinari 2000).

The conclusions of the round table of specialists organized in November 1999 by the Center for Historic and Archaeological Research of the University of Salta constitutes another important precedent for the discussion of the ethical implications of the discovery of human remains. In this meeting the case of mummies found in high-altitude sanctuaries was discussed, due to a claim made by a Colla indigenous community concerning the Inka mummies taken from the Llullaillaco Volcano (see Reinhard 1999, also Politis 2001). Among the recommendations adopted, the need that political authorities and legislation take into consideration the rights and interests of local communities and indigenous peoples to participate in the management of cultural heritage was emphasized (app. 1d). In addition, it was pointed out that ethic professional standards should consider the need to engage local communities and indigenous people in the management of their cultural resources (app. 2b) (CEPIHA 1999).

In general during the last years, archaeologists have changed their attitude toward the respect for the sacredness of sites and the engagement of indigenous communities, although few researchers openly and voluntarily offer opportunities to participate to the communities with whom they interact. Indigenous groups, on the other hand, were hardly visible in relation to ritual and symbolic issues during the first years of the democratic return. It was not until before the celebration of the fifth centenary of America's discovery that these groups reacted to the official celebrations and began to gain importance. Among the numerous demonstrations, it is worth mentioning the celebration of the "last day of freedom" (October 11, 1992) in different archaeological sites, such as the Pucará in Tilcara, the Quebrada de Humahuaca, and Fuerte Quemado in the Calchaquí Valley. Nowadays, local authorities, moved by tourist interest, tend to encourage the performance of traditional celebrations in areas with strong indigenous roots (such as the *camarucos* in Neuquén and Río Negro, the Pachamama celebration, and the Intiraimi in the Northwest region), which some decades ago were questioned by the Catholic Church and even banned by military authorities.

Recently, an important step has been taken to establish a joint dialogue between archaeologists and indigenous communities concerning archaeological heritage. In May 2005, the Declaration of Río Cuarto was signed during the First Forum of Archaeologists–Native People carried out in the city of Río Cuarto, Córdoba, and organized by the Plenary of the XV National Congress of Argentinean Archaeology, celebrated the previous year. Some issues in the declaration are (1) the non-exhibition of human remains in museums, as well as the need to make the public aware of the reasons for such decision; (2) the respect for the ancestral sacredness of human remains and indigenous sites, and the need to tailor archaeological techniques and procedures to match that respect; (3) the mutual collaboration to achieve the restitution of indigenous human remains in public and/or private collections, as well as the amendment of the current law on archaeological heritage; (4) the need for archaeologists to responsibly appreciate the social and political consequences of archaeological research in relation to the rights of the indigenous communities; and (5) obtaining the previous consent of indigenous communities for the realization of archaeological research and taking extreme care for them to have the relevant information for decision making. This declaration is still in the process of gaining steadfast support in the archaeological community in the country.

THE CASE OF BRAZIL

The Federal Constitution

The federal constitution of Brazil of 1988 confirmed some basic rights for indigenous people, mainly the respect for ethnic and cultural diversity and the right to preserve part of their lands.[3] It also created mechanisms to link such communities with the state. Articles 231 and 232 of the federal constitution establish the political guidelines for the relations between indigenous people and the Brazilian state. In this way, there are explicit orientations, for example the obligatory referendum to indigenous people in case of hydro projects or the exploration of minerals on their lands.[4] However, the final decision is left to the national Congress, which possesses exclusive competence.[5]

Indigenous people have the same rights and legal rights as other Brazilians due to the fact that, according to the constitution, all those who are born in the territory are Brazilian citizens. They also have the Indigenous Statute, created by Law 6001, which grants special rights. Yet, when considering indigenous people as citizens, the state considers their lands as part of the national territory, and thus it does not recognize them as people who occupy a delimited territory with their own laws. In 1973, the Indigenous Statute incorporated the view that prevailed during the 1970s, which defended the progressive and harmonious integration of indigenous people into the national society (Art. 1).[6] The most recent proposal of the national Congress for the amendment of the Indigenous Statute was in December 2004, substituting Bill 2957/91.

The constitution does not define indigenous people, which results in difficulty for a country like Brazil without adopting racial, cultural, and other inappropriate and reductionist criteria. In contrast to this line of thought, in 1957 Darcy Ribeiro (1970:254) adopted the criterion of ethnic self-identification,[7] similar to the one recently adopted by the Brazilian government in the program for Afro-descendants at universities. If we analyze the current federal constitution, it can be seen that, among the ethnic minorities, indigenous people are privileged with a specific chapter and the recognition of several rights. This was the result of a strong movement by indigenous people, environmentalists, and NGOs. The Indigenous Statute (Law 6001/73) includes the following definitions:

> Art. 3. For the purposes of the law, the following definitions are established: I. Indigenous or *silvícola*: any individual of pre-Columbian origin and ancestry who feels identified and is identified as part of an ethnic group whose cultural features distinguish it from the national society; II. Indigenous community or tribal group: a group of indigenous families or communities, either living isolated from other areas of the national community or with sporadic or permanent contact, without being, however, integrated to them.

Article 8 of the current project to modify the Indigenous Statute contains the following definitions:

> I. Indigenous communities: groups that are distinguished among themselves and from the rest of the society in virtue of their historical bonds with communities of pre-Columbian origin; II. Indigenous person: individual who is a member or comes from an indigenous community, where she/he shares uses, customs, and traditions and is recognized by its members as such.

For the 1973 statute the indigenous, whether individually or in a community, must be of pre-Columbian origin and must not be integrated into the national society. On the other hand, the new project demands historical bonds with pre-Columbian inhabitants, customs, and traditions and, finally, recognition by the other members as such.

The legislation embeds scarce references to other ethnic minorities, such as Afro-descendants who are rather numerous in Brazil, the most important ones being those whose ancestors lived in the *quilombos*. Originally, *quilombos* were places made up of fugitive slaves in inhabited regions. Later, they were formed by freed slaves and their descendants, and nowadays communities with their own organization and lifestyle, keeping social-cultural bonds with their ancestors. However, there is disagreement with regard to the definition of *quilombo*, for the Brazilian Association of Anthropology proposed some time ago self-definition as a sole criterion, without any need for archaeological reference that could show the continuity between the current inhabitants and the period of slavery. Most archaeologists, however, do not share this stance.

Article 216 of the federal constitution establishes the declaration of public usefulness and legal protection of all related documents, as well as the areas traditionally occupied by the communities descending from ancient *quilombos*.[8] It still guarantees in Art. 68 the definite ownership of those lands to the remnants of the communities of the *quilombos* occupying them.[9] Consequently, the benefit is not restricted to the areas of the *quilombos* or the ones constituted by descendants of fugitive slaves, but it adopts a wider concept. For the Brazilian Association of Anthropology, the concept must reach "all the rural black community with slave descendants living in a culture of subsistence and where cultural manifestations have a strong bond with the past" (Governo do Estado de São Paulo 1997:47).

Concerning cultural heritage, the main article of the federal constitution is Art. 216, where material and immaterial objects are incorporated as related to the memory of different groups of society:

The Brazilian cultural heritage consists in material and immaterial objects, individually or jointly, that make reference to the identity, action, and memory of the different groups comprising Brazilian society, including: I. Forms of expression; II. Ways of creating, doing, and living; III. Scientific, artistic, and technological creations; IV. Works, objects, documents, buildings, and spaces for artistic and cultural manifestations; V. Urban groups and sites with historic, landscape, artistic, archaeological, palaeontological, ecological, and scientific value. 1. The State, with the collaboration of the community, will provide and protect the Brazilian cultural heritage through inventories, reports, custody, declaration of protected possession and of public usefulness and appropriation, and other ways of protection and preservation. 2. The public administration will, as stated by legislation, manage the government documentation and precautions to provide any assistance. 3. The legislation will establish incentives for production and the knowledge of goods as stated by law.

4. Damages and threats to the cultural heritage will be punished as stated by law. 5. All documents will be legally protected, as well as the sites that contain historical remnants of the ancient *quilombos*.

Regulations on Archaeological Heritage

Federal Law 3924/61 uses many imprecise or incorrect terms, and they are limited by the knowledge of archaeology in Brazil in the 1960s. Consequently, it refers to "archaeological or prehistoric monuments" and "archaeological or prehistoric sites," considering also all the objects contained within them as under the custody of the state. The term "site" alone is used to refer to the natural deposit of mineral or oil substances for commercial exploration. But the legislation also specifies some of the types of sites included in the terms used, including indigenous cemeteries, *sambaquis* (shell middens), stone shelters, ceramic lithic sites, or cave paintings, among others.[10] The following regulations on archaeological heritage are also available:

> *Portaria*[11] IPHAN 07/1988: this regulation from the Institute of the Historical and Artistic National Heritage (IPHAN), the federal organ in charge of the management of the national archaeological heritage and of possessions protected by national law, establishes the regulations and procedures for archaeological research and excavations, as well as the custody of recovered artifacts. *Portaria* IPHAN 230/2002: this regulation was the most important regulation since Law 3924 in 1961, which protected archaeological sites. *Portaria* 230 combines the preservation of archaeological heritage with environmental discharges in projects potentially detrimental to the environment. Therefore, it obliges the party responsible for the project to assess archaeological impact and to rescue possible archaeological sites found that would be destroyed by works such as hydroelectric works, oil pipelines, roads, division of lands into plots, water systems, and others established by the Resolution of the Environmental National Counsel (CONAMA) in 1988. In its text it defines the procedures for archaeological diagnosis in each phase of the environmental discharge and also for the rescue of the sites found. It was innovative when it defined that the custody of these archaeological traces "must be guaranteed by the project, whether in the modernization, extension, strengthening of existing units, or in the construction of museum units specific to the case." Until then, the maintenance of most heritage generated by archaeological research remained under the responsibility of public institutions, producing conservation, preservation, and communication expenses. Another important aspect was the compulsory programs of heritage education, "which will be determined in the contract among entrepreneurs and archaeologists responsible for the studies, both in terms of funding and schedule."
>
> Decree IPHAN 28/2003: this decree establishes that water reservoirs in hydroelectric plants of any size or dimension within the national territory must include in the application for the renewal of an environmental working license the execution of maps, surveys, and archaeological rescue projects of the area under water. The IPHAN considered the enormous losses of archaeological heritage produced by hydroelectric plants in Brazil.

These plants have recently been the target of environmental impact studies, and the variable of protection for archaeological cultural heritage has only recently been incorporated. It also considered the need to repair, minimize, and mitigate the negative effects potentially caused by such plants.

Decree 108/DPC 2003: a regulation from the Ministry of Defense, General Direction of Navigation, Ports, and Coasts, this establishes the regulations of sea authority for the investigation, exploration, removal, and demolition of things and possessions sunk, submerged, run aground or lost (NORMAN-10/DPC). It governs authorization for doing research and underwater tourism in archaeological sites incorporated to the state.

Resolution from the Secretary of the Environment of the State of São Paulo (SMA)-34/2003: this establishes the necessary measures to protect archaeological heritage in case of environmental discharge and activities that may generate a significant environmental impact, being subject to an assessment of environmental impact (EIC/RIMA).

However, there are no federal legal regulations that expressly guarantee the participation of indigenous people in the management of their material cultural heritage. Article 41 of the Indigenous Statute states that personal property does not constitute indigenous patrimony.[12] And yet if it did, management of indigenous heritage would be in charge of the competent authority of the Brazilian government, as stated in Art. 42.[13]

Generally, there are difficulties in enforcing the analyzed laws completely. With respect to the regulations on indigenous people, the main problem is the delimitation of their lands. In 1988, the constitution stipulated a five-year period to carry out its reforms. However, after 16 years of enforcement, hardly 275 of the 554 indigenous areas known in the country have been delimited. A total of 279 areas still remain, of which 133 have already been identified, the first step in the process of delimitation, or are in the process of identification.

In the field of archaeology, there are problems in the structure and lack of staff in the organizations in charge of heritage protection. Such as in the case of the Institute of Historical and Artistic National Heritage (IPHAN), the federal organ for archaeological heritage management in Brazil. Currently, there are only six archaeologists in the IPHAN, despite the existence of 13,000 sites registered, apart from thousands that have not been registered, and dozens of research and process reports and projects to be analyzed monthly. This makes it impossible for the organ to achieve national archaeological management, despite the efforts made by the technicians.

Standards of Professional Ethics and Indigenous Participation

In Brazil, a code of ethics for archaeologists does not exist, although this subject has been discussed in congresses and meetings. The profession has never been regulated and, therefore, there are no controlling organs, apart from the IPHAN, that authorize and control archaeological research. Historically, there are not many precedents that show archaeologists' preoccupation for the rights of current indigenous people over the cultural possessions belonging to their ancestors. Law 3924/61 itself only allows the custody of such possessions in public or research institutions. There are several cases of archaeological excavations in areas of abandoned villages some years ago and all the material recovered was taken to research institutions. As a consequence, there is no legal mechanism today that allows indigenous people to own archaeological material that must always be in the hands of public institutions.

For the same reasons, there are few concrete experiences of restitution of collections to indigenous communities or their management of site museums, basically due to the lack of legal support. There are no cases of indigenous engagement similar to that of the Afro-Brazilian communities, for example the case of the Quilombos Los Palmares, where fieldwork, custody, and study of the material had the support of the Nucleus of Afro-Brazilian studies at the Federal University of Alagoas. Archaeological investigations in the famous fugitive site of the seventeenth century, Palmares, have had the institutional participation of the Afro-Brazilian center and, through this, of activists such as Zezito de Araújo (Funari 1999).

Nevertheless, since the democratization of the country in 1985, there have been significant changes in archaeologists' attitudes. There are an increasing number of archaeologists (e.g., Francisco Silva Noelli, André Luiz Soares, Josè Luiz de Moraes) who are devoted to the discussion of these issues from the legal and practical points of view. These changes in attitude were more evident in some centers such as the Museum of Archaeology and Ethnography at the University of São Paulo, Federal University of Mato Grosso do Sul, and Federal University of Santa María, which had, in general, less impact in areas in the northeast of Brazil.

Finally, scientific dissemination books for children such as *Os Antigos Habitantets do Brasil* have contributed in the last years to improve the knowledge of indigenous people in relation to their own heritage, even if only a few people are concerned with the archaeology of Brazil.

CULTURAL POLICY AT MERCOSUR

The process of regional integration started by Argentina, Brazil, Paraguay, and Uruguay in 1995 created the economic and political agreement Mercosur; its Cultural Parliament (PARCUM) seeks to establish a legal framework to facilitate policies that promote cultural integration (Alvarez and Reyes 1999:96).

In this sense, recommendations and a Protocol of Regional Integration were enforced in December 1996, which include principles and orientations for the Cultural Mercosur. In such protocol, there are two articles concerning cultural heritage, as follows:

> Art. III: The state parties will promote a direct link among historical records, libraries, museums, and the organizations whose responsibility is the architectural heritage and monuments, aiming at establishing institutional agreements that consider other issues, the agreement of criteria relative to the classification, recording, and preservation leading to the creation of a record of the historical and cultural heritage in the region.
> Art. IV: The state parties will make an effort to institutionalize such record, conserve and strengthen the different traditions considered as relevant manifestations of the cultural heritage.

Currently, the information relative to different areas of the cultural policy has been systematized, and some improvements have been made in order to combine and complement the legislation referring to the circulation of cultural properties and training programs. However, the task of adopting common rules on cultural legislation is still pending. On the other hand, the protocol has been criticized because it reflects "a definition preferably preservationist and conservative of the culture and an integration approach based mainly on traditional cultural institutions (architecture, books, music, arts, museums)" that hinders the recognition of the richness of cultural dynamics (see Alvarez and Reyes 1999).

DISCUSSION

As can be observed, there are several meeting points in Argentinean and Brazilian legislation in relation to indigenous people. First of all, both in the national constitution of Argentina and the federal constitution of Brazil, there is an explicit recognition of the existence of indigenous people, their cultural diversity, and their right to legally own the lands they have traditionally occupied. In indigenous legislation in both countries, moreover, the criterion of self-recognition is predominant as a basis to defining the indigenous population (e.g., National Law 23.312 in Argentina, the Indigenous Statute in Brazil, and the amendment projects).

Indigenous participation, on the other hand, is widely recognized in Argentina, particularly since the ratification of the ILO Convention 169, while in Brazil the referendum to the communities is more restricted to hydro projects or mine exploration. However, in both legal systems, in general, the recognition of the rights of indigenous people to participate in the management of natural resources is much more advanced than it is in cultural resources, although the exercise of those rights in practice seems to be below the expectations that both constitutional amendments generated at that time. Doubtless, both in Argentina and Brazil, a significant division between legislation and practice can be observed.

Another coincidence appears in the case of heritage legislation, which ignores the issue of indigenous cultural heritage and, thus, does not apply the general principles of recognition, respect, and participation that arise from the framework of legislation in each of these countries, leaving communities without constitutional rights. In the case of Brazil, the Indigenous Statute, which is outdated in relation to the last constitutional amendment, does not include indigenous heritage management, which remains under the control of the heritage authorities of the Brazilian government. In Argentina, the sole exception in favor of indigenous participation is the repatriation Law 25.517, whose new reglamentary decree opens new challenges in the relationship between the National Institute of Indigenous Affairs (INAI) and the Institute of Anthropology (INAPL), which is in charge of implementing Law 25.743 on archaeological heritage.

The ignorance toward indigenous cultural heritage in heritage legislation is not a simple distraction, especially in the most recent regulations, but a clear position in the underlying dispute over the control and intellectual ownership of sites, to which most of the academic and scientific community of both countries are not likely to yield.

Neither of the two countries has managed to advance on the adoption of a mandatory professional code of ethics for archaeologists, although the subject has been part of the agenda of professional organizations in both countries in the last years. A greater interest in these issues is observed, however, in some researchers and academic centers, sometimes influenced by proindigenous ideas or stances that dominate the debate in ruling countries, particularly the USA.

Unlike Brazil, Argentina has pioneer cases of the restitution of human remains to descendant communities, as well as a certain experience of joint site management that, despite being exceptional, constitutes precious precedents for the region. In the last decades, indigenous communities in Argentina found a favorable political context to advance their claims. Obtaining legal status and the devolution of their lands has helped to direct their claims and interests in symbolic issues, such as the development of their own cosmology and the control over archaeological sites and their ancestors' human remains. Nevertheless, the fundamental obstacle indigenous groups face for the recognition of their claims is the fact that most authorities and researchers regard their leaders with suspicion. The fact that they have not made any claims until recently tends to be the main cause to reject their legitimacy. In addition, internal divisions and leadership conflicts among indigenous associations have hindered the development of a strong position on issues relative to heritage. Meanwhile, indigenous heritage is presented in most museums as part of a remote past in time, space, ethnic origin, and cultural tradition and, above all, without recognizing any link with contemporary indigenous communities (Endere 2007). Some university museums are an exception (e.g., the Ethnographic Museum of Buenos Aires, the Anthropological Museum in Córdoba, the Museum of Archaeology in Tucumán), where policies and modes of exhibition represent an encouraging shift.

On the other hand, in Brazil there is a growing and significant recognition of the necessity of interacting with local, indigenous, Afro-descendant, or traditional communities. Many historical sites show an important indigenous or ethnic engagement, and archaeological research begins to have the participation of the local population, originally indigenous. The case of the Laboratory of Biological Archaeology at Rio de Janeiro State University (LAB/UERJ), under the direction of Dr. Nanci Vieira de Oliveira, is paradigmatic of the new tendencies. Here, archaeological research is supported by indigenous communities (Oliveira 2004). Therefore, the perspectives are positive.

Final Remarks

In this framework, it is worth wondering if the inclusion of indigenous engagement in issues relative to cultural heritage in Argentina and Brazil is possible. Could a possible integration of both legislations into the framework of Cultural Mercosur be considered as an opportunity toward the recognition of such rights? Is indigenous participation in research and conservation projects of sites and collections a utopia?

From our perspective, in the recognition of cultural diversity as it is considered by UNESCO and the national legislation, an increasing demand and concern to ensure indigenous participation in archaeological management is evident. Cooperation among neighboring countries in South America is a strong aspect that must not be discarded, for it allows deeper planning and cultural management. Besides, cultural diversity, so evident between Argentina and Brazil, enables a deeper appreciation of the ethnic and cultural richness of indigenous communities. Obviously, there are numerous and well-known difficulties, such as the challenges imposed by the economic conditions of peripheral capitalist countries such as ours. There are not enough resources especially for the preservation of culture in ethnic and social groups that, in historical terms, have been undermined. On the other hand, cooperation among countries, which is essential, is always subject to the fluctuations of diplomatic relations and to periods of agreement and cooperation followed by others of indifference and official hostilities. Common scientific programs are affected by these same avatars. However, we believe that cooperation will continue as an important aim for both countries and, above all, for the proper interaction among ethnic and social groups. Lastly, but not least, the appreciation of cultural diversity implies a proactive policy in favor of action with the communities, to which we subscribe as citizens and as archaeologists, aware of the fact that only this humanist way can lead to an effective development of our people.

NOTES

1. "Indigenous communities will be understood as the groups of families recognized as such due to the fact that they descend from groups who lived in the territory at the time of the conquest or colonization and the members of such communities constitute the indigenous people" (Art. 2, Law 23.302).
2. In 2010 the Council of Archaeologists of Tucumán Province was created by provincial Law 8337. It is mandatory for local researchers to be registered members.
3. Chapter VIII, Indigenous People, Art. 231: "The indigenous social organization, customs, languages, beliefs, and traditions, and the original rights over the lands they traditionally occupy are recognized, being the Union authorized to limit them, protect, and respect their possessions. 1. The lands permanently occupied by indigenous people are the lands used for their productive activities, the lands essential for the preservation of environmental resources necessary for their welfare and for their physical and cultural reproduction according to their uses, customs, and traditions. 2. The lands traditionally occupied by indigenous people are aimed at their permanent possession, and they own the exclusive right to use the riches of the soil, rivers, and lakes."
4. Art. 231, Section 3: "The exploitation of hydric resources, including the energetic potential, the search, and exploration of mineral resources on indigenous lands will only be effective with the authorization of the national Congress, after having considered all the affected communities and having assured them participation in the results of the exploration, as stated by law."
5. Art. 49: "The national Congress will 16. Authorize the exploration and exploitation of hydro resources and the search and exploration of mineral resources on indigenous lands."
6. Indigenous Statute, Art. 1: "This law regulates the legal status of indigenous people or *silvicolas* [forest people] and indigenous communities, with the purpose of preserving their culture and integrating them into the national community, progressively and harmoniously."
7. "In today's Brazil, a native is that part of the population that presents problems for adapting to Brazilian society, in its various diversities, encouraged by the conservation of their customs, habits, or simple loyalty that links them to a pre-Columbian tradition. Or, even more widely, a native is any individual recognized as a member of a community of pre-Columbian origin who identifies him-/herself as ethnically different from the national community, and is accordingly regarded by the Brazilian population he-/she is in contact with."
8. Art. 216, Section 5: "All documents and sites that possess historical remnants of ancient *quilombos* will be protected by law."
9. Art. 68: "To the remnants of the communities in the *quilombos* who occupy their lands and have the definite ownership, the state will issue the corresponding titles."

10. Law 3924/61, Art. 1: "Archaeological or prehistoric monuments of any origin existing in the national territory and all the elements within contained will be under the custody and protection of the state, according to Art. 180 in the federal constitution … 2. Archaeological or prehistoric monuments will be (a) sites of any nature, origin, or purpose representing cultural testimony of Palaeoamerindians from Brazil, such as *sambaquis*, artificial mounds or treasures, burial holes, mounds, burying, and any other thing unspecified here, but with identical significance for the federal authority; (b) the sites where positive traces of occupation by Palaeoamerindians were found, such as caves and shelters under rocks; (c) sites identified as cemeteries, tombs, or places of prolonged or 'ceramic' and 'stationary' settlements, where human traces of archaeological or palaeoethnographic interest exist; (d) cave inscriptions or places such as traces of tool polishing and others of Paleoamerindian activity."

11. *Portaria* is an administrative action used by the heads of governmental organs to give general or individual instructions, administrative processes, etc.

12. Art. 41: "The indigenous patrimony does not include: … II. the room, furniture and domestic tools, personal objects, work tools and products of agriculture, hunting, fishing, and collection or work in general of the *silvicolas*."

13. Art. 42: "The competent authorities will manage the indigenous patrimony, encouraging, however, the participation of *silvicolas* and tribal groups in the exclusive administration of their possessions when they demonstrate the effective capacity for doing so."

REFERENCES

Alvarez, Marcelo, and Patricio Reyes 1999 El patrimonio según el Mercosur. In *Temas de patrimonio cultural II*, edited by the Comisión para la Preservación del Patrimonio Histórico-Cultural de la Ciudad de Buenos Aires, pp. 95–107. EUDEBA, Buenos Aires.

Barié, Cletus 2003 *Pueblos indígenas y derechos constitucionales en América Latina: un panorama*. Instituto Indigenista Interamericano, Mexico.

Biset, Ana 1989 El museo de sitio de Añelo. In *Actas, jornadas sobre el uso del pasado. Simposio Administración de Recursos y Manejo de Bienes Culturales Arqueológicos*. Universidad Nacional de La Plata, La Plata.

Carrasco, Morita 2000 *Los derechos de los pueblos indígenas en Argentina*. Vinciguerra-IWGIA, Buenos Aires.

CEPIHA 1999 Hallazgos arqueológicos, entre la ciencia y la identidad. *Andes* 10:245–248.

Cúneo, Estela 2004 Huellas del pasado, miradas del presente: la construcción social del patrimonio arqueológico del Neuquén. *Intersecciones en Antropología* 5:81–94.

Endere, María Luz 2000 *Arqueología y legislación en Argentina. Cómo proteger el patrimonio arqueológico en Argentina*. UNCPBA, Tandil.

———. 2002 The reburial issue in Argentina: A growing conflict. In *The Dead and Their Possessions: Repatriation in Principle, Policy and Practice*, edited by Cressida Fforde, Jane Hubert, and Paul Turnbull, pp. 266–283. Routledge, London.

———. 2007 *Management of Archaeological Sites and the Public in Argentina*. BAR International Series 1708. Archaeopress, Oxford.

Funari, Pedro Paulo Abreu 1994 Paulo Duarte e o Instituto de Pré-História, *Idéias* 1:155–179.

———. 1999 Maroon, race and gender: Palmares material culture and social relations in a runaway settlement. In *Historical Archaeology: Back from the Edge*, edited by Pedro P. A. Funari, Martin Hall, and Siân Jones, pp. 308–327. Routledge, London.

———. 2002 Class interests in Brazilian archaeology. *International Journal of Historical Archaeology* 6:209–216.

Funari, Pedro Paulo Abreu 2004 *Os antigos habitantes do Brasil.* UNESP e Imprensa Oficial do Estado de São Paulo, São Paulo.

Governo do Estado de São Paulo 1997 *Quilombos em São Paulo.* Imesp, São Paulo.

Hualpa, Eduardo 2003 *Sin despojos. Derecho a la participación mapuche-tehuelche.* Cuadernos de ENDEPA, Trelew.

Molinari, Roberto 2000 ¿Posesión o participación? El caso del Rewe de la comunidad Mapuche Ñorquinco (Parque Nacional Lanín, Provincia de Neuquen, Argentina). Paper presented at the Segundo Congreso Virtual de Antropología y Arqueología, UBA, Buenos Aires.

Oliveira, Nanci Vieira 2004 Arqueologia e historia: estúdio de um poblado Jesuítico em Rio de Janeiro. In *Arqueologia histórica em América del Sur. Los desafios del siglo XXI,* edited by Pedro P. A. Funari and Andrés Zarankin, pp. 73–92. Universidad de los Andes, Bogotá.

Podgorny, Irina 2000 *El argentino despertar de las faunas y de las gentes prehistóricas. Coleccionistas, museos, estudiosos y universidad en la Argentina, 1875–1913.* EUDEBA, Buenos Aires.

Podgorny, Irina, and Laura Miotti 1994 El pasado como campo de batalla. *Ciencia Hoy* 5:16–19.

Podgorny, Irina, and Gustavo Politis 1992 ¿Qué sucedió en la historia? Los esqueletos araucanos del Museo de La Plata y la Conquista del Desierto. *Arqueología Contemporánea* 3:73–79.

Politis, Gustavo 1995 The socio-politics of the development of archaeology in Hispanic South America. In *Theory in Archaeology: A World Perspective,* edited by Peter Ucko, pp. 197–228. Routledge, London.

———. 2001 On archaeological praxis, gender bias and indigenous peoples in South America. *Journal of Social Archaeology* 1:90–107.

Reinhard, Johan 1999 A 6,700 metros niños incas sacrificados quedaron congelados en el tiempo. *National Geographic* 5:36–55. Spanish language edition.

Ribeiro, Darcy 1970 *Os índios e a civilização.* Civilização Brasileira, Rio de Janeiro.

Serbín, Andrés 1981 Las organizaciones indígenas en la Argentina. *América Indígena* 41(3):407–434.

Slavsky, Leonor 1992 Los indígenas y la sociedad nacional. Apuntes sobre políticas indigenistas en la Argentina. In *La problemática indígena. Estudios antropológicos sobre pueblos indígenas in Argentina,* edited by Alejandro Balazote and Juan Carlos Radovich, pp. 67–79. Centro Editor de América Latina, Buenos Aires.

Zeballos, Estanislao 1986 [1878] *La conquista de quince mil leguas.* Hyspanoamérica, Buenos Aires.

CHAPTER 9

INDIGENOUS KNOWLEDGE AND ARCHAEOLOGICAL SCIENCE: THE CHALLENGES OF PUBLIC ARCHAEOLOGY IN THE ÁREA INDíGENA DO UAÇÁ

Lesley Green, David R. Green, and Eduardo Góes Neves

INTRODUCTION

At the Fourth World Archaeological Congress (WAC4) held in Cape Town in 1999, a strong case was made that archaeologists should work in ways that might assist the communities associated with their work. At the WAC4 Executive Meeting it was recommended that, among other things, WAC should engage communities in the production of archaeological knowledge. Proposed strategies included public education; professional education and training and action research with the intention of exploring issues relating to conservation and preservation; the management of archaeological resources to ameliorate poverty; and debating the ethical and epistemological frameworks as well as philosophies and principles of archaeological practices (Hassan 1999). Collectively, these strategies form what has become known as public archaeology.

Expressed in the abstract, the above appears to be a reasonable set of goals that can, with sufficient commitment, be included in the pursuit of archaeological and ethnographic enquiry. Seeking to explore postcolonial research methodologies, we set out to establish a public archaeology project in an indigenous area in northern Brazil and sought to implement

A longer version of this chapter was originally published as "Indigenous Knowledge and Archaeological Science: The Challenges of Public Archaeology in the Reserva Uaçá" by Lesley Fordred Green, David R. Green, and Eduardo Góes Neves in the *Journal of Social Archaeology* 3:366–398 (2003). Reprinted with permission from SAGE Publications.

many of the kinds of goals that were under discussion at WAC4. During 12 months of ethnographic fieldwork combined with two months of site surveying and archaeological excavation, however, the complexity of turning ideals into practice is described well by Johannes Fabian's (2001:4) words in *Anthropology with an Attitude*: "The foremost problem [is] the meeting—I prefer confrontation—of kinds of praxis, ours and theirs."

This chapter describes key moments in the confrontation of practices in an indigenous people's reservation known as the Área Indígena do Uaçá, in the Brazilian state of Amapá on the coast between the Amazon River and French Guiana (Figure 9.1). The argument we wish to make is that public archaeology is comprised not of a series of goals and activities additional to the task of archaeology, but rather that public archaeology constitutes a different approach to the production of knowledge (Figure 9.2). This chapter aims to demonstrate that when public archaeology emerges from the interests of communities and not solely from communities of scholars, alternative research questions can develop and practices in the field can begin to be reshaped in the direction of mutuality rather than control. This has significant benefits: a wider range of knowledge about sites can be drawn upon and oral tradition can enrich and indeed transform understanding of the meanings of places.

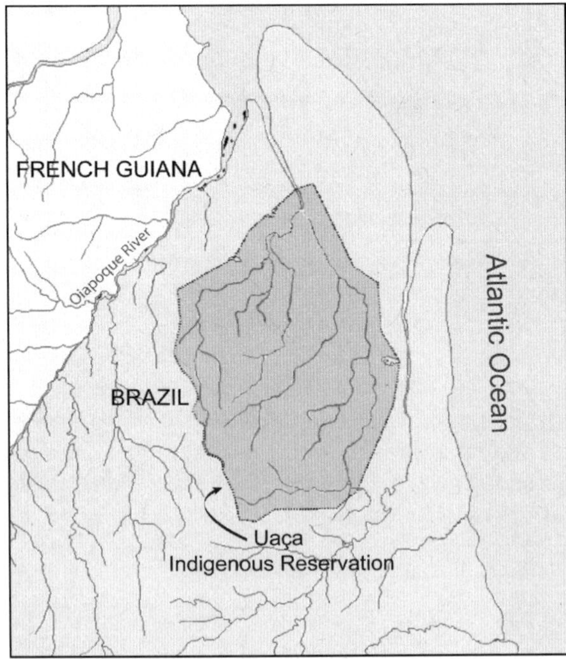

Figure 9.1   Map of the study area.

Figure 9.2 Public archaeology: one of the anthropomorphic urns in the Aristé style that was found by hunters in the region in 2000.

Moreover, by rethinking the range of products of research, the definition and conservation of heritage can be articulated in ways that may have more local value, which ultimately is the only reason that remote sites might find any protection at all.

None of this was easy to implement, however. Some of the challenges we encountered (and discuss later) included having to rethink our own assumptions about "empowerment," particularly if it is considered a one-way process, that archaeological work almost inevitably promotes the commodification of artifacts, and that some historical mythologies about particular sites would make participatory archaeology difficult, if not impossible. Self-consciously working in the domain of the politics of knowledge engendered many inner struggles as we began to question every aspect of the way in which we were working. Yet only through confronting different practices—theirs and ours—could we proceed and, difficult as it might have been, that confrontation was ultimately what produced the qualitatively different knowledge that begins to emerge from participatory work. To cite Fabian (2001:25):

There is an agonistic connotation to "confrontation" that we need to maintain for at least two reasons: (a) to counteract the anodyne, apolitical, conciliatory aura that surrounds "communication" (and for that matter "dialogue") and (b) to indicate that the "move toward ethnographic knowledge" can initiate a process only once it encounters resistance in the form of incomprehension, denial, rejection, or, why not, simply Otherness.

Public archaeology as a methodology generated an engagement in the field that, while tough, was more productive than an alternative could have been. While the question of ethical practice in postcolonial archaeology came into a relief that was sharp enough to be uncomfortable, perhaps—as Martin Hall suggests in a paper on the topic—the resolution of many of the dilemmas we faced is necessarily situational (Hall 2003).

BACKGROUND

The understanding of the impact of European colonization on Amerindian precolonial patterns of sociopolitical organization is one of the most important topics of contemporary Amazonian archaeology. Indigenous oral tradition and early historical reports both attest that, during the last 500 years, native Amazonian societies were deeply transformed, if not exterminated, due to slavery, diseases, or displacement, but the archaeological data on which to base such claims is still ambiguous (Brochado 1980; Lathrap 1968, 1970; Neves 1999b; Roosevelt 1991). Given such a picture, it is important to identify areas in the Amazon where there is a minimum of discontinuity between contemporary societies and precolonial occupations, as they have a greater potential to be understood through archaeological fieldwork. In situations such as these, archaeological information can be combined with ethnography and indigenous oral tradition. The Área Indígena do Uaçá or Uaçá Indian Reservation seems to be one of the few areas of the Brazilian Amazon where a task such as this could be accomplished. Early historical reports indicate that the Oiapoque and Uaçá basins were occupied, in the sixteenth century, by the ancestors of some of the contemporary Indigenous societies who are settled in the region (Arnaud 1971, 1984; Coudreau 1886; Gallois and Ricardo 1983; Grenand and Grenand 1987; Harcourt 1967 [1613]; Keymis 1968 [1596]; Nimuendajú 1926; Williamson 1923). Among these are a group currently known as the Palikur.

Archaeological work in the region was previously conducted by Hilbert (1957), based on the work of Meggers and Evans (1957) and preliminary explorations by Goeldi (1900), Nimuendajú (1926), and Nordenskiold (1930). More recently, Rostain (1994a, 1994b) has studied the material record of indigenous settlements on the French Guianan side.

Palikur populations along the Urucauá River in the Uaçá basin had been decimated by the mid-1920s when, according to Curt Nimuendajú's records, only 238 survived (Nimuendajú 1926:22). Four hundred years earlier, Palikur Indians had been numerous enough at the mouth of the Amazon for the early Spanish explorer Vincente Yañez Pinzon to testify, according to a deposition made to a Spanish court in 1513, that in 1500 he found the lengthy coastline west of the Amazon to have been known to Indians as "the Province of the Paricura" (Williams 1975:6). Based on this information, many early maps labeled it thus. Indeed, the Amazon River itself was called Paricura by one of Pinzon's companions, who testified to this in court in 1515 (Williams 1975:6, citing De Navarrete 1954:321). Grenand and Grenand (1987) paint a picture of a populous alliance of clans consolidated under the name of Palikur. These settlements stretched the length of what is today the state of Amapá and adjoining French Guiana.

Contemporary Palikur speakers number approximately 2000, with approximately one-half living in semiurban settlements in French Guiana and the other half resident in villages along the upper reaches of the Urucauá River on the Brazilian side of the border: a landscape that is regarded as homeland and heartland. Near the confluence of the Urucauá and the Uaçá is the small village of Flexa, home to people self-identified as Galibi-Marworno Indians who speak a French Creole. Some Palikur have settled in Flexa, but little Palikur is spoken in the village despite the dominance of the Palikur language on the Urucauá.

Relations between Palikur and Galibi-Marworno are in some respects strained, as the Arawak-Carib wars that ended in the seventeenth century played a significant role in the decimation of both groups. Consequently, cultural essentialisms became, at times, a source of difficulty in relation to archaeological sites.

Oral history research among the Palikur by David (a fluent Palikur speaker) and Lesley in 1997 brought up a wealth of narratives about the past with many references to places with archaeological significance, including boot-shaped caverns similar to those described by Emílio Goeldi in 1895 in the region of the Rio Cunani (Goeldi 1900) and sites that were landmarks in wars with Galibi Indians that occurred in the sixteenth and seventeenth centuries (Harcourt 1967 [1613]; Keymis 1968 [1596]; and the sixteenth-century voyages of Leigh, cited in Williamson 1923). On survey it was apparent that several sites had been damaged, reportedly both by some people looking for commodities to sell and by others who saw no value in the ceramic or stone artifacts and destroyed them for the "no particular reason" that is that our sense of "heritage" was not shared. The cause of the apparent sense of the worthlessness of the sites was one of the major reasons for pursuing this project.

Initially we hypothesized that the lack of a sense of history and heritage derived from a pervasive feeling of disempowerment related to political change as well as to religious change—though ethnographic research taught us to pay attention to the ways in which different forms of historiography are grounded in particular ontologies of space and time. Believing that the sites were worth investigating further for these reasons as well as their archaeological value, David and Lesley Green met with Eduardo Neves during WAC4 in 1999 to discuss the beginning of an interdisciplinary collaboration. Fieldwork took place over a total of 12 months in three separate excursions to the region in 2000 and 2001, thanks to generous grants from the Wenner Gren Foundation, the National Research Foundation of South Africa, and the World Archaeological Congress.

RESEARCH ACTIVITIES

Ethnographic enquiry—the responsibility of Green and Green—had the goal of collecting a comprehensive set of oral-historical texts and information about possible sites, as well as seeking to understand local power and practices that would need to be accounted for in any archaeological work. An ethnographic understanding of local lifeways proved vital, particularly with regard to the articulation of landscape, historiography and myth, sociality and approaches to power, and the production and appropriation of local identities. Over a dozen storytellers were interviewed in seven Palikur villages along the Urucauá River, with multiple versions of particular stories sought for comparative purposes. These were transcribed and translated into Portuguese by Palikur speakers. Currently, some 230 performances of stories on digital video are in our database. Since the majority of stories refer to particular places in the landscape—of particular interest in an archaeological enquiry—a number of people were invited to participate in the production of a large-format memory map of contemporary Palikur lands.

For several months in 2001, a program of public education included setting up the poster display and a small library, as well as a television and video player powered by a solar panel to show videos on related subjects as well as footage from the sites.[1]

After several months it was planting season and people began to visit carrying fragments of pots, whole pots, and stone axes that they had found in the ground where new fields were being planted; this was material that usually would have been thrown away. Among the most interesting finds was an ancient wooden paddle, the size, shape, and decoration of which no one remembered but which was remarkably similar to a seafaring paddle drawn in 1743 by P. Barrere (illustrated in Rostain 1994a, vol. II:Fig. 209). Photographs of ceramic figurines also elicited much interest, with indications from some that they had found similar items before but had simply thrown them away.

Archaeological investigations were directed by Eduardo Neves. The major goal in 2000 was to investigate sites that were identified in popular memory as those at which key events in ethnohistory took place. We sought to visit these and assess the conditions for further, systematic, research in the area. Recognizing that the only way to ensure the preservation of remote sites would be if local people attributed value to doing so, we sought a process that would integrate archaeological research with indigenous ways of doing history, including local people in decisions and research activities. A key issue was that informed consent was almost impossible to assure in the absence of any prior exposure to archaeology. For that reason, three Palikur—Avelino Labonté, Tabenkwe Manoel Labonté, and Ivanildo Gômes—were invited to attend three weeks of an archaeological field school near Manaus in July 2001 (Figures 9.3a and b), and on the basis of their report back to local leadership, permission was granted to proceed with the first formal excavation work in November 2001. Accompanying Neves for the excavation work was a team of three Brazilian archaeologists who worked both as excavators and trainers. The location of the work was decided in conjunction with leaders and in consultation with residents at a public meeting.

At that meeting interested people were invited to sign up to work on the excavation of a large site at a place called Kwap. We sought to train as many people as possible and brought in a fresh crew of four every three days, with three working the entire period in order to provide some continuity. When the excavation was completed we held an Open Day. Four boatloads of people—about 100 in all, or one in 10 of the Palikur population on the river—made their way upriver to visit Kwap (Figures 9.4 and 9.5) and were guided by Neves from test pit to test pit (Figure 9.6) as he explained the soil profiles, described the artifacts found, and suggested links with oral history. The degree of interest and enthusiasm far outweighed our expectations.

Rethinking Research Questions

The research questions with which we began asked whether the Aristé-style artifacts found at two of the sites were more widespread, whether additional styles could be located at deeper levels at particular sites, and whether archaeological research, supported by oral-historical research, could illuminate questions about the complexity of occupation in this part of the coastal Amazon region. In particular, we were interested in the possibility of anthropogenic landscapes. An additional interest was investigating frequent mention of a shellmound (known in Brazil by the

Figure 9.3   Tabenkwe Manoel Labonté (a) and Ivanildo Gômes (b), two of three Palikur who attended an archaeological field school near Manaus in July 2001, in order to be able to make an informed judgment on whether or not an excavation should proceed on home ground.

Tupi word *sambaqui*). At all of these sites, we were interested in whether and how they are present in memories, their particular histories, and whether they could be said to constitute heritage to local people.

Within days of arrival in May 2000, we had learned the awkward truth that however important and relevant our research questions had seemed, the scholarly debates from which they emerge are worlds apart from everyday life along the Rio Urucauá. There, dominant concerns are the daily struggle to produce enough food, protect access to Indian

Figure 9.4 November 2001: the day's team of participatory archaeologists en route to the excavation at Kwap. In the foreground is Eduardo Neves (left) and Avelino Labonté (right).

Figure 9.5 On the Rio Urucauá, Tabenkwe Manoel Labonté points out the limits of the old village of Kwap to Eduardo Neves.

Figure 9.6 Kwap, November 2001: after the augur tests came the task of delineating the test pits. On the team are, left to right, Geo Iôiô, Juvenal Felício, Lega Labonté, and Matías Labonté.

lands, ensure health, and, at least in 2000 in the biggest Palikur village, keep right with God in preparation for a Pentecostal rendering of Y2K and its possible apocalyptic outcomes (Capiberibe 2007; Passes 1998). In that context, our interest in the past and in the ceramic sherds that we claimed were worthless in monetary terms proved difficult to explain—especially given that we had funds for wages, solar panels, and an outboard motor. The constant fear of many Palikur that Brazilians were going to come and take their lands made some doubly suspicious. Thus, one of our biggest challenges was to develop research questions that had resonance and interest to local people, while trying to explain archaeological work.

One of the ways we chose to do the latter was by bringing with us a large-format, full-color book on Brazilian archaeology, which we acquired at the exhibition known as the "Brasil + 500 Mostra de Redescobrimento," which had opened in São Paulo in 2000 as part of the Brazilian celebration of the 500th anniversary of its "discovery" (despite protestation from some of the more vocal indigenous groups that they had been there all along). Part of a celebratory discourse of the state's capacity to collect, the archaeological exhibition focused on the most prized ceramics in Brazil, most of which were labeled by place of origin, the contemporary collection from which they were sourced, and, for the most part, the culture that they were purported to represent. Unfortunately, in this context the collection of photographs of urns and ceramics in the book (Scatamacchia 2000) was interpreted as proof that archaeology was seeking after treasures, implicitly promoting the idea of artifacts as commodities and undermining our claims that we were not there to collect pots or make a profit.

Reflecting on our idea of archaeology, the phrase we came up with, in conjunction with local leadership, to describe archaeology was *ikiska anavi wayk'* or the study of "things left behind in the ground." Eighteen months later when 22 people had been trained in excavation techniques and were learning to read soil profiles at the test pits, the dialogics of reciprocal learning had produced a very different phrase—*ivegboha amekenegben gidukwankis* (reading the tracks of the ancestors). The switch of explanatory terms for archaeology reflects the extent to which participatory and ethnographic research had shifted our focus from an object-based archaeology to something closer to a relational ontology. Understanding what that meant required careful, long-term ethnographic research that sought to unpack, in the first instance, the idea of a spatiotemporal history (Green and Green 2003) in which archaeological questions can be formulated around the relationalities that are embedded in the landscape. Chronologies and dates, in this view, are deemphasized. Such emphases have many connections with the kinds of landscape archaeology that have become dominant in contemporary Brazilian archaeology—in particular, Roosevelt's work on moundbuilders (1991) and Heckenberger, Neves, and Petersen's (1998) project on *terra preta* (black soils) in the central Amazon. By emphasizing environmental skill and social complexity, our questions about indigenous history became of greater interest to local people.

After reviewing the oral-historical data that had been collected during two field trips in 2000, we chose to focus archaeological research on the long war between what are now identified as the Palikur (Arawak) and the Galibi (Carib), and their complex allegiances with European forces (particularly English, Dutch, Portuguese, and French) that were contesting the Oiapoque region. These questions (together with practical considerations concerning access to sites afforded by the low water level in November and December) made the old village of Kwap a logical choice for the first excavation work. Kwap was, according to oral history, a very big village ("like a city," said many) that on survey had yielded up to 1.8 m of *terra preta,* which, in a landscape of soils that are otherwise a deep orange, was indicative of either lengthy or intensive occupation. The settlement was destroyed in the final battle of the war, which the Palikur won against the Galibi. Oral tradition holds that so many died that they were buried where they had fallen and a portion of the site is today the main cemetery for settlements on the upper reaches of the Urucauá.

One of the leaders' conditions for excavation was that it be outside the known cemetery area. Using a theodolite, the area was mapped and systematic augur tests conducted; thereafter a number of locations were selected as test pits, of which soil profiles were examined. In addition, a profile was dug across what appeared to have been a defensive ditch and a wide pathway going up a steep hill to the old village site, both features that were detailed in oral histories collected prior to the excavation.[2]

Reworking Research Practices

Mutuality, rather than control, is not easily achieved if a particular notion of science is dominant. The methodologies required to produce valid results produced encounters that forced us to rethink our assumptions about empowerment, consultation, essentialism, and historiography.

Power, Empowerment, and "Community"

The notion of "community" is not only deconstructed by many academics but also by several residents who are all too familiar with the use of the word in development discourse. Some were quick to challenge our occasional use of the term, asking who within the community would benefit the most from the work we proposed. The questions pointed to awareness that the power that comes with empowerment cannot be considered neutral or without a context. An entire community cannot be empowered simultaneously; certain individuals will be more empowered than others, with the implication that empowerment activities alter the social landscape as they proceed.

Consultation, Debate, and Mutuality

Participatory action research (PAR) appeared to be the most useful strategy for pursuing a public archaeology project of this kind. Yet PAR assumes that a style of vigorous public debate is possible. In the context of our work, however, vigorous debate is frowned upon (Passes 1998, 2000). By contrast, public agreement is valorized. In the Kumenê village where we lived, public meetings generally go on for many hours, during which many people step forward one by one to reflect on the topic non-confrontationally, after which a recognized leader proposes a way forward, initiating a fresh round of opinion offering. Difficult issues might be considered for several evenings over several weeks. In our case, attempts to make decisions collectively with fieldworkers when site surveying in 2000 were problematic, as some could and often did seize the moment to claim to speak for all, while those who had been present but had not spoken their disagreement aloud would discreetly offer their opinion privately in the days that followed. After a while it became clear that, even with a small group, achieving consensus was a complicated matter. In 2001, during the second phase of the work, we adopted the strategy of seeking advice from a smaller group of respected people prior to major decisions and to advise as many as possible that the meeting was to be held with an open door so that those who wished to listen or join in could do so. It was also important for us to listen to privately offered counsel, after meetings and publicly-offered gossip (the latter being difficult to deal with, but a primary mode of censure if people disapprove of or are uncertain of one's actions), and take both into account in our decision making. Despite all this, key decisions effectively remained ours. It was not the total mutuality we had hoped for, but given our experiences we would doubt any claim made of complete mutuality in a comparable project. A research team with a cargo of expensive goods and the weight of science behind them has tremendous power, however delicate their reflexivities.

Identity Claims and Essentialism

Archaeological and ethnohistoric work is inevitably drawn into questions of "beginnings" and "authenticity"—and easily complicit in the formation of narratives of ethnicity that are by definition exclusionary. Among the most frequently told historical narratives along the upper Rio Urucauá is that of a long war between the Palikur and the Galibi. However, several scholars, notably Francoise and Pierre Grenand (1987) and Lux Vidal (1999), argue convincingly that the identities indexed by these names now are significantly different from those that carried them in the 1600s and 1700s in terms of social organization, ancestry, cultural activities, and language. Grenand and Grenand make a strong case that contemporary Palikur identity emerged out of alliances between many groups against common enemies.

Despite this extensive disruption of societies and associated identities and in response to it, contemporary Palikur identity can be characterized as strongly felt. In large measure this is due to the survival of a language now known as Palikur, in contrast to many other Indian groups in the region, which use Creoles and have lost the languages of their forefathers. Palikur-language oral testimony recalls the formation of alliances of what are now known as "clans" and the decision to adopt the dialect of a dominant group now known as the Kamuyune, or the Sun Clan[3] (Grenand and Grenand 1987; Passes 2002).

A major challenge, then, is to find context-appropriate ways to distinguish between the historical emergence of identities and the appropriation of history to support contemporary structures of social power as they engage state politics based on cultural identity.

For many politically engaged scholars there is, in the words of Brubaker and Cooper (2000:12), "an uneasy amalgam [in scholarship] of constructivist language and essentialist argumentation ... [reflecting] the dual orientation of many academic identitarians as both analysts and protagonists of identity politics."

One has to ask the question, if essentialism has local value, how is one to avoid appealing to it? In the context of working with a group whose numbers have dropped below that which is considered viable for the survival of their language, should one seek to work against essentialisms, even if they elide the complexities and contingencies of historical processes of identity formation?

During fieldwork our strategy was to identify our work as recording the histories of the river (which includes settlements from both sides) rather than a history of the Palikur or the Galibi. Yet essentialist sentiments were a frequent undercurrent in our river of fluid identities. The two issues, then, are how to speak of these matters in analysis and how to speak of them in the field. Discussing the analytical use of the term "identity," Brubaker and Cooper (2000:20–21) offer a way forward:

> The point is not ... to turn from commonality to connectedness, from categories to networks, from shared attributes to social relations. Nor is it to celebrate fluidity and hybridity over belonging and solidarity. The point ... is rather to develop an analytical idiom sensitive to the multiple forms and degrees of commonality and connectedness and to the widely varying ways in which actors ... attribute meaning and significance to them.

A public archaeology process with a deep investment in oral-historical research provides the resources that enables one to debate, with research participants, contemporary versions of a story that promote the reification of identities and minimize the appropriation of archaeological work to essentialist ends.

Archaeology and Mythological History: Confronting the Question of Historiography

The question of historiography was a constant challenge, not least in that the distinction between history and myth is not an emic one (Passes 2002). In this corner of the Amazon, as elsewhere, history may take very different forms from those of the West. Perhaps one of the main reasons for this is that

> we commonly define historicity as embodied in chronological or linear narratives, without accepting that these are characteristics of the European

theory of time, inextricably bound up in the process of the European conquest of the globe ... [W]e have come to accept our own temporal framework as natural and given, according second place to the historical schema of the conquered. (Rappaport 1990:11)

Over time, we began to grasp the tenets of a way of speaking about the past that cohered neither chronologically nor around historical figures, but around spatiality—constituting a spatiotemporal history (Green and Green 2003).

At the same time, such a notion—or cultural history—of a landspace includes the underworld and the upperworlds, and all the spirits and shape-shifting creatures that move between them and the surface world. A historiography of this kind poses significant challenges for an archaeology in which the fantastical and the fabulous are generally excluded from explanations (although archaeological finds are all too readily appropriated to fabulous ends in nationalist myth making).

While there are several sets of stories that might approximate the "chapters" of the canon of Palikur oral history, they should not be understood as a consecutive chronology, although some clearly refer to earlier times than others. Rather, they may be seen as comments on a range of issues that are considered important in times past. These narrative sets or chapters within the canon appeal to different conditions of truth; to put it another way, they constitute a range of historical principles. For our purposes what was important to recognize was that the histories of different sites draw on different historiographical forms, some of which pose greater challenges for archaeological work than others.

The challenge, then, was to understand that where a single site has multiple appropriations, excavation can dismember some meanings at the expense of others. Histories based on laboratory results and soil profiles are meaningful in a particular context and are not unencumbered truths that make sense universally.

One route for public archaeology here would be to prioritize local versions of history over professional assessment of the material record. Yet such an approach is unsatisfactory assuming only incommensurability. The question becomes this, in a public archaeology project, is it possible to proceed at archaeological sites with as much caution over narratives and sensibilities as artifacts?

If unthinking excavation can bury meaning, one has to accept one of two conclusions. The first possible conclusion is that where radically opposed understandings of the past surround a particular site or series of sites, one should retreat from further work there. The second is more delicate: to explore the value of multiple historicities, without assuming that one is engaging only a singular culturalist historiography. Key to an equitable public archaeology, in our view, is the recognition that multiple forms of history are possible in any context, which might have different kinds of validity from those that are dominant in the generally sanctioned archaeological episteme. A genuinely *public* archaeology, then, would be open to engaging multiple ways of finding and forming histories.

RETHINKING THE OUTCOMES OF RESEARCH

Research products are always both tangible and intangible. The tangible research products of a public archaeology project are in progress and include the creation of an oral history archive; educational materials based on archaeological, ethnographic, and oral research; and contributions to archaeological debates. In several respects the intangibles are ethnographically more interesting—the consequences of the verification of oral history; the consequences of training three people from the Urucauá in the craft of archaeological work well enough to participate in contract work elsewhere; the possibility that the work might contribute to the independent effort to establish a community museum and assist in creating the conditions that would enable an Amerindian engagement with sciences and dominant rationalities.

While comment on many of these issues can only be speculative, the case of the pots found in an underground burial cavern (Figure 9.7) with no attached oral history, near to a Galibi-Marworno settlement, brought the twin issues of heritage and its commodification into sharp relief.

Heritage, Its Ownership and Commodification

While beginning an oral history project in the area in 1997, David heard about a man who, some years before, had found a small cave in which were lodged about nine beautiful pots. The man had taken them to his home. By 1997, only four remained. David visited him, filmed the pots, and went with him to the cavern in which they had been hidden. Study of the photographs suggested that they were very similar to the Rio Cunani style found some 200 km south by the Swiss naturalist Emílio Goeldi in 1895, in one of the more celebrated finds of Brazilian archaeology. At the beginning of this project, we sought to make contact with the man once again. Circumstances had changed, however, and he had left his village. His brother and father controlled the site and wanted to limit access to it.

After protracted negotiations, they agreed to let the three of us and four field guides visit the site to photograph and sketch it and take a few samples for ceramic analysis. While walking to the site, three of the four

Figure 9.7 Zecão Iôiô with a tiny urn found in an underground cavern.

field guides engaged us at length on what we—the researchers—would do in the hypothetical situation that whole pots were found. Would we take control of them? Would we take them away? Would we tell the government? Could anyone still sell them?

Some weeks later a story emerged that two of the field guides had found four pots on the same island a year before when lost while hunting. It had been a dry year with very little rain and in the darkness, they said, they had crossed the dry creek that separates the islands without realizing it. Under a rocky outcrop they discovered four extraordinarily beautiful pots, but had never found the place again. To prevent anyone else taking the pots, they had hidden them under a tree, where they had remained for a year. When we journeyed to the island, they said, they had recognized the area, searched for, and found them. They described beautiful painting and anthropomorphic features on the urns, similar to the Aristé-style urns depicted in the archaeological book we had brought with us.

The pots and the manner of their discovery presented a series of ethical dilemmas. People who find artifacts want the individual right to dispose of them as they please; in addition, there were competing senses of entitlement to the site. The field guides felt entitled to the pots because they found them and because historically they believed their ancestors had made them (although we were not able to find any oral history teller with any knowledge of them). By contrast, the family who had discovered the urns earlier felt entitled to the site because it was close to their settlement, on an island where they had hunting rights.

All of this brought into focus the ethics of practice in public archaeology, in the context of the consequences that we could foresee of various possible courses of action.

Our first question to ourselves was that if our archaeological work is committed to the furtherance of scholarly debate (which it is), could we find ways to address the question of the production of knowledge from such urns without seizing them in the name of science? We believed that photographing and sketching was sufficient in the short term and believed that the social network around the pots was unlikely to lead to their sale to an unknown buyer.

A second question was whether public archaeology ought to be focused on the mobilization of cultural material for the advancement of indigenous people and the creation of "subaltern publics" (Hall 2003:16–20) or whether the material ought to have been considered national patrimony and crated immediately for dispatch to an archaeological storage facility. If the latter were to be the course of action, the consequence would be the closure of access to similar sites and the promotion of artifact commodification.

In the situation in which we found ourselves, the beginnings of a community ecomuseum in the region offered the possibility of an acceptable location, although, as there was no immediate plan to equip it with humidity control, it could not yet offer the appropriate storage environment, making the museum at Macapá, 500 km away, the nearest facility.

One of the team of field guides suggested that the urns be returned to the underground cavern from which they had come. But, if that were to be done, there was little guarantee that others would neither take them nor break them. If, on the other hand, the advancement of indigenous people was a goal, is "advancement" to be defined individually or collectively?

Rightly or wrongly, we felt we had to hold to the principle that we were not there to buy pots. We would also not seize any artifacts, as that would destroy relationships and frustrate further archaeological work.

Recognizing that both ethical practice and commodities are defined by social consensus, our decision was to seek to protect the urns through establishing a network of social relationships around them. We discussed the situation with both the Chefe do Posto and the *cacique*. Both expressed the opinion that whole urns ought not to leave the reservation, although as per our prior agreements, sherds could be taken away for analysis and returned at some future date.

Public archaeologists, ourselves included, need to debate these questions with the publics we seek to serve and with national statutory bodies that control material heritage. For ethics in such situations are, we believe, necessarily situational and need to be decided in terms of the primary purposes of each project. In our case one of the primary purposes of the project was to foster a sense of the importance of material heritage—a principle shared directly with the Brazilian Instituto do Patrimônio Historico e Artistico Nacional (Institute of National Historical Patrimony and the Arts, or IPHAN), which is in charge of archaeological licensing in Brazil. In choosing not to take away the urns, we were protecting many more sites in the region than this one, yet that course of action risks censure.

In considering the question of ethical practice in politically engaged archaeology, World Archaeological Congress President (1999–2003) Martin Hall (2003:18) concludes:

> If one accepts the case for situational ethics and the inevitable alignment between the researcher and one or more reference groups within the society that is being studied, then it follows that ethical research will recognize the nexus of knowledge, power and politics and declare its alignments explicitly ... Recognizing the role of power and politics in research is, then, central to an appropriate ethics.

CONCLUSIONS

While many archaeologists remain dismissive of public archaeology, in contexts like the jungle on an indigenous people's reservation in northern Brazil the only practical means by which archaeology might be pursued is via a process of public participation. Participatory research shifted our understanding of heritage from one that focuses on material culture to one that focuses on the heritage of skills that are required, historically and contemporarily, to dwell in this landscape. In our experience, this shift enabled an engagement with different ways of understanding time and land and compelled the rethinking of the production of archaeological knowledge. The work challenged notions of heritage, ethics, historiography, practices of research, and assumptions about community participation. Such an approach to field research is challenging, and via these kinds of encounters public archaeology can begin to engage the politics and contingencies of epistemological practices.

NOTES

We are grateful to the following archaeological colleagues who assisted with the excavation: Rafael Bartolomucci, Carlos Augusto da Silva, and Marcos Castro, and to Palikur assistants Lega Edivaldo Labonté, Avelino Labonté, Tabenkwe Manoel Labonté, Ivanildo

Gômes, Fernando Iaparra, Matias Labonté, Qualeyn Batista, and Xoni Batista. We also wish to thank Martin Hall, Lynn Meskell, and the reviewers of the *Journal of Social Archaeology* for comments on this paper. The financial assistance of the National Research Foundation, the World Archaeological Congress Educational Fund, the University of Cape Town, and the Wenner Gren Foundation for Anthropological Research toward this research is gratefully acknowledged.

1. The library resources and the television with solar panels were donated to the village.
2. Laboratory work on soil samples and ceramic fragments is in progress but was delayed by a range of factors, including the political question of in which Brazilian state such work should proceed.
3. Information from one of the leaders of the church in Kumene village, João Felício, in 2001.

REFERENCES

Arnaud, Expedito 1971 Os indios Oyampik e Emerilon (Rio Oiapoque). *Boletim do Museu Paraense Emílio Goeldi* 47. Belem.

———. 1984 *Os indios Palikur do rio: tradição tribal e protestantismo*. Museu Goeldi Publicações Avulsas 39. Belem.

Brochado, José Proenza 1980 The Social Ecology of the Marajoara Culture. Unpublished Master's thesis, Department of Archaeology, University of Illinois, Urbana.

Brubaker, Rogers, and Frederick Cooper 2000 Beyond identity. *Theory and Society* 29:1–47.

Capiberibe, Artionka 2007 *Batismo de fogo: os Palikur e o Cristianismo*. Annablume Editora, São Paulo.

Coudreau, Henri 1886 *Etudes sur les Guyanes et L'Amazonie*. Librarie Coloniale, Paris.

———. 1887 *Voyage a travers les Guyanes et L'Amazonie*. Librarie Coloniale, Paris.

De Navarrete, Martin Fernández 1954 *Colección de los viajes y descubrimientos que hicieron por mar los españoles desde fines del siglo XV*, vol. 3. Ediciones Atlas, Madrid.

Dreyfus, Simone 1983 Historical and political anthropological interconnections: The multilinguistic indigenous polity of the Carib islands and mainland coast from the 16th to the 18th century. *Antropologica* 59–62:39–55.

———. 1993 Les reseaux politiques indigenes en Guyane occidentale et leurs transformations aux XXVII et XVIII siecles. *L'Homme* 126/128:75–97.

Fabian, Johannes 2001 *Anthropology with an Attitude*. Stanford University Press, Stanford.

Gallois, Dominique, and Carlos Alberto Ricardo 1983 Os Palikur. In *Povos indigenas no Brasil*, vol. 3, pp. 18–39. CEDI, São Paulo.

Goeldi, Emílio 1900 *Excavacoes archeologicas em 1895. I parte: as cavernas funerarias artificiaes de indios hoje extinctos no rio Cunany (Coanany) e sua cerámica*. Memorias do Museu Goeldi, Belem.

Green, Harold, and Diana Green 1997 The war with the Galibí, versions 1–4. Interlinear texts. Sociedade Internacionale de Lingüistica, Belém.

Green, Lesley, and David Green 2000 Of historiography and public archaeology: Explorations in the Área Indígena do Uaçá, northern Brazil. Paper presented to the Department of Social Anthropology Seminar Series, University of Cape Town.

———. 2003 From chronological to spatial histories? The challenges of mapping heritage in Arukwa, Área Indígena do Uaçá, Brazil. Paper presented at the 99th Meeting of the Association of American Geographers, New Orleans.

Grenand, Francoise, and Pierre Grenand 1987 La cote d'Amapá, de la bouche de l'Amazone a la baie d'Oyapock, a travers la tradition orale Palikur. *Boletim do Museu Paraense Emílio Goeldi* 3(1):1–77.

Hall, Martin 2003 Situational ethics and engaged practice: The case of archaeology in Africa. Paper read at the Centre for African Studies, University of Cape Town.

Harcourt, Robert 1967 [1613] A relation of a voyage to Guiana. In *A Relation of a Voyage to Guiana by Robert Harcourt 1613*, edited by C. Alexander Harris. Nendeln, Liechtenstein.

Hassan, Fekri 1999 Notes on the WAC Executive Meeting, Cape Town, World Archaeological Congress IV conference website, http://www.wac.uct.ac.za, accessed January 1999.

Heckenberger, Michael, Eduardo Neves, and James Petersen 1998 De onde surgem os modelos? As origens e expansões Tupi na Amazônia Central. *Revista de Antropologia* 41(1):69–96.

Hilbert, Peter 1957 *Contribuicao a arqueologia do Amapá*. Museu Paraense Emílio Goeldi, Belem.

Keymis, Laurence 1968 [1596] *A Relation of the Second Voyage to Guiana*. Da Capo Press, New York.

Lathrap, Donald 1968 The hunting economies of the tropical forest zone of South America. In *Man the Hunter*, edited by Richard Lee and Irven DeVore, pp. 23–29. Aldine, Chicago.

———. 1970 *The Upper Amazon*. Thames and Hudson, London.

Meggers, Betty, and Clifford Evans 1957 *Archaeological Investigations at the Mouth of the Amazon*. Bulletin 167, Bureau of American Ethnology, Smithsonian Institution, Washington, DC.

Neves, Eduardo 1998a Twenty years of Amazonian archaeology in Brazil. *Antiquity* 72:624–632.

———. 1998b Paths in Dark Water: Archaeology as Indigenous History in the Upper Rio Negro Basin, Northwest Amazon. Unpublished Ph.D. dissertation, Department of Archaeology, Indiana University, Bloomington.

———. 1999a Complexity or not in the Amazon? Paper presented at the IV World Archaeological Congress, Cape Town.

———. 1999b Changing perspectives in Amazonian archaeology. In *Archaeology in Latin America*, edited by Gustavo Politis and Benjamin Alberti, pp. 216–243. Routledge, London.

Nimuendajú, Curt 1926 *Die Palikur indianer und ihre nachbarn*. Elanders Boktryckeri Aktiebolag, Gotemburg.

Nordenskiold, Erland 1930 *L'archeologie du bassin de l'Amazone*. Les Editions G van Oest, Paris.

Passes, Alan 1998 The Hearer, the Hunter and the Agouti Head. Aspects of Intercommunication and Conviviality among the Pa'ikwene (Palikur) of French Guiana. Unpublished Ph.D. dissertation, Department of Anthropology, University of St. Andrews, Edinburgh.

———. 2000 The value of working and speaking together: A facet of Pa'ikwene (Palikur) conviviality. In *The Anthropology of Love and Anger*, edited by Joanna Overing and Alan Passes, pp. 97–113. Routledge, London.

———. 2002 Both omphalos and margin: On how the Pa'ikwene (Palikur) see themselves to be at the centre and on the edge at the same time. In *Comparative Arawakan Histories: Rethinking Language, Family and Culture Area in Amazonia*, edited by Jonathan Hill and Fernando Santos, pp. 171–195. University of Illinois Press, Urbana.

Rappaport, Joanne 1990 *The Politics of Memory*. Cambridge University Press, Cambridge.

Roosevelt, Anna 1991 *Moundbuilders of the Amazon: Geophysical Archaeology on Marajó Island, Brazil*. Academic Press, San Diego.

Rostain, Stefan 1994a L'occupation amerindienne ancienne du littoral de Guyane. Unpublished Ph.D. dissertation, Centre de Recherche en Archaeologie Precolombienne, Université de Paris I, Paris.

———. 1994b The French Guiana coast: A key area in prehistory between the Orinoco and Amazon rivers. In *Between St. Eustatius and the Guianas: Contributions to*

Caribbean Archaeology, edited by Aad Versteeg, pp. 53–99. The St. Eustatius Historical Foundation, St. Eustatius.

Scatamacchia, Maria Cristina Mineiro 2000 *Arqueologia*. Fundação Bienal de São Paulo, São Paulo.

Shanks, Michael, and Randall McGuire 1996 The craft of archaeology. *American Antiquity* 61(1):75–88.

Vidal, Lux Boelitz 1999 O modelo e a marca, ou o estilo dos "misturados": cosmologia, historia e estetica entre os povos indígenas do Uaçá. *Revista de Antropología* 42(1):29–45.

Williams, Donn Alan 1975 Brazil and French Guiana: The Four-Hundred Year Struggle for Amapá. Unpublished Ph.D. dissertation, Texas Christian University, Fort Worth, Texas.

Williamson, James 1923 *English Colonies in Guiana and on the Amazon 1604–1668*. Clarendon Press, Oxford.

PART II

INDIGENOUS ARCHAEOLOGY, ARCHAEOLOGY FOR INDIGENOUS PEOPLES

CHAPTER 10

VINDICATIONS OF A MESOAMERICAN MARGINAL GROUP: THE OTOMÍES FROM THE VALLEY OF THE MEZQUITAL

Fernando López Aguilar

THE CONSTRUCTION OF AN IMAGE

When Hernán Cortés first arrived in the territory that today is part of the Mexican nation, he found a large medley of different groups, political associations, and languages that brought him face to face with a complex reality not easy to understand for a Western mind. Almost all people could without any trouble speak two, three, or four languages. Most political entities (*altepeme*) were in a permanent state of war among themselves, even if they could recognize a common enemy, the Anahuac empire, that, guided by its leader (*Huey-Tlatoani*) Moctezuma II, dominated the southern half of the current Mexican territory.

Using as a comparison their experience with the native groups of the Caribbean they had met some decades before, the Europeans initially thought that it was possible to impose the Catholic faith in the newly discovered territory with order and force. Yet, the images, ideas, and cultural discoveries made by the conquerors (both military and religious) during the years of the conquest and evangelization, sifted through their views and preconceptions, led to a representation of the social medley that was far from the homogeneity they expected (Guzmán 2002:22).

When bursting into the nuclear territory of the Aztec empire, the central highlands (Figure 10.1), they not only were surprised by the magnificence of the capitals of the Triple Alliance, but also discovered that there were two languages in common use—Mexican, as Nahoa was called back then, and Otomí. Other languages were also spoken, but with less frequency, such as Chichimeca (Grijalva 1624:166; Mendieta 1945:92). Otomí speakers were located in the northern half of the central highlands, particularly in the areas that are now known as the Mezquital Valley and Jilotepec Province, at the ends of the northernmost expansion of the Mexica empire.

It was from the very first impression that the Spanish conquerors received of the Otomíes from speaking to Tlaxcala combatants that a common opinion about them as a wild and senseless people started to grow. Bernal Díaz del Castillo (1977:211) in his *Historia Verdadera de la Conquista de la Nueva España,* despite what other authors said, reintroduced the idea that the word Otomí also meant the "order of knights," warriors distinguished because of their bravery and the fact of their wearing an over-the-ear hair cut tied with a hair lock (Durán 1967:167).

It is possible, as Guzmán (2002:26) points out, that this image was transmitted from the pre-Hispanic ruling group to the Spanish, but it is

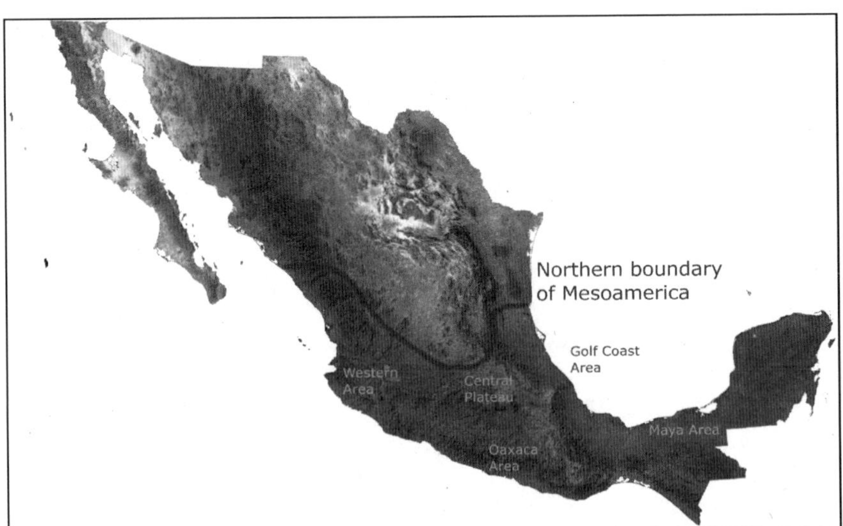

Figure 10.1   Cultural areas in pre-Hispanic Mexico.

also possible that Otomí social customs reinforced this preconceptions; the sixteenth-century missionaries not only strengthened the prejudice of the Otomíes being wild and senseless, but also emphasized other qualities that prevailed over their reputed virtues. For example, Bernardino de Sahagún (1975:603–604), using Nahoa informants from the Tepeapulco area located to the north of Teotihuacán, wrote in 1560:

> The Otomíes were very lazy people, although very tough, and worked the land; they were not very diligent either in obtaining their own food nor in prolonging their ordinary job, because as soon as they finish farming the land they loafed around, with no other occupation than hunting rabbits, hares, quails and deer, using nets and arrows, or birdlimes or corks ... They also made holes in the maguey to drink the honey or to make *pulcre* and get drunk every day ... They ate stinky skunk and snakes and dormouse and all kind of mice, and weasel and other bugs from the countryside or the mountain, and all kinds of lizards and bumblebees and locusts of all sorts.

This quote tells how the Otomíes obtained their food, but also emphasizes their laziness. In the report on the Yzmiquilpa mines the priest pointed out: "It is convenient to remediate the way the natives get drunk since because of this they do and commit terrible crimes and offenses against the Lord God" (Paso y Troncoso 1905:102).

In the second half of the sixteenth century, the Spanish Crown ordered a poll taken in order to determine the situation in the territory of New Spain; instructions were distributed to several colonial authorities in which Otomí settlements and tendencies were described. A quite detailed manuscript from Tornacuxtla, written by Alonso López, stated that the Otomíes were "populated with no order," "the neighbors spread and apart one from the other" (Acuña 1986:47), "they are people of a low understanding and wild manners" (ibid:128), "they badly attend to the doctrine and to the goverment," "they frequently get drunk with an alcoholic beverage made from maguey honey" (ibid:143), and "most of them are clumsy, and only know how to plant, harvest, and load" (ibid:172). In the *Relación de Yeytecomac* they are described as the following:

> It is to be understood they die from the way they get drunk, very common among them. They are populated in towns made by streets, they are of barbarian tendencies, as drunkness is; they are lazy people, so much that if they can eat without working they would be lying all their lives; they are poorly governed, and badly attend to the doctrine; most of them are humble to the elders. (Acuña 1986:134)

The *Relación de Queretaro*, written by Francisco Ramos de Cárdenas and considered by Acuña as a "well-intentioned account" given that it was meticulously researched (Acuña 1987:209), stated that the Otomíes are of low understanding, with no honor, are timid, dirty in dressing and eating, vile, cowardly and ungrateful, slow in understanding good manners, cruel and ruthless, great thieves, superstitious to the point of sacrificing an eleven- or twelve-year-old girl and taking her heart out of her chest when the 1576 epidemic hit hard. The main problem observed is that they get drunk daily, especially on holy days or when the weather is warmer. Pulque makes them speak in Spanish, even if they do not know how to; it also makes them fall asleep everywhere on the streets and fields; they kill each other and they become lustful with their women, no matter if they are their own children, sisters, or even their mothers (Acuña 1987:224–229). Yet the writer qualified his statement:

> Although they are lazy, they work harder than other nations in these lands. They are more diligent in farming than in any other activity, although they farm so slowly and calmly that a Spaniard accomplishes more in one day than the Otomíes in ten. They love to dwell in wild and remote places, where they cannot be seen, mainly for avoiding working. They hardly appreciate what they are paid when working; it often happens that they leave after working a week with no payment. (Acuña 1987:228)

But immediately afterwards, he insists:

> In lust they are very warm, women or men. Women are of easy access; they are good friends with blacks and mulattos and with those of their generation, and when one of them asks them for their bodies they answer, "You know." They are enemies of the Spaniards. They are a generation that multiplies greatly and kindly; it is thought that few of them arrive [intact?] to the nuptial bed, since even younger than ten years old they practice these bad habits. (Acuña 1987:228)

Maybe the most conclusive statement used by sixteenth-century elites and even by twentieth-century researchers to describe the Otomíes literally or metaphorically was written by the Franciscan chronicler Bernardino de Sahagún (1975:603):

> The Otomí were clumsy, rough, and unskillful; when scolding them because of their clumsiness, it is very common to offend them by telling them, "How unskillful you are! You are like an Otomite, it is not enough what you are told. By any chance, are you one of them? Right, you are not like one, you are an Otomite after all." All this was said in order to insult all those who were unskillful and clumsy, scolding them because of their lack of capability or ability.

It is not easy to grasp in sixteenth- and seventeenth-century sources how this perception developed and matured in the collective mind of the non-native inhabitants of the Mexican central highlands, but in the second half of the twentieth century the opinion of some local *caciques* reflected the same ideas:

> The hundreds of years they have lived in this infertile land have originated no ambition; most of the people are lazy because of this last reason. Heat, dust, and lack of water make it difficult for the body to have a normal activity. So these people have enough with coming down every Monday to the market; they bring their *ayates* (textiles), their *lechuguillas*, their *shité* (a by-product of the lechuguillas), which they obtain from Friday to Sunday, because Monday is the day they arrive; they come and get drunk; on Tuesday they recover from the hangover, on Wednesday, the same; they don't have any activity. (Bartra 1984:76)

ANTHROPOLOGY AND ETHNOGRAPHY OF THE NINETEENTH AND TWENTIETH CENTURIES

During the sixteenth and eighteenth centuries, the Otomíes were specially treated; once they became allies of the Spaniards during the conquest they received benefits not usually given to any other Mexican indigenous group. The *caciques* were entitled to carry daggers and ride horseback; they were the main players in the colonization of north-central Mexico (building settlements just as those from the places they came from), and their colonial presence was important to confront the Chichimeca's uprisings in the region (Crespo and Cano 2006). Besides, 144,412 ha of the Mezquital Valley were given to the Otomíes for cultivation, livestock, and grazing (López 2005:103–107). The Otomíes were able to buy community lands and build their churches with gold altarpieces. Their population increased, which allowed them to gain independence from the *pueblos de indios* who governed them originally in the seventeenth and eighteenth centuries (López 2005:275–278).

It was only during the second half of eighteenth century, by strange synchronous processes (the application of the Borbonic reforms in New Spain coincided with one long decade of drought that gave rise to an agricultural crisis), that the Otomíes found themselves in a condition of poverty. That circumstance explains why they did not support the revolutionary party during the wars of independence. For instance, the Orizabita and Tlazinta communities supported a party of king's sappers and in many cases they were allies of the Royalist army (López 2005:383–384).

The national project that resulted from Mexican independence constructed a civilized past; it was proposed by criollo intellectuals who had originated in the Enlightment movement of the previous century. The search for pre-Hispanic history was focused on the Toltec, since indigenous and colonial sources spoke of a wise ruler and of the Toltecs as patrons of the arts and sciences. History became interspersed with a biblical image and the extant knowledge about pre-Hispanic groups, mainly through written sources, especially those of the Nahoas (Rozat 2001:64–66).

Toward 1845, Manuel Crisóstomo Nájera (1984 [1845]:24–25) wrote about the Otomí language as follows:

> The people who spoke this language were ignorant, with a poor life, almost wild, and still divided here and there, banished from their homes by the Spaniards, whose luck has not improved ... If they immortalized the triumph that gave stillness and peace to their language, calling it Hiā hiū, in the name they used for themselves they retained the memory of their very long pilgrimages, and of the many times they had to move their residence to go to the place where they could call themselves the Othomi because *otho* means nothing, and *mi*, sitting or still. The Othomi therefore is a pilgrim, a wandering man; sad is the fate of a people sentenced never to enjoy the peace of home! The Othomites seemed to be devoted to this erratic life in ancient times, and even four centuries ago, because the Mexicans fought them consistently to extend over them the empire of their eagle. The Spanish who defeated the Mexicans also defeated the Othomites; their land was apportioned and they were confined to colonies established amidst other peoples to weaken the settlers and their neighbors, thus fulfilling their destiny as wanderers and pilgrims.

In the nineteenth-century conflict between Liberals (seeking to build citizens and private property) and Conservatives (defending communal property, including those of the church and Indian towns), the Otomí reacted against the former. During the war against the government of Benito Juárez, they militated on the Conservative side and were led by an Otomí general close to Emperor Maximilian, Leonardo Márquez; influenced by the Utopian socialist movements that followed the ideas of Fourier and Proudhon, in 1868 the Otomíes adhered to the manifesto *"A todos los pobres y oprimidos de México y el universo con la petición de los pueblos de Ixmiquilpan"* (To all poor men and the oppressed of Mexico and the universe with the request of the towns of Ixmiquilpan). In both cases they were defeated and the main leaders executed by the Juarez government (López 2005:389–391).

The expropriation of communal property, the capitalist reforms of the end of the nineteenth century, the expansion of large estates, and the construction of a rural and urban working class influenced the conscience of the Creoles and the mestizos who, from the emergent anthropological discipline, sought to know this sector of the population that had just been categorized and discovered, the contemporary Indian, decadent heir of the civilized pre-Hispanic Indian. "When this mass of robots recovers the dynamism that it had in its past and acquires the effectiveness that characterizes modern action, then it will indeed operate and take advantage of the almost virgin sources of the country" (Gamio 1993:22). The application of policies at the end of the nineteenth century only had impact decades later, with the revolutionary governments. In the words of Juan Comas (1964:18):

> Theoretically at least, from 1910 the indigenous preoccupation was oriented toward scientific objectivity to obtain an exact and total knowledge of the Indian in all its aspects based on integral studies that allowed specifying their deficiencies and the way to correct them.

It fell to the Mexico of the twentieth century to discover the poverty and marginalization of the Indians and to attempt their integration in many regards and from multiple campaigns and institutions, sometimes by integral (or multidisciplinary) policies, sometimes by addressing specific aspects such as health and language. In the Mezquital Valley, identified as one of poorest places in the country, rural schools (Escuelas Rurales) and cultural missions (Misiones Culturales) were developed in the 1920s, as well as indigenous boarding schools to train rural teachers who would educate the population according to national values. In 1937 the Intersecretarial Committee of Planning and Study (Comisión Intersecretarial de Estudio y Planeación en el Valle del Mezquital) was created and research projects were carried out by the Institute of Social Investigations (Instituto de Investigaciones Sociales) of the Autonomous Mexican National University (UNAM) under the leadership of Lucio Mendieta y Núñez (1939). The Summer Institute of Linguistics (Instituto Lingüístico de Verano) (1935) was in charge of studying native languages in order to integrate them by teaching Spanish, a task entrusted to the Institute of Literacy for Monolingual Natives (Instituto de Alfabetización para Indígenas Monolingües). In 1950 the Interamerican Indigenist Institute (Instituto Indigenista Interamericano), led by Manuel Gamio and in collaboration with UNESCO, approved a project to integrate the culture of the indigenous people of the Mezquital Valley into the national culture, while in 1951 the Indigenous Patrimony of the Mezquital Valley (Patrimonio Indígena del Valle del Mezquital) was created, and in 1960 the Coordinating Center of the Indigenist National Institute (Centros Coordinadores del Instituto Nacional Indigenista) came into being (Comas 1964). Finally, in 1970 the Institute of Social Investigations of UNAM made a new study of the Mezquital Valley.

Through time, the Otomíes were considered poor; yet, in an act that recalled the land purchases made by the communities during the eighteenth century, the *caciques* of Capula in 1938 acquired 900 ha from the Hacienda Debodé, threatened by expropriations; they were later sold to the neighbors, who became small landowners (Mendizábal 1947:241–243).

All policies and research undertaken in the Mezquital from the second decade of the twentieth century onward emphasized the integration of the Indian into national life. The improvement of conditions was sought after by creating monolingual, Spanish schools and agricultural institutes; Spanish-speaking rural teachers were trained, and industries were developed to make baseballs, uniforms for the Mexican Institute of Social Health (Instituto Mexicano del Seguro Social), Temoayan rugs, shoes, bedspreads, fabrics, and wool rugs. A system of waste water irrigation was also developed. These investments did not produce great achievements. Thus a new preconception came into being—the Mezquital Valley as a place of poverty incapable of resolution.

Applied anthropology carried out so many anthropological studies in a functionalistic, structuralistic, or economic vein that the contemporary Otomíes considered their families as consisting of a "father, mother, son, and a social anthropologist" (Francisco Luna Tavera, personal communication 1998). The assessment made by project of UNAM's Institute of Social Investigations in 1985 expressed the motivations and emphasis that a Marxist-inspired anthropology put forward for the observation of the Otomíes in the 1970s:

> Those of us who collaborated in the research considered that one of the main problems was the way capitalism, as a form of organization and as a social regime, ordered in a definite way the diverse communities of the Mezquital Valley. (de la Peña 1991:24)

The economic emphasis of such research hardly managed to hide the great deficiency in the Mexican anthropology of the Otomíes from the Mezquital Valley. Luisa Paré wrote on this regard:

> The study downplays the importance of indigenous investigation. Being an indigenous zone, and taking into consideration our institution's concern for the agrarian and ethnic problems, the way we approached them was deficient. Personally I cannot say that I have come to understand the Otomí in all their cultural characteristics. (Paré 1991:31)

Sergio de la Peña (personal communication,1988) confessed that "we did not do ethnography." The few ethnographies about the Otomíes are deeply traditional, almost pintoresque. Guerrero (1983), a local-born ethnographer sent to the Mezquital by Manuel Gamio in 1950, recognized that

> in 1950 Dr. Manuel Gamio, the eminent Mexican anthropologist, then director of the Interamerican Indigenous Institute, invited me to participate in an ethnographic and folklore research to get to know the ways of life of the Otomíes from the Mezquital Valley, in our state of Hidalgo. It

was the reason I came back to visit many of their towns in search of their inhabitants in order to inquire about their interests, ideas, concepts, and the practices of their daily life. (Guerrero 1983:15)

The twentieth-century ethnographer, when rescuing the ethnography and the ways of life of the Otomíes, had intellectually assumed their marginalization from Mesoamerican cultural development and civilization as much as the vision of the Otomíes as impoverished by the Spaniards and the Mexicans. It was Manuel Gamio at the beginning of the twentieth century who introduced a novel statement. From his archaeological explorations in the Basin of Mexico, he affirmed, after observing certain pottery patterns of the Archaic period, that

happily we can already make sure in a positive way, according to what was above demonstrated, that the archaic civilization is the oldest civilization of the valley, and according to the historic sources, the archaic civilization identified by archaeology is the Otomí civilization to which history refers. (Gamio 1972:89)

This declaration caused controversy, and it was refuted by Mendizábal, although toward 1927 Gamio had commented that "he had new arguments in favor of the identity of the archaic people with the Otomíes, based mainly upon the similarity of the motifs of the archaic pottery and the products of the Otomí industry" (Mendizábal 1946:459). Supported by "research and critique of historical data," "investigation of the kinds of life, nutritional regimes, and technology," "the geographic distribution of the Otomí linguistic group," and by "research and critique of the distribution of archaic and later pottery," Mendizábal concluded that

in order to accept the Otomíes, clumsy even according to the indigenes themselves, as authors of the oldest pottery of Mexico and, consequently, inventors of that invaluable art and of corn agriculture, the highest American achievement in the material order, it is necessary to have more solid arguments than those adduced to date. (Mendizábal 1946:474)

Nevertheless, certain anomalies existed. One of the main polemics since the nineteenth century (and subjected to discussion by anthropologists in the first half of the twentieth century) was the civilizing origin of the Mexican groups. Although ethnohistoric sources pointed to the existence of the Toltecs and their time as the climax of pre-Hispanic history, archaeology could not find where Tula, their capital, was located. This controversy led to the First Round Table of the Mexican Society of Anthropology (Sociedad Mexicana de Antropología, SMA) in 1941. Although ethnohistorical sources pointed to the Tula ("Tollan" in nahuatl) located in the Mezquital Valley, where Otomí population was dominant, as the ancient captial, the archaeological evidence leaned toward Tollan Teotihuacán, considered of Nahoa origin (Medina 1988:520).

The Round Table concluded that the Tula in the ethnohistorical sources corresponded to the archaeological zone of Tula in the Mezquital Valley (SMA 1987). The old controversy about the civilizing role of the Nahoas was reflected in the words of Mendizábal criticizing Orozco and Berra and some other authors of the nineteenth century who, using an eighteenth-century chronicle, affirmed that Tula was the dwelling place of the Otomíes and that in their language it was called "Mamenhi" (Mendizábal 1946:464). Twentieth-century archaeology discarded Tula as the civilizing center, following the idea of the emigrant Otomí, and considered that the splendor of the city could only have had a Nahoa origin.

The absurd interpretation of Betancourt's words has been accepted, according to our old custom, without any criticisms or verification by Chavero (1981 [1884]) and by some other historians. The Otomíes were a demographic element mobilized, according to their needs, by the Nahoa peoples during time of the Aztecs and by the Spaniards later on. They were instrumental for the population policies of Aztecs and Spaniards, who used them to establish towns and villages in Hidalgo, Queretaro, Guanajuato, and San Luis that served as barriers between urban centers or densely populated regions and the hunting-harvester hordes of the Pames, who maintained their aggressiveness until the end of the sixteenth century (Mendizábal 1946:464).

These ideas guided the archaeological research that has been carried out in Tula since the 1940s in order to confirm if it really was the place where Quetzalcóatl ruled (López 1988:273–274); yet, new evidence was about to be revealed.

DIALOGUES AT THE END OF THE TWENTIETH CENTURY: CURRENT VINDICATIONS

The seed planted by Manuel Gamio reached the Otomíes during the second half of the twentieth century, because by this point they started to consider themselves the founders of the great cities of central Mexico: Teotihuacán, Cuicuilco, Tula, and Cholula. Yet, archaeological and ethnographic anomalies began to increase, and the Otomíes themselves pointed them out by arguing with the anthropologists of the new generation. The Mezquital Valley Archaeological Project revealed the existence of more than 100 sites with cave paintings (Figure 10.2) that showed a

Figure 10.2   Cave painting from the Mezquital Valley.

sacralized space that included the representations of rites and ceremonies linked to deep Mesoamerican traditions, including pyramids, ball games, and shields (López et al. 1998:27–28).

The pre-Hispanic regional history was shown as disquieting, non-linear, and contradictory as compared to what was known up to that point. Although occupation could be traced back to 12,000 years BP, it was only toward the year AD 400 that it was possible to talk about an occupied place with settlements that shared a *Mesoamerican* worldview, although they were independent and autonomous from the great ceremonial centers of the Basin of Mexico. The Xajay Regional Development was identified as an autonomous entity from Teotihuacán that, despite being contemporaneous, survived the collapse of the Classic period in AD 650. It had been restructured and was an important antecedent for the foundation of Tula when its settlements were abandoned around AD 900 (López et al. 1998:31–32).

The Xajay groups were interpreted as the beginning of the Otomí peopling of the Mezquital region (Morett 1996). It was also shown that the design of their settlements not only represented the Mesoamerican worldview (the representation of the holy mountain, the *axis mundi* in the temple, the course of the universe, the view of the calendar, and the geometry of space), but that it also expressed the F proportion or golden ratio arising from the repetition of magnitudes that has been discovered in several Mesoamerican societies (Cedeño 1998:63).

Surface surveys also revealed the existence of a ceremonial center associated with the mythical Coatepec hill, the founding place of the Mexicas and where a mythical combat between Huitzilopochtli and the "one hundred southerners" took place. Archaeological research also discovered the site that regional oral traditions indicated as the "place that was going to be Mexico" (Gelo and López 1998:65).

The question immediately arose of why this site had not been discovered by previous investigations (Gelo and López 1998:78). Even more, this question was associated with other absences in the ethnohistoric evidence. For instance, the Queretaro Relation did not mention the existence of Coatepec, and other geographic-historic relations showed a deep silence about the places where important ceremonial centers had been found archaeologically. Although in pre-Hispanic times the region was known as Teotlalpan ("Land of Gods" or "Land of the Ancestors"), no ethnographic or archaeological research was carried out to address this issue. Only a few statements were made on this regard after about 100 years of anthropological research:

> In the Mezquital Valley during the nineteenth century, the entire population professed the Catholic religion and only some remains of the pre-Hispanic cult were preserved in the Itzmiquilpan-Yolotepec zone, where there were on a nearby hill two stone idols, whose importance in the yearly February 5th celebrations were fundamental. (Arellano 1966:631)

Margarita Nolasco indicated that after the revolution, superstitions remained in the Valley along with small ceremonies celebrated on the farms, including a truly idolatrous adoration of the Señor de las Maravillas, the Señor del Calvario, the Virgin of Guadalupe, the Niño de Atocha, the Cross, and the Holy Spirit (represented by a white dove). Yet, she scorned those practices as a proof of syncretism that included offerings to the Holy Cross in the form of "promises" of animals (Nolasco 1966:654–655). She also recognized that

> their special pagan-religious form takes part in all aspects of their life; it controls them from sunrise to dusk, from birth to death. It controls their ideas, their wishes, their aspirations; in short, it controls everything. (Nolasco 1966:654)

She was astonished by the syncretism implied by the strange ceremony executed in the Portezuelo town "in which some boys and girls participated; most importantly, the game consisted of chickens and hens being strongly whipped by the girls on the boys' backs. Nowadays this ceremony is no longer celebrated" (Nolasco 1966:655).

The answer to such a syncretism lay in a vindication process by the Otomíes themselves (marginal to the glance of the anthropologist): the isolated evidence that had informed ethnology and archaeology were part of a continuous whole unnoticed by the investigators. The Otomíes, now educated and avid readers of anthropology, saw with caution the way to vindicate themselves and looked for a dialogue with the investigators. Thus, during the 1970s they ensured that their name was not Otomí but Hñahñu. Because of the tonal language complications in some colonial references, it was said that this term meant "the one who speaks with the nose" or "a third language" (Buelna 1893); nevertheless, they expressed that in fact it meant "the one who speaks of the road," as a metaphor of one who speaks of history (Luna et al. 2005).

The Otomíes looked for a dialogue with the academics in search of vindication. On one hand, they would no longer permit being referred to in terms of poverty and marginalization and, on the other hand, they were willing to vindicate their role as collaborators in the construction of a Mesoamerican worldview, understanding that their rituals and ceremonies not only were a product of syncretism but also disclosing associations unnoticed by ethnographers and archaeologists. Recently an official cultural television channel asked our collaborator and informant to show them old-style, poor houses made from maguey and now completely marginalized in order to film a documentary. The answer was "there are no such things here ... but if you like we can make a stage scene for you" (Luna Tavera, personal communication 2006).

In 2006 the community of El Espítiru invited us to observe the ritual cycle of Carnival occurring between January and April; the occasion allowed us to see the proximity that exists between their long ceremonies carried out during the year and the celebrations of the pre-Hispanic Mesoamerican calendar in which coherence of the ritual process depends on the articulation of events that had been observed in a fragmentary way. The ritual process involves the harvesting of mistletoe in Coatepec, the investiture of the ancestors (*xitá*), the elaboration of the offerings and the flags that represent the elders, the preparation of sacred food for the participants, the ritual sweep of roads and sacred places, and even a battle with oranges (Figure 10.3), a simulation of a sacred battle where one side represents the sun and the other side represents the night, the eagle against the jaguar, opposed (Luna Tavera, personal communication 2006). In other communities the Carnival culminates with the so-called "chicken killer" (the ceremony Nolasco found to be so strange in the 1960s) or with the simulation, after the dance of the Moors and Christians, of the removal of the flesh from the body of a personage, a distant remembrance of the pre-Hispanic god Xipe-Totec, the flayed one (Bernardo Guízar, personal communication 1990).

Figure 10.3 Battle with oranges at the end of Carnival.

The sacred spaced signaled by Teotlalpan acquired sense when Luna Talavera described that, with the conquest of Mexico Tenochtitlán, the priests tried to protect the sacred bundles from the Spaniards. They transferred them to Tlatelolco and later walked with them retracing the mythical peregrination of the Aztecs; they finally buried them in the place where everything started, the fortress of Copil, the one who had faced Huitzilopochtli from Tezcatepec Hill and, when defeated, whose green-stone heart had been thrown from Coatepec to fall in the place where Mexico Tenochtitlán was founded. The sacred bundles were buried in the Tezcatepec Hill in the Mezquital Valley, a place known by the Mexica *teomamas* (carriers of the sacred bundles) (Luna Tavera, personal communication 2005). The Hñahñu used to perform a ceremony at the Coatepec called the Flag Flowering (Figure 10.4), or Panquetzaliztli, carried out in a square that represents the four corners of the universe, with the *axis mundi*, the heart of the world, located in the center.

Investigations in search of the Tula of colonial sources during the 1940s and 1950s ignored the existence of this ceremonial center, in spite of there having been an excavation made in a pyramid in the cemetery of Mixquiahuala, a town located on the slopes of the hill. In 1989, excavations in a locality known as Elephant Hill were made, and there a sculpture was discovered of a standing male personage with a cavity

Figure 10.4   The Flag Flowering at Coatepec.

in his chest where surely a green stone had been incrusted (Martínez 1994:143–145). With the passage of time, the name of the Martínez Hill was changed to Elephant Hill and only a small town with the original name remained by its side. Recent archaeological surveys have associated Elephant Hill with Tezcatepec, interpreting the sculpture as a representation of Copil, following a suggestion made by the Otomíes. The *Relación Geográfica de Tezcatepec* noted "as far as the fourteen chapter[s]: they didn't have any idols neither did they adore anything; they only watched the sky" (Acuña 1986:147).

Nowadays the Otomíes are revealing their prominence in the construction of the Mesoamerican worldview, previously unknown to anthropologists and archaeologists, whose academic preconception may have blocked their capacity to observe and to assign meaning to the fragmentary and dispersed information they received from archaeology and contemporary events and rituals. Recent interdisciplinary archaeological research has allowed the Hñahñu voice to emerge and express itself. Dialogues with the Otomíes not only allow the construction of regional hypotheses but also consolidate lines of investigation for the Otomíes to reinterpret what anthropologists have written about them; they do so vindicating their own historicity. For instance, the finding of a rich Toltec burial was a reason for a cointerpretation, reading it as part of the *mäkapönti* (the sacred cross), still celebrated among the contemporary Otomíes (Olivares 2004).

Perhaps the best expression of this intellectual search has been the creation of the Hñahñu Culture Museum in which, for the first time, the idea of marginality and poverty has been left behind in order to rescue Otomí ceremonial objects and give expression to the role Otomí themselves assume they had in pre-Hispanic history. Such a prominence is expressed by emphasizing that in the region each pre-Hispanic community was governed by two *tlatoanis*, that is to say, it was a dual system of dual heads, equivalent, where the Nahoa governor was not higher than the Otomí. This information came from the reading of the colonial sources written about Ixmiquilpan (López 2005). It was thematized in the museum, along with the finding of a codex and the recognition of the Otomí landscape as a sacred landscape (Luna et al. 2005).

The conception of sacred landscape is hidden in endless metaphors and representations. A double language exists that makes the Otomí words ambiguous, it is the sacred language (*boxaxni*) that is only used by some elders. In this language the Otomí words have an esoteric and ritual meaning (*boxaxni* is a plant known as cat nail, but in sacred language means "the sacred language." [Luna Tavera, personal communication 1995]). Nevertheless it has been possible to recognize that the world has been conceived in the following form (Figure 10.5): a four-corner square joined by a cross with each course having a color. The north (the place where the *mähuifi* wind blows) is blue in color and corresponds to the summer solstice (June 21). The south (place of the greenness, place of emerald, *mäk'angi*) is green and represents the winter solstice (December 22). The east (the place where light comes from, *máhyats'i*) is white and corresponds to the spring equinox (March 21). The east was the place of genesis, pleasure, and sin, and the dominion of the Goddess Mother. The west (place of concealment, *mäpuni*) is red and represents the autumn equinox (September 23). It is the space of the giants, the *uemä*, the ancestors transformed into rocks because of their fall.

The corners of the Otomí world are joined in the east and the west by the path of the Moon and the path of Venus, by the path of the Sun in the north and the path of Man in the south. In the center is the Heart of the World (*Kungri rä Ximhai*), along with the Navel of the World (*Ts'ai rä Ximhai*): all spatial coordinates converge there. It is the space of communication among different worlds (*Ximhai*)—the three aerial worlds, the terrestrial plane, and the three underground worlds (Luna et al. 2005).

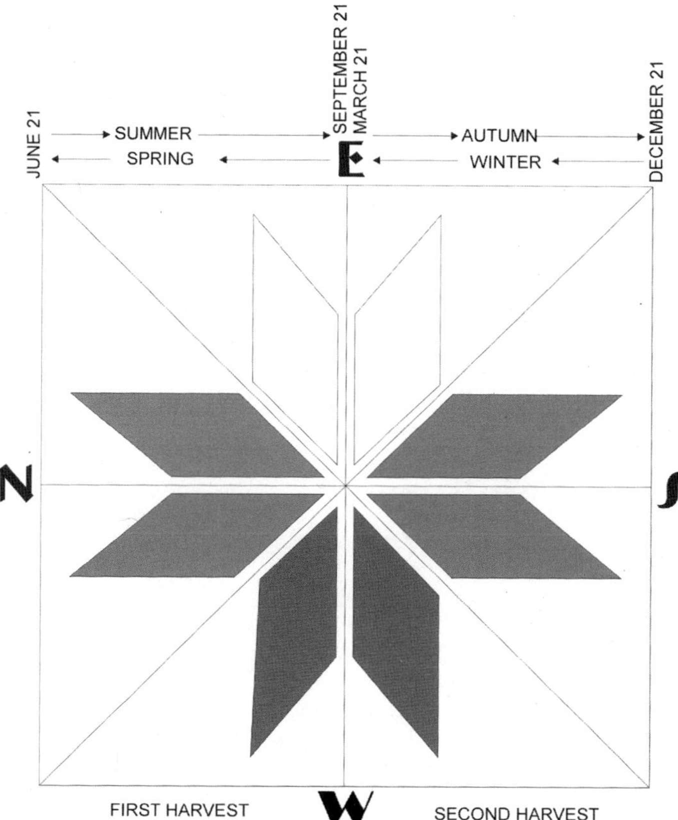

Figure 10.5   Representation of the Otomí world.

The active participation of the Otomíes in the knowledge about the sacred space of the Mezquital Valley has given the project new views that have acquired a deeply transdisciplinary character. The permanent discussions with them are a source of hypotheses to conjugate knowledge and interpretation from ethnography, ethnohistory, and archaeology in order to build a new way of seeing history, their history. Taking this history as a starting point, everything seems to indicate that, indeed, in pre-Hispanic times rather than being a subordinated people they played a leading role, at least during the last thousand years. The interactions that took place from AD 650 to AD 900 were remarkable. During this period still undefined political parties interacted actively toward the construction of the Toltec *altépetl*.

It is feasible to suppose that from that moment on, the double-headed systems were created (perhaps Tula Mamenhi or Tula Xicocotitlán, which were consolidated during the Aztec hegemony). It is also possible to assume that the Otomíes were co-protagonists in Aztec history by creating the founding myths of Coatepec-Tezcatepec, which later would be called Teotlalpan (Land of the Gods, Land of the Otomíes). Thanks to the lineage bonds they established with the Mexica *tlatoani*, at the beginning of the Colonial period a great number of territories of the region were denominated "Moctezuma territories." The rest is still waiting to be revealed, and surely the enrichment of anthropological practices would result in a new construction of the way the Otomíes have been regarded, contributing to their vindication in the present century.

REFERENCES

Acuña, René (editor) 1986 *Relaciones geográficas del siglo XVI*, vol. 2. UNAM, Mexico.
———. 1987 *Relaciones geográficas del siglo XVI*. UNAM, Morelia.
Arellano, Manuel 1966 Síntesis de la situación económica, política y social de la zona árida del Valle del Mezquital durante la primera mitad del siglo XX. In *Summa antropológica en homenaje a Roberto J. Weitlaner*, pp. 613–636. INAH, Mexico.
Bartra, Roger 1984 *Campesinado y poder político en México*. Era, Mexico.
Buelna, Eustaquio 1893 *Luces del otomí o gramática del idioma que hablan los indios otomíes en la república mexicana*. Imprenta del Gobierno Federal, Mexico.
Cedeño, Jaime 1998 El culto al lugar central. Posibilidades en torno a un problema arqueológico. *Arqueología* 20:53–64.
Chavero, Alfredo 1981 [1884] Primera época. Historia antigua. In *México a través de los siglos. Historia general y completa del desenvolvimiento social, político, religioso, militar, artístico, científico y literario de México desde la antigüedad más remota hasta la época actual*, vol. 1, edited by Vicente Riva. Editorial Cumbre, Mexico.
Comas, Juan 1964 *La antropología aplicada en México*. Instituto Indigenista Interamericano, Mexico.
Crespo, Ana María, and Yolanda Cano 2006 Políticas de doblamiento en frontera: asentamientos otomíes en Querétaro. In *Caleidoscopio de alternativas. Estudios culturales desde la antropología y la historia*, edited by Ana María Crespo and Rosa Brambila, pp. 13–36. INAH, Mexico.
de la Peña, Sergio 1991 El contexto de la discusión. In *Nos queda la esperanza. El Valle del Mezquital*, edited by Carlos Martínez and Sergio Sarmiento, pp. 22–27. Consejo Nacional para la Cultura y las Artes, Mexico.
Díaz del Castillo, Bernal 1977 *Historia verdadera de la conquista de la Nueva España*. Porrúa, Mexico.
Durán, Diego 1967 *Historia de los indios de la Nueva España*, vol. 2. Porrúa, Mexico.
Gamio, Manuel 1972 Las excavaciones del Pedregal de San Ángel y la cultura arcaica del Valle de México. In *Arqueología e indigenismo*, edited by Eduardo Matos and Manuel Gamio, pp. 70–89. Sep-Setentas 24, Mexico.
———. 1993 Estado actual de las investigaciones antropológicas en México y sugestiones sobre su desarrollo futuro. In *Dos aportaciones a la historia de la antropología en México*, by Manuel Gamio and Andrés Medina, pp. 9–38. INAH, Mexico.
Gelo, Eduardo Yamil, and Fernando López 1998 Hualtepec, Nonohualcatepec y Cohuatepec. Lecturas a un cerro mítico. *Arqueología* 20:65–78.
Grijalva, Juan de 1624 *Crónica de la orden de nuestro santo padre Agustín en las provincias de la Nueva España. En cuatro jornadas desde el año de 1533 hasta el de 1592*. Imprenta de Juan Ruíz, Mexico.

Guerrero, Raúl 1983 *Los otomíes del Valle del Mezquital (Modos de vida, etnografía, folklore)*. Centro Regional Hidalgo INAH, Mexico.

Guzmán, Ignacio 2002 El otomí, ¿lengua bárbara? Opiniones novohispanas y decimonónicas sobre el otomí. In *Episodios novohispanos de la historia otomí*, edited by Rosa Brambila, pp. 15–46. Instituto Mexiquense de Cultura, Toluca.

López, Fernando 1988 La arqueología en Hidalgo. In *La antropología en México. Panorama histórico*. Vol. 14, *La antropología en el centro de México*, edited by Carlos García, pp. 271–286. INAH, Mexico.

———. 2005 *Símbolos del tiempo. Inestabilidad y bifurcaciones en los pueblos de indios del Valle del Mezquital*. Consejo Estatal para la Cultura y las Artes del Estado de Hidalgo, Mexico.

López, Fernando, Laura Solar, and Rodrigo Vilanova 1998 El Valle del Mezquital. Encrucijadas en la historia de los asentamientos humanos en un espacio discontinuo. *Arqueología* 20:21–40.

Luna, Francisco, Anastasio Botho, and Fernando López 2005 Guión del Museo de la Cultura Hñahñu. Unpublished manuscript, on file at the Consejo Estatal para la Cultura y las Artes del Estado de Hidalgo, Mexico.

Martínez, Ricardo 1994 Un rescate en el cerro del Elefante, Tunititlán, Hidalgo. In *Simposium sobre arqueología en el Estado de Hidalgo. Trabajos recientes*, edited by Enrique Fernández, pp. 143–150. INAH, Mexico.

Medina, Andrés 1988 Miguel Covarrubias. In *La antropología en México. Panorama histórico*. Vol. 9, *Los protagonistas (Acosta-Dávila)*, edited by Lina Odena and Carlos García, pp. 518–532. INAH, Mexico.

Mendieta, Gerónimo de 1945 *Historia eclesiástica indiana*, vol. 2. Editorial Salvador Chávez Hayhoe, Mexico.

Mendizábal, Miguel Otón 1946 Los otomíes no fueron los primeros pobladores del Valle de México. In *Obras completas*, vol. 2, pp. 455–474. Talleres Gráficos de la Nación, Mexico.

———. 1947 Monografía de Capula. In *Obras completas*, vol. 6, pp. 237–256. Talleres Gráficos de la Nación, Mexico.

Morett, Luis 1996 El desarrollo regional Xajay en el poniente del Valle del Mezquital. Unpublished Master's thesis, Escuela Nacional de Antropología e Historia, Mexico.

Nájera, Manuel Crisóstomo 1984 [1845] *Disertación sobre la lengua othom leída en latín en la Sociedad Filosófica Americana de Filadelfia*. Editorial Innovación, Mexico.

Nolasco, Margarita 1966 Los otomíes del Mezquital. Época post-revolucionaria. In *Summa antropológica en homenaje a Roberto J. Weitlaner*, pp. 637–658. INAH, Mexico.

Olivares, Juan Carlos 2004 Una aproximación al significado de las ofrendas asociadas a entierros del sitio Sabina Grande en el Valle del Mezquital. Unpublished Honor's thesis, Escuela Nacional de Antropología e Historia, Mexico.

Paré, Luisa 1991 Balance de un proyecto de investigación. In *Nos queda la esperanza. El Valle del Mezquital*, edited by Carlos Martínez and Sergio Sarmiento, pp. 28–37. Consejo Nacional para la Cultura y las Artes, Mexico.

Paso y Troncoso, Francisco del 1905 *Papeles de Nueva España. Segunda serie: geografía y estadística*. Vol. 3, *Relación de las minas de Yzmiquilpa*. Sucesores de Rivadeneyra, Madrid.

Rozat, Guy 2001 *Los orígenes de la nación. Pasado indígena e historia nacional*. Universidad Iberoamericana, Mexico.

Sahagún, Bernardino de 1975 *Historia general de las cosas de la Nueva España*. Porrúa, Mexico.

SMA (Sociedad Mexicana de Antropología) 1987 *Memoria de la I Reunión de Mesa Redonda: Tula y los Toltecas*. Sociedad Mexicana de Antropología, Mexico.

CHAPTER 11

INDIGENOUS ARCHAEOLOGIES OR THE FIGHT AGAINST THE THIRD TRANSFORMATION OF FAUST: REFLECTIONS FROM COLOMBIAN AND ARGENTINEAN COMMUNITIES

Wilhelm Londoño
Translated from the Spanish by Lilén Malugany

MODERNISM AND ITS EXPERIENCE: A THEORY OF MODERNITY

You are in the West but you are free to live in your East, as ancient as you need—and to inhabit it to your own pleasure. Do not let yourself be beaten.

Arthur Rimbaud (2003 [1873]:68)

In his famous book *All That Is Solid Melts into Air*, Marshall Berman (2001) proposed to distinguish between modernity, modernism, and modernization, useful to differentiate the system of ideas that stimulates the formation of industrial and democratic places from the customs that are generated in that new cultural space. For Berman modernity is an experience, modernization a process, and modernism a logic of values. Through the critical review of modern thinkers (Baudelaire, Marx, and Goethe), Berman showed how modernity, modernism, and modernization received special meaning in the work of those authors. In his analysis of Goethe's *Faust*, Berman identified how a panegyric of modernist values was spread; in order to do so, Berman deconstructed Goethe's work in three phases that lead from the restlessness produced by tradition to the sense of expectancy caused by the launching of modernization projects. In the first scene, Berman presents a fearful Faust, rooted in traditional, local values—in sum, indecisive. In the second scene, he shows a transformed Faust who widens his eyes and throws himself into the whirl of the world. Finally, he displays a Faust committed to the transformation of tradition, who dreams about humanly modified spaces and who looks for the mutation and taming of nature at all costs. In this way, Berman registered the boom of modern values that Goethe portrayed through the relationship of Faust and Mephistopheles.

The third transformation of Faust can be characterized as the most critical point of a series of changes whose poles are defined by the duality between tradition and modernity. One pole is the bucolic society in which individuals depend for their incorporation into the communitarian logic, anchored in face-to-face relationships, and controlled by networks of large families. The other pole is the great change consisting in the aggregation of an amorphous and anonymous whirlpool where individualities are constructed, sheltered, and protected by citizenship.

Within the literary tradition that Berman tries to unravel, modernity is the experience that is formed in the middle of industrialization processes, possible by the staging of modern values. This experience is characterized by individualism and fragmentation, that anonymity that Baudelaire (cf. Berman 2001) found so annoying in the boulevards of nineteenth-century Paris. Along with the rupture of communitarian logic, where the individual emerges, occur the marks of the modern experience: proletarization, urbanization, the creation of ghettos, the formation of nuclear families, the spatial separation of society between the rich and the poor, secularization, and the formation of the body as an instrument for production (Foucault 1996) and desire (Lipovetsky 2004).

The indigenous fight in America, which has occurred from end of the sixteenth century, looked for at all possible cost, in addition to the encounter of points of intermediation with the imperial logic, the maintenance of traditional values that, be what they may, had the aim of preventing Faust's macabre plan to domesticate nature and to displace it by means of the formation of great cities with enormous architectonic constructions—in sum, the place where fragmentation would be possible. Although the colonial documentation shows that the Crown wished to maintain the indigenous towns with a certain internal coherence (Barona 1993), putting in practice the Bourbon policies and those from the formation of the American republics, people tried to consolidate a modern experience by means of strong industrialization accompanied by the strengthening of a system of representation of individualities: democracy (Londoño 2003). In the following pages, some cases will be presented where it is possible to appreciate how archaeology is used in the indigenous context of South America to continue the opposition to the dissolution of the communitarian bonds and the taming of nature.

ARCHAEOLOGY WITH INDIGENOUS COMMUNITIES[1] IN COLOMBIA: THE FIGHT AGAINST FAUST'S DESIRE OR THE STAGING OF A CULTURAL POLICY

It is said that the landscape is a state of the soul, that we see the landscape outside with the eyes of inside; maybe so because those extraordinary inner organs of vision did not know how to see these factories and these hangars, this smoke that devours the sky, these toxic dusts, this eternal mud, these soot coatings, the sweepings of yesterday's garbage on the sweepings of every day's garbage, the garbage of tomorrow swept on the garbage of today; here the simple eyes of the face would be enough to teach the most satisfied of souls to doubt the venture in which it was supposed to be pleased.

José Saramago (2004:112)

The third transformation of Faust is the desire to configure space for the realization of the modern experience; this agenda, identified by Berman in the work of several thinkers of the nineteenth century, finds its real semblance in the desires of modernization that accompanied the formation of nation-states in America in the nineteenth century (Jaramillo 1982) and in Africa and Asia in the twentieth century (Geertz 1989). In the case of the indigenous communities of Colombia, several legislative acts promoted by Simón Bolívar at beginning of the nineteenth century claimed that all citizens were equal; this was achieved by dissolving communal life (Gnecco and Londoño 2008). Most legal norms related to natives advocated their conversion into citizens by becoming land owners. The basic idea was to turn colonial *resguardos* (reservations) into centralized towns where city life was recreated. The logic of the process was simple: to split in two equal parts colonially recognized *resguardos*; to take one part and divide it in equal parts according to the number of registered families; then to divide the remaining part in two, one for the town, with *ejidos* (communal lands) that could be rented, and the other for sale to pay the surveyors in charge of the land process and the priests, in charge of teaching constitutional and religious principles (Gnecco and Londoño 2008).

Although several towns were formed, mainly in regions where modernization was more pressing (Rojas 2001), it did not happen where state presence was negligible. In the nineteenth century, Colombian modernization was characterized by unequal development: in some regions it achieved its goal, in others feudal relations survived. Paradoxically, the latter—in which landowners owned all available land—allowed the permanence of family groups that eventually demanded their lands back, mainly from 1970 onwards.

In southwestern Colombia, near Popayán, an important political and administrative center (Barona 1995), the republic did not succeed in dissolving surrounding *resguardos*; many of them remained to provide servants for the rich families of the city or manual labor for the activities of agricultural estates. Before the 1970s many Nasa, a community that historically has inhabited southwestern Colombia and that defines itself by the use of a language (Nasa Yuwe) and by a common history based on the existence of the important colonial *cacique* Don Juan Tama (Rappaport 2000), worked small plots of land as sharecroppers. Sharecropping was characterized by small-scale food production for local commercial circuits. Oddly, the survival of sharecropping until the end of the twentieth century allowed the reproduction of the communitarian logic that gave coherence to the Nasa political project in the 1970s (Findji 1992). The Nasa project was fundamental in the history of Colombian indigenous movements because it consolidated an organizational platform for the construction of more horizontal proposals; its point of inflection was, perhaps, the new Colombian constitution, enacted in 1991 (Rappaport 2000). Several indigenous communities emerged through political and territorial recognition, even though their articulation with the national political system was not clear. From the time of their recognition as ancestral communities to the promulgation of the 1991 constitution, many groups have suffered, especially from governmental institutions that identified them using essentialist criteria.

This context of discrimination witnessed the creation of the History Committee of the Guambiano community in 1984. The Guambianos are another ethnic group from southwestern Colombia with their own language and history. Accompanied by an archaeologist (Urdaneta 1987, 1991), members of the community appropriated the symbolic value of the discipline to generate a discourse that counterbalanced arguments denying its historical continuity (Vasco 1997 and this volume). Several sites were identified, both their own and foreign, and ancestral practices for managing the space were recognized. Although the extensive and focused interpretation of the archaeologists was not transcendental, the Guambianos used the research to discuss the rooted historicity of their community and how fair their territorial demands were. This process was similar to the one described by James Clifford (1999) for North America, where several communities created spaces of encounter—*contact zones*—through the interpretation of archaeological material culture. He also noted how those spaces were used to generate representations and/or discourses that made it possible to visualize colonial scenarios and strategies to surpass histories of subjection.

Besides authenticating the handling of their own space, the History Committee used archaeology to objectify local senses of time and to provide pedagogical contents for the reproduction of communitarian practices. Archaeology, as a scientific and Western practice, became a device for unfolding a cultural policy (Álvarez et al. 1998): communitarian diacritical values were mobilized to generate recognition outward and coherence inward (Londoño 2002b). Archaeology is a part of the strategies feeding a political culture that, in the case of the Nasa and Guambiano people, configure history as a space of self-representation amidst relations of inequality and subjection and generate agencies leading to a political leveling.

The main goal of the collaborative archaeological research with the Nasa of Novirao, 10 km north of Popayán, was to find empirical support to relate them with the inhabitants of the mythical region of Tierradentro, an important archaeological site in Colombia (Langebaek 1995); although it ended up just determining the presence of Tierradentro pottery types in Novirao (Londoño 2000), it succeeding in providing the proofs demanded by state bureaucrats to activate the system of positive discrimination in favor of the people of Novirao.

Archaeological research highlighted how the archaeological record evokes non-discursive feelings (Londoño 2002a). Through collaborative excavations, we came to understand how sherds focalized people's feelings of belonging to a historical tradition; the latter is informed by Nasa worldview, which posits Tierradentro as the place of origin. While for the archaeologists historical relations are woven around similarities in pottery types scattered in different geographic areas, for the Nasa material culture is used as a metaphor to locate their own genesis. Given that this symbolic operation is not part of a verbal discourse that specifies how the archaeological record can prove historical ties, material culture fulfils a poetic function—a "poetry of sherds" (Londoño 2002a)—that escapes archaeological logic.

The use of archaeology by the Guambianos and Nasa tends to mobilize historical senses that, once sifted by the discipline, become discursive objects that feed a political culture characterized by the use of written documents that overflow communitarian circuits. The configuration of archaeology as a political tool that evokes historical and mythical meanings—up to then nonexistent in verbal discourse—supports new processes of a native political culture that cracks traditional definitions of democracy. This process happens to the extent that the local use of archaeology, accompanied by a reconsideration of the positivist epistemological platform of the discipline (Shanks and Tilley 1992), questions the worth of the truth of official discourses; the latter create a chronological route in which the indigenes locate themselves in a primeval past that was cut short, abruptly, by the foundation of the republic. The participation of archaeology in these new directions of native political culture happens in Colombia through archaeologists like myself and others who collaborate with the communities. These dynamics are not tantamount to an indigenous archaeology but to a practice that, as seen from the academy, result from negotiations with local communities. Although the pedagogical projects of many Colombian groups aim to professional curricula (Laurent 1998), there are as yet no native archaeologists who might permit us to talk about an indigenous archaeology.

Links between the academy and local communities contribute novel contents to native cultural policies in Colombia, underscore how the natives are represented in scholarly discourse, and form powerful symbolic devices to generate a locality based on communitarian principles—a communal land possession, a subjective meaning of territory, and the coexistence with diverse temporalities (Vasco 1997 and this volume). These projects, located midway between academic research and collaboration with communitarian policies, create points of reference for inward educative projects and outward dialogical representations. They invite the modification of the classic definitions of archaeology as the study of culture systems (Binford 1965) or the study of the formation processes of the archaeological record through behavioral patterns (Schiffer 1976). Collaborative archaeological projects with indigenous people turn disciplinary definitions into methodological means for goals more related to local needs.

The strengthening and delimitation of communal territories (sometimes going beyond the official recognition of the Colombian state) break free from the foundational principle of the monopoly of force by the state, that is, the defense of private property. The dichotomy of culture-nature that legitimizes the representation of nature as a resource that must be taken care of and maintained for its rational exploitation (under the metaphor of "sustainable development") crumbles in the face of the native communities' consideration of territory as a subject of rights. A fundamental axiological axis of modernity, a lineal time that legitimizes an empty vital experience (Lipovetsky 2004), is placed in tension when seen only as a transit toward other rationalities (Mumford 1998).

During my own research with Nasa communities (Londoño 2000), archaeological surveys were done following an imaginary line, that of the communitarian territory. We were not allowed to divide the space according to individual plots or activity areas. It was finally divided according to historical names that evoke mythical events, sometimes expressed in Nasa Yuwe. When we discussed where to excavate, the community agreed not to dig tombs; it was implicit that they did not belong to the community but to subterranean beings, with whom one negotiates with specific rituals. Nature, as understood by the West (Escobar 1999), is differentially perceived by these communities; the subsoil belongs to entities with whom there are agreements about things that can or cannot be extracted. The agreements regulate relationships with dimensions that relativize archaeological research.

Research with native communities arranges archaeology as a node on a network of discursive and non-discursive representations that signal the impossibility of the dream of Faust—an accumulation of individuals scattered in urban spaces living a unique, flat, temporal experience with no return amidst an inert and insensible space of which it is not possible to take control. Although archaeology was defined by modernity as a machine to produce empirical evidence about the linear advance of time and the dissolution of tradition (the reality about which Faust fantasized), its use by native communities serves to verify that modernity is an illusion from which we can escape.

INDIGENOUS ARCHAEOLOGY AND INDIGENOUS MOVEMENTS IN ARGENTINA: FAUST IN THE PUNA OF ATACAMA

Maybe the interest to know the past of the oasis, interest that has mobilized scores of people in vehicles of all size, to open up ways in the sand by journeying on their own previous tracks, to construct a stone building that pompously has been called camp, is, at the same time, an instrument of the own settlers of the oases. In the end, they know, better than anyone else, how to imagine, in each traveler who approaches their oases, even in those who approach it for their past, to articulate their future.

Alejandro Haber (1999:452)

Guambianos and Nasa from Colombia have incorporated archaeological studies in their cultural policies to produce powerful discourses that feed, maintain, and help to reproduce their political culture. In doing so, they generated strategic alliances with scholars. In the case of the Atacameño Collas of Argentina the process has been different.

Colla communities have a long tradition of handling the territory of the Puna (Haber 1999) and the Atacama Desert (Molina 2004); the Collas have been characterized by their amazing handling and reproduction of the oases in an area where anthropic intervention is necessary to maintain permanent agricultural conditions. After the 1994 constitution, a group of Colla families in the Antofalla salt flats (northwestern Argentina) initiated a political process seeking recognition as indigenous communities, which will permit them to enjoy the system of positive discrimination offered by the government in favor of historically marginalized groups. In this process of cultural revitalization, these communities have chosen to subvert nineteenth-century images that described the Puna of Atacama as a desert with extensive archaeological remains and a scarce population. Investigators of that time stated that the current population could not be the descendants of the people who left the great archaeological deposits they were investigating (e.g., Ambrosetti's work in the Atacama region, cited in Haber 1999:47). Images of desolation and abandonment registered by the archaeologists of the nineteenth century and the beginning of the twentieth century (Haber 1999:51–53) portrayed the Puna of Atacama as a space in need of modernization; mining projects followed, which nowadays flood the region, displacing and penalizing the peasants who had lived there for centuries.

Given that the Puna was depicted as having no cultural content, it was considered an adequate place for unfolding the dreams of modernization of the emergent Argentine nation. General Daniel Cerri (cited by Haber 1999:51), one of its first governors, proposed to generate a research agenda for discovering investment possibilities in the region for "those who wish to use their money well." Interestingly, these examples of how a cultural policy was enacted show that the appropriation of Western legal logic weakens the dominant images created by the Faustic perspective; in fact, the recognition of cultural differences by the Argentinean government demands a written document about local norms and customs.

The Collas of Antofalla have decided to make theirs norms objective, revealing their ethnic markers to correspond with the essentialist language of the Argentinean government. In this game of political relations, archaeology has not been directly appropriated to note diacriticals that they can use for the recognition of ethnic particularities; daily practices have been contributed to the task of the archaeologists to aid a more consequent interpretation of the archaeological record (Haber et al. 2005). Most investigations have highlighted cultural continuities in the handling of the space between pre-Hispanic and current contexts. The Collas have supported archaeological research for more than a decade; their active participation has helped to make more reasonable interpretations of historical events that otherwise would have been considered from a different, biased point of view. That collaborative work has shown continuities in practices such as the reproduction and handling of the landscape, the permanent dialogue with space as an entity defined through the concept of Pachamama (Mother Earth), the care and raising of camelids, and the maintenance of hydric resources in one of the driest zones on the planet.

One difference between this process and the one occurring in Colombia is that the use of archaeology in this community of northwestern Argentina has not been the main tool for the exhibition of diacritics for the recognition of their cultural particularities. In the fight against state-imposed modernization, as demanded by the National Institute for Indigenous Affairs (Law 23.302),[2] the objectification of their own normativity and their self-identification with original peoples are sufficient for recognizing particularities in order to activate the system of compensations offered by the Argentinean state through its adherence to international treaties, such as Convention 169 of the IWO; nevertheless, the organizational process of this community is not generalized in the Puna of Atacama and, apparently, it maintains substantial differences from cultural policy projects in the Atacama Desert on the Chilean side (Molina 2004). In the regional capital, Antofagasta de la Sierra, modernization has not been met with differentiation or identification, perhaps due to the impact of mining projects and tourism. These two opposing forces—one resisting modernity, the other one not—have militated against a collective project for an ethnic community. Such is an ideal scenario for Faust-like dreams of individuation and fragmentation. In Antofagasta de la Sierra touristic services are offered, not communitarily but individually, following the logic of individual development stimulated by state policies. The pace of these civilizing processes is vertiginous. The 2006 legislature had lands measured and given to individuals; this policy is consistent with the assault on communal lands from investors, especially for tourism.

Two discourses about archaeology can currently be distinguished. On the one hand, the support of archaeological interpretations favors academic investigations and potentializes actions that show a cultural continuity in preceramic and ceramic contexts (the case of Antofalla). On the other hand, there is archaeology as a powerful tool suiting touristic projects in the region (the case of Antofagasta de la Sierra). In his inaugural speech at the 2006 Puna of Atacama fair, the governor of Catamarca mentioned that archaeology was an unquestionable resource that would bring economic benefits to the region, just like the production of handcrafts and the improvement of camelid products such as llama wool and meat. This Faust-like speech finds its favorite place of reproduction in the local museum. That space of small rooms shelters a chronological version of the cultural diversity of the Puna of Atacama. One room is devoted to the "pioneers," not the first inhabitants of the zone but the archaeologists of the nineteenth century who, sometimes, wrote contemptuously about the natives. The weight of a memory disciplined by archaeology is so heavy that a poster indicates, "If the archaeologists are those who recover lost memories, the people are their owners and guardians." There is no direct appropriation of the discipline by a local political culture. The discipline is just seen as a tool to attract investors for local development, traditionally understood as increased profits isolated from any collective project.

There are two different appropriations of archaeological discourse in the Puna of Atacama: one supports disciplinary practices and directs them by allowing scholars to arrive at the best interpretations; in the other the discipline becomes, forcefully, the keeper and guardian of a memory constructed by its own rhetorical machinery. In the former, scholars recognize local knowledge that surpasses nineteenth-century representations based on contemptuous tropes; communities, albeit not explicitly (as in the Colombian case), use the machinery of science to generate connectors that dilute the past-present dichotomy, so fundamental for the formation of modernizing scenarios. In the latter, there is the discourse that considers archaeology the sole device for the configuration of certain cultural reminiscences to follow the steps of Faust toward a total transformation, as if the presence and action of the archaeologists predict the deep and forceful success of modernization.

The success of this memory agenced by the archaeologists but not by the community, as in the case of Antofalla, is a cultural mechanism objectified by the official discourse and its appropriation of archaeology to represent the traditional as something surpassed and located in an inaccessible temporality. Nevertheless, other discourses exist, some non-verbal; they reject the eagerness with which the provincial government stimulates the archaeological connections of northwestern Argentina with the Incas. Such a rejection has gained momentum with the exhibition of two mummies; according to some locals, they have been uprooted from their resting places not to express historical value but the eagerness for profit of foreign investors and others, not necessarily from Antofagasta de la Sierra, interested in the antiques market.

The Recognition of Cultural Difference: New Postmodern Merchandise or the Achievement of Social Movements?

> *They must help us to criticize the society we created so that we could build sophisticated intellectual apparatuses, deconstruct our history, or create imagined communities (civil society, social movements, transnational communities, social forums, networks of the "Third World," or virtual ecological transnational communities) ... All this while we are comfortable, safe, protected, and well paid in our houses, offices, research centers, universities, libraries, congresses, seminaries, forums, classes, or hotels speaking about them, thinking about them, and imagining them. They are our last better hope.*
>
> *Astrid Ulloa (2004:364)*

The enactment of NAGPRA at the beginning of the 1990s (Platt 1991) signaled a rupture with traditional archaeological research in charge of verifying the end of tradition. Yet, it remains to be seen if archaeology has broken free of its discursive rules (Foucault 2002) or if it has just produced new enunciations without modifying its ontological structure based on the panegyric of modernity. The discourse of modernity positioned individuality as the basis of experience. Communal life was condemned because it limited the right of individuals to enjoy their bodies and their minds amidst anonymous social structures. Cities were portrayed as the normal spaces where citizens could develop their potentialities. The nation-state created social spaces where anonymous relations, controlled by tight legislation, dominated face-to-face relations. Although these processes were against the natives and their communal culture, since the 1970s cultural differences have been revaluated, and now indigenous peoples are pleading for their conservation and respect. Since then, archaeology has shifted from positivism toward hermeneutics (Hodder 1995) and has created new spaces for negotiation, such as repatriation (Ferguson 1996).

Before this peculiarity, Faust's dream (which fomented urban spaces by taming nature) stumbles as an opposite discourse emerges. Why contemporary political projects make room for differences and communal forms? Panegyrists of political change see the recognition of difference as resulting from years of struggle and political education (Brysk 2000). Others consider it a capitalist strategy to produce market niches for fragmented consumers who search for green commodities to satiate their nostalgia of a pristine nature, lost since the dream of Faust became real (Ulloa 2004:363–364). Yet, no one explains why certain indigenous demands became governmental agendas worldwide; nevertheless, it seems that the recognition of difference followed the recognition of the environmental crisis generated by modernization. The fact that many indigenous groups maintain no modern relations with ecological niches makes them representative of acceptable behaviors within environmental sustainability. An emergent discourse that promotes and facilitates ecologically sustainable behaviors, which Astrid Ulloa (2004) labeled as the "ecological native," is accompanied by the opposition to modernity. In this context the recognition of difference is not a concession to decades of native struggle to conserve social, economic, and political preferences, neither is it a way to sell green products to dissatisfied citizens. Recognition emerges from the interstices located between the political motivations of the marginalized groups and the conservationist eagerness that oscillates between the rational use of nature (understood as natural resources) and the identification of investment opportunities in the green market. The nostalgia of a pristine nature becomes an ideal scenario for economic investment by constructing natural spaces with natives who, in spite of global transformations, are presented as immediate descendants of pre-Hispanic communities. The nexus between desires structured by a communal political base and those generated by diminishing energy resources (and the consequent emergence of business opportunities) allows an epistemic dynamic that pleads for the existing native knowledge and stimulates the search for new knowledge.

Archaeology with and of indigenous communities cannot escape this structuring. The relationship of indigenous groups with scholars strives to counter modern images that locate them as objects of the past. Indigenous archaeologies try to generate connectors that dissolve the past-present dichotomy by ritualizing what scholars call the "archaeological record." A reflection on the relationship between archaeology and indigenous peoples must consider that it is partly due to, and receives stimuli from, the market instrumentalization of green discourses that posit Western science as responsible for contemporary social maladies. It also results from the functionalization that native groups make of Western sciences that, as in the case of archaeology, level local knowledge so it can enter international academic, communitarian, and market networks.

In this mutual functionalization, many communities have found the satisfaction of fundamental necessities, such as the recovery of bone remains (Ferguson 1996) that, conceived as scientific objects, had been uprooted from their localities and exposed in metropolitan museums (Clifford 1999). This instrumentalization has also produced profits from ethnotourism; indigenous groups are thus obtaining income without transforming nature and without breaking the principles that consider it a subject.

In sum, a discourse that enunciates the experiences of indigenous archaeologies and archaeology with natives is located in the interstices of market instrumentalizations that turn differences into commodities. Such experiences are stimulated and fed by grassroots strategies to obtain both inward historical coherence (a shared discourse on what nature, community, and territory are) as well as outward (to legitimize native readings of the environment, the ethnic group, and the socially constructed space). The utopias that we, as archaeologists, can construct with indigenous communities must be shielded against the ways that the market reads historical continuities or communally produced historical versions. Archaeology with indigenous peoples and indigenous archaeologies must include an awareness of the interstitial space that oscillates between the reproduction of capitalism (Lipovetsky 2000) and communitarian expectations.

TOWARD THE REFORMULATION OF ARCHAEOLOGY: THE FOLLY OF A SCIENTIFIC ARCHAEOLOGY

Just as archaeology came to be when the Eurocentric bourgeoisie needed to give scientific status to an overwhelming collection of objects disconnected from their original contexts by the colonial journey, the discipline will be transformed when the logic of capitalism destructures the center-periphery dichotomy. Through ethnic museums resulting from policies of creation in traditional communities, archaeology will become, unavoidably, a tool of local use and the scientific status of the discipline will be an anachronistic remembrance.

Wilhelm Londoño (2002a:153)

Since its inception as a discipline in charge of pronouncing, through the description of monuments and ruins, the dissolution of the communitarian bonds that gave sense and coherence to tradition, archaeology configured itself as an epistemological device that corroborated the success of Faust's dreams. The extremes of the transformations experienced by Faust go from the collective principles of the community to the fragmenting of the individual. Although archaeology never pretended to account for those processes, its fundamental task was and still is the description of the perennial nature of the first moment (that is, the end of tradition); its practice recreates and reproduces the second moment (the triumph of modernity), so fragmentation is lived and experienced as real and unquestionable. Nevertheless, the current context—a continued disciplinary depoliticization challenged by its very repoliticization seeking more horizontal and communitarian relationships (Tilley 1998)—it is foolish and paradoxical that the archaeologists still fight for academic agendas based on the scientific reconstruction of the past.

No matter how convincing the critique of epistemological models based on objectivism is, and in spite of the increasing popularity of hermeneutic and symbolic agendas in archaeology (Hodder 1995), in many parts of the world research projects that plead and stimulate logocentric, disciplinary studies still operate. It is as if in the middle of the revitalization of tradition, archaeology opened spaces to contradict the very forces that gave it its dynamic and discursive force; instead, what emerge are alternative disciplinary practices that do not controvert the principles of modern logic. To be sure, the future of the discipline will be determined by the resolution of this paradox and how a horizontal practice can bloom within a colonial and asymmetrical space.

Although a community-oriented archaeology is now part of the grain, disciplinary practices are basically rhetorical; their passage to intercultural and more balanced actions is largely inhibited. The declaration of archaeological sites by transnational corporations, like UNESCO, turns sacred and secular spaces into world heritage; this means that those who could claim to be direct heirs of those places have their hands tied. Although several scholars have sided with the recognition of ancestral knowledge that superimposes academic interpretations, academia preserves a vertical structure in which the teaching of native knowledge is forbidden due to the pedagogical incompetence of natives as measured by Western standards. The "others" always speak through "us" or by the appropriation of Western epistemological devices. Native ontologies try to navigate through discourses like archaeology, protected by an elaborate epistemological construction; as a result, a traditional construction is packed and adorned with the tones of modernity. It would make more sense to formulate these discourses in the extensive margins of their own logics.

Perhaps the only way of leaving the tight margins of archaeology, a device that supports Faust's dream by proving the end of tradition with each ruin that it describes, is to recognize the failure of that globalizing project given the resistance emerging from localities, even though the latter are presented just as gracious concessions of modernity. Although Faust is all over the world, his footsteps have been closely followed by furtive hunters who have erased his tracks, following other ones that lead home, to the community. The only thing left to Faust is a utopic return to home, now torn apart. What will be his last transformation? Surely the return home, the reencounter, the recognition that no matter how much asphalt has been laid, the Earth is still there to receive human beings, not as individualities but as an accumulation of cultures. Sociability must be reinvented.

NOTES

1. I see a difference between "archaeology with natives" and "indigenous archaeology." The former is characterized by an association between non-native scholars and indigenous communities; negotiation of interests occurs and scholars have room for action. That is not the case in the latter. Nevertheless, concrete differences are yet to be established.
2. Available at http://www.bioetica.org

REFERENCES

Álvarez, Sonia, Evelina Dagnino, and Arturo Escobar (editors) 1998 *Cultures of Politics, Politics of Cultures: Re-visioning Latin American Social Movements*. Westview, Boulder.

Barona, Guido 1993 *Legitimidad y sujeción: los paradigmas de la invención de América*. Colcultura, Bogotá.

———. 1995 *La maldición de Midas en una región del mundo colonial: Popayán 1730–1830*. Universidad del Valle, Cali.

Berman, Marshall 2001 *Todo lo sólido se desvanece en el aire. La experiencia de la modernidad*. Siglo XXI, Mexico. First published 1983.

Binford, Lewis 1965 Archaeological systematics and the study of culture process. *American Antiquity* 31:203–210.

Brysk, Alison 2000 *From Local Village to Global Village: Indian Rights and International Relations in Latin America*. Stanford University Press, Stanford.

Clifford, James 1999 *Itinerarios transculturales*. Gedisa, Barcelona.

Escobar, Arturo 1999 *El final del salvaje. Naturaleza, cultura y política en la antropología contemporánea*. ICANH-CEREC, Bogotá.

Ferguson, Thomas J. 1996 Native Americans and the practice of archaeology. *Annual Review of Anthropology* 25:63–79.

Findji, María Teresa 1992 The Indigenous Authorities Movement in Colombia. In *The Making of Social Movements in Latin America*, edited by Arturo Escobar and Sonia Álvarez, pp. 112–134. Westview, Boulder.

Foucault, Michel 1996 *La verdad y las formas jurídicas*. Gedisa, Barcelona.

————. 2002 *La arqueología del saber*. Siglo XXI, Mexico.

Geertz, Clifford 1989 *La interpretación de las culturas*. Gedisa, Barcelona.

Gnecco, Cristóbal, and Wilhelm Londoño 2008 Representaciones de la alteridad indígena en el discurso jurídico colombiano. In *Representaciones legales de la alteridad indígena*, edited by Herinaldy Gómez and Cristóbal Gnecco, pp. 25–94. Colciencias-Universidad del Cauca, Popayán.

Haber, Alejandro 1999 Una arqueología de los oasis puneños. Domesticidad, interacción e identidad en Antofalla, primer y segundo milenios DC. Unpublished Ph.D. dissertation, Department of Anthropology, Universidad de Buenos Aires, Buenos Aires.

Haber, Alejandro, Marcos Quesada, and Miguel Ramos 2005 Tebenquiche chico en la superficie del tiempo. Unpublished manuscript, on file at the Escuela de Arqueología, Universidad Nacional de Catamarca, Catamarca.

Hodder, Ian 1995 Interpretation in archaeology. *Cambridge Archaeological Journal* 5(2):306–309.

Jaramillo, Jaime 1982 *El pensamiento colombiano en el siglo XIX*. Temis, Bogotá.

Langebaek, Carl 1995 Informe preliminar sobre actividades del Proyecto Tierradentro. *Revista de Antropología y Arqueología* 8(1–2):226–236.

Laurent, Virginie 1998 Pueblos indígenas y espacios políticos en Colombia. In *Modernidad, identidad y desarrollo*, edited by María Lucía Sotomayor, pp. 85–109. Instituto Colombiano de Antropología, Bogotá.

Lipovetsky, Gilles 2000 *El crepúsculo del deber. La ética indolora de los nuevos tiempos democráticos*. Anagrama, Barcelona.

————. 2004 *El imperio de lo efímero*. Anagrama, Barcelona.

Londoño, Wilhelm 2000 Reflexiones sobre un trabajo de campo en Novirao. Una comunidad Nasa. Unpublished Honor's thesis, Department of Anthropology, Universidad del Cauca, Popayán.

————. 2002a La poética de los tiestos: el sentido de la cultura material prehispánica en una comunidad Nasa. *Arqueología del Área Intermedia* 4:137–157.

————. 2002b Arqueología y política cultural en una comunidad Nasa en el suroccidente de Colombia. *Revista de Antropología y Arqueología* 13:78–100.

————. 2003 La "reducción de salvajes" y el mantenimiento de la tradición. *Boletín de Antropología* 34:235–251.

Molina, Raúl 2004 Los collas de la cordillera de Atacama. In *La memoria olvidada: historia de los pueblos indígenas de Chile*, edited by José Bengoa, pp. 45–78. Cuadernos Bicentenario, Presidencia de la República, Santiago.

Mumford, Jeremy 1998 The taki onqoy and the Andean nation: Sources and interpretations. *Latin America Research Review* 33:150–165.

Platt, George 1991 The repatriation law ends one journey—but opens a new road. *Museum News* 70:91.

Rappaport, Joane 2000 *La política de la memoria. Interpretación indígena de la Historia en los Andes colombianos*. Universidad del Cauca, Popayán.

Rimbaud, Arthur 2003 [1873] *Una temporada en el infierno. Iluminaciones*. Longseller, Buenos Aires.

Rojas, Cristina 2001 *Civilización y violencia: la búsqueda de la identidad en la Colombia del siglo XIX*. Norma, Bogotá.

Saramago, José 2004 *La caverna*. Punto de lectura, Bogotá.

Schiffer, Michael 1976 *Behavioral Archaeology*. Academic Press, New York.

Shanks, Michael, and Christopher Tilley 1992 *Re-constructing Archaeology: Theory and Practice*. Routledge, London.

Tilley, Christopher 1998 Archaeology as socio-political action in the present. In *Reader in Archaeological Theory: Post-processual and Cognitive Approaches*, edited by David S. Whitley, pp. 305–330. Routledge, London.

Ulloa, Astrid 2004 *La construcción del nativo ecológico*. ICANH-Colciencias, Bogotá.

Urdaneta, Martha 1987 En busca de las huellas de los antiguos Guambianos. Unpublished Honor's thesis, Department of Anthropology, Universidad Nacional, Bogotá.

———. 1991 Huellas de pishau en el resguardo de Guambía. *Boletín del Museo del Oro* 31:3–30.

Vasco, Luis Guillermo 1997 Para los Guambianos la historia es vida. *Boletín de Antropología* 11(28):115–127.

CHAPTER 12

ARCHAEOLOGY AND IDENTITY: THE CASE OF THE GUAMBIANOS

Luis Guillermo Vasco
Translated from the Spanish by Cristóbal Gnecco

The Guambianos are indigenous peoples who dwell in the highlands of the Cordillera Central in southwestern Colombia. They call themselves Namuy Misak, "our people," or speakers of the Wam language, "our language," initially classified as Chibcha but currently unclassified. Spanish conquest and domination fractured Guambiano society in several *parcialidades*, a division that still lingers in the communities of Guambía, Quizgó, Totoro, Ambaló, La María, San Vicente, and others of smaller size. In this chapter I will only refer to Guambía. For their subsistence they depend almost exclusively on agricultural production, both for local consumption and for the markets: potato, onion, *ulluco* (a highland tuber), lima beans, corn, garlic, and wheat, plus domestic animals such as guinea pigs, chicken, horses, pigs, sheep, and cattle. They buy foodstuffs, cloth, and other consumer goods from the local markets. A few Guambianos work as teachers, government clerks, carpenters, shoemakers, or have transportation vehicles. Some old production processes are still retained, especially those regarding cloth making. Women weave wool on four-log vertical looms of pre-Columbian origin, making their skirt-like *anacos* and the ponchos used by their men. Smaller, forked looms are used for weaving *chumbes*,[1] with which anacos are tied to the waist and children are secured when carried on the back. A few men still make rounded hats, *tambalkuari*, made with a long band woven with vegetal fiber.

Guambiano territory, measuring 20,000 ha, is recognized by Colombian law as a *resguardo*,[2] communal land that cannot be sold

---

This chapter was originally published as "Arqueología e identidad: el caso guambiano" in *Arqueología en América Latina hoy*, edited by Gustavo Politis, pp. 176–191 (Fondo de Promoción de la Cultura, Bogotá, 1992). Translated and reprinted by permission of the publisher.

or given away and is allotted by the *cabildo*[3] to the members of the community. A large part of their best land, especially that suitable for corn and wheat, had been taken away by landlords gradually since colonial times and converted to cattle farming. The workforce was recruited among Guambianos themselves through sharecropping—in "exchange" for small plots and poor housing, they had to perform free work for the landlords a number of days every month. Sharecroppers were outside communal life and beyond the authority of the *cabildo*. A severe land scarcity determined the current settlement pattern. Most people cluster in a few narrow valleys along the main rivers (Piendamó, Cacique, Michambe, and Juanambú), although many have *trabajaderos* (work places) in the highlands further up or farther away from their dwellings, where they stay for variable periods devoted to agriculture. Cold, rain, and strong winds are good reasons the Guambianos have for avoiding steeper hills or mountain ridges. Land scarcity, the need to diversify agricultural products, and the influence of the values of the national society have resulted in the division of extant communal lands in minute plots; very little land is allotted to each family and it is normally located in several places, both inside and outside the *resguardo*. Thus, many Guambianos were forced to emigrate, but conserve social ties with those left in the *resguardos*; they are still considered part of the community and participate in exchange networks of goods, work, and marriage.

Despite the long-time strong pressure from landlords, politicians (basically from the two traditional Colombian parties, Liberals and Conservative), priests, and white teachers, Guambianos preserve an identity based on their own thought, language, beliefs, cloth, family organization, communal works, kinship system, authority, and territory; however, these aspects and their own identity have been diversely affected, shattered, and weakened as a result of domination. Since 1980, the almost 17,000 members of Guambiano society started a fight for "recuperating everything," from authority and territory to language, education, thought, history, and autonomy. In this fight the need to rediscover and strengthen their identity plays a central role.

As victims of negation and deculturation for almost 500 years, many things have been lost, others are "hidden" or only remain in the memory of the elders, while the younger people decry them, ashamed. But now the leaders and many members of the community are willing to uncover those things, retrace the steps of the forebears, and become themselves again. Only so, they reason, will they be able to resolve the complex and difficult current problems without recurring to outside people and without compromising their identity. But, how to proceed? Let the Guambianos speak for themselves:[4]

"In the old times, before Columbus, we Guambianos had everything to live: our territory, our authority, our economy, our organization, our customs, our thoughts, everything our own."

"When the whites came many changes happened and are still happening; those changes were leaving Guambiano society as if empty, not really empty but silent."

"The invader cut the tree, our tree, and left a single trunk. And we Guambianos ask how the rest was."

"In 1980 we started to recover our own things: our *cabildo* and our lands. And the question about how was the rest of the tree was became important because we now want to recover everything, our whole life."

"We want to know how are the roots and the branches to let it be know to the *cabildo*, to the people, to the kids. We must follow the steps of the forebears."

"Archaeology must excavate from the trunk downward, looking for the roots. We did archaeology; we are currently doing it. And we have found some things. We have come to know something. And we have gained some clues."

"In order to follow those clues, in order to interpret what we are finding, we found it necessary to talk to the elders, because in their heads rests the knowledge of Guambiano history and our own thought is preserved. We did studies of oral tradition." (Script of the House and Museum of Guambiano Culture)

Thus, Guambianos want archaeology to uncover the objects of the forebears, their material remains, their traces. In doing this job they have been discovering that things do not speak by themselves, that the objects recovered during excavation are mute by themselves, and that it is necessary to make them speak so they can utter the words. In this regard two discourses are heard: one is that of archaeologists and ethnohistorians, which Guambianos take in consideration but which does not satisfy them; the other one is that of the elders, who talk about what they know but which is not enough in the current conditions. Thus, it was necessary to find the words jointly, confronting both discourses: "We had to confront the stories (of the elders) with the histories that come from the papers."

The Guambianos summoned archaeologists Martha Urdaneta and Sofía Botero, with whom they shared their problems. Guambianos know by oral tradition that they belong there, that these lands have been their own forever although they were invaded for centuries by white landlords. But whites despise these arguments and maintain that the Guambianos were brought from Peru and Ecuador by Spanish conquistadors as *yanaconas*, "service Indians." To face the white's word, Guambianos want archaeology, also a white's word and thus authority and power, to show with white's arguments their continuity in these lands "well before Columbus."

In order to live now and to recover their identity they need to find roots, history, memories, and the words of the past for walking along them toward the future, following the steps of the ancestors. In Guambiano thought the past is ahead and the future behind. Thus, the history that is being currently lived needs to travel the road opened by the forebears with their steps, the traces they left; only so will it be a true Guambiano history. Many of these things are "hidden," and those that are remembered or remain have no arguments of authority any longer before many members of Guambiano society, greatly influenced by teachers, priests, and other agents of Colombian society. The hidden has to be uncovered, excavated, and presented with arguments of authority and power in order to allow recovery, to allow the Guambianos to walk again "following the thoughts and steps of the Guambiano *taitas*."[5]

At the beginning of the archaeological collaborative research between scholars and the community, the *cabildo* appointed 15 Guambianos to "accompany" (*linchap*) us, so three of them could work every day; but dozens of men, women, and especially children have participated, coming to the roads to give us bags with sherds from all over the *resguardo* or telling stories about the "steps of the ancestors." We have discussed with the *cabildo* when and where to dig and how to preserve the sites from agricultural activities while archaeological research lasts. The *cabildo* has obtained from landholders the permissions needed to carry out excavations, some of them in the middle of planted fields.

Numerous terraces are found throughout the *resguardo*, most of them likely for dwellings. Two main types can be defined: (1) isolated and placed at the bottom of hills and on top of small elevations in flat lands (according to Guambianos this type is the most recent and may belong to the houses of sharecroppers and commoners), and (2) clustered and located on high hills and along mountain ridges above 3000 m. More than 350 terraces of this type have been found and seem to be the oldest since they do not accord to the Guambiano settlement pattern, as "nobody would live that up high because the wind would tear off the roofs of the houses."

The ridges of some mountains are cut by large parallel ditches, called "snake trails" by Guambianos. James Ford (1944) found similar ditches to the north, in Jambaló, and thought they were made for defensive purposes; yet, the very nature of these traces renders that explanation unlikely.

Few tombs, both isolated and clustered, have been excavated so far in order to avoid possible suspicion by commoners about easy gain and because Guambianos consider that bones and burial goods are dangerous and can cause disease and even death upon entering in contact with them. Many say that those remains do not belong to Guambianos but to *pishau*, about whom there is no agreement whether they are their ancestors or not (an elder, for instance, thinks that the *pishau* were *kallimachik*, ancient Nasa).[6]

Participation of Guambianos in the research group has posed methodological and operational problems. Their solution demands confronting their points of view and those of archaeology, their way of doing things and that of archaeology; yet, they are also a source of enrichment on how to plan objectives, ask the pertinent questions, and carry out the survey, excavation, laboratory work, and interpretation. During the two field seasons completed so far, there have been obvious difficulties with the Guambianos "accompanying" excavations because "the levelings of the ancients have too much force and can make us sick." But once in the task, we all decide how to proceed. For instance, during excavation "the basic horizontal control was done just by 1 x 1 m units, because doing such a control inside the units themselves was not popular among Guambianos," who argued that materials roll down the slope, roots and worms bring together what was formerly separated, digging tools separate what was formerly together, and, at the end, everything is mixed up. What is horizontal control needed for, then? Thus "it was not possible to avoid that, often, little mountains of sherds were created inside the units."

Discussions about stratigraphic control were and still are endless: What is the meaning of 30 cm of archaeological material on house floors? Continuous occupation of people who did not sweep? Several occupations? If so, how to define the limit between them? What happens if the house was expanded, remodeled, or torn down to be rebuilt in the same spot? When work stops due to these discussions we resort to the elders and traditional wise men to bring the work back and keep going ahead. For instance, the *mørøpik* think that "the large butterflies forced people to abandon the terraces ... The butterfly was the spirit of the dead and with that spirit (*trør*) the medicine man said that no one could live there and the place had to be abandoned ... because the house did not burn but rotted. [It collapsed and] this increased the deposit 10 cm"; this is a more plausible hypothesis than that of people not sweeping, burying themselves in their own dirt.

At the beginning, the decision about when to stop an excavation was hard to make. Sometimes it was necessary to decide, somewhat arbitrarily, to stop at a certain depth after levels containing material culture.

At some point we established that there was no cultural material in the brown yellowish stratum (the D stratum of an "ideal" profile) nor below it; we called excavations to a halt when we found such a stratum, although if doubts remained we dug around to make sure.

What should be done when community members come to "accompany" for the first time? Sometimes the entire excavation area was flooded by people willing to participate in the dig, so we had to introduce certain order, explanations, and orientations, about which even the Guambiano members of the team were not convinced. But, we are dealing with them themselves, with their own history.

During the first season Guambiano specialists in house building and wood differentiated between holes made by larvae, those resulting from the burial of umbilical cords (normally made near the hearth), and possible postholes. When the latter was identified "the work was closed for the Guambianos"; one of them said, "Now this has to start having meaning," an expression of Guambiano vision conveying that everything begins in the house and, within this, in the kitchen. Even the territory develops in concentric circles with the house at its center; thus, it is an expansion of the house as much as the community is an expansion of the domestic group. The Guambianos say that their territory, the *nupirau*, is a large house where a single and large family dwells, the Guambiano family. When a house floor was identified, it was a starting point to unfolding the knowledge of the totality. In the lab the dialogue is continuous because, among other things, according to the purpose the Guambianos attribute to the work we do, "the labor of sorting out ceramic material is thought of as a medium and not as an end ... It is a matter of defining criteria for a classification that helps to reflect about socioeconomic organization, technology, relationships with other people, etc."

That is why "the idea is not to classify just for the sake of classification but to search for pottery elements that can reflect central aspects of the society whose remains, seen through factors external to pottery itself, can start speaking about the live systems behind classifications." Archaeological categories, based on paste, decoration, tempers, and forms are confronted with those of the Guambianos, preexistent in the memories of the elders and basically based on function, with form and size playing a secondary role: pots for cooking during the *mingas*,[7] pots for domestic cooking, pots for carrying and storing water, pots for preparing medicines, pots for fermenting the *chicha*, dishes for eating, skillets for roasting corn tortillas, and the like.

For the Guambianos paste differences, central to most classifications, mean that the clay comes from various sources, generally not rich and so prone to exhaustion, and, therefore, a change of sources within the same area. Paste differences can also mean provenience from several sources with different clays, all in the same temporal plane. The same behavior could be indicative of changes in temporal succession, preferred materials for certain pots, differences between potters, or trade. From the beginning the Guambianos argued that the most elaborate and decorated pottery belonged to the ancients and the less elaborate to the most recent inhabitants; these criteria can also be found among other Colombian native societies, such as the Embera-Chami of the Garrapatas River in the Cauca Valley, and was found to hold true in Guambía as the research went on. In the general analysis done by the Guambianos, however, "time seems to dissolve because the material was placed in a single temporal plane," just as it happens in their historical thought, in which time is compressed until becoming "flat." Archaeology has to reestablish, using its sequences and dates, the temporal depth necessary to face the arguments of the whites.

A central issue for the Guambiano members of the research team, both during excavation and the analysis of the cultural material, was the idea that the remains we were dealing with were their own, were "traces of the old Guambianos." This represents a rupture with the previously held idea—widely shared by the Guambianos and popularized by the whites as a mechanism for severing their historical continuity, depriving them of their past and the consciousness surrounding it—that the remains belong to *pijaos* or *pishau*, which were strange and enemy people. Thus, the development of the research under this idea created the bases for reestablishing the continuity of Guambiano history.

But, what to do when using the results to achieve the expectations Guambianos have regarding archaeology? The date obtained in the first excavation, AD 1620 ± 50 years, affirmed the presence of Guambianos during that time in Santiago, one of the former farms recovered some years ago, a presence testified by Spanish chroniclers and by archive documents found through ethnohistorical research, especially the visit by Tomás López (see Calero 1997:62–64). Besides, the beginning of the work allowed us to define whatever "Guambiano" there was in the pottery.

According to the Guambianos, the paste comes from five different sources: (1) a paste with white dots, (2) a paste with red dots, (3) a paste with quartz, (4) a black paste with mica, and (5) a paste with a lot of mica. Pinpointing the sources appeared, then, as a must; this process is just beginning. But based on traditional archaeological criteria such as paste (color, hardness, texture, porosity, surface color, finishing, manufacture technique, decoration), the pottery recovered during the first season (9,098 sherds) was organized in seven basic groups. The second field season forced us to add a new group and to make small modifications in the definition of the initial groups.

Group 1 contains 70.7% of the material and Group 3 contains 19.5%; these groups are similar and their differences may be due to clay sources, firing, or use. This fact points to the hypothesis that they were produced and used by the same people, and that the pottery in other groups belong to other people and was "imported." The Guambianos sorted out pottery function according to sherd thickness, size, and curvature in the following manner:

1. Single function, such as flat *cayanas* (of three kinds: for tortillas, for roasting corn, and for frying), large bowls for *mingas*, medicinal pots, water-carrying pots, and pots for fermenting corn beer.
2. Multiple functions, such as large-size pots for cooking during *mingas*, medium-size pots for domestic use, small size for cooking for two or three people, and extra small size for the use of one person, and bowls for eating (medium, small, and extra small).
3. Other objects, such as bases for supporting pots over the fire, figurines, and "candlesticks."

This classification, however, leaves out most of the pottery, particularly small fragments. From the point of view of traditional archaeological classification, Guambiano pottery does not present radical discontinuities, except in form and decoration, through which to follow a developmental sequence established by dated sites; on the contrary, it is markedly homogenous. Thus, the classification just presented was adjusted to include seven formal categories using both the criteria of archaeologists and those of the Guambianos, although function was not worked out enough because it was considered that it was "too premature" to do it:

1. Globular or semi-globular pots of rounded or bell-shaped base and everted rims, some of which have traces of red paint as well as incised and imprinted decoration. This group accounts for 51.8% of the material.
2. Pots similar to the former but with everted rims. This difference has been established because, according to the Guambianos, these pots are smaller and handled by the rim. Some have imprinted decoration toward the rim. This group accounts for 5.1% of all the pottery.
3. Globular or sub-globular pots with neck and straight or semi-straight rim. About half of them have imprinted, painted, or incised decoration. This group accounts for 11.2% of the pottery.
4. Narrow-mouth pots (n = 7). Three of these have imprinted decoration toward the rim.
5. Bowls with straight-everted rims. Some have painted, printed, and/or incised and incised-applied decoration. This group accounts for 18.8% of the material.
6. Bowls with straight-inverted rim. Some have painted or imprinted decoration. This group accounts for 6% of the material.
7. One fragment of an everted rim bowl.

There are also 41 pot bases (most of them bell-shaped; others are leg-shaped), circular, flat, or conical spindle whirls, rollers, handles, and a few figurines. Fragments belonging to pots account for 68.9% of the sample and bowl fragments 24.9%.

The oldest pottery is similar to that of the Clásico Regional (Duque 1963) or lsnos (Reichel-Dolmatoff 1975) from San Agustín, a nearby region. Some sherds decorated with imprints and incisions resemble the "incised-pointed A" type defined by Julio César Cubillos (1959) in the Morro de Tulcán, in Popayán, while the imprinted sherds are similar to the "deep-incised" type defined by Cubillos for the Morro de Tulcán, Pubenza, and Tinajas phase (1984). The more recent material has traits in common with pottery found by Cháves and Puerta (1985) in Tierradentro.

Further research has given depth to the human occupation of Guambiano territory, taking it back to several centuries before the Spanish conquest in La Campana and Ñimbe, above an altitude 3,200 m. Those evidences date to before the Christian era, although it is still not possible from archaeological evidence to affirm if this oldest occupation was Guambiano; yet oral tradition has it that way. In this form the sense of "we belong here" has been confirmed and is strongly supported by Guambianos; even more, the Derecho Mayor[8] has been endorsed from the point of view of the whites and has become the base for the fight to recover the territories they claim as being legitimate Americans, the first inhabitants of these lands.

But, what to do with archaeologically derived materials and data in order to make them speak to the community? "We also found that the members of the community keep materials of times past: archaeological, from burials and excavations, and ethnographic, used by the elders and even currently by some people. They were eager to donate these traces to the *cabildo*."

"Thus, the idea of this museum arose out of the necessity to preserve the results of our work and for them to speak to the community."

"But we do not want a museum like the ones the white people have in the cities—mute museums that are good only to show the works of the tribes—because in the hands of the whites the things of the Indians cannot speak; they are silent."

"On the contrary, in our own hands these objects talk because they are not separated from their people and history. At first glance they look mute but upon discussing they talk a lot; even a tiny thing has a lot reasons to speak up."

"We want to know the past, not just for the sake of knowledge but for tracing the road ahead."

"In the time of the ancients and during the time of the chiefdoms there was a word, a very important one: 'very pretty sunset, very pretty dawn.'

That was the word. It indicated to all of us the management, the unity, the community."

"In the fourth generation the custom of parents advising their children was terminated. The word we have spoken became silent."

"With the fifth generation our things are dimming, our thinking is terminating. In the sixth generation things are even worse. Some have produced eight generations and in them everything has been finished. The unity of the people is over."

"That is why this museum must talk, must lift up this silence, must address the governor, the body of the *cabildo* Guambiano, the people, and the children, must transmit to the people what is to be done tomorrow and bring to all *veredas*[9] the words of the ancients."

"With the museum we want to show that all the pottery and all the traces found in our territory are our own and not of other people, that the *pishau* are our ancestors and not strange people. Thus we were born right here, in these lands and waters; we have not been brought from elsewhere, neither are we *venideros*[10] from other worlds. This is our home."

"We also want to show that the Guambiano people has traveled a long road, and that during that time these hearths were used, as much as these beds, these pots, these things that are in the roots."

"And we want the museum to be the base for recovering our own education. The ancients were able to resist outrages because they had their own education; that is the basis of the community."

"Because we strive for the right, we want to create a country of laws based on our beliefs; not for creating laws between Guambianos but in order that our rights are recognized. Such is the purpose of our work."

"To teach our children, to establish an organization, to maintain a multiplication."

"Our own education started in the house, the family, and from there it was amplified to the global. From the kitchen (*nakchak*), with the family reunited around the hearth, flows the management of a community. And from there another thread starts: the respect for love. It is passed on to the new life and to multiplication, entering the living room (*wallikatø*) and the *pishiya* (a small room, separated from the house, where the valuables are kept)."

"This museum is a house from where to nurture the *cabildo* and the people."

"During the time of the chiefdoms this land was global, it was a territory, it was the house of the Namuy Misak, our people."

"The house is the family itself; it gives life and management, and it also multiplies itself until reaching a territory. From there flows the whole unity of its people."

"That is why we want the museum to be a house that gives life with its kitchen, its room, and its *pishiya*."

"*Nak* is the fire, but it is for cooking many things, not just meals. *Chak* is the place of the fire, is the work of the organism, is the function of how to live."

"The *wallikatø* contains many things in the global sense of the community."

"The *pishiya* is for storing the valuables that cannot get lost and that must be kept; it also keeps an eye on the behavior of fiancés in order to give advice."

"This museum is not only for showing things. The objects, once on display, look silent. To make them speak we have to find their words with the community elders, we have to investigate our past. When we recover the words these things will speak out and will be silent no longer. In this way teachings could be delivered."

In order to "find the words," Guambianos began researching oral tradition with elders and traditional wise men. I was invited by the *cabildo* to "accompany" this research and to work with the community's History Committee; they expected that my word as anthropologist, together with that of the elders, would produce new words, based on tradition but adequate for the new living conditions. The ethnographic, archaeological, and ethnohistorical words must "accompany" those of the community to talk to the people, to recover the voice, and to break the silence. Thus, it is spoken about the kitchen, the heart of the house, and the society:

"In the kitchen lies the fire, like a mother to us because it gives us meals and heat. It is the cradle of the youngsters who live with their parents before finding a mate."

"From it arises the management of the community. From it the thread of respect for love is taken. That is why we say that our laws come from the kitchen."

"There, around the hearth, sitting on their wood benches, the elders talk and in their voices the wisdom and knowledge of the ancients walk. Through their advice the children learn to behave; there the Guambianos are made."

"Likewise, just to make a comparison, a pot for cooking in the house stores many things, so many that one can get tired mentioning them."

"So, when her father-in-law arrives the daughter-in-law must serve him first, then serve her mother-in-law, then her husband, then her brother-in-law, and then the others. But not as it pleases her: she must not spill on the ground, neither throw the kitchen ware, nor serve in the same plate. She must serve and mix things properly, not just water or little water, not too much to some and too little to others. This is the advice of respect and equality; this is the advice that comes from women."

"The large pot used for *mingas* tells us how much to serve to each one so there will be enough for everybody. And the woman knew how to distribute because she had the dream and her hand is healed. In only two *veredas* are there women capable of distributing food during *mingas*. If they die, whom shall we ask to come and distribute food?"

"And the advise given to the men—how to love their families, how to receive meals from their wives without forgetting to say *dius pay unkua* (God thanks you). Today men receive without saying a word and then leave."

"There in the museum, the children sitting on their little benches around the hearth, in the *nakchak*. The things will give new voice to the words of the ancients, and the silence will be over."

"This is the way of this museum. Because in order to teach all this it is not necessary to read, write, sing, or pray; the only thing needed is to see the people, to be recognized as Guambianos, and to fight for unity" (Script of the House and Museum of Guambiano Culture).

In the old house of one of the recovered farms the Guambianos built a museum, which reproduces a traditional dwelling; the purpose was to erect a house in the Guambiano way, with kitchen, rooms, and *pishiya*. The museum is visited by schoolchildren, youngsters, and elders. There they hear the word and listen to the objects speak through the voice of the elders who know, who have investigated. The visitors are reached by the voice of the forebears, who point to the road that must be followed in order to live. From this place, from this house, the forebears expand their voice to the community. In *veredas*, schools, *mingas*, and the *cabildo*, daily activities are being shaped by these voices, although with difficulty and effort. And from that point of departure, with the bases provided by the museum and the continuing works, the other Guambianos are contributing to retrieve the voices of the once-forgotten ancestors.

NOTES

1. Translator's note: *chumbe* is a colorful band made of wool.
2. Translator's note: *resguardo* is equivalent to "reservation," although it has precise connotations, both in colonial and republican terms; that is why I use the Spanish word instead of its English equivalent.
3. A political-administrative corporation, the most important communal authority; it is renewed every year and is headed by a governor elected annually by all Guambianos older than 10 years of age.
4. Unless noted, all citations are taken from Urdaneta (1985, 1987, 1988), from where the archaeological information also derives.

5. Translator's note: *taita* is a title reserved for wise men, especially those with political authority.
6. Translator's note: Nasa is the vernacular name of a neighboring group, once known as Paeces, enemies of the Guambianos until recent times.
7. Translator's note: *minga* is a communal gathering for carrying out, basically, public works for the benefit of the community as a whole.
8. Translator's note: Derecho Mayor is the name given by Guambianos to their own legal system.
9. Translator's note: *vereda* designates clusters of dwellings, normally separated from each other. The word is used to single out relatively discrete groups in an otherwise homogenous settlement pattern.
10. Translator's note: *venidero* is a Spanish word that means someone who has recently arrived from abroad. It usually conveys a negative meaning, because it implies lack of roots and recent arrival, as compared to other people living in the area well before.

REFERENCES

Botero, Sofía 1982 Relaciones familia-comunidad en Guambía. Unpublished manuscript, on file at the Department of Anthropology, Universidad Nacional, Bogotá.

———. 1984 Tras el pensamiento y pasos de los taitas Guambianos. Intentos de aproximación a su historia, siglos XVI-XVII-XVIII. Unpublished Honor's thesis, Department of Anthropology, Universidad Nacional, Bogotá.

Calero, Luis Fernando 1997 *Chiefdoms under Siege: Spain's Rule and Native Adaptation in the Southern Colombian Andes, 1535–1700*. University of New Mexico Press, Albuquerque.

Cháves, Álvaro, and Mauricio Puerta 1985 *Tierradentro*. El Áncora, Bogotá.

Cubillos, Julio César 1959 El Morro de Tulcán (pirámide prehispánica): arqueología de Popayán, Cauca, Colombia. *Revista Colombiana de Antropología* 8:54–112.

———. 1984 *Arqueología del valle del río Cauca. Asentamientos prehispánicos en la suela plana del río Cauca*. FIAN, Bogotá.

Duque, Luis 1963 *Reseña arqueológica de San Agustín*. Instituto Colombiano de Antropología, Bogotá.

Ford, James 1944 *Excavations in the Vicinity of Cali, Colombia*. Yale University Publications in Anthropology, no. 31. Yale University Press, New Haven.

Reichel-Dolmatoff, Gerardo 1975 *Contribuciones al conocimiento de la estratigrafía cerámica de San Agustín*. Banco Popular, Bogotá.

Urdaneta, Martha Lucía 1985 En busca de las huellas de los antiguos Guambianos. Unpublished manuscript on file at the Department of Anthropology, Universidad Nacional, Bogotá.

———. 1987 En busca de las huellas de los antiguos Guambianos. Unpublished Honor's thesis, Department of Anthropology, Universidad Nacional, Bogotá.

———. 1988 Investigación arqueológica en el resguardo indígena de Guambía. *Boletín del Museo del Oro* 22:54–81.

Urdaneta, Martha Lucía, Cruz Trochez, and Miguel Flor 1990 En busca de las huellas de los antiguos Guambianos. Unpublished manuscript on file at the Fundación de Investigaciones Arqueológicas Nacionales, Bogotá.

Vasco, Luis Guillermo, Abelino Dagua, and Misael Aranda 1989 *Somos raíz y retoño*. Fundación Colombia Nuestra, Cali.

———. 1990 *Calendario Guambiano y ciclo agrícola*. Colombia Nuestra, Colección Historia y Tradición Guambianas no. 2. Fundación Colombia Nuestra, Cali.

CHAPTER 13

INDIGENOUS REPRESENTATIONS OF THE ARCHAEOLOGICAL RECORD: SPECTRAL REFLECTIONS OF POSTMODERNITY IN ECUADOR

O. Hugo Benavides

*Y no le hablo con las palabras que sólo han servido para no entendernos,
ahora que ya es tarde empiezo a elegir otras, las de ella, las envueltas en eso
que ella comprende y que no tiene nombre, auras y tensiones que crispan el
aire entre dos cuerpos o llenan de polvo de oro una habitación o un verso.
¿Pero no hemos vivido así todo el tiempo, lacerándonos dulcemente?*
Julio Cortázar, Rayuela

Contrary to other important communities in South America, it is the indigenous population that holds a monopoly over the historical definition of the pre-Hispanic past. This period holds as its historical subject a set of diverse and complex indigenous communities that saw their numbers and power dwindle as a result of the European invasion and centuries of similar colonial and republican adaptations. This particular kind of racial/ethnic classification of the past has had a series of implications that have not only helped legitimize the ideological foundation of national identities but has also contributed, in different ways, to incorporate the pre-Hispanic contribution in a continental Latin American mentality. Therefore, it is not surprising that this preference of an Indian past was not an obstacle in the xenophobic structuring of a Latin American identity that always opted for the white and European as the highest moral component to be emulated in the nation and the household. The great Indian feats were incorporated into a particular way of believing and writing Latin American history in which the Indian was hailed as a historical subject emptied of any real agency. This type of historical hermeneutics has allowed various Indian activists to state that a Latin American history has yet to be written because where there is any written account the Indian (and all indigenous communities) has been erased through that same representational process.

This hermeneutical process, however, is not an isolated factor; on the contrary, it is an essential element as well as a central motor of a culture in permanent formation. Indigenous communities were not erased as much as they were incorporated into a distant and sanitized version of the past that allowed Indians to be seen as the nations' pasts but not their present, and even less, their future. Muratorio's work (1994) has analyzed the construction of indigenous representations in different republican periods of the nation as well as at the international fairs held in the United States at the turn of the century. These fairs, although held thousands of kilometers away, strongly contributed to support the xenophobic attitude of a foreign European ethos. These modes of representation contributed two kinds of ideological representations. On the one hand, the recovery and definition of the pre-Hispanic past as a static object that could be used to reinforce mythical stories about the Incas, Waris, and Moches, among other past indigenous communities. And on the other hand, these same historical myths became essential mechanisms for the reproduction of the nation and defining an indigenous mentality as the racial/ethnic other of a Latin American identity that was a necessary reflection of an alien European constitution. Far from it, these two processes were not contradictory and allowed an indigenous presence in the contemporary ideological make-up of the nation, albeit slightly different from what both the indigenous communities and the national elites had in mind, or even attempted to frame.

The Archaeological Condition

Latin American archaeology has never been at the margins of the process of historical production. Despite archaeology's consistent attempts in maintaining empirical objectivity and a positivist tradition, it is precisely this obsessive attempt for objectivity that evidences its close association with the mechanisms of social power and hierarchy. Archaeology has become, as all disciplines are, both an element and an arbitrator of those same historical truths over which it looks to deliberate. This reality does not in any way question the scientific validity of Latin American archaeology but rather contributes to understanding how it is impossible to think that any scientific discipline could not be inherently involved in culture's social reproduction.

The development of Ecuadorian archaeology shares many similar traits with the discipline's evolution throughout the continent but also has slight differences in terms of its relationship to identity process formation and, in this present context, to the idea of global citizenship. To this degree it is not insignificant that a country like Ecuador with an enormous amount of archaeological remains and a limited research infrastructure also experienced the largest Native American uprising the American continent has seen in the last three decades. At the same time it must also be pointed out that these struggles for indigenous rights have been carried out without any direct claims to archaeological sites per se. Although far from this being an expression of disdain for archaeology or the pre-Hispanic past, the evolution of Ecuadorian archaeology and indigenous rights shows a unique manner of understanding the past as a central player in the nation's future, which is inscribed and erased in multiple manners in the nation's social reality.

Similar to a mythic Indian past that never really existed, both Indians and archaeologists have used archaeology and its disciplinary structure to reconstruct a more congruent manner of expressing their identity, both in national and local contexts. Archaeological discourses are essential fixtures of the national formation, contributing in multiple manners to what is understood to be an Ecuadorian identity. The burgeoning national identity is both fed and feeds a strong Indian social movement that in the last three decades, contradictorily, would seem to reproduce a mentality different from its republican history.

In Ecuadorian archaeology there are two central characters at the beginning of the twentieth century, Jacinto Jijón y Caamaño (1890–1950) and Emilio Estrada (1916–1961), who marked the beginning and development, respectively, of the discipline and not unrelatedly expressed clear ethnic (if not racial) and personal differences that were reflected in their research endeavors. Both men belonged to the cultural, political, and financial elite of the country and made use of white racial legitimization that positioned them at the apex of the country's social hierarchy. Jijón y Caamaño came from and represented the *"latifundistas"* (large landholders) elite that at the turn of the century were losing their hegemony in a new changing market that opened its doors to the mercantile opportunities of the coastal bourgeoisie. And it would be Estrada that represented these new socioeconomic spaces opened by the country's liberal revolution (1895–1905) that, far from emancipating Indians and blacks, was able to reaccommodate these national subjects to the new shifting forms of exploitation of the global market.

Ecuadorian archaeology owes its disciplinary origins to Jijón y Caamaño. His studies consolidated a different manner (defined within new global parameters of scientific objectivity) of analyzing the past and the material culture found within the country's borders. This new approach represented a significant improvement from the archaeological studies carried out in previous decades in its more systematic manner of studying the pre-Hispanic past. At the same time his collaboration with different colleagues during this early period also allowed the consolidation of the first professional archaeology associations and the publication of the first archaeology/history journal in the country. The personal contribution of Jijón y Caamaño only further intensified one of his prime ideological objectives, that of introducing the country's archaeological research into the global setting. As part of this objective (and also as a class rite) he would spend a couple of years in Europe, excavate archaeological sites in other Latin American countries, and invite (financing their research) foreign scholars to work in the country. His support of the German archaeologist Max Uhle's research in the Ecuadorian highlands is a good example of this desire to look beyond the national borders and attempt to put the Ecuadorian past within a global research landscape, an objective that would be central to his disciplinary program and that would define the very evolution of archaeology in the country.

This Eurocentric vision was expressed, with enormous clarity, in one of Jijón y Caamaño's later essays on the relationship between the country's pre-Hispanic past and its national identity. According to Jijón y Caamaño (1992), the Indian, as well as the mestizos, only represented a dead weight that impeded the nation's progress. Contradictorily, the scholar that has most succinctly contributed to recovering and analyzing this "dead weight" argued that the Indian contribution had been at its best in the past and that was all that was left, the remains of a lost splendor impossible to resuscitate. In this manner, from its very beginnings the archaeological discourse in Ecuador not only looked to make history an object of study in itself but also created a historical subject, the Indian trapped in the past, that served as the reflecting Other to consolidate the new white/mestizo control of the territory. Therefore, far from contradictory, Jijón y Caamaño's xenophobic discourse was an essential part of a globalizing national identity that was legitimized by the Indian past but left behind the contemporary Indian communities that were closer descendants of the original Indian constructors of these lost civilizations.

Emilio Estrada (1954, 1957, 1962) would enter into dialogue with this archaeological discourse in the 1950s. His main differences with Jijón y Caamaño can be best understood through the regional discrimination between highlanders (*serranos*) and coastal (*costeños*) communities that marks a national form of governmentality. This regional animosity started to lose (or at least shift) some of its stronghold after a main railroad system was built to unite the two major cities, Quito in the highlands and Guayaquil on the coast. This railroad project was an important part of the liberal revolution that looked to introduce the nation into the new global market as well as align itself to the new ideological demands that Estrada would most succinctly represent.

Estrada was a member of the coastal agro-exporting elite infrastructure and was also part of one of the most influential financial and banking families in Guayaquil. From a very early age he took on less traditionally minded interests and hobbies that landed him on the fringe of the political concerns of his family. On top of archaeology and politics, he also pursued a career in car and boat racing. Although it would be for his contribution to archaeology that he would be most remembered, his "playboy" or "man of the world" image would accompany not only his archaeological contribution but his untimely death at the age of 45. If Jijón y Caamaño had dedicated himself to archaeological research with extreme dedication and close commitment to the country's Conservative Party (Partido Conservador), Estrada would do almost the exact opposite. It is not so much that his work lacked scientific seriousness, but rather that Estrada would have a different way of focusing on the pre-Hispanic past. Although both were part of the elite, Estrada would use his class position to carry out the work in a more leisurely and carefree manner, although this more relaxed style is absent from his rigorous publications. Ultimately Estrada would both shift the focus of Ecuadorian archaeology from the highlands to the coast and also in a sense open up archaeology to a more easygoing and worldly mode.

There are also several other interesting elements of Estrada's contribution; paramount among them is the trust he would bestow upon another Ecuadorian archaeologist, Julio Viteri Gamboa, who would become his faithful assistant in all his field excavations. Therefore it would be Viteri Gamboa who would run the excavations and be present full time while Estrada was kept busy with his many interests, including at one point being mayor of Guayaquil. However, for many this relationship was problematic since it was Estrada that appeared as sole author of the publications. Added to this was the racial difference between them—Estrada was white while Viteri Gamboa was mestizo (pejoratively described as *cholo* in the local context)—that highlighted their unequal access to the limelight.

Unlike Jijón y Caamaño, Estrada would look toward the United States not Europe for legitimization for his archaeological work. The Smithsonian Institute, represented by Clifford Evans and Betty Meggers, would be very supportive of Estrada's work and theories. Like Jijón y Caamaño, his archaeological work would not have an ethnographic component and would also be unrelated to any contemporary native descendants in his area of study. However, this kind of historical amnesia would seem more logical in a coastal setting where all indigenous communities had been decimated and almost no contemporary group were still identified as such, rather coastal Indian communities suffered a profound transculturation that put them at the end of the social hierarchy (even below slaves) and almost made them completely dependent on the urban ideology springing from Guayaquil. Categorized as *cholos* (and as *montubios* farther inland), they were not deemed to be Indian (although they shared the same racial discrimination and economic exploitation) and, worse, to be able to claim credit for the rich cultural tradition of their local homelands.

Just as Viteri Gamboa was compared to Estrada, contemporary coastal communities were not deemed racially white, i.e., superior enough, in comparison to the new white/elite of the country. Even more particularly, Estrada's focus on the United States helped to further erase descendant native communities from their past, and alienate them from the political present as well. Not unrelated to this worldview, he readily interpreted the early cultural progress of the formative cultures in the region (3000–1500 BP) in terms of pottery and agriculture as evidence of Asian diffusion to the area (from the Jomon culture of Japan). The implicit racist underpinnings of this diffusionist theory superseded the empirical evidence, precisely because this theory was conducive to explaining away the archaeological evidence as not belonging to present (or even past) Indians. The Ecuadorian nation could claim this archaeological heritage more as a result of the current white/mestizo efforts to recuperate the past rather than by any Indian connection to it. The Ecuadorian archaeological discourse supported both by Jijón y Caamaño's and Estrada's efforts not only erased any Indian genealogy from the archaeological sites but also successful neutralized any direct link with the contemporary uprising or Indian social movement during this period.

Since the death of these two archaeologists, the discipline has not had a similar single person that has monopolized the research focus. Rather it has been different cultural groups and institutions that have defined and represented varied epistemological and political approaches. Perhaps two of the biggest factors within the last four decades of archaeological research in the country, besides the Indian movement and the impact of globalization (both discussed below), are the role of oil companies in the recovery process of sites in the Amazon (where most of the oil refineries are) and the influence of a Marxist-inspired *"arqueología como ciencia social"* (archaeology as a social science) that was part of a continental-wide movement. In this manner, both oil companies and Marxism linked Ecuadorian archaeology to wider social and intellectual networks that went beyond the national or even continental borders. This crux between the local and the global, as well as the process of globalization, is also tackled by the Indian movement which, starting in the 1990s, most explicitly, opens a new way of defining both what it means to be Ecuadorian in a global context as well as what is the past's role in the definition of an Ecuadorian national identity.

THE INDIANIST CONDITIONING

Since the 1990s the "Indian problem" in Ecuador has entered a new postpatriarchal phase, where the state, the Catholic Church, and other social institutions no longer are trusted by the Indians to represent or speak for them. Since the first significant uprising in 1990, associated with an Indian hunger strike in the Santo Domingo convent in Quito, the indigenous communities took upon themselves their own political and ideological representation. In this contemporary context, the CONAIE (Confederación de Nacionalidades Indígenas del Ecuador/Confederation of Indian Nationalities of Ecuador) managed to represent the majority of Indian communities in the territory. The second most powerful Ecuadorian Indian group in this regard is the Evangelical Indian movement (Movimiento Evangelista Ecuatoriano), and to a lesser degree the failed attempt of a Secretaría de Asuntos Indígenas during Abdalá Bucaram's presidency (1996–1997).

The current moment has been defined as "*Indianista*" to distinguish it from the "Indigenist" period of the 1930s that was characterized by a paternalist structure allowing white/mestizo liberals to exhume themselves from their oppressive guilt of two centuries of racial discrimination. However, the CONAIE has in many ways become the single most powerful social movement in the country to represent the political left, replacing the more traditional class-based worker's and teacher's movements (FUT/Frente Unitario de Trabajadores and UNE/Unión Nacional de Educadores, respectively). The Indian movement's social power has also been felt in electoral politics, making the Indian political party (Pachakutik Nuevo País) the most viable leftist option until the election of Rafael Correa in 2008. In association with other national groups, such as their historical enemies, i.e., the Catholic Church and the military, they have been able to contribute to the toppling of three national governments, boycotted the IMF's (International Monetary Fund) structural policies (which included incorporating the US dollar as the national currency), and enabled Nina Pakari to become the first Indian person to hold the office of secretary of state.

The accomplishments achieved by the Indian movement have significantly changed the political discourse in the country and, not surprisingly, affected the relationship between the national political and archaeological discourses. From very early on, the Indian movement has made a claim to the pre-Hispanic past as an important part of their heritage and a marker of their genealogical belonging to the territory. This particular historical approach is explicit in many of the CONAIE's publications, which articulate an alternative history different from the official one put forward in textbooks and the mainstream historiography. In the new history, for the CONAIE, the pre-Hispanic past is not so much a past element but rather a live narrative that is inherently connected to the movement's present political objectives. In this manner, the CONAIE is able to do what over one century of archaeological research was unable: to both recognize the Indian subject as the main character of the pre-Hispanic past and to reaffirm the experiential character of history as an essential contemporary element.

Within these revolutionary objectives the history put forward by the CONAIE (1989) is not a national Ecuadorian history as much as it is a national history of the different indigenous communities that currently occupy the territory. One of the manners in which they achieve this objective is by making the past a first person narrative; it is no longer the Incas or Caranquis but rather "we Indians" and "our ancestors" that carried out these great cultural achievements that are archaeology's object of inquiry. This new alternative history is burdened by the colonial past as well and recreates a series of national, racial, and gendered differentiations in a spectral fashion, similar to the normative history used to represent an official Ecuador. There is a terrifying resemblance in the manner in which the Indian movement's alternative history recreates authoritative categories, to the official history it is looking to debunk, particularly as the new version begins to hold hegemonic sway through publications, political texts, and mainly through a new way of interpreting the national reality.

However, one of the big distinctions between these two histories is the role that archaeology plays within them. While in the official history archaeology is seen as the objective scientific validation for statements about the pre-Hispanic past, in the alternative history archaeology itself is a colonial discipline that needs to be liberated from its oppressive origins. Therefore, just as the contemporary Indian communities were alienated and distanced from their past by the archaeological discourse, it is now the discipline's turn to be removed from its hegemonic hold in defining the past and determining the varied ethical and political implications in today's world. This hermeneutical difference reflects an epistemological divide that opens itself to new ways of doing (and even performing) history, incorporating oral histories in the process, that question the Western positivist promise of the archaeological discourse. It is no longer the Indian that disappears from its relationship to the past but rather archaeology itself that begins to be deconstructed as part of an inherently racist ideology with ambiguous implications in its manner of understanding and assessing that same past.

The Indian movement's critique of the archaeological discourse is clearly a result of a political process that takes into account over 100 years of research that was complicit in the exploitation of Indian communities in the country. This intellectual and political reticence seems doubly linked to the archaeological discourse in itself as well as the postcolonial conditions inherent in the reworkings of an Indian identity in the new millennium. An example of this is the explicit absence of reclaiming archaeological sites by indigenous communities; rather, what you have is the CONAIE's interest in land rights and issues associated to the group's social, cultural, and economic reproduction. It is in this manner that the past plays an important role as ideological legitimization, but at a distance and removed from any direct contact with archaeologists, sites, or archaeological material culture. The few exceptions to this, at sites such as Agua Blanca (on the central coast) and Culebrillas (in the highlands), provide material that heightens rather than questions the differences between native communities and archaeologists.

In both cases the claims over the sites have more to do with access to social-economic resources than to direct material culture. In Culebrillas the construction of a dam not only endangered the archaeological site but the ancestral homeland of the native community of the area. Meanwhile, in Agua Blanca the context is a bit more complicated since it incorporates a local community no longer recognized as indigenous but reorganized in communal form, i.e., *comuna* organization, while still proclaiming their pre-Hispanic ancestry as a central element of their identity. But even in this case the site was preserved as a tourist attraction; not only for fellow Ecuadorians to learn about their past accomplishments but also to provide a much-needed economic resource for the local communities that had been decimated by the agro-export model put into place throughout the coast in the last century.

These two cases reaffirm the Indian movement's prime objective: the social-economic reproduction of its endangered communities. However, culture is understood as an essential component of this process and not as a peripheral element. This kind of organic relationship is not foreign to the traditional structure of indigenous communities. The CONAIE sustains an understanding of the past that reflects its essential' importance in its social reproduction and political strategies. This ambiguous manner of incorporating the past from which the Indian has traditionally been excluded serves to question the relationship between research and progressive transformation, and/or between archaeology and Indian identity.

To this degree, the Indian movement has done nothing more but refocus the ideological exclusion as a central component in their own new manner of fighting for their political livelihood. In this new model the movement incorporates the past but refuses to reaffirm the state's traditional legitimization of archaeology as the prime method to understand and define that pre-Hispanic past. Therefore, even though the movement recognizes the power of the past, it has yet to develop a cohesive method to incorporate the varied unconscious manners in which the past plays out its power over the country's political future. It is quite understandable that the nation and each of the according governments have looked to evade this responsibility, not unrelated to Renan's insight (Renan 1990) that what made a nation as such was its inability to process and represent its own history. The most troubling implication, however, is that unless the Indian movement shifts its historical discourse they could also very well "succeed in similar failures," and continue (like the state they oppose) to usufruct from their own victimization.

The Global Conditioning

Globalization is by no means a condition of modernity (and less of postmodernity) or contemporary technological and theoretical advances that look to make sense of geographical differences. The globalization process has been an essential element of human definition from the very beginning of our hominid evolution, perhaps more clearly emphasized in the first processes of state formation throughout the globe. As Wolf (1992) explains, a globalization structure was already in place before Europe's Westernization process started five centuries ago. Rather, Europe along with the Americas entered modernity together at the end of the fifteenth century. This understanding is vital because it helps to debunk the Eurocentric notion that globalization is exclusively a Western affair, which has the negative implication of neutralizing the pre-Hispanic past as a pre- or aglobalization process (again, a notion easily denied in the most basic type of inquiries into the past). This Eurocentric notion also defines indigenous identity as something pre- or non-modern. The Indian has been traditionally excluded from modernity precisely at the same moment that their interaction with Europeans allowed the latter to enter modernity on their own.

The racial hierarchy instituted between Europeans and Indians (as representatives of the American continent) has been inherently reproduced in the discourse of modernity that denies the historical recourse of offering Americans (continentally speaking) the same sense of subject formation offered to Europeans. An example of this historical denial is the inability to recognize the globalization processes present in the Americas before the onslaught of European colonialism, even when for over a century archaeologist have systematically offered evidence of a complex set of geographical networks that covered the continent in its entirety. The complexity of this American process of globalization is such that one could easily argue that it is yet to be succinctly written, mainly because our postcolonial condition has only made it possible to register it at this late time. In this endeavor the Indian movement in Ecuador has its own unique insight since, as they have so adamantly expressed, they are quite aware that the Indian history is yet to be written as well. In a manner of speaking the movement is a form of autodefinition that is still not completely tolerated either in ideological or emotional fashion.

Therefore it is more realistic to understand the current forms of globalization, not as completely new, but rather as new forms of old processes of the transformation of capital or, as Stuart Hall (1997) refers to them, "new old" forms of identity relationships and economic articulations. This new period of globalization is intimately tied to late (or cybernetic) capital, which neo-Marxist theorists like David Harvey and Frederic Jameson describe as a moment of capitalist transformation in which theoretical definition is in itself compromised by the transformation.

This "new old" globalization process has powerful implication for the future of the continent but even more for the production of a historical future (which includes notions of the past) of the archaeological mentality. This period of capital flows and transformation of identities is what many define as postmodernity: a contemporary moment in which traditional schools of thought no longer hold sway but rather all forms compete to determine what we are, and the manner in which we see and represent ourselves. This postmodern crux of changing identities, migrant movements, and cybernetic capital has solidified an Indian identity that makes use of a symbolic capital of the past in quite contradictory fashion.

García-Canclini (2002) has pointed out how in Latin America this postmodern moment is defined by a global debt, migrants, and soap operas, which turn out to be our specific contribution to globalization. It is through these mechanisms of economic dependency, cultural representation, and a search for better livelihood that Latin Americans define themselves as such within and across the national borders. In Ecuador this is not only translated to a greater closeness to the reflection of our foundational racist origins and a powerful Indian movement but also to the fact that a significant amount of the population now constructs diasporic notions of "Ecuadorianness" in places like the United States, Italy, Spain, and Venezuela (to mention the most important migrant destinations). These migrants now provide new ways of defining ourselves within and outside of the traditional national canons.

Again, in this globalization process the archaeological discourse has been relegated to a secondary plane, perhaps even less explicit than in the official and alternative historical versions of the nation. There is no doubt that archaeological discourse has its own place in a globalization enterprise in which cultural identities have superseded old class manners of defining oneself. However, archaeology's secondary role in the globalization process has both worldwide and national implications that demand further analysis. A denial of archaeology's political role is a central concern of a postprocessual approach to the discipline that takes to task an understanding of the discipline that does not account for the pervasive political impact of archaeological research. This allows many of these self-defined postmodern archaeologists to recognize that archaeology has always been a political enterprise, with its greatest political work being carried out by the silent manner in which it is performed: always contributing to maintain (even when many times the archaeologists are in direct opposition) an exploitative and hierarchical status quo.

This particular global conflict contributed to the creation of the World Archaeology Congress (WAC) that looked to incorporate the diverse cultural voices that archaeology studies, but has also silenced over the decades. In this context native and/or indigenous voices are vital agents in the recovery of their own history, and concurrently, of the manner by which to enter into their own definition of postmodernity. Therefore, it is in this fashion that the Indian movement in Ecuador is a product of these highly unstable and ambiguous forms of capital flow and identity production. As many other entities, both the WAC and the CONAIE are products of globalization that contest the traditional manner in which archaeology is performed and cultural identity reproduced.

Unfortunately archaeology in Ecuador, as the locus of both the WAC and CONAIE in the national context, has failed to live up to this historical moment in terms of constructing a new counterhegemonic contribution, although not surprisingly, there are concise reasons for this type of disciplinary limitation. The presence of oil companies in the country (both state and privately owned) has made them the single most important source of funding of archaeological research, which immediately limits the scope of the theoretical findings but also any kind of committed political association with the indigenous communities being displaced by this economic enterprise. This type of funding source supports salvage or CRM (cultural resource management) archaeology that is less concerned with a revitalized understanding of the country's past. In other words, the archaeological contribution is limited in its scope and fails to fulfill the more ambitious program of organisms such as the WAC or CONAIE.

Ecuadorian archaeology's dependency on oil funding is visible evidence of the state's inability to support large-scale long-term cultural projects. If on top of this one takes into account the continuous development of a traditional history that has consistently looked to exclude cultural differences, it is no surprise that the archaeological discourse is most memorable for its absence rather than anything else. However, it is precisely through these forms of transnational dependencies that Ecuadorian archaeology is being permeated by postmodern forms that define what, when, and where archaeological excavation take place, both literally and theoretically speaking.

SPECTRAL REFLECTION OF POSTMODERNITY IN ECUADOR

This chapter looks to assess a central imperative: to understand the relationship (or its absence) between the Ecuadorian archaeological discourse and the Indian movement. At the same time it is impossible to even begin to ponder this relationship outside of the specific conditions imposed by postmodernity. It is precisely for this reason that I have looked to develop each constitutive element (archaeology, Indian identity, and globalization) in their separate contexts to better understand their intricate dependencies upon each other. These postmodern conditionings better allow us to appreciate how archaeologists and natives (or more generally, the archaeological discourse and an alternative vision of the state) have been placed within different settings of the same historical moment, which most importantly helps us define and produce that which is the Ecuadorian nation.

In this fashion one could understand postmodernity as a sociopolitical entity defined by the shifting hierarchy of its constitutive parts. Unlike modernity, postmodernity needs and is nourished by difference; not as separate entities of identities but rather as essential elements of differentiation that must be maintained at all costs. This is the new logic of late capital where homogeneity and the denial of difference amount to political death. This particular form of highlighting difference is present in the economic and cultural flows, from the role of Latin America soap operas worldwide to the fact that the Ecuadorian currency is the US dollar. However, what is harder to explain is how this difference is both a product and constitutive element, at one and the same time, of a postmodern reality and of the new Ecuadorian historical discourse in a constant state of transformation.

This particular manner of reflecting and being reflected is part of what I call the spectral residuals of postmodernity in Ecuador, not at all because the imaginary center of our current existence is lodged in Europe or the United States but because the idea of a holding center itself is a symptom of what postmodernity looks to dislodge itself from. Difference and heterogeneity are essential mechanisms of Otherizing in an unequal and hierarchical fashion. The ambiguous production between (archaeological) discourse and (Indian) movement helps to keep the Ecuadorian nation constantly questioning its own, essentially ontological, historical development. In a way, the absence of a direct relationship between both marks, in paradoxical fashion, a primordial way of relating and maintaining cohesiveness in a postmodern world of reflections where homogeneity and similarity are only artificial productions of an impossible attainment of cultural authenticity.

Because of this it would be a mistake to reconstruct an alternative archaeological discourse that looks to provide a theoretical solution to our historical conundrum, as it also would be a mistake to encourage Indian communities to explicitly engage a more committed relationship to their own past as if that relationship were not already in place. My argument is that the current moment obligates a different manner of understanding the past and the nation, and a particular way of assessing global relationships between constitutive and local identities. In this sense both are cultural products that allow a "new old" way in which to reconstruct the colonial project that defines the American continent from the inside out in its new postcolonial setting.

Therefore the problem is not resolved by accusing the Ecuadorian archaeological discourse of being reactionary and conservative (which it is) or defining the Indian movement as authentically inauthentic (which it also is), but rather by understanding how both are interrelated, over and over again, and in a systematic manner sustain plausible scenarios for imagining the nation. It is no longer an issue of defining victimizing identities that have been constituted as such but instead of understanding them as unequal cultural products that do nothing better than reflect, in non-homogenous fashion, the new postmodern enterprise. The unequal collaboration between discourse and movement evidences the stubborn mutual alienation of the multiple social actors that produce the fiction that is the Ecuadorian nation (as are all nations).

The troubled national context is a visible symptom of the manner in which difference is the most plausible articulation of a political formulation. The contents and contours are not essential elements as much as external parameters that are preferred at times over others and that are articulated in a spectral motor in which object and reflection, subject and Other, are integrated in all cultural products. It would be a mistake, therefore, to question an authentic identity or a group's political contribution without taking into account their productive parameters or the palimpsest history that has been scratched and written over several times (Foucault 1993). For Oscar Wilde (1964), as for Marx, reality can never be wrong because it is both product and constitutive element. The essential difference (and even this is left open to theoretical exploration) is to recognize how these spectral reflections get represented in our imaginary caves of who we are and who we believe to be, of who is and who we believe the nation to be, and of how this past/future articulation is carried out.

Life is by definition confusing, and our existence cannot be anything else but similar except when we impose an artificial homogenous reality and a rational hermeneutics to a reconstruction of the past, to which both archaeologists and Indians are equally committed. Therefore it is important to recognize what our most intimate central failings are in reproducing coherent histories that legitimize our present-day identity narratives. In this fashion we can begin to understand the supposed non-relationship between archaeologists and Indians no longer as a theoretical or political flaw as much as simply a method for reconstructing the past. This spectral difference serves to open up and assess the manner by which theory is produced and singularly redefines us in the process.

The archaeological discourse and the Indian movement are committed to different ways of understanding and constructing the nation. It is this contrast that one can perceive as an element of a greater power relationship constituted by this difference. It is no longer understanding difference as a limitation that fuels the state or multiple national communities. Social differences are the very pillars of alternative mentalities essential for the nation's hegemonic production of what we must believe is Ecuador. In this fashion, it is quite impossible to answer if Ecuador is real or not, since the question takes its very existence as a point of reference, looking to deny that the varying social, cultural, economic, religious, ethnic, and racial differences, structured in an unequal manner and marked by a supposed absence of theoretical formulation, are really what defines the present moment (and, necessarily so, the future) of the nation.

The spectral reflections work because they more clearly outline a contemporary existence impossible to define and provide an incoherent tone to an incoherent reality that we insist in reordering, further ignoring that the history produced and reconstructed by Indians and archaeologists are inherent elements of our own national identity production. In this supposed conflict between a coherent past and present is precisely where we could better view the global production of postmodernity, which also belies Ecuador's contribution to globalization. In this trying context it is important to recognize the fragmentation of the historical subject that no longer supports new attempts at homogeneity or differentiation but rather inclusive parameters in which one and the other are constitutive parts at one and the same time: spectral reflections of a greater formation in constant movement.

Conclusion

No necesita saber como yo; puede vivir en el desorden sin que ninguna conciencia de orden la retenga. Ese desorden que es su orden misterioso, esa bohemia del cuerpo y el alma que le abre de par en par las verdaderas puertas. Su vida no es desorden más que para mí, enterrado en prejuicios que desprecio y respeto al mismo tiempo. Yo, condenado a ser absuelto irremediablemente por la Maga que me juzga sin saberlo. Ah, déjame entrar, déjame ver algún día como ven tus ojos.

Julio Cortázar, *Rayuela*

This chapter looks to problematize the relationship between archaeologists and Indians in Ecuador at the beginning of the twenty-first century. Contrary to the more traditional positivists' point of view, I would argue that the problem is not one of political will or of a simplistic official and state appropriation of history. Rather, I believe the ambivalent relationship between archaeologists and Indians evidences a tortuous history of colonial domination that goes beyond what we can consciously know or ever completely define. Therefore, instead of proposing theoretical utopias that are as vague as they are productive (in the discursive sense of the word), I analyze this non-relationship as a relationship in its own right, that is, a relationship that not only highlights different histories but also a fragmented historical subject in a constant process of reconstruction.

The difference between the archaeological discourse and the Indian movement marks a new manner of constructing the nation and constituting the state within the new shifting postmodern parameters. It is no longer about reconstructing homogenous histories (beyond their superficial enunciation) but of understanding their differences as belonging to wider social formations that implicate all of us in multiple ways. I propose that a spectral vision is the closest manner in which to understand how these shifting identities form continuously different political projects, different not only to what the social subjects initially proposed but even what one could predict from their constitutive elements.

It is in this context where the silences, desires, fantasies, and imagination are able to offer links where before we only saw emptiness and absence (as Cortázar elaborates in the quote above). Only in this fashion can we understand how the absence of a coherent theoretical model between archaeologists and indigenous communities is anything but absent or a social void, but rather a spectral reflection more powerful than we could understand, a reflection that sustains us during this long postcolonial century in a constant search for emotional, existential, and historical fulfillment, and autoproducing ourselves in the permanent desire to, in the words of Cortázar, "go in and see."

REFERENCES

CONAIE (Confederación de Nacionalidades Indígenas del Ecuador) 1989 *Las nacionalidades indígenas en el Ecuador: nuestro proceso organizativo.* TINCUI-CONAIE-Abya-Yala, Quito.

Cortázar, Julio 1987 *Rayuela*. Alianza Editorial, Madrid.

Estrada, Emilio 1954 *Ensayo preliminar sobre la arqueología de Milagro*. Editorial Cervantes, Guayaquil.

——. 1957 *Los Huancavilcas: últimas civilizaciones pre-históricas de la costa del Guayas*. Museo Victor Emilio Estrada, no. 3. Guayaquil.

——. 1962 *Arqueología de Manabí Central*. Museo Victor Emilio Estrada, no. 7. Guayaquil.

Foucault, Michel 1993 Nietzsche, genealogy, and history. In *Language, Counter-Memory, Practices: Selected Essays and Interviews*, edited by Daniel Bouchard, pp. 139–164. Cornell University Press, Ithaca.

García-Canclini, Néstor 2002 *Latinoamericanos buscando lugar en este siglo*. Paidós, Buenos Aires.

Hall, Stuart 1997 The local and the global: Globalization and ethnicity. In *Culture, Globalization and the World-System: Contemporary Conditions for the Representation of Identity*, edited by Albert King, pp. 19–39. University of Minnesota Press, Minneapolis.

Jijón y Caamaño, Jacinto 1952 Antropología prehispánica del Ecuador: resumen 1945. La Prensa Católica, Quito.

——. 1992 La ecuatorianidad. *Museo Histórico* 59:233–268. First published 1943.

Muratorio, Blanca (editor) 1994 *Imágenes e imagineros: representaciones de los indígenas ecuatorianos, siglos XIX y XX*. FLACSO, Quito.

Renan, Ernest 1990 What is a nation? In *Nation and Narration*, edited by Homi K. Bhabha, pp. 8–22. London, Routledge. [A lecture, first delivered in 1882.]

Wilde, Oscar 1964 *De profundis*. Avon Books, New York.

Wolf, Eric 1992 *Europe and the People without History*. University of California Press, Berkeley.

CHAPTER 14

ARCHAEOLOGICAL RUINS: SPACES OF THE PAST, EXPECTATIONS OF THE FUTURE. TOURISM AND HERITAGE IN NOR LÍPEZ (DPT. OF POTOSÍ, BOLIVIA)[1]

Francisco M. Gil García

We live in a global world characterized by a magnificent—even fictional—reality, by mass tourism, and by a consumer fever of the past through heritage.[2] All this has promoted a qualitative and quantitative change in the valuation and use of ruins and the remains of past times; it is a process activated by the logic of entertainment, leisure, and consumerism. In this postmodernity without rules that favors the production of images, representations, and symbols, the (re)discovery, revaluation, and invention of the past and heritage arise everywhere. I am not going to theorize in this chapter about what heritage is or what elements are active in it; I will only assume it is a social construction about the ethos of a community and a representation of selected referents at the service of contextual discourses. The demand for a historical link between the "traditional" and the "authentic" becomes the key for understanding the relationship between heritage and tourism.

According to the concept of an "illusionary kaleidoscope of tourism" (Augé 1998:16), any community, big or small, all over the world, shows and promotes its own heritage because tourism is considered fundamental in any development strategy. While Augé (2003:27) interpreted ruins as "footprints of the past and stigmas of defeat," Bromberger (cited in Prats 1997:85) argued that the greater part of the current local activation of heritage emerges as a kind of "museification of frustration," creating a variety of reconstructions of identity, alternatives to economical development, or both. Several vestiges of the past are transformed into touristic attractions; through the ruins of a lost past, people seek a ludic approach to it, so different than and distant to our own present. The activation of heritage serves the search, reconstruction, or (re)invention of identity and the attempts to achieve community cohesion through identification with it and the benefits resulting from its exploitation.

The analysis of the relationship between heritage and tourism can be examined from two different points of view, although both converge in a fundamental issue, central for the politics of heritage management and tourism: how to turn heritage into a touristic attraction. From a technical perspective, solutions contemplate the mystification of heritage, the construction of a metastory around it, the emphasis on its singularities/otherness, its transformation into show or fantasy, or the generation of an amazing, funny, and participative experience around it. Based on these elements the general tendency in the investigation of tourism has been centered on heritage's ideology and myths. In spite of myths and propaganda, the pitfalls of uncontrolled tourism began to be reported by mid-1970s (Jurado 1992; Kandt 1991; Santana 1997; Smith 1992; Turner and Ash 1991). However, this maelstrom has only increased; its consequences have branched, more and more, into social, economic, cultural, and ecological realms. Social analyses have focused on these issues, although biased by a logocentric perspective that negates the voices of implicated parties (host communities and tourists).

This chapter poses a different standpoint: the consideration of the equation between tourism and economic development from an *emic* point of view. The following pages broach the myth of the pursuit of tourism by two Bolivian highland communities: Santiago and Santiago Chuvica (Chuvica from here on) in Nor López Province (Department of Potosí, Bolivia), self-designated guardians and managers of the Laqaya archaeological site. Considering the moments before the full entry of these two communities into the regional touristic system, I will analyze (1) the local interpretation of the heritage/tourism relationship and (2) the value conceded to archaeological ruins as they become cultural commodities for economic development.

When I started my fieldwork in Santiago in August 2001, my ethnographic and ethnoarchaeological interests were focused on the local view of archaeological ruins—the representation of the past and its inhabitants according to an emic interpretation of the archaeological record and the myths, metaphors, fears, and desires of the people about the ruins (Gil 2005, 2007a, 2007b). However, I discovered early on that the social dimension of the Laqaya stones is not only fixed in a past/present temporality but projected strongly into the future. A complex psychosocial, identifying, esthetic, mythic, strategic, and spatial transformation has occurred over the ruins. During the last years the archaeological site has stopped being contemplated as a simple stage for oral tradition about the time of the *chullpas* (the time of ancient people);[3] it now plays an active role in the communities' development expectations (Gil 2004, forthcoming). With tourism looming over the region, the ruins become an emblem of a utopian progress, a flag of a current commodity project. This fact forced me to change my research design.[4] The new ad hoc analysis tipped the scale toward Santiago, where I was working; however, methodology and ethics demanded the incorporation of Chuvica as well.

From different impulses Santiago and Chuvica have learned to value and sense the Laqaya ruins, connecting it with their hopes for the future, maybe by comparison with nearby San Juan, where tourist hostels and a small site museum have been operating for some time. Given their lack of "attractions of remarkable touristic interest" and infrastructure, Santiago and Chuvica were originally excluded from the touristic circuits of the Uyuni salt flats and the Eduardo Avaroa Wildlife National Reserve (REA from here on) which attract thousands of tourists annually. Yet, both communities nowadays value the interest and attractiveness of "their" ruins and are trying to gain space in the booming regional economy. This chapter is not a detailed analysis of the impact of tourism on Uyuni and Lípez through the case study of Laqaya. Rather, my purpose is to reflect on the local interpretations and representations of the myths of tourism as access to regional circuits.

The Phenomenon of Regional Tourism in the Uyuni Salt Flats and the Lípez Highlands

Different labels are given to the concepts of heritage and tourism. Travel agency advertisements tempt us with choices of different kinds of tourism for different kinds of tourists. The tourist industry must generate its own attractions, constructing narratives and spaces for consumption. This is key for the great variety of touristic choices. If modern society condemns individuals to an artificial and alienated life, tourism offers them the possibility of introducing authenticity into their lives. The tourism industry is always pressing for an improved product: it appeals to hyperrealism, fantasy, imitation, or invention for the building of magical landscapes and stages that tourists will consider authentic. Authenticity is key for tourism because those images are produced and organized around the ideas of exoticism, magnificence, tradition, savagery, and virginity—this last one especially in relation to ecological tourism.

The tourism industry has nature and culture as its principal sources of income, uses them as attractions, ignores them, or considers them as simple locations for other activities, generally stereotyped (Prats 1997:44–52). Heritage is integrated into the touristic system according to three categories (Prats 1997:42–43): (1) as a touristic product per se, qualified for building, in union with others services, an autonomous commodity; (2) as related to a touristic package in organized travels that combine it with other cultural and recreational products; and (3) as added value to touristic destinations that, without having it among their principal attractions, take advantage of it for completing a high-quality touristic offer.

The Uyuni salt flats are normally marketed along with the REA environmental attractions—touristic products per se according to the preceding categories—in the promotion of the so-called "Route of the highland jewels" (Ruta de las joyas altoandinas) or "Route of white deserts and colored lagoons" (Ruta de los desiertos blancos y las lagunas de colores) (Figure 14.1). However, and in order to complete such a high-quality touristic offer, tour operators and travel agencies working in the area add ethnicity and culture to the beauty and grandeur of savage nature. Landscapes are humanized by the communities' "traditional way of life" and by archaeological ruins.

For understanding the logic of this system, I will describe the itineraries offered by travel agencies, whose services can be contracted in any office in La Paz, Potosí, Oruro, Sucre, Villazón (on the Bolivia–Argentina border), or Uyuni, where their headquarters are housed for backpackers and independent travelers searching for emotions, landscapes, and proximity to native peoples.

Tourists are taken northwest early in the morning from Uyuni to Colchani, a community devoted to the extraction, packaging, and trade of salt. Then they access the Uyuni salt flats, visiting the Salt Hotel and Pescado Island; these are the only "remarkable touristic points" in 12,000 km² of salt flats.

What is a "remarkable touristic point"? Heritage is a raw material modeled by discourses about culture in a recreated or invented stage. Tourism needs to generate its own images for selling a product; when the latter does not exist tourism invents them, generating diverse plays of perception, experimentation, emotion, and sensation, searching for effectiveness to satisfy the expectations of tourists. When the images have been selected, it is necessary to stop space and time and to define those images more representative of their own reality; their identification and recognition are clues for singularizing the new touristic product. In the case of environmental heritage, this process derives in landscapes construction through the perception and representation of sociocultural rationalizations of natural elements. The tourist industry in Uyuni needs to transform the monochromy of salt and the apparent monotony of the Lípez highlands into singular scenes worth a photograph. Such is the compositional logic of all postcards in this voyage: Pescado Island and its cactus forest, Ollagüe volcano, briny lagoons with their flamingos,

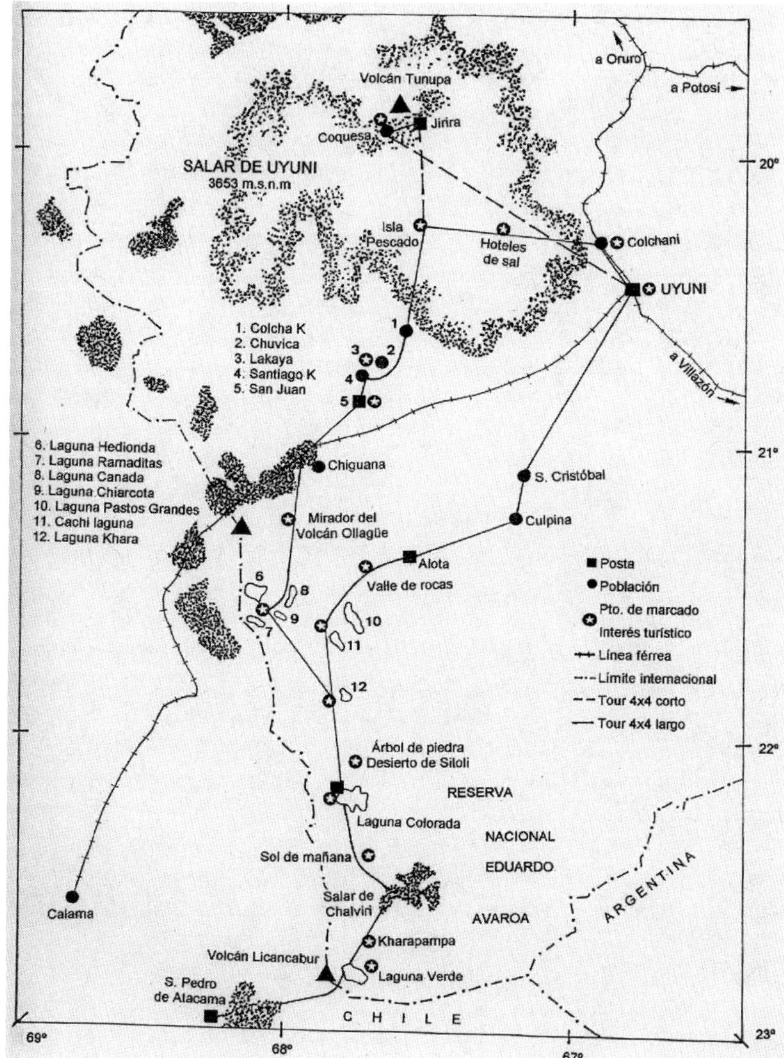

Figure 14.1 "White deserts and colored lagoons": touristic circuits across the Uyuni salt flats and Lípez highlands.

Rocks Valley and the Salvador Dali Rocks, the Stone Tree, Red Lagoon, Morning Sun Geyser, and Green Lagoon.

There are two possible itineraries from Pescado Island: a two-day circuit to the north and a four-day circuit to the south, crossing the Uyuni salt flats and the Lípez highlands. The shorter option arrives at Jirira and then, watched over by the Tunupa volcano, on to Coquesa; tourists can visit the church and the *chullpas* cavern[5] there. Going though Jirira again, the tourists then return to Uyuni. The long circuit exits Uyuni via the Colcha K peninsula to San Juan, a village with some hostels and attractions—a small archaeological and ethnographical museum, capricious geological forms, and archaeological ruins. Then, crossing the Chiguana salt flats and the highlands, passing small briny lagoons, tourists enter the REA by the Red and Green Lagoons. At this point some agencies offer the option to cross the Bolivia–Chile border to San Pedro de Atacama, although the most common practice is to go back to Uyuni via the alternative eastern routes. Along this journey, the tourists enjoy scenes included in the 368,000 Google links for the Uyuni salt flats.[6]

I would like to point out some aspects of the touristic services offered along this journey. These notes allow for an understanding of the problems created by the construction of a hostel in Santiago,[7] which was basic for the transformation of Laqaya into a touristic commodity.

The tourists that choose Uyuni and Lípez as destinations enjoy a mixture of "ecotourism" and "adventure tourism," especially when they arrive in this area full of environmental delights. They are mostly backpackers in search of landscapes, inner experiences, and intercultural contacts, especially if they are "authentic" and "traditional." However, in spite of age and budget, the travelers are not willing to give up security, comfort, intimacy, hygiene, or Western food, all of them significant for travel operators when they evaluate hostels and services wanting to be incorporated into the touristic circuit.

As Nielsen et al. (2003:372) indicate, the development of tourism began in this area without planning and as a result of a few particular initiatives. Local communities had no time to prepare themselves or enough options to participate in the design of touristic products, development, and administration. Communities have been fighting to attract tourists to their villages and to keep them away from their neighbors. Hostels and heritage managers lure tourist convoys to their communities. According to the expectations of tourists and the requirements of tour operators, hostels ought to become "lodging oases" with parking areas and rooms for four to six tourists, a driver, and a cook. Besides common areas, privacy is a must for bedrooms and toilets. No matter how cultural interaction is promoted, tourists hardly ever interact with local people; at the most, while tourists walk about the communities taking photographs, children may benefit from playing with them and receiving trinkets.

The Myth of Tourism among Santiago Community Members

We were only three or four people who wanted to build a hostel and wait for visitors. I asked in Potosí and La Paz, and all agencies told me the same, that if we would like to operate correctly, we ought to have an archaeological site with good advertisement and brochures. Then we understood the need for all community members to work together. (JCL, 40 years old, Santiago, 2001)[8]

My *compadre* Justino Calcina Lupa placed emphasis on the transit from individual initiative to communitarian management while talking about a group of community members looking after the myth of tourism to Uyuni and Lípez that started to colonize those virgin spaces at the beginning of the 1990s. People from Santiago remember how touristic convoys went right to San Juan, where community members had already built some hostels.

Santiago, in Nor Lípez Province, is made up of some 350 people devoted to potato and quinoa agriculture; they are also shepherds in crisis. The village is 100 km southeast of Uyuni and 15 km from Route 701, which goes from Potosí to the Bolivia–Chile border, so it is strategically located on the touristic circuit. It has plenty of archaeological ruins, of which Laqaya is the most relevant. Burgeoning tourism, the proximity to roads, and potential heritage attractions were important incentives for the local touristic project. Héctor Saturnino Lupa remembers 1992 as the year when particular initiatives were opened to the rest of the community:

We were planning our own project, without thinking in the others. But then we assumed that maybe we must count on the community, and we made them participants in our idea. Most people didn't correspond. We were delayed till 1996–1997 for this reason. Then we began to walk, with the collaboration of archaeologists ... and we go on! (HSL, 32 years old, Santiago, 2002)

Héctor, *corregidor* in 2002, told me about the project. He insisted on the interest of the original group in sharing profits with the community and on the disinterest of most community members at that time, which he interpreted as a consequence of ignorance: "We did not find any answer in the community because people didn't know what tourism was." Could it be that they did not ignore "tourism," but rather considered it an aggression to their spaces and traditional way of life? Ideologic and economic issues were also at stake. On the ideological side people expressed their preoccupation with the possibility of the Laqaya ruins being "disturbed," an idea directly related to local knowledge about archaeological sites as borderline spaces where forces of the remote past are concentrated; such forces inhabit the *chullpas*. Tradition requires respect for the ancients, forbids transit across the ruins for fear of their anger—a cause of illness and calamities—and demands *pagos* (offerings) to the ruins if they happen to be in *chacras* (agricultural plots) or crossroads. These beliefs are apparently disappearing as a consequence of modernity. The psychosocial interpretation of the ruins is changing from their conception as places of memory, experience, and fear to places onto which the ideal of progress is projected (Gil, forthcoming).

On the economic side, building a hostel implies a high spending and there are not enough funds in Santiago. The building of the hostel has been fairly irregular. Even when it is finished, accessing the touristic circuit will demand marketing, which also requires funds. Besides, as the project is based in the local management of the ruins,[9] negotiations with culture and heritage state, provincial, and departmental institutions would soon follow. For even considering these plans, local management bureaucracy demands a technical assessment. But neither individuals nor the community could afford archaeological research. The arrival in Santiago of the Southern Highland Archaeological Project in 1996 was a point of inflexion in the development of events: Santiago obtained a long-awaited archaeological study and the work of archaeologists helped to change the people's view of the ruins, this time as valued goods of the archaeological heritage.

The Laqaya Project: An Experience of Local Management and Intercultural Dialogue

About 7 ha in size and having a chronological sequence spanning from the twelfth to the fifteenth centuries, Laqaya is one of the most important archaeological sites in the north of the Lípez highlands. Located at the edge of a rocky peninsula from where the visual control of a fertile farming plain is possible, the site is divided into two well-defined sectors: the upper sector, Alto Laqaya, is protected by steep slopes and a rocky cliff and houses a *pukará* (fortress) from the Regional Developments period previous to the Inca expansion; the lower sector, Bajo Laqaya, is a village from the Inca period, perhaps settled as a tributary community devoted to farming state lands. A *chullpa* tower area is located between these two sectors (Figure 14.2).

Laqaya means "village in ruins" in Quechua. According to oral tradition, the site was the capital of Lípez during *chullpa* times. Powerful warriors inhabited the *pukará* and its walls witnessed several battles, the last one against the Incas: their tyranny and/or the first sunrise—varying from myth to myth—caused the extinction of the *chullpas* and the beginning of a new era (Gil 2005, 2007a). At the beginning of this century, Santiago and Chuvica are fighting a battle

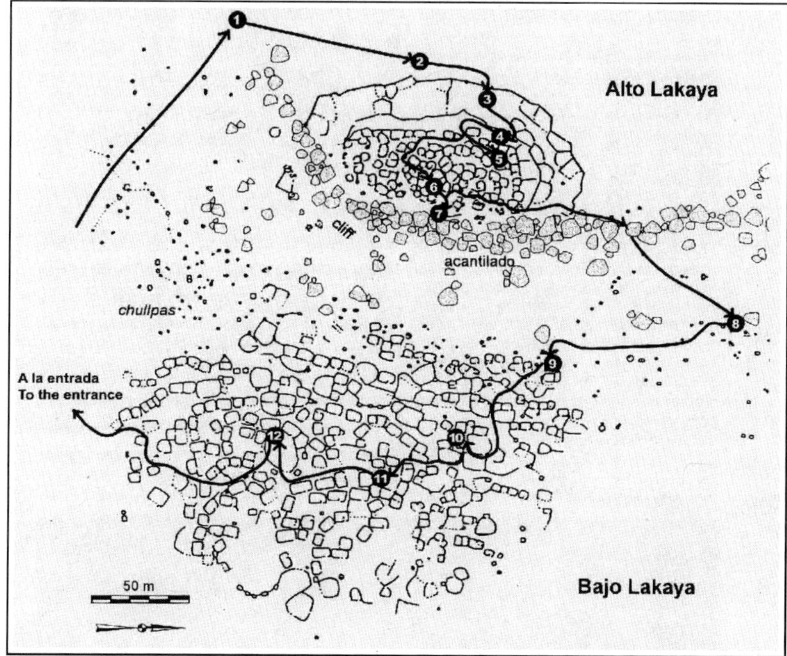

Figure 14.2 Plan of the Laqaya archaeological site with the interpretative path and stations indicated. (From *Lakaya. Tierra de Chullpas/Land of Chullpas.* South Altiplano Archaeological Project, Axel E. Nielsen director, p. 2.)

to include Laqaya into the touristic regional system and to achieve their idea of development. Before dealing with this issue, I will briefly consider the heritage management project that aims to revaluate this archaeological site.

The Laqaya Project—part of the Southern Highland Archaeological Project—started in 1996 as a joint effort between archaeologists and the communities of Santiago and Chuvica. Axel Nielsen, its director, noted:

> The goal is to support the regional communities so they can take advantage of their archaeological heritage in the function of tourism, furthering their participation in management and profits, and to minimize the negative environmental, social, and cultural impacts of tourism.(Nielsen et al. 2003:374)

The Laqaya Project is an example of an archaeology engaged with local peoples in which archaeologists and communities participate in an intercultural dialogue. The project allows communication between archaeological and traditional knowledge and helps local communities to obtain new tools for their own future. The project started as a collaboration between archaeologists and people from Santiago; afterwards people from Chuvica also joined. The two communities decided to share work and profits. Although they state that they work in harmony, periodical conflicts arise, especially regarding deadlines and differences about profits.

The Laqaya Project is based on two criteria inspired by self-management and interculturalism. Archaeologists surveyed and partially excavated the site, consolidated damaged architectural structures, rebuilt some of them, and designed an interpretative path. Community members actively participated in these activities, and hundreds of people attended a guide-training course. The project published *Laqaya. Tierra de Chullpas—Land of Chullpas* in 2001–2002, a Spanish-English bilingual brochure explaining the interpretative path's 12 stops and including details of the traditional way of life and oral traditions about the ruins.

The project seeks the declaration of Laqaya as an archaeological park and a national monument. In 2002 Santiago and Chuvica asked the Vice-Ministry of Culture and the Bolivian National Archaeological Office (UNAR, from here on) for their recognition as stewards of the site. The request was initially turned down but finally granted in 2004. The ruins opened that same year. The opening ceremony was attended by officials from those two governmental bodies, members of the project, and local and national TV and radio channels. Nowadays, Santiago and Chuvica continue self-managing the site.

ARCHAEOLOGY AND TOURISM FROM THE PERSPECTIVE OF LOCAL DEVELOPMENT

Tourism creates attractions and transforms them into commodities through different development myths, just what the community members from Santiago did when they started to consider Laqaya from the logic of tourism:

> We think that the self-management of archaeological ruins is a unique source of income that we could have to progress. As we have no other income, people emigrate. So we are thinking of tourism in order to prevent this situation because we see that there are a lot of tourists arriving in Uyuni. We compare our reality with other places and see that they receive tourists and get an income from them. Why not here? For this reason we have started to work in that direction and have expectations about our project. (HSL, 32 years old, Santiago, 2002)

Tourism changes local views about the ruins. While tradition holds that ruins are borderline spaces inhabited by a dangerous ancient Otherness, the current dual feelings about the ruins are interesting: people respect archaeological sites out of fear but they nevertheless exploit them for tourism (Gil, forthcoming).

At the beginning of the Laqaya Project, Santiago and Chuvica appointed committees to oversee the management of the ruins. In 2000 the Santiago Tourism Committee (Laqaya Park Committee since 2001) was appointed "to carry on all needed procedures to obtain a legal resolution for Laqaya, to manage and conserve the archaeological site, and to build an archaeological museum and a hostel." On July 4th, 2001, two days after filing in La Paz the request for the declaration of Laqaya as an archaeological park, the committee sent a letter to the Vice-Minister of Tourism asking to include Santiago in regional touristic circuits as a "land of *chullpas*"; the letter argued that the community was in charge of the Laqaya ruins, working on a hostel, and had applied to the local telephone company for a phone. These arguments—remarkable touristic point of interest, accommodation, and services—not only show how well Santiago community members knew the rules of tourism, but also that they were constructing an attractive product for tourists.

While walking across Laqaya with Wilson Condori Vilca, he told me spontaneously:

> Our archaeological site must be attractive for tourists. We hope it is. People are working in order to obtain this. For this reason tourists will come here, and we will tell them what happened in this place, how people lived here. (WCV, 30 years old, Santiago, 2002)

Justino Calcina, who worked as a driver in the 2001 tourist high season for a Uyuni travel agency, knows that the tourist comes first, and thus his/her expectations ought to be satisfied:

> Thus, it is very important to give good information to tourists. If we give them bad information and bad services they will not be satisfied. For this reason we are preparing the economic part as well as the guides. Only when we are really well qualified, we won't have troubles. (JCL, 40 years old, Santiago, 2001)

Travel agencies in Uyuni asked the community to finish work in Laqaya and the hostel in Santiago before including the ruins in their circuits. Santiago and Chuvica started to work together to finish the needed infrastructure at the ruins: an interpretative path designed by the Southern Highland Archaeological Project, a parking lot, a reception office, and toilets. They also agreed on how to share profits.

Apparently everything was going well, but I learned of disagreements, especially about the allocation of activities, the location of the archaeological museum, and the future distribution of profits. For example, as early as 2001 Chuvica wanted to receive tourists in Laqaya, even though their neighbors had not finished their assigned works. Santiago did not accept, arguing that the museum was part of the Laqaya Project but only as a plus for tourists arriving at the archaeological ruins; thus the entrance ticket should include both the guided visit to the ruins and the museum. However, rushing to file for the declaration of Laqaya as an archaeological park, work on the museum was delayed. Yet, people in Santiago talked about the museum in spite of its inexistence; even children, as could be seen in a drawing done by students of the Miguel Cuzco Educational Center. While doing fieldwork in 2001 and 2002, part of a research project on how people experience and represent places, I called a drawing competition for elementary and high school students. The theme of the 2001 competition was "My Community." One of the 65 drawings included a building identified as the museum (Figure 14.3), five explicitly related Santiago to the Laqaya ruins, and 11 included archaeological ruins (especially *chullpa* towers) in or nearby the village. I found these numbers to be indicative of the ruins as an important reference in

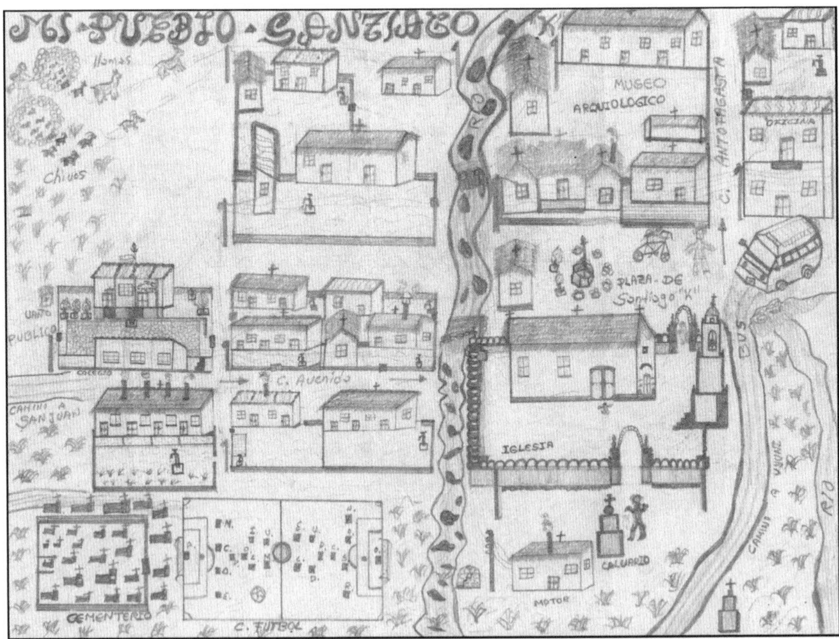

Figure 14.3 Drawing of Agustín Orlando Bernal (19 years old) from Santiago, 2001. Note that a nonexistent "archaeological museum" building is included in the village representation, even though at that time it was only a long-term objective.

the representation of the community's social space. "The Laqaya Ruins" was the theme of the 2002 competition. Out of 62 drawings, 12 showed the interpretative path and six included large huts with different labels: a "souvenir store," an "office," two labeled as a "museum," and two more as a "touristic stop" (Figures 14.4 and 14.5). The numbers not only show that children were aware of the project but also how important it had become for the people.

In Santiago in 2002 Erasmo Condori Ticona—a former community authority, respected elder, and founding member of the Santiago Tourism Committee—told me what had happened during my absence:

> Well, it seems that if Laqaya is not yet in operation it is because we probably set too high a price for the entrance ticket. Tourists do not come here. One, two, three vehicles arrived last week, but no more, and I do not know why. OK, we are delayed, but we have not stopped working during all this time. (ECT, 60 years old, Santiago, 2002)

That year before going to Santiago, I visited several travel agencies in Uyuni to check if Laqaya was included in the tours offered. The result

Figure 14.4 Drawing of the Laqaya ruins by Héctor Elio Quispe Ferrer (13 years old), Santiago, 2002. In the lower left on the path, note the indication "Parada de Turismo" (tourism stop); a hut identified as "Museo" (museum) is located nearby.

Figure 14.5 Drawing of the Laqaya ruins by Franz Gonzalo Quispe Cayo (14 years old), Santiago, 2002. In the bottom center note the building labeled "Museo" (museum); next to this building is a sign inviting people to visit the ruins.

was negative, indicating that the archaeological site was not yet in operation. What then was Erasmo talking about? It was not long before I found out. The episode, maybe just anecdotal in another context, had become gossip for some people in Santiago, who accused Chuvica of being impatient and convinced themselves of the need to be better prepared for receiving tourists. Justino Calcina told me what had happened: the communities did not agree about the price of the entrance ticket. Chuvica suggested $5, all included; Santiago thought $1 would be enough, without the brochure. One day, when Chuvica community members were working at the site, some tourists arrived; they were charged an expensive price without receiving full benefits. Santiago community members thought this was a terrible mistake. Discussions were renewed about the need to complete pending works before offering *their* ruins to Uyuni travel agencies.

Héctor Saturnino added a relevant argument about the relationship between heritage and tourism:

> We didn't resolve the issue of ticket prices ... There is a lack of communication between both communities and the solution could be to lower

the price. I think $1 is a good price, because $5 is the entrance price to Eduardo Avaroa [Wildlife National] Reserve. You pay that much but get to see a lot of different things there. However, you can only visit the archaeological site here, Laqaya ruins ... This is the problem. (HSL, 32 years old, Santiago, 2002)

In November 2004 I checked again the travel agencies in Uyuni. Tour operators were still not taking tourists to Santiago or Laqaya. Shopkeepers in the market and several passengers in the bus to Santiago told me about "a lot of vehicles" arriving at the archaeological site. When I discovered that they were Chuvica inhabitants or relatives, I wondered if they were not just defending their own community. Yet, I also discovered that some Chuvica community members had started to offer lodging on their own, and the travel agency Colque-Tour had apparently come to an agreement for the construction of a hostel there for its tourist clientele. As I could confirm later through informal talks with San Juan hostel owners, this move was not well received by the community because community members felt it threatened their regional lodging monopoly. Santiago people considered it an unfair competition. I talked about this situation with Justino Calcina, who considered it a mistake in local development terms and argued for projects from and for the communities, not for a fictitious short-term personal profit:

> I believe that the community should benefit from tourism, and then open the options to individuals if there is room for them. My view is that we have to work together to earn benefits collectively ... The community loses when we work as individuals and only some people obtain profits. I don't know what Chuvica thinks about it, but I think that my neighbors' initiative doesn't benefit anyone, even individuals. If a travel agency controls the hostel in the end, the single beneficiary will be the businessman. However, when the project benefits the whole community, it is possible to pay attention to educational or sanitation necessities, for example water ducts or sewer systems. (JCL, 44 years old, Santiago, 2004)

This was the opinion among Santiago people, who have not stopped criticizing Chuvica for its unilateral decision, detrimental to both communities. They thought it necessary to finish the works in Laqaya first and then proceed on with building the hostel.

PROJECTING HOPES TO THE FUTURE: ON LOCAL VIEWS ABOUT TOURISM

When Héctor Saturnino Lupa talked to me about the debate over entrance prices and the 2002 disagreements, he remarked that Laqaya ruins were less attractive than sites at the Eduardo Avaroa Wildlife National Reserve: "You can see a lot of different things there. However, you can visit only the archaeological site here, the Laqaya ruins." During all my fieldwork seasons in Santiago since 2001, this was the only time someone talked to me in those terms. Optimism is rampant about works at the archaeological site, the hostel, and even the still-nonexistent museum; in spite of difficulties and delays, nobody questions how precarious is the raw material in which people deposit their hopes. Knowing Héctor Saturnino and his Protestant ethic, I don't believe his statement was a slip. I think he was just implying that Laqaya, as a heritage commodity, was still far from being ready for tourism; as Prats (1997:41–48) would have it, it needed the addition of other elements to make it attractive.

Taking into consideration the equation of tourism with development and the community members' idea that the arrival of tourists in Laqaya and Santiago will bring much-needed resources, I pose two questions: How is the profit from tourism thought about in local, practical terms? What feedback circuit is established from this equation?

One day in 2001 I was chatting with children and teenagers in Santiago. We were talking about archaeologists and ruins, when one of them, Jorge Condori Suna, asked me to record his testimony:

> In Laqaya there will be a museum. There we will sell some things. Archaeologists will also arrive. And here in Santiago we will sell weavings, socks, *chulos* (Andean wool caps), shawls, gloves. It will be just like that. There are *chullpas* in Laqaya, and there will be a hostel here in Santiago … The archaeologists have studied the ruins. We have repaired them, we have cleaned the places. We have done everything so they can come! (JCS, 12 years old, Santiago, 2001)

This testimony is not spontaneous. It springs from the community's feeling about tourism as an important future source of income. The more complete the product offered is (ruins, museum, souvenir store, hostel), the more profits will be earned. So, a hut for a visitors center is planned for Laqaya. Thinking about sales, some individuals started the production of handcrafts. Tourism is thus considered an important opportunity for economic gain, although most expectations are not met.

By the end of 2002, people from Santiago had planned to finish the hostel with the income from tourist visits to Laqaya. They had also planned to use the profits to improve the local school and health services. However, as a result of the disagreements about the ticket price, profits from tourism never materialized. The community's expectations were covered by small development projects funded by an Italian missionary group (a greenhouse in 2003) or by the Municipality of Colcha K/Villa Marín (a sanitarian facility for cattle and a new classroom in 2004). In the meantime, Santiago people still hope that the opening of Laqaya as an archaeological park and the building of the hostel will earn them needed profits.

In 2002 I conducted workshops with highschoolers to understand their idea of progress and to see if tourism was contemplated as a part of it. Most of them, especially those from upper grades, wanted to leave the community to continue studying elsewhere. Those willing to stay pointed to agriculture and tourism as their sole options; yet, they were opposed to considering tourism as a panacea to mitigate all community needs. They thought it necessary to get a better preparation for accessing the touristic system and agreed that there was still a long way to go. For those in the lower grades, the idea of progress derived from the profits of tourism was centered on a satellite dish to watch news and movies[10] and in the embellishment of the main square for dances and parties—not thinking about themselves but as a way to lure tourists.

FINAL CONSIDERATIONS

Nowadays, we are witnessing an unparalleled revitalization of the past, a recovery of the "authentic," an exacerbation of identities. The local strongly rises against the backdrop of the global, eagerly searching for its roots. In this context, heritage has been defined as a historical and cultural legacy that connects past and present and that is symbolically manipulated by different social agents for the (re)construction of identities. However, heritage commodities are only accepted as such when claimed and valued by a (sometimes complex) selection process encouraged by ideologies and discourses. Tourism is one of those heritage-making ideologies, perhaps one of the most powerful ones. As an industry of images and the commodities they generate for the market, tourism transforms heritage into an attraction, a product subjected to market rules and to the despotism of economic gain. Such is the funding logic of the equation between tourism and development, the main reason behind local activations of heritage, precisely those Bromberger (1996) defined as the "museification of frustration," a mechanism of cultural and economic survival from which to rebuild identities or derive profit, or both. The Laqaya Project promoted by Santiago and Chuvica fits this argument.

In this ethnographic study I tried to answer how the past is transformed into a heritage commodity, how the process unfolds, and who is behind it, theorizing from general arguments to local contexts. Contrary to classic studies on the impact of tourism, I have adopted an emic perspective to consider local perspectives on development and local interpretations of the myths of tourism. This is not a detailed study about the paradoxes surrounding the building of Laqaya as a heritage commodity for the tourism market; I have rather recorded the voices of one of the communities involved in order to understand its idea of progress and its perception of tourism as a clue for change and development and on which its hopes are built.

I am aware of my discursive bias: the local testimonies I presented all come from individuals actively implicated in the touristic project. However, I am confident that the whole community shares the same stereotyped discourse based on the same key issues: a burgeoning regional tourism, the equation between tourism and economic development, the Laqaya ruins, the archaeological study, the work on the ruins for the tourism market, a cooperation with neighboring Chuvica, the hostel in Santiago, the museum in Laqaya and/or Santiago, the complexity of the whole process, the consequences brought about by its delay, the context of economic crisis, the need for an official declaration of Laqaya as an archaeological park, the conflicts that arose between the communities, and the anecdotal and frustrating experiences with the first tourists to arrive in Laqaya in 2002.

Just as societies and cultures are in a permanent state of transformation, tourism has further changes, permanently generating new images and forcing the implicated parties to (re)built their scenarios. For essentialist and romantic anthropology (or archaeology), native peoples or local communities must approach their pasts for reasons of tradition and ancestral identity, never for money. Yet, and possibly due to globalization and the loss of traditional values, communities are eager to hop onto the wagon of modernity and progress; thus, they think in economic terms, no matter how politically incorrect the association between heritage, tourism, and profit may look. The Laqaya ruins are much more than stones. The tourist who contemplates them may sense a journey back in time, but the people from Santiago and Chuvica strive to build a present and a future from them, although their utopian acts may not seem real. As they work hard to get Laqaya into tourism, they also continue their communal life.

NOTES

1. A longer version of this paper was published in Spanish in *Textos Antropológicos* 15, no. 2 (2006):197–228 as "*Cuando vengan los turistas … ruinas arqueológicas, turismo y expectativas locales de futuro en Nor Lípez (Dpto. Potosí, Bolivia).*" I worked this new, rewritten, and revised English version with the collaboration of Antonio J. Gil García.

2. The heritage concept is usually accompanied by adjectives such as historical, artistic, monumental, archaeological, cultural, ethnographic, intellectual, or natural. Yet, heritage always goes through management policies of diverse kinds. In this chapter

I will consider "heritage" as the legacy of a community and their identity through time.

3. *Chullpa* is an ambiguous concept of complex specification. In Andean archaeology the term is used to refer to post-Tiwanaku (ca. 10th century AD) Aymara highlands funerary towers; they were built and/or reused until early colonial times. By extension, the term is also used to refer to any similar architectural feature, burial and deposits alike. Metonymically *chullpa* is also the body placed inside these towers, although it would be better used to refer to a funerary bundle. For ethnography, fantastic *chullpa* creatures are classificatory units of Otherness related to pre-solar ancient peoples and, by extension, pre-Inca peoples (who the Spaniards called *gentiles*). In this sense, *chullpas* as *gentiles* are also underworld tutelary entities who inhabit the ruins, causing illness and even death to those who do not respect archaeological sites or objects.

4. This paper is the result of three fieldwork seasons in Santiago between 2001 and 2004, two of them linked to the project "Archaeology and local knowledge in Lípez (Dpt. of Potosí, Bolivia)," promoted by the Directorate of Cultural Issues of the Bolivian Embassy in Spain and approved by the National Archaeological Unit of Bolivia (UNAR, its Spanish acronym).

5. The *chullpas* cavern is surely the principal attraction sold to tourists by the Coquesa community. In an inner rock shelter, community members have stored under key several mummified bodies collected in the area. The official version is that by doing so these *chullpas* (ancestors) were rescued from the ransacking of the community's archaeological heritage. However, oral tradition is more romantic: this cavern was the last shelter of a *chullpa* family, escaping from Spanish conquerors. Desperate, they sought refuge in this cavern, where they died of starvation and sadness (tale collected in Jirira, August 2001).

6. Updated as of November 19, 2008.

7. Since 2008 there has been an active hostel in Santiago. It is managed by the cultural association Our Roots (Nuestras Raíces), the same group that promotes the majority of touristic projects in this community; this group not only manages the Laqaya ruins but is also involved in cultural activism around history and tradition. The incorporation of Santiago into the regional touristic system has generated new sociocultural situations that I am currently studying.

8. All testimonies quoted in this chapter were originally recorded in Spanish. Local usages were eliminated in order to obtain a better accommodation to English.

9. As Héctor Saturnino Lupa stated in 2002, the ruins "could be an attractive place for tourists." This point of view articulates with the functioning of the touristic system and its production of images.

10. The long-awaited satellite dish and phone box arrived in Santiago in 2003 when Héctor Saturnino Lupa was finishing his term as *corregidor*. The arrival of TV was an important social event in Santiago, even though a diesel engine provided power only two hours a day, and even though there was only one channel available.

REFERENCES

Augé, Marc 1998 *El viaje imposible. El turismo y sus imágenes.* Gedisa, Barcelona.
———. 2003 *El tiempo en ruinas.* Gedisa, Barcelona.
Bromberger, Christian 1996 Ethnologie, patrimonies, identités. Y a-t-il une spécificité de la situation française? In *L'Europe entre cultures et nations. Cahiers d'Ethnologie de la France* 10, edited by Daniel Fabre, pp. 10–23. Maison des Sciences de l'Homme, Paris.
Gil, Francisco M. 2004 Arqueología y pensamiento local en Lípez (Potosí, Bolivia). "Historias de ruinas" y gestión integral del patrimonio cultural en la modernidad. *Espacio y Desarrollo* 16:101–135.

Gil, Francisco M. 2005 Batallas del pasado en tiempo presente: "guerra antigua," civilización y pensamiento local en Lípez (Dpto. Potosí, Bolivia). *Bulletin del Institut Français d'Etudes Andines* 34(2):197–220.

———. 2007a Las ruinas, la iglesia, la mina. Identidad local y construcción del discurso histórico de una comunidad del Altiplano de Lípez (Dpto. Potosí, Bolivia). In *Actas del XI Congreso Internacional de la Sociedad Española de Americanistas*:663–676. Spanish Society of Americanists, Murcia University, Murcia.

———. 2007b Expropiando el pasado para la construcción del presente. Discurso histórico e identidad en una comunidad del Altiplano de Lípez (Dpto. Potosí, Bolivia). *Nuevo Mundo, Mundos Nuevos*, 7, http://nuevomundo.revues.org/document3662.html.

———. Forthcoming Cuando los ideales de progreso se impusieron al miedo. Modernidad, arqueología, turismo y transformaciones del pensamiento local en torno a las ruinas (Nor Lípez, Potosí, Bolivia). In *Espacios del miedo y etnografía de lo fantástico en las fronteras amerindias de la globalización*, edited by F. M. Gil García. Abya-Yala, Quito.

Jurado, Francisco 1992 Los mitos del turismo. In *Los mitos del turismo*, edited by F. Jurado, pp. 15–88. Endymion, Madrid.

Kandt, Emanuel de (editor) 1991 *Turismo: ¿pasaporte al desarrollo? Perspectivas sobre los efectos sociales y culturales del turismo en los países en vías de desarrollo.* Endymion, Madrid.

Nielsen, Axel, Justino Calcina, and Bernardino Quispe 2003 Arqueología, turismo y comunidades originarias: una experiencia en Nor Lípez (Potosí, Bolivia). *Chungara* 35(2):369–377.

Prats, Llorenc 1997 *Antropología y patrimonio.* Ariel, Barcelona.

Santana, Agustín 1997 *Antropología y turismo. ¿Nuevas hordas, viejas culturas?* Ariel, Barcelona.

Smith, Valene L. (editor) 1992 *Anfitriones e invitados: antropología del turismo.* Endymion, Madrid.

Turner, Louis, and John Ash 1991 *La horda dorada.* Endymion, Madrid.

CHAPTER 15

THE MESSAGE OF THE KUVICHE IN THE LLEW-LLEW

Juana Paillalef Carinao

Llew-Llew Lake is one of the territorial landmarks that the Mapuche people of the coast of Chile have conserved and fought for in order to keep it intact through the years. The conviction of belonging and the certainty that these old places full of history and spiritual meaning are the places of their ancestors are sufficient reasons to reaffirm the patrimonial rights of the Mapuche *lavkenche* (people of the lake or coastal region) over these territories.

In 2002, a woman of the Llew-Llew region informed the Mapuche Museum in Cañete that a *menkuwe* (burying vessel) had been found on the north shore of the lake along with some accompanying objects. The members of the community, or *lov*—the basic family-political unit of the Mapuche people—who discovered it mentioned that the finding occurred in November while doing agricultural tasks and while repairing and building a fence, because there was wheat planted that needed to be protected from animals. When they were digging, they came upon some objects that they thought were stones, without realizing that these stones could have belonged to an old Mapuche cemetery. They immediately stopped the task and excavated deeper, finding this old vessel in which the corpse of a person had been placed long ago.

The landowners proceeded to remove the find carefully, leaving it in a shack near their house, protected and kept away from curious people; in order to reach the spot it was necessary to secure permission at the main house of one of the *lov*, or community, members. The people who moved the objects told us that they consisted of pottery sherds, a large ceramic vessel, and some teeth found inside this old grave. After seeing the objects we requested to see the exact place of the find. Accordingly, we were taken there, walking down a trail along a fence protecting a potato field; then we took a trail near the place where we could see the excavation left after the objects were removed.

This landscape was situated in a scenario whose principal actor was the Llew-Llew Lake; we had it around us as a loyal companion during the time we walked toward the cemetery. Upon arriving there we realized how privileged was this space that had been occupied for such a long time by this ancestral grave.

They Want to Tell Us Something

After some time, some people who lived nearby invited us to talk about the situation they were witnessing and of which they were protagonists. They invited us to come inside the house, which also had a special location in the landscape because the lake could be seen in all its magnificence from the trail on the south side of the house, where the find was made. This led to reassessing its importance in the social space of this Mapuche family. While we were talking about the find, we were served water with roasted flour and strawberries by the *lamgen* (sister), the owner of the house. She was the old mother of the person who reported the find, and she talked to us in *chedugun* and in Spanish, her second language, saying that this had never happened to her before and that she was worried because if the deceased allowed him-/herself to be seen, it was because he/she wanted to say something positive or negative; that is, he/she was advising us about something that would happen. "For doing this we had to pray for the deceased to be pleased and not upset because the belongings he/she had for his/her other life had been stolen." As I listened to this woman I remembered the many conversations I had with my grandparents when they referred to those who had already departed. They said that they talked with the deceased and that the deceased warned them about some things that were to happen. With this I confirm, once again, that the elders knew what there was in the afterlife because they achieved an important communication with those spaces and times, with the other world, the world where "the dead dwell." Today it is difficult to see and promote those acts due to the current lifestyle and the ignorance of that which is really important for our culture.

At some point one of our companions proposed that a *llellipun* (a little ceremony of salutation and gratitude to the spirits that dwell in places that have been altered) should be staged at the place in order to perform the mortuary rite the ancestors did when giving the farewell to those departing for the afterlife. "How could we do it," the *lamgen* said, "if many of the Mapuche living around here profess other creeds and have abandoned our Mapuche traditions. The churches and schools have stolen what we are and what our grandparents and parents have left to us." I thus understood what the oldest *lamgen* wanted to tell us; maybe she was telling us why the dead who appear bring us their messages.

I was able to understand that the answer was in the analysis that the *lamgen* was sharing with us regarding what we have forgotten about the spiritual and the daily practice of our traditions; just facing an unforeseen event of special meaning related to our recent past is not enough to reflect on nor to know what to do before such a revelation. Doubtlessly, we are facing a history and familiar elements from a Mapuche point of view that makes us different from other cultures.

The dead are telling us that we must return to our own things because not everything is lost, just retained in our subconscious. Not in vain has this find shown up in a territory in conflict, where the *lamgen* are fighting to recover part of their cultural heritage, of which the land is a fundamental part. One of the community leaders referred to this fact, saying:

> This is a very important finding to us because we are recovering our land; we have no more land to sustain our families and this *menkuwe* helps us to demonstrate to this *winka* (non-Mapuche), to the *winka*, that we are in an ancestral Mapuche territory. It allows us to demonstrate to them with tangible things that we have always been here … Some people have recovered land in other places; these objects give us the right to demand the restitution of our spaces.

We are aware that the viewpoints that can be recovered are multiple and depend on the interests we have or on the importance assigned to them from inside the culture. This interest can be demonstrated analyzing the treatment that exists when dealing with works or interventions. The cemeteries of Westerners are protected by the law and whoever dares to withdraw objects from a grave is prosecuted. This does not happen when dealing with an indigenous cemetery, such as the one I am documenting here. This is not illegal—it is "science," say the archaeologists.

Relations with the Archaeological Science

When this event was reported, some archaeologists were more interested in the "object" than in the subject; in this case the "object" was the bones and other items that were found on the shores of Llew-Llew Lake. For them the subjects living here were not important; I am not referring only to those living here and who have coexisted for so long with these remains without even knowing it, but also to the *newen* (natural forces that live in these spaces with the Mapuche, not only with the living beings but also with those who have departed) who have existed and exist here since times immemorial. Yet, we cannot ask these professionals to understand what is happening inside those communities that still keep and practice rituals loyal to their traditions, that live these events from within their own culture.

On one hand is the reprehensible treatment of something sacred as an object of research, disrespectful of the human and historical aspects, given that Mapuche people and their departed ancestors were here long before others. I remember when Marco Antonio de la Parra, in his book *El Cuerpo de Chile,* analyzed the behavior of doctors toward working, dogmatic, and personal matters. I am referring to the behavior of a doctor who him-/herself is also a parent, when performing an autopsy on a child. The author states that it is very difficult for a doctor to perform an autopsy on a child whose cause of death is perfectly known because he or she does not understand such an act. Maybe this is not the best example, but I think it is pertinent to the conditions experienced by the communities when they face these events and the professionals working on this endeavor.

On the other hand, there are the community members who, at the start, are impressed by the work done by these individuals inside the communities, especially when they listen to the bases these professionals rely on for fulfilling their goals, which normally are unrelated to the interests and wills of the community. I cannot ignore the fact that this situation might be easier for these professionals in some landless communities that have "lost their being," as the elder mentioned before, because the community members want to get rid of these ancient objects in order to occupy the once sacred land that, supposedly, will then be vacant. They also think that getting rid of these objects, once considered sacred and as containing spiritual forces that protect the Mapuche people, is tantamount to getting rid of "the ignorant past of their ancestors" and the rejecting by the *kuifiche* (the community elders) of the new creeds that arrive to make them forget who they are and the knowledge passed down by their ancestors.

It is important to note that the Mapuche people of this place do not have large tracts of land but save whatever they have because they are microagriculturalists; their lands are smaller than 10 ha, unlike the lands of the timber industries and the Chilean farm that borders the Mapuche community. They support themselves only with the products of the land. Migration is high at some times of the year, given that they go out looking for jobs to support their families.

New Relationships

The difficulties with archaeology in some Mapuche contexts are related to the information obtained from the surveys that are carried out. The communities, aware of the value that this information has for them and also for archaeology, are demanding a more inclusive participation and respect. Currently some archaeologists, conscious of this scenario, are willing to dialogue with the communities and to negotiate the due respect. For instance, in Elikura (Contulmo), an emblematic sector and community for the *lafkenche* Mapuche world in Arauco Province, the authorities refused for the archaeologists to survey Mapuche sites; this was a work commissioned by the CONADI and the regional government of Bio-Bio for a consulting company to complete the survey of archaeological sites in the province. Thus it was only possible to survey the sectors inhabited by some colonists who also live in the region. I must mention and highlight the attitude of the archaeologist in this narrative. Initially she suffered and was shocked when she had to face the community; she had the institutional requirement of the CONADI but, once in the field, noted that the task was not as easy to carry out as it had been done before by her predecessors (archaeologists), who without any respect broke into the cemeteries and sacred sites of Mapuche territory. What she had not planned was that she would have to negotiate her situation as a professional and her goals in a cultural context and in a non-neutral territory unknown to her; thus she was placed in the position of considering the apprehensions presented by the Mapuche community members, dialoguing in a horizontal and consensual plane in order to understand the objections of the leaders and take into account their position in undertaking her anthropological work.

This situation also happened with the people in Llew-Llew because, when they were informed what was the procedure to be followed or the regular conduct of information, they refused for several reasons. One of the reasons was the situation surrounding their lands and the unstable or bad relationships with the police. The judge was to send policemen to perform the customary procedure, that is, for them to be given a sample of bones for analysis at the Medical Examiner's Institute. The people refused to bring the remains to the museum for analysis, documentation, and study; they only let the museum photograph the find in situ and collect a few sherds. They wanted the find to remain in situ and not to be moved or taken out of their territory. This is how the objects remained in the hands of the Mapuche, who salvaged this cultural heritage that brought them hope for their life plans, whatever they are, especially those related to relevance and belonging.

Mapuche Mapu Mew, *Pewun* 2004.

CHAPTER 16

ARCHAEOLOGY AND *CABOCLO* POPULATIONS IN AMAZONIA: REGIMES OF HISTORICAL TRANSFORMATION AND THE DILEMMAS OF SELF-REPRESENTATION

Denise Maria Cavalcante Gomes
Translated from the Portuguese by David Rodgers

INTRODUCTION

In this chapter I shall discuss the impact of archaeological research among Amazonian *caboclo*[1] communities. Guided by concepts related to public archaeology, the interaction between archaeologists and communities involves issues such as consultation, negotiation, access to the investigated areas, power relations between local groups, the appropriation of scientific discourse, identity construction, and the destiny of archaeological heritage, all of which may considerably affect the course of the research. Although these questions are common to various contexts in Latin American, the production of information on the relevance of Amazonian archaeological heritage presents additional challenges: *caboclo* populations of Brazilian Amazonia have experienced a singular process of identity construction, historically marked by social marginalization and denial of their indigenous history. The purpose of this chapter is to examine the sociopolitical implications of participatory archaeology in a multifaceted social landscape.

The archaeological research project conducted between 2001 and 2003 in the community of Parauá, located on the left bank of the Tapajós River some 100 km south of Santarém in the Tapajós-Arapiuns Extractivist Reserve in the Brazilian state of Pará, provides the elements for a case study on concrete forms of community participation and the appropriation of archaeological discourse within the community's own strategies of constructing identities. The local population's interaction was fairly turbulent at the outset since many residents were suspicious of archaeological work, especially when this meant opening transects (long transversal clearings) in the area occupied by the community, which led to the formation of a group of people opposing the work and another group supporting it. The solution found was to allow the community partial control of the decisions made concerning the project. As Layton observed (1994), resolving the conflicts of interests between researchers and local communities necessarily implies this kind of solution, which results in a sociopolitical and reflexive form of archaeological practice (Allen et al. 2002; Clarke 2002:250; Rodríguez 2001, 2006).

While contract archaeology in Brazil is required by law to include the development of heritage education activities, academic research is not. Ethical concerns involving the rights of indigenous and traditional populations over the control of Brazil's cultural and archaeological heritage are recent (Funari 2001:241). Few examples exist of research projects that reflect a commitment to participatory archaeology (Funari 1995, 1996, 1999; Gomes 2005, 2006; Green et al., this volume). Generally, Brazilian archaeologists are not adequately trained to deal with local communities or with situations that could jeopardize projects developed in remote areas of the country. The project in question was also part of this reality. It was primarily focused on the cultural development of the Santarém region rather than being interested in local identities and strategies of self-representation. However, these concerns increasingly came to the fore as the research developed and with it various conflicts, making it evident that the only form of ensuring the viability of this kind of research project in Amazonia was through the public involvement of the local communities.

THE REGIONAL ARCHAEOLOGICAL CONTEXT

Until the 1970s, the prevailing interpretation of the cultural development of Amazonia was that produced by the archaeologist Betty Meggers (1971), who depicted Amazonia as an illusory paradise that contained precolonial cultures originating from other lowland areas and from the Andes. The classic example was represented by Marajoara culture, identified by Meggers as Andean in origin with a social organization of the same level found in the rest of the circum-Caribbean region, but which, due to the limits posed by the Amazonian environment, had declined to the level typical of the tropical forests. In the following decade, a new discourse emerged that constructed a grandiose image of Amazonia, describing many of its late precolonial societies as powerful chiefdoms with a complex social organization, political hierarchies, and settlements comparable to the societies found in the Andes and Mesoamerica. Roosevelt

(1980, 1987, 1991, 1992) was responsible for this shift in the interpretative paradigm concerning the cultural development of Amazonia, which has since had a strong influence on the work of various researchers.

The research conducted by myself (Gomes 2005) in the community of Parauá was designed to test the model of a complex, centralized, and hierarchical society that had supposedly developed in the region during the late precolonial period (Figure 16.1). In archaeological terms, one way of testing this model would be to find in the lower Amazon region, close to Santarém and along the Tapajós River, remains of ancient villages or satellite communities that demonstrate an ideological and political dependence on the center of the chiefdom in Santarém. This study was conducted in an area thought to be on the periphery of this regional system, employing a strategy that looked to reconstruct the ancient community and its regional interactions (Canuto and Yaeger 2000; Kolb and Snead 1997) based on data from settlement patterns and the internal organization of the sites, as well as an understanding of everyday subsistence practices through the analysis of pottery.

Parauá pottery—a basically utilitarian ceramic industry with decorative elements composed of vertical and transversal incisions—is associated with the Amazonian Incised Rim tradition (Meggers and Evans 1961), whose later phase shows stylistic affinities to the ceramic industries of the Upper Xingu River (Ipayu phase) and central Brazil (Uru tradition) (Heckenberger 1996; Wüst 1990) (Figure 16.2). The chronology indicates continuous occupation of the site over a long time scale, with initial dates reaching as far back as circa 2000 BC. These dates document the development in the Santarém region of one of the most ancient formative complexes of horticulturist potters in Amazonia, as well as more intense occupations from AD 700 onwards, associated with the formation of anthropogenic *terra preta* (dark soils), which subsequently vanish between AD 1100 and 1200.

Faunal and archaeobotanical remains indicated that the subsistence of these marginal groups, situated in an area of riverine *terra firme*, was based on the hunting of small animals, fishing, cultivation, and gathering. Along with domesticated species, such as manioc and maize, evidence of palm fruits demonstrated the importance of gathering for late precolonial populations and implied a lifestyle marked by a mixed, non-intensive economy, as recently observed in central Amazonia (Neves 2006; Neves and Petersen 2006).

The precolonial communities that developed in Parauá, though partially contemporaneous with Santarém, maintained a relationship of political autonomy from it toward the end of the occupation sequence. During the late period, along with rare artifacts revealing the influence of Santarém ideology (Gomes 2001, 2002), we predominantly see vessels

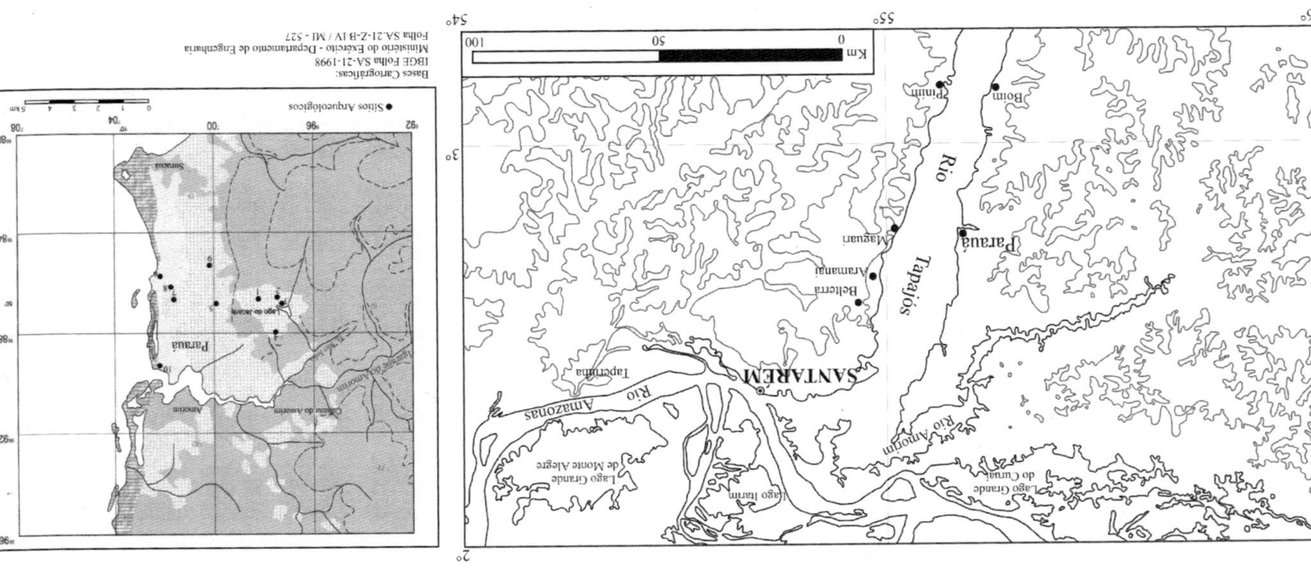

Figure 16.1   Map of the research area.

Figure 16.2 Formative pottery from Parauá, Santarém, PA.
(Photo by Wagner Souza e Silva.)

with mammiform appendages used in public contexts (female initiation ceremonies), whose symbolism looked to actively communicate social roles and group affiliations. These markers were an expression of identity, which in the regional setting comprised a symbol of resistance to the emerging political center. These communities disappeared between AD 1100 and 1200 during a period subsequent to the emergence of the Santarém chiefdom after AD 1000 (Roosevelt 1999). This date suggests the existence of political pressures, but also the regional coexistence of sociopolitical formations of different scales, a situation that did not inevitably lead to domination. These findings contribute to a less essentialist vision of the relations existing between the *varzea* (floodplain) communities and those of the peripheral *terra firme* areas that developed during late prehistory and undermines the notion of political centralization as an inherent attribute of Amazonian chiefdoms.

CONSTANT CULTURAL REINVENTION

The *caboclos* constitute the traditional peasant population of Amazonia. Although schematically described in the literature as a mixed population of indigenous and Portuguese ancestry, they represent distinct social groups that emerged from historical processes beginning in the seventeenth century during Portuguese colonization and lasting until the nineteenth century and the rubber cycle (Parker 1989:251). In the seventeenth century the concentration of indigenous populations promoted by Catholic missionaries united different groups in the same settlement, contributing to the homogenization of the Amazonian region's ethnic and cultural diversity. In the eighteenth century, the Indian Directorate issued by the Marquis of Pombal put an end to the missions and declared their indigenous populations free, though on the condition that they become part of colonial society. Other strategies for miscegenation were developed, such as encouraging marriages between indigenous women and European colonizers. In the nineteenth century, workers from Brazil's northeast—and with them minority groups (such as Jews) coming from North Africa—arrived in Amazonia to work in rubber extraction and joined these mixed populations (Arenz 2000).

The term *caboclo* combines various meanings. Employed by anthropologists and other social scientists as an analytic category to designate historically formed populations, use of this term, even today, carries a negative connotation among the local elites, who think of *caboclos* as a subaltern labor force due to a long history of socioeconomic domination. Though the word has rarely been used as a self-designation, examples found in various parts of Amazonia indicate that this situation tends to change where identities are in the process of being reconstituted. Another expression used as a synonym for *caboclo* is "traditional populations," which emerged with the creation of the Conservation Units and Extractivist Reserves, protected by IBAMA (Brazilian Institute of the Environment) and, from 1992 onwards, managed by the CNPT (National Council of Traditional Populations).

The indigenous cultural influence is revealed in the recurrence of certain religious practices (shamanism) and cosmologies based on beliefs in forest spirits and hybrid beings. These are mixed with Iberian religious traditions such as, for example, the patron saint festivals (Arenz 2000; Vaz 1996; Wagley 1957). Subsistence, settlement, and community organization patterns, as well as forms of managing and perceiving the forest resources, are aspects that have been highlighted by various scholars as clear evidence of the adoption of indigenous adaptation strategies (Adams 1994; Balée 1989, 1998; Roosevelt 1989). A partial explanation for these patterns resides in the persistence of a regional economy heavily based on extraction activities (Parker 1989). Although *caboclo* populations are the main contributors to this economy, their access to land ownership is restricted, and they usually live as tenant farmers and more recently as occupants of the Extractivist Reserves.

More than an efficient form of adapting to the environment, the *caboclo* way of life can be seen as a historical experience of resistance to the effects of colonization and of continual transformation and cultural reinvention, which combines the preservation of a technological inventory of indigenous origin and a mixed religiosity with the appropriation of material innovations. In this sense, the *caboclos* are themselves the agents of their historical transformation. New consumption habits mean that industrial goods now mix freely with artifacts inherited from the indigenous tradition. At the same time, these populations—previously marked by their marginal status and social invisibility—are becoming increasingly involved in political discussions with the different actors who today promote the development of Amazonia.

Contemporary *caboclo* identities initially emerged within a context shaped by the denial of their indigenous origin and affirmation of the attributes of civilization. This is the most common form of responding to the identity issue among Amazonia's *caboclo* populations. Nonetheless, today self-representation strategies vary greatly. While some groups affirm their status as modern citizens, others seek to recuperate—albeit in generic form—an indigenous inheritance by reinventing rituals, habits, and forms of governance attributed to their ancestors. This is what can be observed in the Tapajós River region. The movement is related to the emergence of political leaders among the groups of Amazonian rubber tappers and *caboclos* who organized at the end of the 1980s, proposing solutions toward sustainable development (Almeida 2002). In a wider sense, this echoes Sahlins's idea (1997a) of an "indigenization of modernity" through which indigenous groups and other marginalized sectors of society respond to globalization and constitute themselves as political actors. The success of these strategies depends on the ability to create connections with the centers of power and on the proposal of solutions to global problems such as those related to environmental conservation (Andrello 2006:48).

The fact that certain *caboclo* communities of Amazonia have opted to reinvent an indigenous identity can be understood, therefore, as part of a process of social legitimization, connected to the struggle for the recognition of political rights in an area dominated by the discourses and demands of indigenous and environmental organizations. However, government agencies such as FUNAI (the National Indian Foundation) do not consider the *caboclos* to be authentic Indians since it is impossible to trace them back to a specific ethnic origin. On the other hand, *caboclo* communities opposed to these forms of identity reconstitution refer to their neighbors as opportunists and pour scorn on their reinvented indigenous discourses and practices, which gives a measure of the diversity of actors present in the contemporary Amazonian social landscape.

The Community and Fieldwork

In 2003, when I embarked on my last period of fieldwork, Parauá had 500 inhabitants, most of them children and adolescents (Figure 16.3). Subsisting primarily on an extractivist economy, the majority of families live off fishing, manioc cultivation, and gathering activities for domestic consumption with some income derived from the sale of surplus production. Other income-generating activities were limited to work in the three local stores, teaching, and running the community's two schools. A single health post attended the population, while emergency cases were sent by boat to Santarém. There was no electricity, though an oil-powered generator allowed less than two hours of television (news and soap operas). Immune to the projects developed by internationally funded non-governmental organizations (NGOs), the community lacked piped water and basic sanitation. A wooden building served as the community center, hosting political meetings, parties, and dances.

Timber houses, roofed with straw thatch or asbestos and built along two roads parallel to the Tapajós River, formed the town's three neighborhoods: Mangal, Centro, and Retiro (Figure 16.4). Most of these houses were home to nuclear families, though some contained extended families with couples, adult children, and their respective spouses, grandparents, and grandchildren. A number of these residences had a "flour house" (a traditional structure used to make manioc flour and its subproducts) (Figure 16.5), as well as televisions, radios, and gas stoves. The

Figure 16.3 View of the Parauá community, Santarém, PA.
(Photo by Maurício de Paiva.)

Figure 16.4 Thatched house, Mangal district, Parauá. (Photo by Denise Cavalcante Gomes.)

Figure 16.5 Flour house, Parauá, Santarém, PA. (Photo by Denise Cavalcante Gomes.)

political disputes between rival factions enlivened the day-to-day life of the community, which as well as an elected president had various leaders whose position was based on accumulated prestige. These leaders evoke similarities to the indigenous leaderships of egalitarian societies, defined by their skill in representing the group and speaking in public, their generosity, and their practical work for the community. However, the organization of the groups around such leaders is also related to class interests and political and party affiliations based in Santarém.

Another form of political alliance found among the community groups derives from the relations established with the employees of IBAMA, responsible for managing the Tapajós-Arapiuns RESEX (Extractivist Reserve) in which the Parauá community is located. While a small group supported the creation of the extractivist reserve, the majority opposes the regulations set out by IBAMA and the changes that resulted in the area being constituted as an environmental conservation unit, since these have imposed restrictions on fishing and extraction activities and legal restrictions on the right to ownership of their land.

From the outset, the development of the archaeological project was heavily affected by the conflict between the community's political factions. In 2001, despite the authorization of the community's president for implementing the archaeological work, one of the divergent groups denounced the research to IBAMA, accusing it of biopiracy: this resulted in the paralyzation of the activities and my physical removal from the locale by armed agents until the situation was cleared up with the help of IPHAN (the National Institute of Historical and Artistic Heritage). Aside from political motivations stemming from the fact that an opposing group was supporting the archaeological research, the false accusation of biopiracy could be explained by the community's insecurity with respect to the ownership of their lands. The lack of familiarity of riverine populations with archaeological work is also an important factor, since the excavations, instruments, and methods used are usually associated with land demarcation activities, mining, and the sale of archaeological artifacts. Bielawski (1994:231) reports similar views of archaeological research conducted among Inuit communities in Canada. In Mexico, some communities in the Yucatán region also took archaeologists working there to be land invaders (Rodríguez 2001, 2006).

The solution for continuing the research in the Parauá community was negotiation. After formalization of the project with IBAMA and the CNPT, each phase of work was preceded by a meeting in the local school held in the presence of political leaders and other community members interested in discussing the schedule of activities and the interim results. Another form of involving the community more was to establish a work team in the community itself. This made it possible to learn about the local way of life and establish personal connections with various people. The inclusion of local workers and a cook in the research team, as well as the help of the family of one community leader, who provided lodging for the researchers, facilitated the archaeological work. The involvement of the team in the social life of the community (during holy festivals, dances, anniversaries, sports events, football tournaments, and weekends at the beach) enabled community members to become used to the presence of the outside researchers. However, not even these strategies for involving the community could prevent the partial paralyzation of the systematic archaeological survey, including the opening of various 6 km long transects, and the alteration of the initial research design. The transects, which served as access routes through the vegetation to dig test pits every 50 m, crossed swiddens and house terrains, as well as various areas of community forest. Various people felt invaded, which severely constrained the activities of the work team. After an impasse, the solution found was to reduce the intensity of the work, which compromised the survey to some extent since it became limited to just five lines with a 1.3 km distance between them. This situation illustrates the partial control of the community over decisions in the field.

On the other hand, the local workers contributed decisively to the execution of all phases of the research project. During the site survey, they undertook important tasks such as clearing the trails that allowed the team to move through the dense vegetation and improved the surface visibility (Figure 16.6). They also excavated test pits and helped with the identification of plant species. The most skilled were incorporated in the larger excavation teams (Figure 16.7) and encouraged to interpret the contexts and draw profiles under the supervision of the researchers, enhancing the work and improving the team's cohesion.

However, the production of archaeological knowledge was also affected by this interaction with the workers, which, contrary to the myth of scientific neutrality, supports the idea of the sociopolitical environment having a decisive influence on the production of scientific knowledge (Gero 1994; Shanks and Tilley 1987, 1989). As well as a distinct perception of environmental resources and their relation to the places where the sites were inserted in the landscape, other territorial markers were signaled by the workers, revealing aspects not initially foreseen by the research. These markers were associated with the *caboclo* communities and reflect the way in which riverine populations relate with supernatural beings (the owners of the rivers, game, and forests, the inhabitants of the lower cosmic levels, and the spirits that live among the river stones and around the lakes). Discovering these relations meant that the archaeological sites and their insertion in the landscape were apprehended from a perspective that avoids the separation between nature and

Figure 16.6 Clearing transects at the Lago do Jacaré site, Parauá, Santarém, PA. (Photo by Denise Cavalcante Gomes.)

Figure 16.7 Excavation at the Lago do Jacaré site, Parauá, Santarém, PA. (Photo by Denise Cavalcante Gomes.)

culture, as well as recognizes the existence of a highly transformational world with distinct subjectivities populating the universe (Descola 1986; Viveiros de Castro 2002). It was also possible to identify the continuity of indigenous cosmological patterns over a lengthy time scale, which was gradually and more recently transformed by the *caboclo* populations. Accounts of women who failed to observe a period of reclusion after childbirth and went mad because of the harm sent by the spirit owners of the rocks when the women went to the riverbanks to wash clothes, or of old and young women being seduced by the river dolphin when the animal transforms into a man, are mixed with descriptions of the fantastic beings, animals, and spirits who people the creeks, lakes, and forests. These examples demonstrate the continuance of a historically modified pan-Amerindian ideology.

During the archaeological survey, when the team was traversing an area of *igapó* forest (a kind of marshy terrain that floods periodically during the rainy season and that contains large trees with exposed roots where snakes are abundant), one of the workers, who also acted as shaman in the Parauá community, asked for the activities to be interrupted so that he could ask permission from the owners of the *igapó* forest, described as two large snakes with the head of a woman, wide-open eyes, and a body covered with yellow scales. On another occasion, the same shaman recounted that he had been visited in his dreams by the dolphins that live near the rocks, in the lower substrate of the cosmos corresponding to the depths of the river. These beings, who reside at a location close to one of the archaeological sites, were furious about the presence of the archaeologists and wanted to know who these people were and what they were doing there. The explanations were given and the danger threatening the team dissipated. Thereafter, the archaeological research acquired another dimension, ceasing to be strictly objective and materialist in order to interact with the *caboclo* beliefs and cosmologies.

APPROPRIATION OF THE ARCHAEOLOGICAL DISCOURSE

The meetings held in the local school, in the presence of students, teachers, political leaders, and other interested people, enabled discussion of the interim findings of the archaeological research, along with the public divulgation of these findings through lectures and the distribution of written material. Issues discussed included the importance of preserving archaeological sites, the illegality of the trade in archaeological finds, and the final destination of the collected material. This was the first time that hundreds of people had contact with a type of research that connected material remains with indigenous history. However, we observed the community's apparent indifference to the recovered archaeological heritage. The pottery artifacts that emerged from the excavations failed to stir much interest among those present because they were just like the sherds they themselves found when working their swiddens and there was nothing particularly attractive about them.

On the other hand, the cultural-historical contextualization of the formative societies that lived in the same locality in the past revealed a lifestyle based on manioc cultivation, very similar to that of the *caboclo* populations (Gomes 2005). The archaeological remains obtained in the Parauá community indicated various elements in common with the current population, such as settlement patterns, the construction materials used, a diet based on manioc growing, fishing, and palm fruit gathering (such as *chontaduro*), and the consumption of fermented manioc drinks, similar to those produced today during celebrations. However, these findings were not seen by the population as a connection with the past. People's responses stressed an alterity in relation to indigenous peoples, describing the pieces as "the Indian's pot," "the Indian's house" or "the Indian's coffin" (a funerary urn). These issues only became clarified, though, when the discourses on local identities began to emerge during these meetings.

While the Parauá community displayed a strong resistance to any identification with an indigenous heritage, some of the neighboring communities had recently opted to recreate traditions attributed to indigenous peoples who once inhabited the region and to reassert their identity as Indians, albeit without formal recognition from government bodies. In addition to fighting politically for formal recognition of their identity, these groups reinvented this heritage, as well as various indigenous rituals, on a day-to-day basis. Nonetheless, the archaeological work did not directly affect these groups since its scope was limited to Parauá. Although I visited some of these communities personally, talking with their political leaders and observing their way of life, there was no opportunity to discuss more deeply some of the questions related to the archaeological work being developed in the region. It is very likely that had the research been conducted in one of these communities, it would have been more readily welcomed. On the other hand, many of the residents of Parauá refer to their neighbors in a joking way, labeling them "fake Indians," making fun of the clothing used during the recreated indigenous ceremonies, and showing even more scorn for some of the dances performed by unclothed youngsters (according to the dancers, like the ancestors). Among other things, this suggests a contrasting process of constructing identities.

The expectations generated by middle-class values, shared by the archaeologists, tend to induce a rapid identification of communities with archaeological artifacts, especially when the latter reflect analogous social contexts or suggest some kind of ethnic connection. Funari et al. (2005:106) argue that archaeology can perform a significant role by demonstrating diversity, providing evidence of how everyday life was in the past, and celebrating a shared architecture, allowing local people to recognize themselves in the archaeological discourse and to use the past to construct alternative texts about the present. But in the Parauá community, it was not precisely in this order, nor following the same logic, that the archaeological interpretation was used to generate discourses of self-representation in the present.

When asked about their history and their ancestors, the Parauá residents almost always referred to their recent past, evoking an origin connected to the immigrants from Brazil's northeast and, in some cases, the Moroccan Jews who had come to this region of the Tapajós River to work in rubber extraction in the nineteenth century. Few people mention an indigenous heritage, although this is implicitly recognized by everyone. People continue their day-to-day existence as traditional communities with their own practices and forms of conceiving the world that clearly demonstrate an indigenous legacy. However, in contrast to their neighbors, their discourses of self-representation emphasize the fact that they see themselves as modern citizens rather than Indians. I heard them repeat on countless occasions that they were not indigenous and they did not want to be treated as such. This helps explain the distance maintained in relation to archaeology and, especially, those aspects shared with the way of life of indigenous populations in the past. In my opinion, there was no great interest in archaeology among the Parauá residents precisely because they perceived the cultural continuities. They rejected precisely that which bothered them about their lives, the indigenous heritage, seen now from the perspective of their own technological and symbolic aspects and those of earlier populations.

From a strictly cultural-historical point of view, the adoption of a perspective based on a very large time scale identified historical discontinuities between the precolonial occupations and the contemporary *caboclo* communities. In this process of forming the latter-day riverine groups, the indigenous legacy became generalized, mixing with other cultural influences over the course of time and making any recuperation of the ethnicity of their ancestors impossible (Arenz 2000; Ribeiro 1997). By exposing this absence of direct historical continuity, the archaeological discourse provided elements that were rapidly appropriated by the community leaders as a positive argument to reinforce their self-image of modern citizens who deny any connection with the indigenous past. This selective appropriation of one of the aspects of the archaeological interpretation expresses the power of the community members and their partial control of the research findings, incorporating the latter into the historical process of constructing cultural identities. The same archaeological project that initially produced feelings of insecurity and unease ended up being used by political leaders as an additional element in their discourses of self-representation, which emphasize the alterity of indigenous peoples, in opposition to other communities located in the Tapajós-Arapiuns RESEX. This demonstrates the sociopolitical nature of the archaeological practice developed among *caboclo* populations in Amazonia and its relation to the continual process of constructing fluid and polymorphic identities (Jones 1997), negotiated in response to the different demands of the local communities.

CONCLUSION

Based on the example discussed, it is possible to conclude that the benefits of participatory archaeology were various. Firstly, it was possible to familiarize residents of the Parauá community, especially the students, with archaeological research procedures and forms of heritage preservation and with the project's findings. These results demonstrated a formative indigenous occupation over a time scale of millennia (between 2000 BC and AD 1200) with subsistence and settlement patterns possessing a degree of similarity with contemporary populations (Gomes 2005). After the work was completed, various journalistic and academic papers were published associating the Parauá community with scientific discourse, which helped boost local people's self-esteem. The involvement of workers in the research project provided accounts of local cosmologies and their association with distinct features of the landscape, influencing the archaeological interpretation.

Finally, in terms of the emergence of contemporary *caboclo* identities, the implementation of this project using a participatory research framework exposed a reality shared by all the *caboclo* populations living in this area of the lower Tapajós, who possess different strategies of self-representation linked, in various forms, to the recognition of political rights and the issues of land occupation and ownership. Although the denial of an indigenous identity has been the rule among Amazonian *caboclo* populations, those groups that opt to identify themselves as indigenous, despite no longer being able to trace the ethnicity of their ancestors, also do so in legitimate form, as shown by the trajectories of other cultures that move through the globalized world (Sahlins 1997a, 1997b). The dilemmas of self-representation experienced by Amazonian *caboclo* populations are inscribed, therefore, in a dynamic of the reinvention of the past and cultural appropriation that can be better understood in the words of Marshal Sahlins (1997b:133):

> The new planetary organization could be described, therefore, as a world culture of cultures. Given this structural order, there is no sense in lamenting as "inauthentic" the forms in which local peoples adapt to the world system, including when they appropriate Western images of the "native" as signs of their own alterity—whether for apparently benign purposes (as when the "natives" use for their own benefit all the ecological wisdom with which the global environmentalist movement imputes them), or for explicitly commercial purposes (as in the exploration of the tourist market avid for "native" dances, artifacts or the like). This is how cultural history is done today, in a dialectical exchange between the global and the local, since it has now become extremely clear that imperialism is not dealing with amateurs in this business of constructing alterities or producing identities.

It is up to archaeology to recognize the right of self-representation of these groups and of their appropriation of the archaeological discourse, using it as a legitimating source for ethnopolitical discourses. As in other experiences of interaction between archaeology and community actions already reported in the literature, such as the work conducted in Palmares (Funari et al. 2005), researchers evidently have no ownership over their interpretations, despite controlling their data, since there are many forms of interpreting the past and situating it in the present when we accept the tendency toward multivocality (Gnecco 2004).

My interaction with the dynamic reality of *caboclo* communities from the lower Tapajós enabled me to conclude that if the inhabitants of Parauá reaffirmed themselves as modern citizens and not Indians, they must have motives for doing so. At the same time, those *caboclo* communities that identified themselves as indigenous also did so in a legitimate form. The only thing clear to me was that it was not my role to tell these people who they were.

Notes

This chapter is based on data from my doctoral research conducted in the community of Parauá, Santarém, PA, during 2001 and 2003, which received support from FAPESP (Processes: 00/04563-0 and 2002/04916-5), and also on subsequent reflections in a postdoctoral program developed with a grant from CNPq (Process 151577/2005-6). I thank Pedro Paulo Funari for supervising my thesis and Eduardo Viveiros de Castro my postdoctoral project. I also owe thanks to Zenóbio Serique and his family for all the support received during my fieldwork in Parauá.

1. The term *caboclo* is used in this paper as a sociological category to describe mixed-ethnicity Amazonian rural populations. A more detailed explanation of the term is provided later in the main body of the paper.

REFERENCES

Adams, Cristina 1994 As florestas virgens manejadas. *Revista do Museu Paraense Emílio Goeldi* 10:3–20.

Allen, Harry, Dylis Johns, Caroline Phillips, Kelvin Day, Tipene O'Brien, and Ngati Mutunga 2002 Wahi ngaro (the lost portion): Strengthening relationship between people and wetlands in north Taranaki, New Zealand. *World Archaeology* 34:315–329.

Almeida, Mauro 2002 The politics of Amazonian conservation: The struggles of rubber tappers. *Journal of Latin American Anthropology* 7(1):170–219.

Andrello, Geraldo 2006 *Cidade do indio: transformações e cotidiano em Iauaretê*. Editora Unesp-ISA-NuTi, São Paulo.

Arenz, Karl Heinz 2000 *Filhos e filhas do Beiradão: a formação sócio-histórica dos ribeirinhos da Amazônia*. Faculdades Integradas do Tapajós, Santarém.

Balée, William 1989 The culture of Amazonian forests. *Advances in Economic Botany* 7:1–21.

———. 1998 Historical ecology: Premises and postulates. In *Advances in Historical Ecology*, edited by William Balée, pp. 13–29. Academic Press, New York.

Bielawski, Ellen 1994 Dual perceptions of the past: Archaeology and Inuit culture. In *Conflict in the Archaeology of Living Traditions*, edited by Robert Layton, pp. 228–236. Routledge, London.

Canuto, Marcelo, and Jason Yaeger 2000 *The Archaeology of Communities: A New World Perspective*. Routledge, London.

Clarke, Anne 2002 The ideal and the real: Cultural and personal transformations of archaeological research on Groote Eylandt, Northern Australia. *World Archaeology* 34(2):249–264.

Descola, Phillipe 1986 *La nature domestique: symbolisme et praxis dans l'écologie des Achuar*. Maison des Sciences de l'Homme, Paris.

Funari, Pedro Paulo 1995 The archaeology of Palmares and its contribution to the understanding of the history of the African-American culture. *Historical Archaeology in Latin America* 7:1–41.

———. 1996 Novas perspectivas abertas pela arqueologia da Serra da Barriga. En *Negras imagens*, edited by Lilia Moritz Schwarcs and Leticia de Sousa Reis, pp. 139–151. Edusp/Estação Ciência, São Paulo.

———. 1999 Marron, race and gender: Palmares material culture. In *Historical Archaeology: Back from the Edge*, edited by Pedro Funari, Martin Hall, and Siân Jones, pp. 308–327. Unwin Hyman, London.

———. 2001 Public archaeology from a Latin American perspective. *Public Archaeology* 1:239–243.

Funari, Pedro, Nancy Vieira Oliveira, and Elizabete Tamanini 2005 Arqueologia para o público leigo no Brasil: três experiências. In *Identidades, discurso e poder*, edited by Pedro Funari, Charles Orser, and Solange Nunes de Oliveira Schiavetto, pp. 105–116. Annablume Editora-Fapesp, São Paulo.

Gero, Joan 1994 Gender division of labor in the construction of archaeological knowledge in the United States. In *Social Construction of the Past: Representation as Power*, edited by George Bond and Angela Gilliam, pp. 144–153. Routledge, London.

Gnecco, Cristóbal 2004 La indigenización de las arqueologías nacionales. In *Teoría arqueológica en América Latina*, edited by Gustavo Politis and Roberto Peretti, pp. 119–128. Universidad Nacional del Centro de la Provincia de Buenos Aires, Olavarría.

Gomes, Denise M. C. 2001 Santarém: Symbolism and power in the tropical forest. In *Unknown Amazon*, edited by Colin McEwan, Cristiana Barreto, and Eduardo Neves, pp. 134–155. British Museum Press, London.

———. 2002 *Cerâmica arqueológica da Amazônia: vasilhas da coleção tapajônica MAE-USP*. Edusp-Fapesp, São Paulo.

Gomes, Denise M. C. 2005 Análise dos padrões de organização comunitária no baixo Tapajós: o desenvolvimento do Formativo na área de Santarém, PA. Unpublished Ph.D. dissertation, Programa de Pós-Graduação em Arqueologia, Museu de Arqueologia e Etnologia, University of São Paulo, São Paulo.

———. 2006 Amazonian archaeology and local identities. In *Ethnographies of Archaeological Practice: Cultural Encounters, Material Transformations*, edited by Matt Edgeworth, pp. 148–160. Altamira Press, Walnut Creek.

Heckenberger, Michael 1996 War and Peace in the Shadow of Empire: Sociopolitical Change in the Upper Xingu of Southeastern Amazonia, AD 1250–2000. Unpublished Ph.D. dissertation, Department of Anthropology, University of Pittsburgh. Pittsburgh.

Jones, Siân 1997 *The Archaeology of Ethnicity: Constructing Archaeology in the Past and Present*. Routledge, London.

Kolb, Michael, and James Snead 1997 Community analysis in Hawaii and New Mexico. *American Antiquity* 62(4):609–628.

Layton, Robert 1994 Introduction: Conflict in the archaeology of living traditions. In *Conflict in the Archaeology of Living Traditions*, edited by Robert Layton, pp. 1–21. Routledge, London.

Meggers, Betty 1971 *Amazonia: Man and Culture in a Counterfeit Paradise*. Aldine, Chicago.

Meggers, Betty and Clifford Evans 1961 An experimental formulation of horizon styles in the tropical forest area of South America. In *Essays in Precolumbian Art and Archaeology*, edited by Samuel Lothrop, pp. 372–388. Harvard University Press, Cambridge.

Neves, Eduardo 2006 *Arqueologia da Amazônia*. Jorge Zahar, Rio de Janeiro.

Neves, Eduardo, and James Petersen 2006 Political economy and pre-Columbian land-scape transformations in central Amazonia. In *Time and Complexity in Historical Ecology: Studies in the Neotropical Lowlands*, edited by William Balée, pp. 279–309. Columbia University Press, New York.

Parker, Eugene 1989 A neglected human resource in Amazonia: The Amazon caboclo. *Advances in Economic Botany* 7:249–259.

Ribeiro, Darcy 1997 *O povo brasileiro: a formação e o sentido do Brasil*. Companhia das Letras, São Paulo.

Rodríguez, Timoteo 2001 Maya perception of ancestral remains: Multiple places in a local space. *Berkeley McNair Research Journal* 9:21–45.

———. 2006 Conjunctures in the making of an ancient Maya archaeological site. In *Ethnographies of Archaeological Practice: Cultural Encounters, Material Transformation*s, edited by Matt Edgeworth, pp. 161–172. Altamira Press, Walnut Creek.

Roosevelt, Anna 1980 *Parmana: Prehistoric Maize and Manioc Subsistence along the Amazon and Orinoco*. Academic Press, New York.

———. 1987 Chiefdoms in Amazon and Orinoco. In *Chiefdoms in the Americas*, edited by Robert Drennan and Carlos Alberto Uribe, pp. 153–185. University Press of America, Lanham.

———. 1989 Resource management in Amazonia before the conquest: Beyond ethnographic projection. *Advances in Economic Botany* 7:30–62.

———. 1991 Determinismo ecológico na interpretação do desenvolvimento social indígena da Amazônia. In *Adaptações e diversidade do homem nativo da Amazônia*, edited by Walter Neves, pp. 103–142. Museu Paraense Emílio Goeldi, Belém.

———. 1992 Arqueologia amazônica. In *História dos indios do Brasil*, edited by Manuela Carneiro da Cunha, pp. 53–86. Editora Cia. das Letras, São Paulo.

———. 1999 The maritime, highland, forest dynamic and the origins of complex culture. In *The Cambridge History of the Native Peoples of the Americas*, edited by Frank Salomon and Stuart Schwartz, pp. 264– 349. Cambridge University Press, Cambridge.

Sahlins, Marshall 1997a O "pessimismo sentimental" e a experiência etnográfica: por que a cultura não é um "objeto" em via de extinção (Parte I). *Mana* 3(1):41–73.

———. 1997b O "pessimismo sentimental" e a experiência etnográfica: por que a cultura não é um "objeto" em via de extinção (Parte II). *Mana* 3(1):103–150.

Shanks, Michael, and Christopher Tilley 1987 *Re-Constructing Archaeology*. Cambridge University Press, Cambridge.

———. 1989 Archaeology into the 1990s. *Norwegian Archaeological Review* 22:1–11.

Vaz, Florêncio 1996 Ribeirinhos da Amazonia: identidade e magia na floresta. *Cultura Vozes* 2:47–65.

Viveiros de Castro, Eduardo 2002 *A inconstância da alma selvagem e outros ensaios de antropologia*. Cosac e Naify Edições, São Paulo.

Wagley, Charles 1957 *Uma comunidade amazônia: estudo do homem nos trópicos*. Companhia Editora Nacional, São Paulo.

Wüst, Irmhild 1990 Continuidade e mudança: para uma interpretação dos grupos ceramistas pré-coloniais da Bacia do Rio Vermelho, Mato Grosso. Unpublished Ph.D. dissertation, Faculdade de Filosofia, Letras e Ciências Humanas, University of São Paulo, São Paulo.

CHAPTER 17

ARCHAEOLOGY AND PARESI CULTURAL HERITAGE

Flavia Prado Moi and Walter Fagundes Morales

INTRODUCTION

In the Brazilian context, the dizzying growth of archaeological investigations related to heritage preservation is a consequence of the democratization of the country and the adoption of public policies that foster citizen participation in the management of their own cultural heritage. This growth has created a forum for discussion about archaeological and heritage issues and their relationship to the wider realm of economy, culture, politics, ethics, and government as well as to social, educational, and management aspects. There has also been a gradual growth in the promotion of the rights of indigenous people to make and take part in decisions about the treatment, interpretation, and management of their sites and objects.

Our research with the Paresi, an indigenous group of the Chapada dos Parecis (Mato Grosso, Brazil), emerged from the growing concern for the public components of archaeology (i.e., financial planning, social issues, and politics related to the regulatory practices in a variety of contexts). The investigation seeks to discover and discuss the political, sociocultural and economic developments since the 1990s through the lens of environmental impact studies that are being conducted before the construction of small hydroelectric centers (PCHs, the Portuguese acronym) in various rivers in the region. Over the course of fieldwork,[1] we noted that some technical aspects of these studies are related to an emerging awareness of ethnic identity and preservation and to the management of archaeological heritage. As a result, with the knowledge of a larger context of discussion that extended beyond the legal requirements of the environmental licensing process, we began an investigation to help programs that strengthen the application of public policies in the area.

This study aids to assess, manage, and preserve archaeological heritage with the effective participation of local indigenous groups; it also ensures that the results are employed in the service of those communities.

This context inspired the doctoral investigation "Public archaeology in Paresian territory: An analysis of the political, sociocultural, and economic impacts of archaeological research" (Moi 2006),[2] which seeks to identify the strategies of archaeological research programs in the area; their social, political and economic implications; and the extent of the reciprocal relationship established between participants and the ethnic Paresi, in a critical and political dimension, with the goal of amplifying the realm of discussion about the rights and duties of the Paresi and about their cultural environment. The investigation discusses how the Paresi use archaeological information—and what are the ideological applications of this information—and the epistemological questions that address social identities and the political nature of science. The information produced, used, and/or adopted by local populations allows investigators to expand the range and the results of their work and to increase the level of interest and identification with respect to the archaeological heritage, furthering its estimation and preservation.

INDIGENOUS EMANCIPATION, ECONOMIC DEVELOPMENT, AND SUSTAINABILITY

The twentieth century witnessed an economic boom closely related to marked demographic growth, principally in the poorest countries, which produced environmental consequences such as pollution and ecological deterioration; furthermore, the Internet created a swift and intense information transmission. The indiscriminate appropriation of resources worldwide in the postwar era fostered the emergence of social movements in different capitalist countries at the beginning of the 1960s: counterculture, antiracism and student movements rejecting militarism, industrialism, and dominant colonialism and critical of consumer society (Hobsbawm 1995). As time passed by, ecological issues escaped from the limited sphere of specialists and small groups and reached the masses, especially regarding oil spills, nuclear accidents, and large-scale toxic contamination. With the intensification of environmental problems and the recognition that their impact is not just local but global, numerous new international players emerged. In the search for sustainable forms of development, traditional social groups, ethnic minorities, religious groups, and representatives of developing countries began to be heard in the international arena (Acselrad 2004). A result of this trend is the United Nations' declaration of 1995–2004 as the International Decade of the World's Indigenous People and the creation of the Permanent Forum on Indigenous Issues in 2002. Various new ethnic groups have gained ground, especially those who occupy territories that environmentalists consider natural preserves and who apply traditional knowledge that can serve the future of humanity; others have benefited by the recognition of their historical fight against environmental degradation. Globalization has both permitted and stimulated the organization of indigenous peoples; many of them have obtained international funds and participate in international networks, thus achieving a greater impact and political reach than before.

In Brazil, the indigenous cause has also succeeded in making it to the international arena, evolving from a situation of complete dependence in the 1960s to a phase of assemblies (1970s) and interethnic unions (1980s); in the last decade its has established interethnic political, social, and economic projects (Neves 2003). The most important triumphs of the Brazilian indigenous movement occurred in the 1980s with the end of the military regime, mobilization of the movement, and an advantageous political climate. In 1988 the current constitution was enacted, recognizing the right to cultural difference. Ethnic groups have intensified the fight for the demarcation and recognition of their lands, and the new federal constitution has modified the legal framework dealing with environmental and indigenous issues.

Most Brazilian indigenous people live within environmental preserves (Gray et al. 1998; Vicenzo 2003). Since in many of these areas natural resources have been conserved, a strong parallelism was established between environmental and indigenous issues (Berkes et al. 1993; Toledo 1992); both have been treated as inseparable in the last four decades (Alarcón-Cháires 2006). This situation led to the use of the concepts "sustainability" in the environmental arena and "multicultural emancipation" in the indigenous realm, thus emerging intrinsically related semantic linkages between nature and human populations under the term "people of the jungle."

Along with the growing articulation between indigenous policies and sustainable development, pressure has increased on those countries—such as Colombia (Borda and Mejía 2006), Argentina (Gordillo and Leguizamón 2002), and Brazil—that still control a significant part of their natural reserves and that adapted the economic model of developed countries (PNUD 2004). New global needs—but not new phenomena (Harvey 1989, 1996)—accelerated investments in the production of electric energy from non-renewable resources (oil, gas, minerals, and wood), increasing environmental impact and threatening the survival of various indigenous groups living in territories with valuable natural resources. Yet, some of them have gained growing autonomy in the management of those resources. They want to maintain (or gain) a differentiated status as ethnic groups with their own languages and customs, both within and outside their reserves, and, at the same time, to profit from the benefits of the society around them. Nevertheless, the increased involvement of indigenous groups with the world of the "white man" has resulted in confrontations with urban and rural segments of the society; as a result, the saying "a lot of land for a few indigenes" has been replaced by "they are not indigenes anymore."

It is symptomatic that since the 1990s the force and sympathy of various sectors of Brazilian society for the indigenous cause is decreasing at the same time that native societies have won several victories and have considerably improved their health conditions (reflected in their demographic expansion). Among the different reasons that brought about the change is the media-produced image of indigenous peoples as owners of cars and airplanes resulting from the exploration or lease of the natural resources of their reserves. The year 2006 was marked by headlines announcing indigenous demands for financial compensation for damages inflicted to their territories by large economic groups. One of the best-known events was the occupation of the largest open-pit iron mine in the world[3] by the Xikrin; this ethnic group demanded an increase in the annual 4.5 million dollars they received from the Companhia Vale do Rio Doce (CVRD) as compensation for mineral exploration in their territory.[4]

This kind of occupation and the subsequent paralysis of economic activities damage the image of indigenous groups in the eyes of Brazilian society at large. In their imagination, fed by the media and by political circles, the belief persists that indigenous groups should keep living in isolation—receiving trifles, wearing feathers, and painting their bodies—and should wait for the whites to resolve their needs and defend them. Although there is a growing ethnic emancipation as indigenes become independent social agents, the speed of events in the last years created a disconnection between mature ethnic groups and the way they are perceived by Brazilian society. Attempting to keep up with changes that occur to indigenous groups, a series of activities, projects, short courses and training have been carried out by NGOs, universities, religious institutions, and government organizations such as the Fundação Nacional do Índio (FUNAI). Many of these activities seek to support indigenous peoples in their search for autonomy and to help them gain economic independence, achievable by a sustainable exploitation of the richness that exists in their lands. These activities manifest a definition of culture that is supposedly changing and adapting to new realities.

These changes do not occur at the same pace or in the same way in the various Brazilian indigenous groups because there are significant differences in political participation and in the resources and riches that exist in their territories that increase or decrease their ability to interact with the "world of the white man." In Brazil, unknown or isolated indigenous groups still exist. Some ethnic groups have simple and modest plans to raise chickens or create communal gardens for survival. Ethnic groups vary widely, from those that participate in electoral politics to those that cut down the forest for soybean cultivation, permit lumber exploitation, or alter the course of water for the extraction of precious metals within their reserves, something prohibited by Brazilian law. Contact with the white man and the inclusion of these groups in the Brazilian economy brings them closer to desires and needs they can hardly satisfy. The boundary between the dispensable and the indispensible is tenuous and subjective, and relates to the possibility of acquiring commodities.

Indigenous political and economic emancipation has created a divergence between native interests and the way the surrounding society perceives them; between their territorial needs, federal government financial support, preservation of the areas they inhabit, and cultural changes resulting from the use they make of their economic resources. Although indigenous groups are recognized as protectors of the jungle, they increasingly exploit their lands for profit, disrupting their historic opposition to capitalism. In spite of the fact that the justification for large tracts of land earmarked for the indigenous groups rested heavily on the idea of an environmental preserve, the actual use of some of these lands by many indigenous groups has generated a negative and contradictory image that has been cleverly used by sectors that seek to stop the demarcation or the upkeep of the current limits of indigenous lands. Groups maintaining their ethnic identities and cultural differences face a dilemma: how to reconcile traditional needs with consumption demands created by economic opportunities offered by the environmental conservation community.

A Paresi answer to this question is articulated with new international economic policies regarding cultures as financial resources (Yúdice 2004). In 2005 the Paresi-Haliti indigenous association of the Seringal village, along with the government of Mato Grosso and the municipal town council of Campo Novo de Parecis, organized a "State Seminar on Ecotourism in Indigenous Lands," concurrently with the Fifth Festival of Indigenous Culture and Games,[5] in the framework of an ecotourism project underway since the 1990s. Among the themes of the seminar (indigenous diversity, Paresi body painting, and indigenous architecture), indigenous economical sustainability, including ecotourism, was also discussed. The seminar program reserved a space to present archaeological investigations in the region and unpublished reports of ongoing environmental impact studies. Walter Morales, who traveled to Mato Grosso to present the paper "First exhibit of Haliti archaeology," was approached by a Paresi leader who lives in Sacre 2, the town most benefited (or injured, in his point of view) by the installation of the PHC Sacre 2; he requested Walter not to go on with the project or else existing problems in Paresi society would be augmented.

The goal of these events goes beyond disseminating indigenous culture and assessing athletic skills. The seminar sought to structure cultural tourism in Paresi territory. One of the activities supported the idea of constructing a traditional village exclusively for Brazilian and foreign tourists. The intention was to organize a "tourist village" in which the visitors would pay indigenous guides to tour forest trails and watch animals and birds, dive in the crystal waters of the rivers, and enjoy the fantastic waterfalls of the region. Production of handcrafts was to be increased for sale in the village, both because it would provide a source of income and for its cultural heritage value. Due to disagreements on the matter between the leaders and the lack of adequate infrastructure, these goals are still unfulfilled. Tourism is still sporadic, unstructured, and with little intensity or profit. Even so, Paresi youth are still trained in environmental education for developing consistent and sustainable projects.

A CASE STUDY: THE PARESI OF CHAPADA

The Paresi, an indigenous Brazilian group self-defined as Halití (people of the town), speak an Aruák language, although unrelated to any linguistic trunk (Montserrat 1994). The Paresi, well studied by anthropologists (Costa 2002; Costa 1985; Filho 1994, 1996; Pivetta and Freire 1993), are divided into four distinct subgroups (Kazíiniti, Waimaré, Warére, and Káwali); they inhabited well-defined territories in a vast high plain that stretched from the headwaters of the Arinos and Paraguay rivers to the headwaters of the Guaporé and Juruena rivers in central-western Mato Grosso. Written records of Paresi presence in the area go back to the eighteenth century (Costa 2002; Filho 1996; Lévi-Strauss 1996; Silva 1993): Though the Paresi occupied this vast territory since the days of the European colonization, they now live in smaller, politically defined zones (*terra indígena* [indigenous land] or TI) with less environmental diversity.[6] According to FUNAI, the Paresi are now divided into 11 non-contiguous TIs[7] located in the Chapada region. The Paresi inhabit tracts of their traditional territory, including a site known as Stone Bridge, the place of their myth of origin where the world began, 70 km from Campo Novo dos Parecis.

Territory, Myth, and Memory

Imposed contact produced sociocultural and economic impacts in Paresi society but it did not eliminate their culture; instead, new norms and rules were incorporated. Over three centuries the Paresi reformulated, transformed, and adapted their cultural standards; some characteristics were (or still are) unique. Ancient cultural models and symbols were adapted to new realities, absorbing new meanings. While some values were maintained others were transformed or were substituted, without eliminating a common identity or cultural continuity over the long term in the Chapada dos Parecis (Shennan 1994, 2000; Thomas 1996).

Contact between cultural and ethnic standards and social conditions, including domination, resistance, and assimilation, generated articulations and solutions. Some people, individually or collectively, were active agents in the elaboration of a social order and not simply passive recipients of new conditions. Group identity depends on how individuals recognize themselves and others in categories stemming from a common origin or cultural elements. This process creates so-called "ethnic groups" that have the power to define who pertains to their group and who does not (Barth 1969).

The strategy of the Paresi to actively seek out better conditions could be part of the affirmation or negation of their ethnic origin. In some historical moments, such as in the remote period of the "just wars" (Perrone-Moisés 1992), to be "pleasant" and of "good character" was the easiest road to survival. The Nambikwara, their neighbors and ancestral enemies, "opted" to confront expanding colonial borders, which they considered to belong to allies of the Paresi. At the end of this true "proof of resistance," after so many disagreements and obstacles and after a drastic demographic decline, the ethnic Paresi have succeeded in maintaining their language and some of their fundamental institutions. How was it possible? How did they succeed in defending their common values, with increasing determination, without resorting to violence when faced with a surrounding society that sought to annihilate or integrate them? One of the most important factors contributing to their physical and cultural survival was the establishment of symbolic "points of contact" with tangible elements (the territory and existing landmarks); those points helped to integrate generations and to create a sense of belonging and a common unity (Machado 2002). "Points of contact" resulted from historical, social, and cultural events coherently kept by oral tradition over a long period of time. Those events, individually and collectively appropriated, became the basis of Paresi ethnicity (capable of incorporating ethnically distinct groups) when faced with strange and adverse agents and situations. Their point of departure was the fact that the Paresi had occupied the region since long ago; the best-known "point of contact" is the myth of origin from the north of Stone Bridge:

> In the myth of origin of the Halití people, recorded at the beginning of the [twentieth] century by German anthropologist Max Schmidt, a group of siblings emerged from inside the Earth, sprouting from cracks and holes in the rocks of the Sakuriu Wiña River, which the Imóti, the non-Indians, the "civilized people," called Stone Bridge or Sucuruína, a tributary of the Arinos. As they emerged from the rocks the Halití discovered the world and all its rivers, its birds, the trees that existed but had not yet been named. Wazáre, the eldest's of the siblings, guided the others to the exit, installing each in his own territory. (Machado 2002)

For the Paresi, the world began in this location, less than 70 km from Utiariti. Physical evidence was found: the bridge and the house of stone. A telegraph station set up by the Comissão Constructora da Linha Telegráphica Estratégica de Mato Grosso ao Amazonas, led by Colonel Cândido Mariano da Silva Rondon, was installed here, where the indigenous people gathered in search of protection at the beginning of the twentieth century. As Damião, a 100-year-old Paresi who lived in Sacre 2 until his death in 2006 and Rondon's guide, said, "The stone bridge is the proof that we were here, in this land, since the beginning of the world and we were Paresi."[8] The myth of the stone bridge passed from generation to generation, giving a sense of continuity and integration.

The sum of these tangible elements, found in the landscape and oral tradition, fosters a feeling of belonging and union that decreases distance and differences between individuals who, in other situations, could be enemies; it unifies descendents of distinct subgroups such Kaxiniti, Waimaré, Kawáli, Waréré, and Kozarini. To these appropriations of images other "points of contact" are added. As the Paresi have inhabited the region since precolonial times, they have an ethnotoponymic knowledge of their ancient territory (areas of circulation, borders, waterways, hills, paths, geographic accidents, and abandoned villages), which is used to justify their territorial claims (Souza 1997:31). This explains why the villages, including the youngest, are built next to large waterfalls, where previous villages were also located. Archaeological investigations conducted in the area proved this to be true:[9]

> The villages have their definitive localization within a territory that has a mythical significance. As I mentioned before, Wazáre, the hero of the original group of brothers, distributed the Halíti descendents over the vast high plain, that even today retains its name, Planalto dos Parecis. (Machado 2002)

The territory is the support of collective memory and myths. Orality is the integrative agent between generations and people. To be part of the past is to be part of something wider: it is to have an identity that creates differences accepted by others, defining related categories and dichotomies in which "we" is juxtaposed to "others." Real differences, imaginary or imposed, emerge and are constructed from this relationship.

Occupation of the territory has permitted the ethnic appropriation of the land (Jones 1997), which is a political construction over the territory. This appropriation, consisting of language and other cultural characteristics, allowed the Paresi to utilize differentiated spaces for self-determination within the group and to recognize "others" because identity changes according to the way in which the subjects are challenged or represented. Identification is not automatic; it can be gained or lost, it can be politicized in a process that constitutes a political change in identity (of class) in the politics of difference (Hall 2003:21). This phenomenon can be perceived among the Paresi, the "white man," and the Nambikwara. Historically, the Nambikwara and the Paresi were enemies, but since they now inhabit the same territory, recognized as Paresi, they are enemies no more; they have become allies in a pact that does not erase a conflictive past. One of the favorite activities of a Paresi is to complain about a Nambikwara and vice versa; "to speak in bad terms" about one another is common and does not prevent interethnic marriages and good friendships. Counterpointing is just a way to reinforce identity and a common past. In order to distinguish themselves from other indigenous groups, the Paresi define themselves as "Halití" (people of the town) and as such they are known; nevertheless, to differentiate themselves from the "white man" who lives in their zones they use Paresi. For the "white man" the Paresi are, simply, "indigenes."

The stone bridge myth and other transgenerational references give a sense of continuity and integration and are part of the oral universe, underscored by our archaeological research in Paresi territory. Preserving this cultural heritage is not only important for raising the self-esteem of the Paresi but also for better understanding the significance of the transformations and growth of communicative genres, deepening the knowledge of these societies, and highlighting the importance of the methodical use of oral sources for archaeology and its social responsibility.

These types of societies are rooted in notions of memory and orality, among the most vulnerable aspects of their cultural identity; they are of the utmost importance for minorities and indigenous populations because they are vital sources of an identity rooted in tradition. In these communities values, wisdom, celebrations, and expressive forms are orally transmitted. Orality is the foundation of their communal life (Moi 2003).

Intangible heritage is transformed over time because knowledge transmission is collectively recreated and reformulated (Sperber 1996). The study of the oral sources makes it possible (1) to understand their adequacy to the present, guaranteeing knowledge maintenance, transformation, and generation; (2) to understand society by its adequacy to reality; and (3) to construct and/or reconstruct cultural manifestations. Myths of origin, family histories, and narratives allow access to culture and time. Myths serve in the construction and reproduction of differences between those who live in the present and those powerful entities of times past; they not only establish continuity with the place of origin (as is the case with the stone bridge) but also relate to ethnic boundaries, which are available for archaeological verification. Thus, we not only attempt to construct and/or reconstruct social facts or events but also to understand them in their reality (Lummis 1992).

(Re)constructing Identity: Archaeology and Ancestry

Environmental impact studies in archaeology and subsequent surveys and mitigation of identified sites provided the first systematic studies of the precolonial occupation of Chapada dos Parecis, leading to the identification, excavation, and analysis of many archaeological sites.[10] Research is being conducted in nearby regions (Migliácio 2000, 2006; Oliveira and Viana 1989; Vialou 2005) thus far unexplored from an archaeological perspective. Research conducted over the past few years in the region of the valleys and rivers of Ponte de Pedra, Sangue, Sacre, Papagaio, and Juruena uncovered precolonial and historic sites; this research allows us to reconstruct a cultural mosaic of human occupation that could reach back thousands of years and provide a final link to current indigenous activities.

Despite this significant archaeological potential in the Paresi area, more precise regional contexts are still to be discovered. Ancient buried lithic sites are now known (Moi and Morales 2003; Morales 1998; Morales and Moi 2001); sites associated with this activity have been identified around waterfalls and gravel plains now covered by dense vegetation. More recent lithic activities found upstream from Sacre 2, on the Sacre River, are located on small hills close to the river, in fertile soil with dense tree cover.

Settlements of potters are identified by the Paresi as associated with ancient villages; their preliminary field analysis demonstrates that the material is covered by thick vegetation, and is located in areas affected by fire and close to large rivers. The pottery shows great technological diversity, decoration with incisions, marks of basketry in the walls, and the use different types of clay. Some sites are associated with so-called

Uru tradition; some pieces are similar to those identified in the Planalto Central and in Mato Grosso (Morales 2008; Oliveira and Viana 1989; Robrahn-González 1996; Wüst 1990).

Graphisms can be found in two rockshelters near the Sangue and Ponte de Pedra rivers; the latter, as we already noted, is sacred for the Paresi. In Ponte de Pedra there are schematic graphs and concavities for polishing and sharpening axes. Archaeological vestiges are not limited to rocks and artifacts. The landscape has mythological meanings incorporated into the Paresi mentality; here lies the stone bridge, the exact site where a hole was opened for human beings to emerge, and the stone house and sandstone outcrops that give unique contours to this stretch of the river. In this place, decades ago, one of the Rondon's telegraph stations was installed, the Ponte de Pedra station. Few vestiges remain of this historic activity: nickel plates, the foundation of a telegraph post, and an inscription in brittle sandstone next to the stone bridge where the date 1915 and the initials AM can be read. Various petroglyphs have been identified in rockshelters near the Sangue River; one is next to the river canyon in a small concavity created by flooding water, others are located in a more elevated zone and have walls replete with graphs and also have stratified deposits. This outcrop is in a region that oral knowledge, ethnohistories, and ethnographies identify as Paresi territory (Moi 2003; Moi et al. 2009).

Archaeological research has attracted a lot of attention from indigenous communities. For those with a sense of opportunity and more attuned to the changing role of archaeologists, this new "species" in the pantheon of investigators who traverse indigenous lands has generated hope and bewilderment. Bewilderment because the archaeologists always arrive with unusual questions, different from those normally posed by anthropologists or FUNAI officials. The archaeologists, in the indigenes own words, ask questions with difficult answers that, almost always, cause surprise if not indignation. That was the reaction in the case of the Xerente when we asked them if they had heard of an era in which the elders carved in stone, worked leather, and skinned animals (Moi 2007), or with the Nambikwara and Paresi when we asked about the existence of villages "from ancient times." Winds of change can bring new information and unknown facts to the indigenous communities that can be utilized to better understand the territory where they live and the tools that they used in a not-too-distant past. This knowledge is valuable because it revives a cultural heritage that forms part of their daily lives and can serve other purposes in the future. It brings indigenous groups some sort of hope, as they see in archaeological research an opportunity to recognize and demark their former territories. Thus, we instigated the identification of archaeological sites outside the limits of indigenous lands, hoping to incorporate these ancient settlements.

Over the course of this process we could perceive how the maintenance and propagation of myths reinforced Paresi identity and how some archaeological results have been incorporated into their mythological pantheon and oral tradition (Moi 2003; Moi and Morales 2008/2009). Archaeological investigations carried out in Paresi territory revealed a rocky refuge next to the Sangue River, previously unknown to natives. Images of this site were shown to a Paresi woman, who identified the graphic style as that of her own people; some Nambikwar also recognized it as Paresi. The interviews that we conducted at different sites yielded similar results regarding the meaning of the images (Moi 2003). Informants confirmed the association of the graphs with their people because they recognized familiar schematic representations of hunting gear. Thus, archaeological research uncovered a direct relation between the Paresi and ancient rock art, suggesting that the drawings were a kind of "instruction" for the manufacture of hunting weapons (Moi et al. 2009).

Rony Azoinayce Paresi, a professor and important indigenous leader who works in the revitalization of body painting among young people, was brought to the refuge to see and learn more about the graphs; he confirmed the association between ancient geometric designs and those currently used by the Paresi and, as other people had already done, he named them in his language. When we asked him if knew this kind of drawing or if it was regularly used he answered negatively, but said that he would use it from then on because it was associated with others that, undoubtedly, came from his people. Since then the Sangue petroglyphs became (or came to be anew) part of Paresi tradition, myth, and history. The reintroduction of these images allowed us to understand the dimension of the ideological/conceptual context of those Paresi in charge of transmission and communication; these people could and/or were going to act as social and political forces that assimilate, exclude, or manipulate events according to the situation.

Archaeological research amid the Paresi is only a part of a larger context that, besides addressing themes like cultural heritage, also involves political actions for the recognition of ancestral lands and property rights over objects now stored in museums. Archaeological investigations (like other investigations carried out in indigenous areas) should be social responsible, recognizing the historical and social roles of the discipline as well as its political context, striving to make them important for society again; yet, how research results are put to use may escape the control of investigators and can have unexpected consequences.

The interests and actors involved in our work in Paresi territory are many and diverse, forcing us to put aside simplistic viewpoints with two defined and polarized sides. In many cases arguments revolved around the fact that the community (or at least some influential leaders), power and agricultural companies, and the local government of Campo Novo all want development projects in the region. This odd convergence of apparently disparate interests can be explained by showing that works impacting the environmental and cultural heritage also produce profits, higher taxes for the municipality and the state, and improvements in infrastructure, which permit a better circulation of people and commodities.

The Paresi participate in a complex political, economic, and symbolic game on which their physical and cultural survival depends. Indigenous peoples are threatened. The weapons and ammunition they can count on are the riches of their lands, the cultural heritage inherited from their ancestors, and the experiences accumulated by centuries of dealing with the "white man." The Paresi organize themselves into associations, put forward their cause in national and international media, and mobilize environmentalists, indigenous assistance, and politicians genuinely interested in the environmental question or in search of an electoral opportunity. The Paresi do not hide the fact that they want profits from tourism, from power generated by PCHs, or from soybean cultivation. Yet, they cling to their differentiated status within the national society and their constitutional rights, which guarantee them territories, traditions, sacred sites, languages, customs, and government assistance in legal, health, and educational issues. As part of this game, they have begun to use archaeology to reconstruct their past and the history of those indigenous groups that inhabited the region since immemorial times.

Final Considerations

Through this research we sought to delineate and discuss how the Paresi use, ideologically and politically, the results of archaeological research in their territory. We noted their growing interest in that regard (for example, incorporating petroglyph designs in the revitalization of body painting), beyond the already known archaeological use for justifying land claims. Such results are examples of the political and social involvement of archaeology in the contemporary context, even though the discipline is dedicated to the construction of the past.

Notes

1. Flavia Prado Moi coordinated cultural heritage fieldwork in the municipalities located in the area of influence of the PCHs Sacre 1, Sacre 2, and another 11 in the Juruena

River channel. Enawenê-nawê, Nambikwara, and Paresi groups inhabit the area influenced by these projects; they were directly affected by the construction of the PCH Sacre 2, which is dependent on a waterfall near Sacre 2, Terra Indígena Utiariti. Walter Fagundes Morales coordinated archaeological fieldwork around these PCHs (Documento Antropologia e Arqueologia 2001a, 2001b, 2003).

2. The research is being carried out in NEPAM/UNICAMP under the leadership of Pedro Paulo de Abreu Funari.

3. In the mineral province of Carajás (Pará).

4. See http://www.cartamaior.com.br/templates/materiaMostrar.cfm?materia_id=12740.

5. Among those attending were representatives of the Paresi, Irantxe, Mynky, Bororo, Cinta-larga, Rikbaktsa, Arara, Nambikwara, and Umutina groups competing in traditional indigenous games: *jikunahati* (head soccer), *jakatiye* (bow and arrow), *jitsoti* (diving), *temati* (running), and *nolokakakwati* (tug of war).

6. Historical information presented here summarizes field and archival data collected by the authors in an environmental study in the Sacre, Juruena, Sangue and Ponte de Pedra rivers areas in Mato Grosso from the end of the 1990s onwards (Moi and Morales 2003; Morales 1998; Morales and Moi 2001, 2003).

7. Barros (2002) noted that there is a population of about 1273 people.

8. Interview by Flavia Prado Moi and Édison Rodrigues in Sacre 2, 2003.

9. The examples are the ancient villages (in the present-day archaeological sites) of Kotitiko, Salto do Utiariti, Ponte de Pedra, and Sacre.

10. Field reports can be read in Morales (1998), Morales and Moi (2001, 2003), and Moi and Morales (2003); company assessments can be found in Documento Antropologia e Arqueologia (2001a, 2001b, 2003) and (Griphus 2003), and scholarly papers in Moi (2003).

REFERENCES

Acselrad, Henri 2004 Conflitos ambientais. A atualidade do objeto. In *Conflitos ambientais no Brasil*, edited by Henri Acselrad, pp. 7–11. Relume Dumará-Fundação Heinrich Boll, Río de Janeiro.

Alarcón-Cháires, Pablo 2006 Riqueza ecológica versus pobreza social: contradicciones y perspectivas del desarrollo indígena en Latinoamérica. In *Pueblos indígenas y pobreza: enfoques multidisciplinarios*, edited by Alberto Cimadamore, Robyn Eversone, and John-Andrew McNeish, pp. 41–70. CLACSO, Buenos Aires.

Barros, Márcio Carlos Vieira 2002 A questão ambiental e os professores Paresi do município de Tangará da Serra, Mato Grosso: uma análise contextualizada. Unpublished Master's thesis, Faculdade de Educacão, Universidade Federal de Mato Grosso (UFMT), Cuiabá, MT, Brasil.

Barth, Fredrik (editor) 1969 *Ethnic Groups and Boundaries: The Social Organization of Culture Difference*. Little, Brown and Company, Boston.

Berkes, Fikret, Carl Folke, and Madhay Gadgil 1993 *Traditional Ecological Knowledge, Biodiversity, Resilience and Sustainability*. Beijer Discussion Paper Series 31. Beijer International Institute of Ecological Economics, Stockholm.

Borda, Carolina, and Darío Mejía 2006 Participación política y pobreza de las comunidades indígenas de Colombia. El caso de los pueblos zenú y mokaná. In *Pueblos indígenas y pobreza: enfoques multidisciplinarios*, edited by Alberto Cimadamore, Robyn Eversone, and John-Andrew McNeish, pp, 71–86. CLACSO, Buenos Aires.

Costa, Maria Ribeiro Fernandes Moreira 2002 *Senhores da memória. Uma história do Nambiquara do cerrado*. Unicem, Cuiabá.

Costa, Romana M. Ramos 1985 Cultura e contato: um estudo da sociedade paresi no contexto das relações interétnicas. Unpublished Ph.D. dissertation, Museu Nacional do Rio de Janeiro, Universidade Federal do Río de Janeiro, Río de Janeiro.

Documento Antropologia e Arqueologia SC Ltda. 2001a Diagnóstico de patrimônio arqueológico, histórico e cultural para o Projeto PCH Sacre 2. Unpublished report submitted to the Instituto do Patrimônio Histórico e Artístico Nacional (IPHAN), on file at the Documento Antropologia e Arqueologia SC Ltda., São Paulo, SP, Brasil, and the Superintendência Regional do IPHAN do Mato Grosso, Cuiabá, MT, Brasil.

————. 2001b PCH Sacre / MT. Diagnóstico arqueológico e antropológico. Unpublished report submitted to the Instituto do Patrimônio Histórico e Artístico Nacional (IPHAN), on file at the Documento Antropologia e Arqueologia SC Ltda., São Paulo, SP, Brasil, and the Superintendência Regional do IPHAN do Mato Grosso, Cuiabá, MT, Brasil.

————. 2003 Complexo Juruena. Diagnóstico antropológico / diagnóstico do patrimônio arqueológico, histórico e cultural. Unpublished report submitted to the Instituto do Patrimônio Histórico e Artístico Nacional (IPHAN), on file at the Documento Antropologia e Arqueologia SC Ltda., São Paulo, SP, Brasil, and the Superintendência Regional do IPHAN do Mato Grosso, Cuiabá, MT, Brasil.

Filho, Aderval Costa 1994 *Os paresi: sistemas econômicos*. UFMT, Cuiabá.

————. 1996 Mansos por natureza, situações históricas e permanência Paresi. Unpublished Master's thesis, Departamento de Antropologia Social, Universidade de Brasília (UnB), Brasília, DF, Brasil.

Gordillo, Gastón, and Juan Martín Leguizamón 2002 *El río y la frontera: movilizaciones aborígenes, obras públicas y mercosur en el Pilcomayo*. Biblos, Buenos Aires.

Gray, Andrew, Alejandro Parellada, and Helen Newing 1998 *From Principles to Practice: Indigenous peoples and biodiversity and Conservation in Latin American*. International Work Group for Indigenous Affairs (IWGIA) Document 87. Copenhagen.

Griphus Consultoria Ltda. 2003 Relatório final: projeto de resgate arqueológico na área diretamente afetada pela PCH Baruito, MT. Global Energia. Unpublished report submitted to the Instituto do Patrimônio Histórico e Artístico Nacional (IPHAN), on file at the Griphus Consultoria Ltda., Cuiabá, MT, Brasil, and the Superintendência Regional do IPHAN do Mato Grosso, Cuiabá, MT, Brasil.

Hall, Stuart 2003 *A identidade cultural na pós-modernidade*. DP and A, Río de Janeiro.

Harvey, David 1989 *The Condition of Postmodernity*. Blackwell, Oxford.

————. 1996 *Justice, Nature, and the Geography of Difference*. Blackwell, Oxford.

Hill, Jonathan 1988 Introduction. In *Rethinking History and Myth: Indigenous South American Perspectives on the Past*, edited by Jonathan Hill, pp. 1–17. University of Illinois Press, Urbana.

Hobsbawm, Eric 1995 *Era dos extremos. O breve século XX (1914–1991)*. Companhia das Letras, São Paulo.

Jones, Siân 1997 *The Archaeology of Ethnicity: Constructing Identities in the Past and Present*. Routledge, London.

Lévi-Strauss, Claude 1996 *Tristes trópicos*. Companhia das Letras, São Paulo. First published 1955.

Lummis, Trevor 1992 Oral history. In *Folklore, Cultural Performances and Popular Entertainments*, edited by Richard Bauman, pp. 6–13. Oxford University Press, Oxford.

Machado, Maria de Fátima Roberto 2002 Relatório complementar de identificação e delimitação da T.I. Estação Parecis (Decreto no 1775). Coord. do GT Port. no 527/ FUNAI/PRES de 21 jun 2000, Cuiabá.

Migliácio, Maria Clara 2000 A ocupação pré-colonial do Pantanal de Cáceres, Mato Grosso: uma leitura preliminar. Unpublished Master's thesis, Museu de Arqueologia e Etnologia da Universidade de São Paulo (MAE/USP), São Paulo, SP, Brasil.

————. 2006 O doméstico e o ritual: cotidiano Xaray no Alto Paraguai até o século XVI. Unpublished Ph.D. dissertation, Museu de Arqueologia e Etnologia da Universidade de São Paulo (MAE/USP), São Paulo, SP, Brasil.

Moi, Flavia Prado 2003 Patrimônio imaterial e tradição oral: potencialidades de pesquisa. In *Resumos XII Congresso da Sociedade de Arqueologia Brasileira*, p. 168, São Paulo.

Moi, Flavia Prado 2006 Arqueologia pública em território paresi: uma análise dos desdo-bramentos políticos, socioculturais e econômicos decorrentes das pesquisas arqueológi-cas. Unpublished Ph.D. dissertation, Núcleo de Estudos Ambientais da Universidade de Campinas (NEPAM/UNICAMP), Campinas, SP, Brasil.

———. 2007 *Os Xerente: um enfoque etnoarqueológico*. Editora Annablue/Acervo-Centro de Referência em Patrimônio e Pesquisa, São Paulo.

Moi, Flavia Prado, and Walter Fagundes Morales 2003 Relatório de campo para as PCHs do Juruena. Unpublished report produced for Documento Antropologia e Arqueologia SC Ltda.

———. 2008/2009 Arqueologia e gestão de recursos culturais entre os Paresi da Chapada dos Pareci, MT, Brasil. In *Arqueologia Hoje*, edited by Walter Fagundes Morales, pp. 183–218. Dossiê Especiaria–Cadernos de Ciências Humanas/Universidade Estadual de Santa Cruz, vol. 11/12, no. 20/21, Ilhéus, Bahia.

Moi, Flavia Prado, Edison Rodrigues de Souza, Walter Fagundes Morales, and Rony Walter Azoinayce Paresi 2009 Memória e oralidade: interpretação de grafismos rup-estres entre os Aruak do Noroeste do Estado do Mato Grosso, Brasil. In *Cenários Regionais em Arqueologia Brasileira*, edited by Walter Fagundes Morales and Flavia Prado Moi, pp. 205–237. São Paulo: Editora Annablume/Acervo-Centro de Referência em Patrimônio e Pesquisa, Porto Seguro.

Morales, Walter Fagundes 1998 Relatório de campo da UHE Ponte de Pedra. Unpublished report produced for Documento Antropologia e Arqueologia SC Ltda.

———. 2008 *Brasil Central: 12.000 anos de ocupação humana no médio curso do rio Tocantins, TO*. São Paulo: Editora Annablume/Acervo-Centro de Referência em Patrimônio e Pesquisa, Porto Seguro.

Morales, Walter Fagundes, and Flavia Prado Moi 2001 Relatório de campo para a PCH 28. Unpublished report produced for Documento Antropologia e Arqueologia SC Ltda.

———. 2003 Relatório de campo para a PCH 28. Unpublished report produced for Documento Antropologia e Arqueologia SC Ltda.

Montserrat, Ruth Maria Fonini 1994 Línguas indígenas no Brasil contemporâneo. In *Índios no Brasil*, edited by Luís Donisete Benzi Grupioni, pp. 93–94. Ministério de Educação e Deportes, Brasília.

Neves, Lino João de Oliveira 2003 Olhos mágicos do sul (do Sul): lutas contra-hegemônicas dos povos indígenas no Brasil. In *Reconhecer para libertar: os caminhos do cosmopolit-ismo multicultural*, edited by Boaventura de Sousa Santos, pp. 111–151. Civilização Brasileira, Río de Janeiro.

Oliveira, Jorge Eremites, and Sibeli Aparecida Viana 1989 O centro-oeste antes de Cabral. In *Dossiê antes de Cabral: arqueologia brasileira*, vol. 1, pp. 89–142. Revista USP, São Paulo.

Perrone-Moisés, Beatriz 1992 Índios livres e índios escravos: os princípios da legislação indigenista do período colonial (séculos XVI a XVIII). In *História dos índios no Brasil*, edited by Manuela Carneiro da Cunha, pp. 115–154. Companhia das Letras-Fapesp-SMC, São Paulo.

Pivetta, Darci Luiz, and Maria de Lourdes Freire 1993 *Irantxe: luta pelo território expro-priado*. Universidade Federal de Mato Grosso, Cuiabá.

Price, P. David 1983 La pacificación de los nambikwara. *América Indígena* XLIII (3):601–628.

Programa das Nações Unidas para o Desenvolvimento (PNUD) 2004 *Relatório do desenvolvimento humano 2004. Liberdade cultural num mundo diversificado*. PNUD, Lisboa, Portugal.

Robrahn-González, Erika 1996 A ocupação ceramista pré-colonial do Brasil Central: ori-gens e desenvolvimento. Unpublished Ph.D. dissertation, Faculdade de Fisolofia, Letras e Ciências Humanas, Universidade de São Paulo (FFLCH/USP), São Paulo, SP, Brasil.

———. 2006 Relatório final do programa de patrimônio cultural da PCH Paranatinga II. Unpublished report submitted to the Instituto do Patrimônio Histórico e Artístico

Nacional (IPHAN), on file at the Documento Antropologia e Arqueologia SC Ltda., São Paulo, SP, Brasil, and the Superintendência Regional do IPHAN do Mato Grosso, Cuiabá, MT, Brasil.

Sahlins, Marshall 1978 A primeira sociedade da afluência. In *Antropologia econômica*, edited by Edgard Assis Carvalho, pp. 7–44. Livraria Editora Ciências Humanas, São Paulo.

Shennan, Stephen 1994 Introduction: Archaeological approaches to cultural identity. In *Archaeological Approaches to Cultural Identity*, edited by Stephen Shennan, pp. 1–32. Routledege, London.

———. 2000 Population, culture history and the dynamics of cultural change. *Current Anthropology* 41(5):811–835.

Silva, Jovam Vilela da 1993 A capitania de Mato Grosso: política de povoamento e população - seculo XVIII. Unpublished Ph.D. dissertation, Universidade de São Paulo, São Paulo.

Souza, Hellen Cristina de 1997 Entre a aldeia e a cidade: educacao escolar pareci. Unpublished Ph.D. dissertation, Universidade Federal de Mato Grosso, Cuiabá.

Sperber, Dan 1996 *La contagion des idées*. Odile Jacob, Paris.

Thomas, Julian 1996 *Time, Culture and Identity: An Interpretative Archaeology*. Routledge, London.

Toledo, Victor 1992 What is ethnoecology? Origins, scope and implications of a rising discipline. *Etnoecológica* 1(1):5–21.

United Nations Educational, Scientific, and Cultural Organization (UNESCO) 2003 *Convención para la salvaguarda del patrimonio cultural inmaterial*. UNESCO, Paris, France.

Vialou, Águeda Vilhena 2005 *Pré-história de Mato Grosso*, vols. 1 and 2. São Paulo, EDUSP.

Vicenzo, Lauriola 2003 Ecologia global contra diversidade cultural? Conservação da natureza a povos indígenas no Brasil: o monte Roraima entre o Parque Nacional e Terra Indígena Raposa, Serra do Sol. *Ambiente & Sociedade* 6(1):165–189.

Wüst, Irmhild 1990 Continuidade e mudança. Para uma interpretação dos grupos ceramistas pré-coloniais da bacia do rio Vermelho, Mato Grosso. Unpublished Ph.D. dissertation, Museu de Arqueologia e Etnologia da Universidade de São Paulo (MAE/USP), São Paulo, SP, Brasil.

Yúdice, George 2004 *A conveniência da cultura: usos da cultura na era global*. Editora UFMG, Belo Horizonte, MG, Brasil.

BOLIVIAN ARCHAEOLOGY: ANOTHER LINK IN THE CHAIN OF COLONIALITY?

Marcelo Fernández-Osco

Before fully addressing the topic of this work, it is convenient to make clear some issues related to the historical, political, and ideological character of coloniality. Coloniality refers to the logic of domination embodied by colonial structures through which indigenous peoples were subjected and discriminated against since the conquest. The killing of Atawallpa was part of this *habitus* that persists in contemporary Bolivian society, its culture, and its power relations. Thus, I sustain that colonial power relations still exist and have become a sort of common sense within the field of archaeological knowledge, particularly in what pertains to indigenous sacred spaces denominated "archaeological monuments," "remains," or "ruins." For indigenous peoples these spaces or objects are part of contemporary life and are known as *wak'as* (sacred sites) and *achachilas* (ancestors) that partake in the sacred world of Pachamama or Mother Earth; concretely one could say that these sites are the vital source of indigenous political memory and support for their organizations. In the body of this chapter, I will analyze certain symbolic continuities within indigenous peoples' life in relation to coloniality/ modernity and its variants as internal colonialism. Finally I will present some tentative conclusions.

This chapter has been conceived from the Aymara indigenous worldview and through this lens I hope to highlight the possibilities and the limits of archaeology. Archaeologists have carried out their work regardless of the will of native populations, without consulting their programs and concepts. Thus archaeological work can be considered part of coloniality or internal colonialism;[1] that is, a set of mechanisms of exclusion and segregation based on racial differences. However, I also wonder to what extent Bolivian archaeology has contributed to the reestablishment of a collective political consciousness, the identity of the indigenous peoples, and the struggle for political rights in the present context.

In Spite of the Colonization of Souls

The conquest of the New World and colonization became the most immediate antecedent upon which archaeological knowledge in the Andes was based. That is why it is important to begin our discussion with the conquest and colonization,[2] the initial moment of the first modernity. Catholic doctrine was one of the most important mechanisms for exploiting and devastating indigenous spiritual and material values through the application of colonial policies and their several reforms.

The campaigns to extirpate idolatries, which were first presented as legal procedures, were then followed by violence in different forms. One example is Alonzo Ricary in Cajatambo, where indigenous peoples were subjected to trials in order to make them confess their idolatries. Common people were put in front of tribunals for their supposed crimes against the public order: "A witness was asked and he confessed that they adored not God but their *camaquenes guacas ydolos and malques*[3] because they dress and feed them" (Duviols 1986:69). Besides testifying against the accused, the witnesses remained faithful to their idols and hinted at the idea that the idolatry had important practical benefits in both material and spiritual sense, thus grounding the idea that human beings need the support of gods, society, and other entities. As the witness Andrés Chuapis expressed it:

> Mochaban y daban culto las tres bezes al año una por tiempo de Navidad para que lloviese ... otra por febrero quando queria enpecar el aillo ... y por modo de premicias los cogian y los muchachos que tenian señalados hacian el coco azua chicha y con esta hacian ofrendas a los dhos malquis convidaban a los demas y desta manera alternativamente lo iban haciendo todos. (Duviols 1986:53)

The witnesses Francisca Tuctu and Juana Colque reported:

> Fuele preguntado si adora al sol la luna las estrellas y luzero las siete cabrillas el chuchu coyllur. Dixo que es verdad que da culto y veneración como los demás del pueblo y que esto lo hace por que no aya enfermedades ... y por tener de comer y bestir y porque ... las comidas ... y antepasados que hiziesse. (Duviols 1986:75)

From the church's perspective these interrogatories were part of controlling and extirpating indigenous religious practices, which were stigmatized as diabolic sorcery because they were not in consonance with

Catholic values, ultimately determined by the dichotomy between good and evil. In contrast, indigenous religious values were part of a wide system of knowledge and practices based on a pluriverse that connected other lives and the cosmos.

As might be evident, it is difficult to separate the religiosity from the archaeological monument as archaeology does. Even when an indigenous word is lacking to distinguish religion and monument, these have been conceptualized in several ways. For instance, "Viracocha means their god which brings with it several viracochas, or which is the same several gods" (Sarmiento de Gamboa 1943 [1893]:271). We face here a conception in which monuments are ancestors, beliefs, an ethic and practice of life, or a life force that is profoundly mingled with material objects, society, peoples, and cosmos. This conception is not anchored in pure abstraction as happens with the Catholic religion, whose conceptions are imprecise and even vague. For the Aymara culture, orality is "the fundamental space of the critique, not only to the colonial order, but to the whole Western conception of history" (Rivera 1986:33).

In the indigenous vision of history the past does not exist as such, there is nothing back in time that is irreversible—the past is also the present. In Aymara this is expressed as *nayrapacha*,[4] the past presupposes the strength of renovation. Both past and future are reversible; the past is fixable because, as sacred things, it is raised and it lends itself to be raised, in the same way as humans and society do. In this sense, damage such as colonialism and racial discrimination are fixable since all that exists in the world is not self-contained but is part of an interconnected whole. In this world everyone has a meaning in and for life.

Gods or deities must not be understood as supernatural entities that are "beyond" our lives and world, but rather as inhabiting a symbiotic world in which everyone facilitates life for everyone else, regardless of their status. That is why this goes beyond spirituality or materiality. Given the way in which the witnesses presented above spoke, one can assume that those religious premises were organized according to an ethic more in tune with the surrounding world. Since those times and until today, this way of interacting persists even after all the campaigns to extirpate idolatries. The chronicler Arriaga (1920 [1621]:20) recognized the pluridiversity of the gods; for example, Libiac is lightning and "is very common in the mountains, thus many take the name or surname from Libiac, or Hillapa, which is the same." Thus these objects, regardless of size and shape, were taken as living bodies, and many times operated as guarantees of territorial rights.[5] Access to resources is justified by the sacrality and age of the gods— the more ancient they are the stronger the right and the stronger the guarantee they provided.

To expand this interconnective idea between spirituality and people, it is convenient to mention the figure of Pachamama or Mother Earth, an absolutely sacred dimension of the indigenous everyday life. That is why Pachamama is often offered liquor and coca leaves while invoking the *w-ak'as* of each region before starting any work, as Arriaga (1920 [1621]:61) pointed out:

> Y asimismo a uisto este testigo en muchas ocaciones que quando los indios quieren sembrar sus chacaras antes de ararlas les echan chicha cocca y queman deguellan cuyes y adoran del quel disen ... para tener buena cosecha.

The activities cannot be performed without regard for this complex of worlds and entities in which Andean people live immersed. For Quechua and Aymara people, good and evil are not separate worlds. A deity, regardless its value for humans, can bring benefits or can also bring conflicts; much will depend on the communication and interaction that has been sustained with it. The stronger and more intense the relation, the less likely it is that problems will arise and vice versa.

This way of life is part of a wide network of kinship[6] that is also interconnected with the community of sacred things representing nature and the cosmos. This appears clearly in the cosmological scheme made by Santa Cruz Pachacuti (1968 [1613]:35), for whom "all the elements are commanded for service by men." In this scheme the creation of time, religion, and space is expressed. This is not about Western time/space but rather something more complicated where life is privileged. This assumes that the world of multiple lives is sustained by multiple forces or elements. Something similar can be observed in the drawings of Waman Puma de Ayala (1992 [1612–1615]). In the work of both authors we can glimpse the holistic sense of life, and particularly, how certain spaces have dimensions that go beyond simple religiosity and materiality, forming thus a corpus of good living or *suma jakaña*.

Having made this explanation then, it should not surprise us that places have names like Guacaquillay, machayes, guacas, camachicos, mallqui, peñas, arañas, mollo, ciete machaiees, apu libia Cancharco, libiac choquerunto, libiac Runtuy, quebradas, alturas, lucero de la mañana, dos hermanos, siete cabrillas, madre agua, cerro, camaquen una culebra, mar, Guari, Titicaca, puquios, el sol, la luna, las estrellas, rios, paraxes, la pampa, camay, capacocha, Pachacamac, Wiraqocha, camaquen, gentiles, chuzec, lechuza (Acosta 1954 [1590]; Arriaga 1920 [1621]; Duviols 1986; Waman Puma de Ayala 1992 [1612–1615]). Each one of these names articulates different subjectivities that are connected with spaces that are multiple in their dimensions and nature. The same is the case with temples that have been destroyed, as in Cuzco, Mochica, and

Tiwanaku, or diverse chullpares. Of all these only literary monuments remain that under diverse headings narrate the destruction brought about by the extirpation of idolatries. These communities of sacred things are interconnected with the community of inhabitants. They do not live isolated; they have not lost actuality but rather coexist and are part of the everyday life of the indigenous peoples. Even though they have been resignified, in no way has their pluriversal view of life disappeared. At bottom what can be perceived is a kind of autonomy that survived the adversities of coloniality, in spite of the forgetfulness produced by archaeology and by the official Western history, which Gruzinski (1991) has characterized as the colonization of mentality.

DEVASTATIONS AND MISUNDERSTANDINGS

Let us now see what happened with these monuments after the conquest. Tiwanaku, the former center of Wiñay Marka, eternal city or town, is the best example to understand the coloniality of archaeological knowledge.

In 1612 a Catholic church was built on top of Tiwanaku using parts of the stones and figures of the Tiwanaku civilization. Doubtless, this is a valuable architectonic monument that joins gothic elements with pre-Hispanic indigenous elements (Posnansky 1945). In this way the so-called town of Tiwanaku took shape according to the urban norms of the colony, which, following a quadrangular pattern, formed the basis for other dependencies of the colonial administration. The houses of the first Spanish settlers were built with stones carved by the Tiwanaku people (Posnansky 1945). The old buildings became ruins, thus eroding their symbolic and material value. This process deepened when control was taken by the landowning criollo oligarchy who built a railway in the region. Indigenous history had no value, and their spaces were taken to be "Indian things" that had no utility for the Bolivian state.

Archaeology sees material objects and sites as anchored in the past. In studies concepts such as pre-Hispanic, ruins, prehistoric antiquities, the ruins, ancient civilization, archaeological sites, and prehistoric monuments are common (Albarracin-Jordan and Mathews 1990; Bandelier 1911; Posnansky 1910; Velard 1942). There is a clear difference between the "pre" and the "post," and this is not simply a grammatical issue: it is an important issue that consists in disconnecting what these sites meant in the past and what they mean today for those inheritors that still live around Tiwanaku.[7] In this way the indigenous rights and worldviews were delegitimized. This process started with the institutionalization of archaeology, this time in the name of science. What I mean is that the policy of colonial extirpation did not disappear with the constitution of the modern Bolivian state, since the colonial *habitus* continued in different ways and through different mechanisms. The presence of the first archaeologists in the region was framed by this *habitus* marked by the racial difference. In principle the Bolivian state declared Tiwanaku "ruins" (El Comercio 1891:3) and part of its jurisdiction and national patrimony; thus, the *ayllus*[8] or indigenous peoples of the area lost their rights, although from the perspective of the tacit ceremonial rights actually practiced, these were never lost.

Supported by the principle of *res nullius*, archaeological missions without ethics excavated, stole, and negotiated vital pieces that are today owned by museums in industrialized nations. It was never considered that indigenous peoples see those pieces and monuments as deities to whom one must offer veneration and respect. That is why rituals such as *kuchu*, consisting in the sacrifice of a white llama to guarantee good weather or to give thanks for a good harvest, are performed. Indigenous peoples consider Tiwanaku as one of the most important *w-ak'as*, which in turn can be understood as another form of political self-determination.

Tiwanaku attracted all kinds of interests. For instance, travelers seeking indigenous exoticism such as the German naturalist Tadeo Haenke, who visited the site in 1799 and spoke of Tiwanaku as a pre-Columbian monument. At the beginning of the nineteenth century the site was visited by Alexander von Humboldt, who spoke of aboriginal monuments and advised the literate circles to visit them for recreation. Around the same time the site was visited by the French naturalist Alcides Dessalines D'Orbigny, who "during his visit had the opportunity to gather some archaeological sculptures to be taken to France for his collection" (Ponce 1995:17). Another important visitor was Francis de Castelnau, supported by the French government. Although the visits allowed recovering the historicity of Tiwanaku, they also implied its destruction and robbery of important pieces. In contrast to the colonial era extirpation of idolatries, the destruction was now made in the name of naturalism and modern science, such as the archaeology embodied by Arthur Posnansky, considered the father of Bolivian archaeology. He described Tiwanaku as being extremely old and reified the notion of a pure race, reinforcing the racism against contemporary indigenous peoples. Important also were the expeditions of Freidrich Max Uhle, known as the father of Peruvian archaeology, who tried to understand the pre-Hispanic indigenous society through the knowledge of contemporary indigenous peoples (Loza 2004:27); however, the result was an instrumentalization of indigenous knowledge and not the recognition of the indigenous rights over Tiwanaku.

It is not easy at first sight to understand how archaeological knowledge presupposes coloniality, especially in a context were internal colonialism is rampant. This order becomes visible if one follows the connections between one set of work and another. For example, the American archaeologist Wendell Clark Bennett traveled to the Andes for the first time as a staff member of the American Museum of Natural History in New York; later he was sent by Yale University. In 1932 he carried out several excavations in the Andean regions of Bolivia and Peru. In Tiwanaku he found several "*estelas*" (stelae) one of which (the Bennett Monolith) carries his name to commemorate him. Other monuments were renamed, such as the "Friar Monolith." While foreign archaeologists carried out this renaming, national archaeologists did it as well:

> A great discovery was the monolith called Ponce ... The Minister of Education, the writer Fernando Diez de Medina, visited Tiwanaku on Sunday, November 10, and named the monolith Ponce in recognition of the director of the archaeological expedition. (Ponce 1995:230)

I understand the nationalist process of 1952 as the exaltation of Bolivian values but not of Indian values, which were excluded by the neo-nationalists. The new elites of the middle class of Creoles and mestizos reproduced the *habitus* of the modernity/coloniality of power. The attitude of the archaeologist Carlos Ponce is a good example. He participated in the nationalist project and was in charge of decontextualizing the parts of Tiwanaku that had formed a whole before. This is very similar to what happened to Tupak Katari, the indigenous leader dismembered by four horses in 1782 by the colonial power. Today the indigenous movement is trying to restitute the dismembered body, which also means the restitution of the spaces and objects or monuments considered sacred.

For archaeology the value of the so-called archaeological monuments is connected to the "imagined community" of Anderson (1993) and is part of the machinery of coloniality/modernity. In contrast, for the *ayllu* they have a value that has no measure because they have to do with the political well-being and the worldview of the present. They are not only objects anchored in the past but rather they are anchored in another humanity, an indigenous one.

Twentieth-century modernity began with these antecedents, thus implying processes of cultural and material devastation. Large amounts of monumental pieces were used to build the railway to Guaqui and the houses of the landowning classes (Fernández 1996). This is why I speak of the dismembering of the indigenous political memory at the hands of science. However, in the indigenous imagination there still exist a strong linkage between these so-called archaeological sites or monuments and their communities. For the indigenous peoples these are the vital force, the foundation of their cultural and political identity that has allowed resisting the successive forms of oppression the dominant society and modernity have exercised upon the indigenous peoples. In this context ritual and cultural practices are being renovated, for example the emergence of the so-called Aymara New Year (*machaq mara*, *willka kuti*, return of the new sun or *pachakuti*), which is celebrated on the 21st of June through the veneration of Tata Willka, or Lord Sun, in Tiwanaku. This is a way to restore vital political energies. This is happening in several places in the Andes where different celebrations and rituals are being reenacted in the twenty-first century in spite of the devastation suffered for hundreds of years. Bolivian archaeology had little to do with this process until Evo Morales, the first indigenous president of Bolivia, was invested as *mallku* or governor in Tiwanaku, this before going through the state rituals in the legislative palace in La Paz.

TOWARD AN INTERCULTURAL ARCHAEOLOGY

Although archaeological studies of Andean indigenous peoples have treated them as a homogenous unit or as lacking knowledge, the Andean indigenous world is characterized by internal relations that have an intercultural character and great temporal depth. This is exemplified by Waman Puma de Ayala (1992 [1612–1615]:42) and his proposal of a "pontifical world" where he expressed the intercultural character of Tawantinsuyu thought and underscored the integration of Cusco and Castilla in the political-organizational model of *aranzaya* and *urinzaya* (upper and lower), typical of the territorial organization of the *ayllu* and the *marka*. These are not antagonistic entities but rather complementary parts. Another example is that of Eduardo Nina Qhispi (1932)[9] who in the 1930s proposed a renewal of Bolivia on the basis of the restitution of communal lands as they had been granted by colonial titles. This process implied a pluriversal education and should be based on the rights of brotherhood, understood as the reencounter, recognition, and coexistence between different peoples, or, which is the same, a dialogue between peers. This proposal marked a significant moment in indigenous history and was coincident with a growing archaeological interest in Tiwanaku. Nina Qhispi proposed a *pachakuti* by way of dialogue and mutual understanding based on an educational dynamic. Indigenous interculturality makes evident essentialist discourses in scientific disciplines, particularly archaeology, which worked and still works on the basis of a monoculture where the interests of the archaeologist are prevalent, and thereby so are those of the institutions the archaeologist represents, and which are not connected with a pluriversal view in the construction of archaeological knowledge.

Two contemporary examples make my point clear. One is the case of the weavings from the *ayllu* Coroma, which today is part of the

Indigenous Municipality of Coroma. As many *ayllus*, Coroma keeps patrimonies of value beyond measure, such as old weavings, or *q'ipis*,[10] which come from the times of Tawantisuyu or colonial times and which are considered *illas* or spirits of the community. In the 1980s Coroma was visited by rogue traders of antiquities who bought some of these objects at laughable prices. Shortly after, Coroma suffered a series of events climatic, political, and social turmoil that affected the collective. The authorities conducted a series of investigations to find out why this conflictive situation had arisen. The knowledge of the *yatiri*[11] helped to clarify the issue. The results indicated that the ancestors, the *achachilas* or *w-ak'as* of the *ayllu*, were no longer with the community. This produced a state of emergency and the enactment of several actions to convince the ancestors—represented by the *q'ipis* that had been sold to the gringos—to return. This turned into a national and international problem that ended with the repatriation of the weavings to Coroma in 2002 after a long negotiation with the governments of the USA and Canada. Thus, with the assistance of some specialists (some of whom were anthropologists), the objective of having the objects returned was achieved. Currently, the return of *q'ipis* to the *ayllu* has reignited practices around them, not as a living museum but as a town that lives another modernity that does not imply the loss of identity as indigenous.

In 2002 the Bennett Monolith, which had been located in downtown La Paz since 1932, was returned to its original place in Tiwanaku. This was part of a new policy of revalorizing the indigenous heritage regardless of contemporary interests. The return of the Bennett Monolith produced great concerns for everyone. La Paz was flooded by unprecedented rains, which was interpreted as a sign of anger by this *w-ak'a* that had been mistreated for so long. The *yatiri* Valentín Mejillones said, "What happened on Tuesday the 19th and what will happen in the future every time the Bennett Monolith is attempted to be moved without permission of the sacred spirits, who are the owners of the Andean worldview, is what is in the prophecies" (La Razón 2000). The return of this *w-ak'a* to its original place, Tiwanaku, produced favorable and unfavorable comments; rituals were held by numerous people along the road connecting La Paz to Tiwanaku. The monolith is not a stone monument of archaeological value only, its meaning is multidimensional. This must lead us to processes of change; not only in attitude but also in the way we conceive how to treat these objects, sites, and monuments because they are connected to the deep feelings of the people and to cultural identity and are part of a system of political relations with an intercultural indigenous character.

Bolivian archaeology shows the importance of considering how coloniality operates under unequal relations and the monoculture that ignores other kinds of knowledges and the need to democratize knowledge and its praxis (for example, the written works about Tiwanaku are not known among the indigenous peoples). Inclusive and collaborative practices among indigenous peoples and archaeologists could be part of the process of the intercultural democratization of knowledge.

NOTES

1. The basis of this perspective has been laid out in the works of González (1970), Quijano (1992), Rivera (1993), and Mignolo (1995, 2000).
2. The most representative example of the first moment of globalization can be observed in the following passage of Inka Garcilaso (1970 [1605]:81–82):

> Demás desto, deseo saber de aquel bonísimo varón Jesucristo que nunca echó sus pecados, que dices que murió, si murió de enfermedad o a manos de sus enemigos; si fue puesto entre los dioses antes de su muerte o despues della. También deseo saber si teneis por dioses a estos cinco (cmc: dios trino, dios y jesús) que me habéis propuesto, pues los honraís tanto, porque si es así tenéis más dioses que nosotros, que no adoramos más de al Pachacamac por Supremo Dios y al Sol por su inferior, y a la luna por hermana y mujer suya. Por todo lo cual holgara en extremo que me dierades a entender estas cosas por otro mejor faraute ... me proponeis cinco varones señalados a que debo conocer. El primero es el Dios tres y uno que son cuatro, a quien llamais creador del Universo; por ventura es el mismo que nosotros llamamos Pachacamac y Viracocha. El segundo es que dices que es padre de todos los otros hombres, en quien todos ellos amontonaron sus pecados. Al tercero llamais Jesucristo, solo el cual no echó sus pecados en aquel primer hombre, pero que fue muerto. Al cuarto nombraís Papa. El quinto es Carlos, a quien sin hacer cuenta de los otros, llamaís poderosísimo monarca de universo y supremo a todos. Pues si este Carlos es Príncipe y señor de todo el mundo, ¿qué necesidad tenía de que el papa le hiciera nueva concesión y donación, para hacerme guerra y usurpar estos reinos? Y si la tenía ¿luego el Papa es mayor señor que no él, y más poderoso, y príncipe de todo el mundo? También me admiro que digais que estoy obligado a pagar tributo a Carlos y no a los otros, porque no dais razón para el tributo, ni yo me hallo obligado a darlo por ninguna vía. Porque si de derecho hubiese de dar tributo y servicio, paréceme que se había de dar a aquel Dios que dices que nos creó a todos, ya aquel primer hombre que fue padre ...; finalmente se había de dar al papa, que puede dar y conceder mis reinos y mi persona a otros. Pero si dices que a éstos no debo nada, menos debo a Carlos, que nunca fue señor destas regiones ni las ha visto.

3. *"Camaquenes, guacas, ydolos y malques"* are not only religious objects but later will become archaeological objects.
4. This word comes from two Aymara words: *nayra* (eye, back viewing) and *pacha* (time, space, age).
5. Most territories of originary nations were delimited by *w-ak'as* or other landscape features.
6. Often, children in the Andean region refer to strangers as "uncle" or "aunt," and the grown-ups refer to each other as *jilata* (brother) and *kullaka* (sister).
7. I come from the region of Tiwanaku, the Marka Waki. Those of us who are from there consider ourselves to be the inheritors of that great culture upon which the Inca state was built.

8. This is an Aymara and Quechua word that denotes the primordial territorial, political, and socioeconomic unity in the Andes.
9. Nina Qhispi was one of the Indians thrown out of the haciendas in Taraqu (province of Ingavi, Department of La Paz). He lived between his hometown and La Paz and was linked to the struggle of the *caciques apoderados* movement and popular urban movements such as the *matarifes*.
10. Aymara word, meaning "sacred bundle." Given their value, these objects can be considered monuments.
11. *Yatiris* are people of great knowledge.

REFERENCES

Acosta, José de 1954 [1590] *Obras*. Biblioteca de autores españoles, Madrid.

Albarracin-Jordan, Juan, and James E. Mathews 1990 *Asentamientos prehispánicos del valle de Tiwanaku*, vol. 1. CIMA, La Paz.

Anderson, Benedict 1993 *Comunidades imaginadas*. Fondo de Cultura Económica, Mexico.

Arriaga, Pablo José de 1920 [1621] *La extirpación de la idolatría en el Perú*, vol. 13. Imprenta y Librería Sanmarti, Lima.

Bandelier, Adolph 1911 *The Ruins at Tiahuanacu*. Proceedings of the American Antiquarian Society, Worcester.

Duviols, Pierre 1986 *Cultura andina y represión. Proceso y visita de idolatría y hechicerías Cajatambo, siglo XVII*. Centro de Estudios Rurales Andinos Bartolomé de las Casas, Cusco.

El Comercio 1891 Monumentos de Tiahuanacu. 6 October:5.

Fernández, Marcelo 1996 El poder de la palabra: documento y memoria oral en la resistencia de Waquimarka contra la expansión latifundista (1874–1930). Unpublished Honor's thesis, Department of Sociology, Universidad de Mayor de San Andrés, La Paz.

Garcilaso de la Vega, El Inca 1970 [1605] *Historia general del Perú*. Editorial Universo, Lima.

González, Pablo 1970 *Sociología de la explotación*. Siglo XXI, Mexico.

Gruzinski, Serge 1991 *La colonización de lo imaginario*. Fondo de Cultura Económica, Mexico.

La Razón 2002 Bennett, el monolito khencha. 21 February:3–4.

Loza, Carmen Beatriz 2004 *Itinerarios de Max Uhle en el altiplano boliviano*. Instituto Ibero-Americano, Berlín.

Mignolo, Walter 1995 *The Darker Side of the Renaissance: Literacy, Territoriality, and Colonization*. Michigan University Press, Ann Arbor.

———. 2000 La colonialidad a lo largo y a lo ancho: el hemisferio occidental en el horizonte colonial de la modernidad. In *La colonialidad del saber: eurocentrismo y ciencias sociales. Perspectivas latinoamericanas*, edited by Edgardo Lander, pp. 55–85. CLACSO, Buenos Aires.

Nina Qhispi, Eduardo 1932 *De los títulos de composición de la corona de España. Composición a título de usufructo como se entiende la exención revisitaria. Venta de España. Títulos de las comunidades de la República. Renovación de Bolivia. Años 1536, 1617, 1777, 1825 y 1925.* Unpublished manuscript, on file at the Archivo de La Paz, La Paz.

Pachacuti, Joan de Santa Cruz 1968 [1613] *Relación de antigüedades deste reyno del Perú*. Ediciones Atlas, Madrid.

Ponce, Carlos 1995 *Tiwanaku. 200 años de investigaciones arqueológicas*. CIMA, La Paz.

Posnansky, Arthur 1910 *Monumentos prehistóricos de Tihuanaco*. Homenaje al XVII Congreso de Americanistas, La Paz.

———. 1945 *Tihuanacu. La cuna del hombre americano*, vol. 1. J.J. Agustín, New York.

Quijano, Aníbal 1992 Colonialidad y modernidad/racionalidad. *Perú Indígena* 13(29):11–20.

Rivera, Silvia 1986 La historia oral: ¿más allá de la lógica instrumental. *Historia Oral* 1:30–38.

———. 1993 La raíz: colonizadores y colonizados. In *Violencias encubiertas en Bolivia*, edited by Xavier Albó and Raul Barrios, pp. 33–54. CIPCA-ARUWIYIRI, La Paz.

Sarmiento de Gamboa, Pedro 1943 [1893] *Historia de los Incas*. EMECÉ, Buenos Aires.

Velard, Jehan Albert 1942 *Tihuanacu y las principales zonas arqueológicas de Bolivia*. Kollasuyu, La Paz.

Waman Puma de Ayala, Felipe 1992 [1612–1615] *El primer nueva corónica y buen gobierno*. Siglo XX, Mexico.

DECLARATION OF RÍO CUARTO

Translated from the Spanish by Cristóbal Gnecco

In the city of Río Cuarto (Argentina), on the fortieth day of May, 2005, the undersigned gathered in the First Meeting of Indigenous Peoples and Archaeologists and decided to agree on the following:

Considering:

—The mandate of the Plenary of the XV National Congress of Argentine Archaeology, especially the need to establish a dialogue based on mutual respect between indigenous peoples and archaeologists and the acknowledgment of the contribution of archaeology to the understanding of the indigenous past and the legitimate interest of contemporary indigenous communities for the cultural heritage that belongs to them and that is the support of ancestral knowledge, wisdom, and worldviews.

—That the indigenous peoples were not consulted neither included in the current national law of archaeological heritage (24.743/03), violating Article 75, Inc. 17, of the National Constitution.

We recommend:

—To extend the provisions approved by the XV National Congress of Argentine Archaeology regarding the non-exhibition of the Llullaillaco bodies to all other human remains stored in museum collections in the country, taking as a precedent the policies adopted by some museums, such as the Ethnographic Museum of the University of Buenos Aires.

—To sensitize the public about the reasons behind the decision not to exhibit human remains.

—To respect the ancestral sacredness of human remains and indigenous sites and to implement adequate archaeological techniques and procedures to comply with such a respect.

—To mutually collaborate in order to repatriate those indigenous human remains stored in public and/or private collections.

—To promote the necessary mechanisms for the integral revision and modification of Law 24.743/03 after consultation and debate by indigenous peoples, archaeologists, and all other social actors with a genuine interest in such a heritage, taking into consideration a multicultural perspective for its treatment.

—To responsibly value the social and political consequences of archaeological research in relation to the rights of indigenous communities.

—To obtain the previous agreement of indigenous communities for the realization of archaeological investigations of the cultural heritage of such communities and to further steps for them and their authorities to have the relevant information for reaching a decision. To give copies of reports and conclusions to the communities where research has been carried out.

—Finally, we acknowledge the preoccupation of indigenous communities regarding different issues linked to the intellectual property of cultural heritage and express the need to promote an informed and deep debate about the matter in order to extend the points of the agreement.

INDEX

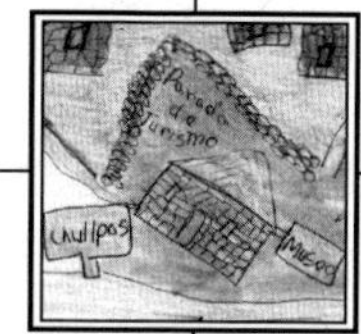

About The Authors

Dante Angelo investigates topics related to cultural heritage, sociopolitical issues in archaeology, the politics of archaeological practice, and the relationships of modernity and urbanism with material culture. He has published "La arqueología en Bolivia. Reflexiones sobre la disciplina a inicios del siglo XXI" (*Arqueología Suramericana* 1(2), 2005), "Interacción, fronteras y nuevos desafíos para la arqueología del sur de los Andes" (In *Esferas de interacción prehistóricas y fronteras nacionales modernas: los Andes sur-centrales*, edited by Heather Lechtman, Instituto de Estudios Peruanos/Institute of Andean Research, Lima, 2006), and "Dominant narratives, social violence and the practice of Bolivian archaeology" (*Journal of Social Archaeology* 5, 2005), with David Kojan.

Patricia Ayala coordinates the office of relationships with the Atacameño community at the Archaeological Research Institute and Museum Gustavo Le Paige of the Universidad Católica del Norte (Chile). As an archaeologist she has studied the Formative and Late Intermediate periods of Atacameño prehistory as well as social interaction between the Circumpuna and the Bolivian altiplano. As an anthropologist she investigates the historically constructed relations and discourses between indigenes, archaeologists, and the state in Atacama, and heritage processes in Chile. She has organized meetings, workshops, and symposia, and co-edited issues of *Chungará* (2003) and *Textos Antropológicos* (2005) on these topics. She has published *Políticas del pasado. Indígenas, arqueólogos y Estado en Atacama* (Universidad Católica del Norte, Antofagasta, 2008).

O. Hugo Benavides is Professor of Anthropology at Fordham University (USA). His books about archaeology and anthropology are *Making*

Ecuadorian Histories: Four Centuries of Defining Power (University of Texas Press, Austin, 2004), *The Politics of Sentiment: Imagining and Remembering Guayaquil* (University of Texas Press, Austin, 2006), and *Drugs, Thugs and Divas: Telenovelas and Narco-Dramas in Latin America* (University of Texas Press, Austin, 2008). He has published papers in *Iconos, Arqueología del Área Intermedia, Arqueología Suramericana, Critique of Anthropology, Latin American Antiquity, Social Text,* and *Journal of Latin American Anthropology.* His main research interests are in archaeological discourse in America, popular culture, and comparative studies of race and sexuality.

Plácido Cali is Director of and Archaeologist at Gestão Arqueológica Consultoria (Brazil). He has conducted historical archaeology in the Juréia region, and founded the Museu Arqueológico de Peruíbe and the Instituto Arqueológico of Ilhabela.

Luis E. Cornejo is Researcher and Curator of the Museo Chileno de Arte Precolombino (Chile). He has researched pre-Columbian settlements in central Chile, the Inka presence in his country, and late hunter-gatherers. He has curated several exhibits about pre-Columbian America, such as "Gorros del desierto" (2006), "Chimu. Laberintos de un traje sagrado" (2005), "El arte del cobre en el mundo andino" (2004), and "Quipu. Contar anudando en el imperio Inca" (2003). He teaches methods in the Archaeology Program of the Universidad de Chile.

María Luz Endere is Associate Researcher at the Consejo Nacional de Investigaciones Científicas y Técnicas, and Professor at the Universidad Nacional del Centro de la Provincia de Buenos Aires (Argentina). Her work focuses on the legal protection of heritage and indigenous claims of cultural heritage. She has authored *Arqueología y legislación en Argentina. Cómo proteger el patrimonio arqueológico* (UNCPBA, Tandil, 2000), "Talking about others: Archaeologists, indigenous peoples and heritage in Argentina" (*Public Archaeology* 4, 2005), "Entre lonkos y 'ólogos': la participación de la comunidad ranquelina en la investigación arqueológica" (*Arqueología Suramericana* 2, 2006), with Rafael Curtoni, and co-edited with Rafael Curtoni *Análisis, interpretación y gestión en arqueología en Sudamérica* (UNCPBA, Tandil, 2003).

Marcelo Fernández-Osco is Researcher at the Programa de Investigación Estratégica en Bolivia (PIEB) and at the Taller de Historia Oral Andina (THOA). He has worked in the implementation of the Sajama National Park and has taught at the Universidad Mayor de San Andrés (Bolivia) on indigenous issues, social movements, and indigenous legal systems. He has published *La ley del ayllu* (PIEB, La Paz, 2000), *La ch'axwa o guerra de los ayllus* (PIEB, La Paz, 2000), and *Resolución de conflictos en la región andina* (PIEB, La Paz, 2007).

Pedro Paulo A. Funari is Professor at the Universidade Estadual de Campinas (Brazil). His research interests are the strategic systems of the Brazilian coast, the archaeology of slavery, and the history of Latin American social archaeology. He is an editor of the *Oxford Encyclopedia of Archaeology*, and his recent publications are *Arqueología de la represión y la resistencia en América Latina, 1960–1980*, co-edited with Andrés Zarankin (Universidad Nacional de Catamarca, Catamarca, 2006), *Arqueología histórica en América Latina*, co-edited with Fernando Brittez (Suárez/Unicamp, Mar del Plata, 2006), and *Global Archaeological Theory*, co-edited with Andrés Zarankin and Emily Stovel (Kluwer, New York, 2005).

Francisco M. Gil García is Professor in the Department of the History of America II (Anthropology of America) at the Universidad Complutense (Spain). He has conducted archaeological investigations in Argentina, Spain, and France and ethnographic research in Argentina, Bolivia, and Spain on issues related to the landscape, identity, the invention of tradition, and colonial taxonomies. His current research interests are the links between the archaeological record and oral traditions in the local construction of the past, and the relationships between heritage and tourism. He edited *Espacios del miedo y etnografía de lo fantástico en las fronteras amerindias de la globalización* (Abya-Yala, Quito, 2009) and co-edited with Gerardo Fernández the dossier "A la sombra de los cerros. Cerros y cultura en el mundo andino" (*Revista Española de Antropología Americana* 38, Madrid, 2008).

Cristóbal Gnecco is Professor in the Department of Anthropology at the University of Cauca (Colombia), where he works on the political economy of archaeology and discourses on the ethnic Other. He has published "Modernity and politics in Colombian archaeology" (In *Handbook of South American Archaeology*, edited by Helaine Silverman and William Isbell, Springer, New York, 2008) and co-edited with Carl Langebaek *Contra la tiranía tipológica en arqueología. Una visión desde Sudamérica* (Universidad de los Andes, Bogotá, 2006).

Denise Maria Cavalcante Gomes is Adjunct Professor at the Universidade Federal do Oeste do Pará-UFOPA. She works on the emergence of social complexity in Amazonia, ceramic iconography in Santarém (Brazil), and public archaeology, and is the author of *Cerâmica arqueológica da Amazônia* (Edusp, São Paulo, 2002) and *Cotidiano e poder na Amazônia pré-colonial* (Edusp, São Paulo, 2008).

David R. Green is a freelance videographer with a particular interest in Palikur oral history and community development. He is a fluent Palikur speaker and is developing a multimedia Palikur-language oral history archive. Prior to this he spent several years working in community development and food relief projects in Mozambique. He is attached to the University of Cape Town (South Africa)–based research project "Tradition, science and citizenship: Interfacing archaeology and indigenous knowledge," for which he is working as a Palikur translator and coordinating the archiving of Palikur historical, geographical, and astronomical narratives.

Lesley Green is Senior Lecturer in the Department of Social Anthropology at the University of Cape Town (South Africa). Her research interests are indigenous historiography in Amazonia, with emphasis in the history of landscapes and the environment, and participative research methodologies in ethnography. Some of her recent publications are "Anthropologies of knowledge and South Africa: Indigenous knowledge systems policy" (*Anthropology of Southern Africa* 31, 2008), "Indigenous knowledge and science: Reframing the debate on knowledge diversity" (*Archaeologies* 4, 2008), and "Cultural heritage, archives and citizenship: Reflections on using virtual reality for presenting different knowledge traditions in the public sphere" (*Critical Arts* 21, 2007).

Alejandro F. Haber is Professor at the Universidad Nacional de Catamarca (Argentina) and Researcher at the Consejo Nacional de Investigaciones Científicas y Técnicas. He has spent a great deal of the last 20 years doing archaeology in the Puna de Atacama or whatever it is that archaeology has become in that place through the years; he has used other parts of that time in recovering (himself and his family) from his long absences. He is nurturing a growing disbelief in the diverse ways of writing in the third person about oneself.

Alexander Herrera is Professor and Researcher in the Department of Anthropology at the Universidad de los Andes (Colombia) and founding member of the Centro de Investigación Andina Punku. Since 1996 he has investigated the archaeology of the north-central sierra of Peru, focusing on the history and complexity of transversal social relations in the Andes.

He is currently doing a comparative and critical study of archaeology as applied to "development" in Argentina, Bolivia, Colombia, Ecuador, and Peru. He co-edited, with Carolina Orsini and Kevin Lane, *La complejidad social en la sierra de Ancash* (Comune di Milano, Milan, 2006).

Wilhelm Londoño is Professor in the Department of Anthropology at the Universidad del Magdalena (Colombia). He has done research in historical archaeology and legal anthropology; he has also undertaken experiments in multivocal archaeology in Colombia and Argentina. His publications include "Los hijos de las quebradas: caracterización cultural de la configuración política Nasa" (In *Contra el pensamiento tipológico en arqueología. Una visión desde Suramérica*, edited by Cristóbal Gnecco and Carl Langebaek, Universidad de los Andes, Bogotá, 2006) and "Representaciones sobre lo justo e injusto en comunidades marginadas de Cali: elementos para la interculturalidad jurídica" (In *Investigación jurídica y sociojurídica en Colombia*, edited by Olga Restrepo, Universidad de Medellín, Medellín, 2006).

Fernando López Aguilar is Researcher at the Graduate Program in Archaeology, Escuela Nacional de Antropología e Historia (Mexico). He has worked in the Mezquital Valley of central Mexico seeking to understand the local processes that produced a specific trajectory of Mesoamerican history. He has been Director of Research at the École des Hautes Études en Sciences Sociales (France) and directs the transdisciplinary project "Valle del Mezquital. Arqueología, etnografía, etnohistoria." He has published *Símbolos del tiempo. Inestabilidad y bifurcaciones en los pueblos de indios del Valle del Mezquital* (Consejo Estatal para la Cultura y las Artes del Estado de Hidalgo, Pachuca, 2005) and *Elementos para una construcción teórica en arqueología* (Instituto Nacional de Antropología e Historia, Mexico, 1990), and co-edited with Fernando Brambila *Fractales y antropología* (Sociedad Matemática Mexicana y CIMAT, Mexico, 2008).

Flavia Prado Moi is Researcher at the Nucleus of Strategic Studies of the Universidade Estadual de Campinas (Brazil) and the Nucleus of Studies and Archaeological Investigations of Bahia at the Universidade Estadual de Santa Cruz. She has conducted ethnoarchaeological research among the Xerente of Tocantins and, currently, among the Paresi of Mato Grosso. She authored *Os Xerente: um enfoque etnoarqueológico* (AnnaBlume, São Paulo, 2007).

Walter Fagundes Morales is Professor at the Universidade Estadual de Santa Cruz (Brazil), Coordinator of the Nucleus of Studies and

Archaeological Investigations of Bahia, and Researcher at the Nucleus of Strategic Studies of the Universidade Estadual de Campinas. He currently investigates the shellmounds of southern Bahia. His publications include *Índios e africanos na Jundiaí colonial* (Secretaria Municipal de Planejamento e Meio Ambiente de Jundiaí, Jundiaí, 2002).

Federico Navarrete, historian and anthropologist, is Researcher at the Instituto de Investigaciones Históricas of the Universidad Nacional Autónoma de México. His work is centered in the history of Amerindian peoples after the conquest, their cultural transformations and, more recently, their relation with nation-states. Some of his publications are *La invención de los caníbales* (Castillo, Mexico, 2006) and *Las relaciones interétnicas en México* (Universidad Nacional Autónoma de México, Mexico, 2004); he is the editor of *Indios, mestizos y españoles. Interculturalidad e historiografía en la Nueva España* (Universidad Autónoma Metropolitana, Mexico, 2007).

Eduardo Góes Neves is an archaeologist at the Museu de Arqueologia e Etnologia, Universidade de São Paulo, Brazil. His major research interest is in the central Amazon, where his work focuses on the structure and functioning of the ancient late precolonial social formations that promoted landscape changes in the region. He has published *Arqueologia da Amazônia* (Jorge Zahar, Rio de Janeiro, 2006), *Arqueologia amazônica* (Edições Governo do Estado, Manaus, 2007), with Helena Lima and Fernando Costa, and co-edited with Colin McEwan and Cristiana Barreto *Unknown Amazon: Culture and Nature in Ancient Brazil* (British Museum Press, London, 2001).

Juana Paillalef Carinao, a Mapuche woman, is Director of the Mapuche Museum of Cañete, Bio-Bio Region (Arauco Province, Chile). She has taught about intercultural and bilingual education at various universities in southern Chile. She has worked to engage the Mapuche-Lavkenche in the knowledge of the material heritage preserved at the Mapuche Museum. She has also worked in the retrieval and revitalization of the Mapuche language and ancestral practices related to the particular form of seeing and interpreting the Mapuche world.

Diego Salazar is Professor in the Department of Anthropology at the University of Chile, and head of the Archaeology Program. He has done archaeological research in northern Chile, especially on indigenous mining and its recent historical transformations; he has also been a consultant for the mining industry and collaborated with various indigenous communities in sustainable development projects. He has co-edited, with Donald

Jackson and Andrés Troncoso, *Puentes hacia el pasado. Reflexiones teóricas en arqueología* (Universidad de Chile, Santiago, 2008).

Luis Guillermo Vasco was Professor in the Department of Anthropology at the Universidad Nacional de Colombia and worked on the ethnography of indigenous societies in order to support their organization and struggles. Some of his publications are *Notas de viaje. Acerca de Marx y la antropología* (Universidad del Magdalena, Santa Marta, 2003) and *Entre selva y páramo. Viviendo y pensando la lucha india* (Instituto Colombiano de Antropología e Historia, Bogotá, 2002).